RANCH HOME PLANS is a collection of our best-selling ranch homes in a variety of architectural styles and sizes. A broad assortment is presented to match a wide variety of lifestyles and budgets. Each plan page features floor plans, a front view of the house, interior square footage of the home, number of bedrooms, baths, garage size and foundation types. All floor plans show room and exterior dimensions.

TECHNICAL SPECIFICATIONS

At the time the construction drawings were prepared, every effort was made to ensure that these plans and specifications meet nationally recognized building codes (BOCA, Southern Building Code Congress and others). Because national building codes change or vary from area to area some drawing modifications and/or the assistance of a professional designer or architect may be necessary to comply with your local codes or to accommodate specific building site conditions. We advise you to consult with your local building official for information regarding codes governing your area.

BLUEPRINT ORDERING - FAST AND EASY

See page 6 for more information on which types of blueprint packages are available and how many plan sets to order. Your ordering is made simple by following the instructions on page 7.

YOUR HOME, YOUR WAY

The blueprints you receive are a master plan for building your new home. They start you on your way to what may well be the most rewarding experience of your life.

CONTENTS

MENARDS RANCH HOME PLANS is published by Design America, Inc., 734 Westport Plaza, Suite 208, St. Louis, MO 63146.

Artist drawings and photos shown in this publication may vary slightly from the actual working drawings. Some photos are shown in mirror reverse. Please refer to the floor plan for accurate layout.

Current printing 5 4 3 2 1

COVER HOME The multi-family plan shown is Plan #M08-007D-0076 and is featured on page 214. Color rendering courtesy of Design America, Inc.

COVER HOME The house shown on the cover is Plan #M08-055L-0748 and is featured on page 14. Photo courtesy of Nelson Design Group.

COVER HOME The house shown on the cover is Plan #M08-013L-0039 and is featured on page 94. Photo courtesy of Atlanta Plan Source.

LET MENARDS® MAKE YOUR DREAM HOME A REALITY

"Thanks to MENARDS®, finding and building our Dream Home has never been easier."

Thinking about building your dream home? Or, perhaps you are interested in a luxury home or possibly a ranch home? Choosing a home plan can be a daunting task.

This book of Ranch Home Plans has been designed to make the search simple and easy. Browse the pages of this book and look for the style that best suits your family and your needs. These plans have been chosen from top designers from across the country and can provide to you the perfect home that will truly be a place of refuge for your whole family for years to come.

This book is the perfect place to begin your search for the home of your dreams. You will find the expected beauty you want and the functional efficiency you need, all designed with unmatched quality.

Also, keep in mind, this book contains helpful articles for understanding what kind of plan package you may need as well as other helpful building aids to make the process even easier.

When you have made this decision visit your local MENARDS® store to place your order and partner with one of their friendly team members to walk you through the process or order your home plans at www.Menards.com.

MENARDS® is dedicated to assist you through the entire home decision process

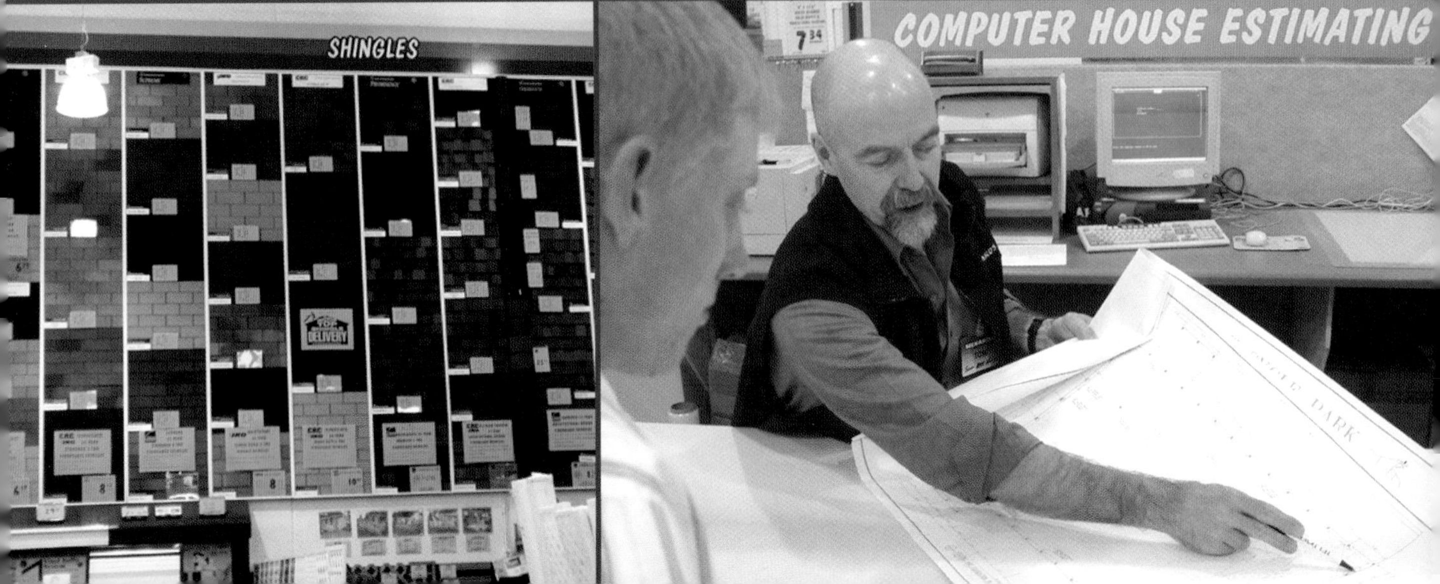

WHAT'S THE RIGHT PLAN FOR YOU?

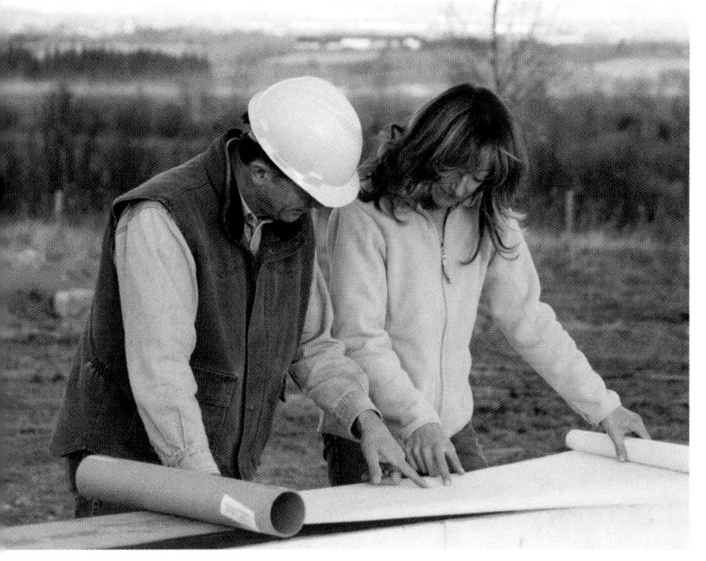

Choosing a home plan is an exciting but difficult task. Many factors play a role in what home plan is best for you and your family. To help you get started, we have pinpointed some of the major factors to consider when searching for your dream home. Take the time to evaluate your family's needs and you will have an easier time sorting through all of the home plans offered in our magazine.

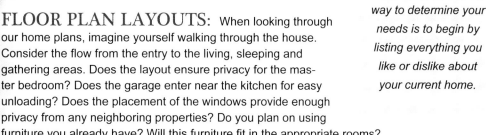

BUDGET: The first thing to consider is your budget. Many items take part in this budget, from ordering the blueprints to the last doorknob purchased. When you find your dream home plan, visit the MENARDS® Building Materials Desk to get a cost-to-build estimate to ensure that the finished product will be within your cost range.

FAMILY LIFESTYLE: After your budget is deciphered, you need to assess you and your family's lifestyle needs. Think about the stage of life you are at now, and what stages you will be going through in the future. Ask yourself questions to figure out how much room you need now and if you will need room for expansion. Are you married? Do you have children? How many children do you plan on having? Are you an empty-nester?

Incorporate in your planning any frequent guests you may have, including elderly parents, grandchildren or adult children who may live with you.

Does your family entertain a lot? If so, think about the rooms you will need to do so. Will you need both formal and informal spaces? Do you need a gourmet kitchen? Do you need a game room and/or a wet bar?

Experts in the field suggest that the best way to determine your needs is to begin by listing everything you like or dislike about your current home.

FLOOR PLAN LAYOUTS: When looking through our home plans, imagine yourself walking through the house. Consider the flow from the entry to the living, sleeping and gathering areas. Does the layout ensure privacy for the master bedroom? Does the garage enter near the kitchen for easy unloading? Does the placement of the windows provide enough privacy from any neighboring properties? Do you plan on using furniture you already have? Will this furniture fit in the appropriate rooms? When you find a plan you want to purchase, be sure to picture yourself actually living in it.

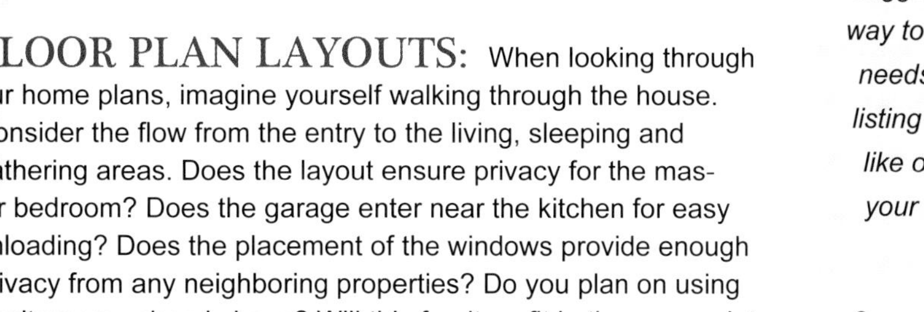

EXTERIOR SPACES: There are many different home styles ranging from Traditional to Contemporary. Flip through and find which style most appeals to you and the neighborhood in which you plan to build. Also think of your site and how the entire house will fit on this site. Picture any landscaping you plan on incorporating into the design. Using your imagination is key when choosing a home plan.

Choosing a home plan can be an intimidating experience. Asking yourself these questions before you get started on the search will help you through the process. With our large selection of multiple styles we are certain you will find your dream home in the following pages.

OUR BLUEPRINT PACKAGES OFFER...

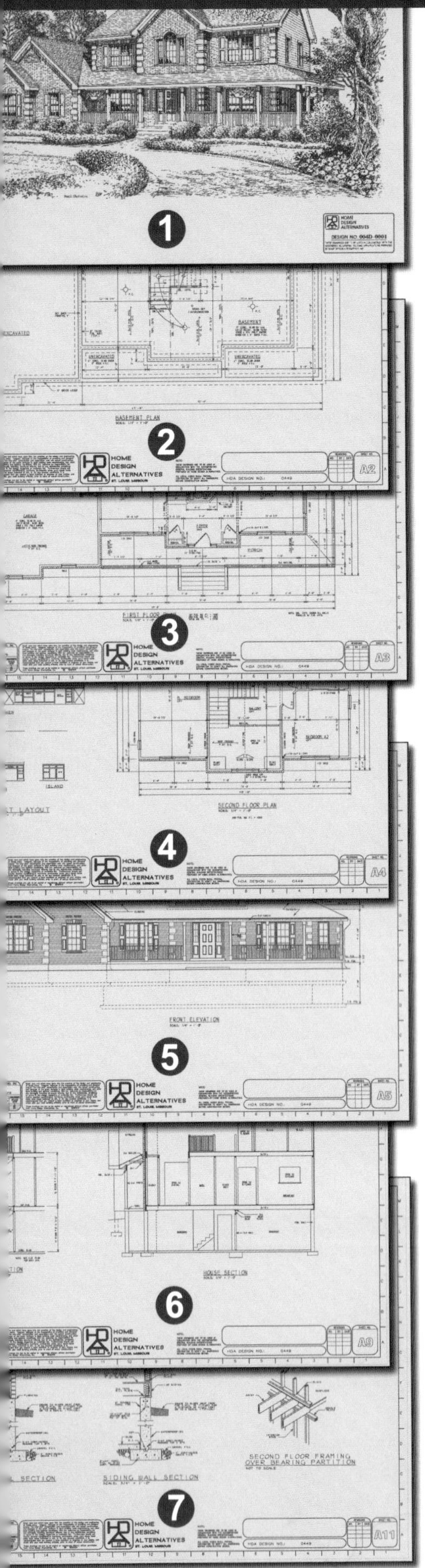

Quality plans for building your future, with extras that provide unsurpassed value, ensure good construction and long-term enjoyment.

A quality home - one that looks good, functions well, and provides years of enjoyment - is a product of many things - design, materials, and craftsmanship.

But it's also the result of outstanding blueprints - the actual plans and specifications that tell the builder exactly how to build your home.

And with our BLUEPRINT PACKAGES you get the absolute best.
A complete set of blueprints is available for every design in this book.
These "working drawings" are highly detailed, resulting in two key benefits:

- Better understanding by the contractor of how to build your home and...
- More accurate construction estimates.

Below is a sample of plan information included for most of the designs in this book. Specific details may vary with each designer's plan. While this information is typical of most plans, we cannot assure the inclusion of all the following referenced items. Please contact customer service for plan specific information, including which of the following items are included.

1. COVER SHEET is the artist's rendering of the exterior of the home and is included with many of the plans. It will give you an idea of how your home will look when completed and landscaped.

2. FOUNDATION plan shows the layout of the basement, crawl space, slab or pier foundation. All necessary notations and dimensions are included. See the plan page for the foundation types included. If the home plan you choose does not have your desired foundation type, see page 8 on how to customize your foundation to suit your specific needs or site conditions.

3. FLOOR PLANS show the placement of walls, doors, closets, plumbing fixtures, electrical outlets, columns, and beams for each level of the home.

4. INTERIOR ELEVATIONS provide views of special interior elements such as fireplaces, kitchen cabinets, built-in units and other features of the home.

5. EXTERIOR ELEVATIONS illustrate the front, rear and both sides of the house, with all details of exterior materials and the required dimensions.

6. SECTIONS show detail views of the home or portions of the home as if it were sliced from the roof to the foundation. This sheet shows important areas such as load-bearing walls, stairs, joists, trusses and other structural elements, which are critical for proper construction.

7. DETAILS show how to construct certain components of your home, such as the roof system, stairs, deck, etc.

OTHER GREAT PRODUCTS

THE LEGAL KIT™

Home building can be a complicated process with many legal regulations being confusing. This Legal Kit was designed to help you avoid many legal pitfalls and build your home with confidence using the forms and contracts featured in this kit. Included are request for proposal documents, various fixed price and cost plus contracts, instructions on how and when to use each form, warranty statements and more. Save time and money before you break ground on your new home or start a remodeling project. Instructions are included on how to use the kit and since the documents are universal, they are designed to be used with all building trades. Since review by an attorney is always advised before signing any contract, this is an ideal way to get organized and started on the process. Plus, all forms are reproducible making it a terrific tool for the contractor and home builder.

Discount Price: $35.00 - Menards SKU 100-3422

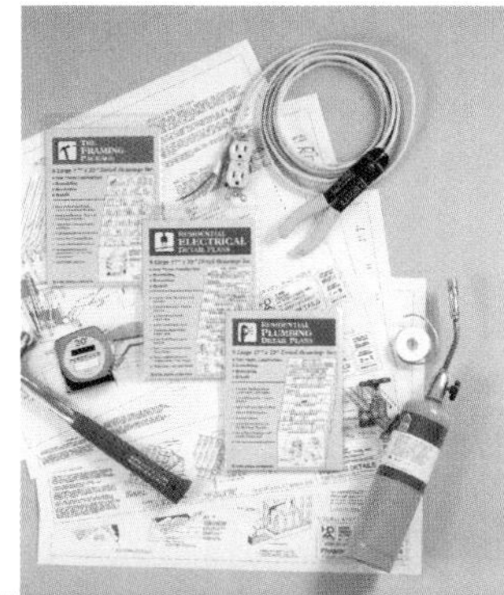

DETAIL PLAN PACKAGES

Framing, Plumbing and Electrical Plan Packages

Three separate packages offer home builders details for constructing various foundations; numerous floor, wall and roof framing techniques; simple to complex residential wiring; sump and water softener hookups; plumbing connection methods; installation of septic systems, and more. Packages include 3-dimensional illustrations and a glossary of terms. These drawings do not pertain to a specific home plan making them perfect for your building situation. Purchase one or all three.

Discount Price: $20.00 each or all three for $40.00 - Menards SKU 100-3422

MORE HELPFUL BUILDING AIDS...

Your Blueprint Package will contain the necessary construction information to build your home. We also offer the following products and services to save you time and money in the building process.

EXPRESS DELIVERY

Most orders are processed within 24 hours of receipt. Please allow 7-10 business days for delivery. If you need to place a rush order, please call or visit any MENARDS® store to order by 11:00 a.m. Monday-Friday CST and specify you would like express service (allow 1-2 business days).

Discount Price: $60.00 - Menards SKU 194-4356

MATERIAL LIST

Material lists are available for all of the plans in this book. Each list gives you the quantity, dimensions and description of the building materials necessary to construct your home. The material list is intended to be used only in conjunction with the corresponding blueprints and specifications, and is not intended to be used solely for ordering purposes. Extreme care has gone into assuring that your material list is accurate. However, due to variations in local building practices and widely differing code requirements, the exact material quanities cannot be guaranteed. To receive a free home plan estimate call or visit any MENARDS® Building Materials Desk.

Discount Price: $125.00 - Menards SKU 100-3422

NOTE: Material lists are designed with the standard foundations only and will not include alternate or optional foundations. It is essential that you review the material list and the construction drawings with your builder and material supplier in order to verify product line, color, measurements, and descriptions of the materials listed.

CUSTOMER SERVICE

If you have questions about a plan, call our customer service department at 1-800-373-2646 Monday through Friday, 7:30am-4:30pm CST. Whether it involves design modifications, or specific plan questions, our customer service representatives will be happy to help you. We want your home to be everything you expect it to be.

WHAT KIND OF PLAN PACKAGE DO YOU NEED?

Now that you've found the home you've been looking for, here are some suggestions on how to make your Dream Home a reality. To get started, order the type of plans that fit your particular situation.

YOUR CHOICES

- ☐ **THE 1-SET STUDY PACKAGE** - We offer a One-set plan package so you can study your home in detail. This one set is considered a study set and is marked "not for construction." It is a copyright violation to reproduce blueprints.

- ☐ **THE MINIMUM 5-SET PACKAGE** - If you're ready to start the construction process, this 5-set package is the minimum number of blueprint sets you will need. It will require keeping close track of each set so they can be used by multiple subcontractors and tradespeople.

- ☐ **THE STANDARD 8-SET PACKAGE** - For best results in terms of cost, schedule and quality of construction, we recommend you order eight (or more) sets of blueprints. Besides one set for yourself, additional sets of blueprints will be required by your mortgage lender, local building department, general contractor and all subcontractors working on foundation, electrical, plumbing, heating/air conditioning, carpentry work, etc.

- ☐ **REPRODUCIBLE MASTERS** - If you wish to make some minor design changes, you'll want to order reproducible masters. These drawings contain the same information as the blueprints but are printed on reproducible paper and clearly indicates your right to alter, copy or reproduce. This will allow your builder or a local design professional to make the necessary drawing changes without the major expense of redrawing the plans. This package also allows you to print copies of the modified plans as needed. The right of building only one structure from these plans is licensed exclusively to the buyer. You may not use this design to build a second or multiple dwelling(s) without purchasing another blueprint. Each violation of the Copyright Law is punishable in a fine.

- ☐ **PDF FILE FORMAT** - A complete set of construction drawings in an electronic format that allows you to resize and reproduce the plans to fit your needs. Since these are electronic files, we can send them to you within 24 hours (Mon-Fri, 7:30-4:30 CST) via email and save you shipping costs. They also offer printing flexibility by allowing you to print the size and number of sets you need. *Note: These are not CAD files and cannot be altered electronically.*

- ☐ **MIRROR REVERSE SETS** - Plans can be printed in mirror reverse. These plans are useful when the house would fit your site better if all the rooms were on the opposite side than shown. They are simply a mirror image of the original drawings causing the lettering and dimensions to read backwards. Therefore, when ordering mirror reverse drawings, you must purchase at least one set of right-reading plans.

- ☐ **RIGHT READING REVERSE SETS** - Right reading reverse is where the plan is a mirrored image of the original drawings, but all the text and dimensions read correctly. This option may not be available for all home plans, so please check the Home Plan Index on page 224 for availability.

- ☐ **ADDITIONAL SETS** - Additional sets of the plan ordered are available for an additional cost of $45.00 each. Five-set, eight-set, and reproducible or PDF packages offer considerable savings. *Note: Available only within 90 days after purchase of plan package or reproducible masters of the same plan.*

COPYRIGHT

These plans are protected under Copyright Law. Reproduction by any means is strictly prohibited. The right of building only one structure from these plans is licensed exclusively to the buyer and these plans may not be resold unless by express written authorization from home designer/architect. You may not use this design to build a second or multiple dwelling(s) without purchasing another blueprint or blueprints or paying additional design fees. Each violation of the Copyright Law is punishable in a fine.

HOW TO ORDER HOME PLANS

You've found your Dream Home, now what?

Follow these simple steps:

1. Review the article on page 6 to decide what type of plan package you need.
2. To order, call or visit any MENARDS® store and go to the Building Materials Desk or visit **www.Menards.com**.

To locate the nearest MENARDS® store, go to **www.Menards.com** and click on the Store locator.

Artist drawings and photos shown in this publication may vary slightly from the actual working drawings. Some photos are shown in mirror reverse or have been modified. Please refer to the floor plan for accurate layout.

BLUEPRINT SKU PRICING
(PRICES SUBJECT TO CHANGE)

PRICE CODE		1-SET STUDY	5-SET PLAN	8-SET PLAN	REPRO. MASTERS	PDF FILE
AAA	Menards SKU	194-3920	194-3933	194-3946	194-3959	194-3960
	Discount Price	$310	$410	$510	$610	$610
AA	Menards SKU	194-3962	194-3975	194-3988	194-3991	194-3995
	Discount Price	$410	$510	$610	$710	$710
A	Menards SKU	194-4000	194-4084	194-4165	194-4246	194-4250
	Discount Price	$470	$570	$670	$770	$770
B	Menards SKU	194-4013	194-4097	194-4178	194-4259	194-4260
	Discount Price	$530	$630	$730	$830	$830
C	Menards SKU	194-4026	194-4107	194-4181	194-4262	194-4265
	Discount Price	$585	$685	$785	$885	$885
D	Menards SKU	194-4039	194-4110	194-4194	194-4275	194-4280
	Discount Price	$635	$735	$835	$935	$935
E	Menards SKU	194-4042	194-4123	194-4204	194-4288	194-4290
	Discount Price	$695	$795	$895	$995	$995
F	Menards SKU	194-4055	194-4136	194-4217	194-4291	194-4295
	Discount Price	$750	$850	$950	$1050	$1050
G	Menards SKU	194-4068	194-4149	194-4220	194-4301	194-4305
	Discount Price	$1000	$1100	$1200	$1300	$1300
H	Menards SKU	194-4071	194-4152	194-4233	194-4314	194-4315
	Discount Price	$1100	$1200	$1300	$1400	$1400
P	Menards SKU	194-4080	194-4160	194-4240	194-4320	194-4325
	Discount Price	$1500	$1600	$1700	$1800	$1800

OTHER PRODUCTS & BUILDING AIDS

MIRROR REVERSE*	Menards SKU	194-4327
	Discount Price	$15
RIGHT READING REVERSE*	Menards SKU	194-4328
	Discount Price	$150
2" x 6" WALLS	Menards SKU	194-4360
	Discount Price	$150
ADDITIONAL FOUNDATION	Menards SKU	194-4329
	Discount Price	$250
ADDITIONAL SETS**	Menards SKU	194-4330
	Discount Price	$45
MATERIAL LIST**	Menards SKU	100-3422
	Discount Price	$125
EXPRESS DELIVERY	Menards SKU	194-4356
	Discount Price	$60
LEGAL KIT	Menards SKU	100-3422
	Discount Price	$35
DETAIL PLAN PACKAGES *ELECTRICAL, PLUMBING & FRAMING - ALL SAME SKU*	Menards SKU	100-3422
	Discount Price	$20 EA. 3 FOR $40

Please note: All blueprints are printed in response to your order, so we cannot honor requests for refunds. However, if for some reason you find that the plan you have purchased does not meet your requirements, you may exchange that plan for another plan in our collection within 90 days of purchase. At the time of the exchange, you will be charged a processing fee of 25% of your original plan package price, plus the difference in price between the plan packages (if applicable) and the cost to ship the new plans to you. Keep in mind, reproducible drawings can only be exchanged if the package is unopened and material lists can only be purchased within 90 days of purchasing the plan package. PDF Files are not returnable or refundable.

License To Build: When you purchase a "full set of construction drawings" from Design America, Inc., you are purchasing an exclusive one-time "License to Build," not the rights to the design. Design America, Inc. is granting you permission on behalf of the home plan designer to use the construction drawings one time for the building of your dream home. The construction drawings (also referred to as blueprints/plans and any derivative of that plan whether extensive or minor) are still owned and protected under copyright laws by the original designer. The blueprints/plans cannot be resold, transferred, rented, loaned or used by anyone other than the original purchaser of the "License to Build" without written consent from Design America, Inc. or the home plan designer.

*See page 6
**Available only within 90 days after purchase of plan package of same plan

MAKING CHANGES TO YOUR PLAN

We understand that it is difficult to find blueprints that will meet all your needs. That is why Design America, Inc. is pleased to offer plan modification services.

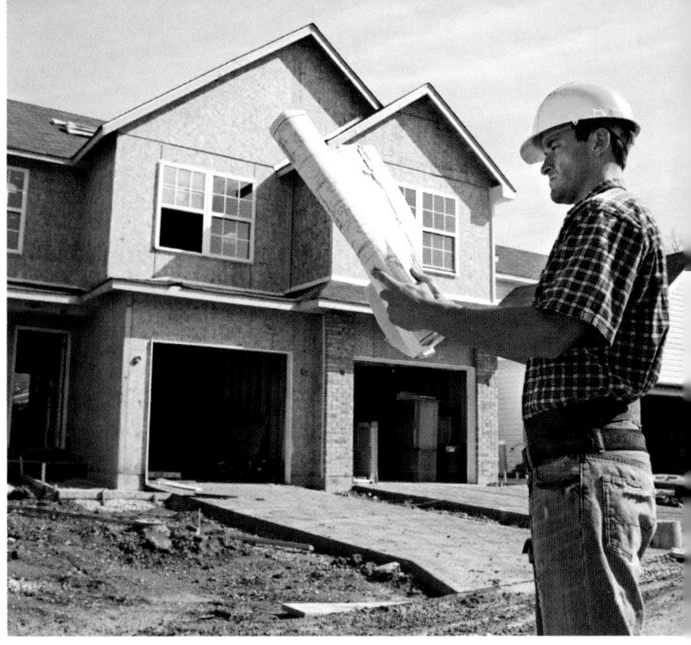

THINKING ABOUT CUSTOMIZING YOUR PLAN?

If you're like many customers, you may want to make changes to your home plan to make it the dream home you've always wanted. That's where our expert design and modification team comes in. You won't find a more efficient and economic way to get your changes done than by using our design services.

Whether it's enlarging a kitchen, adding a porch or converting a crawl space to a basement, we can customize any plan and make it perfect for your family. Simply create your wish list and let us go to work. Soon you'll have the blueprints for your new home and at a fraction of the cost of hiring an architect!

THE DESIGN AMERICA, INC. MODIFICATION ADVANTAGE

- We can customize any plan
- FREE cost estimates for your home plan modifications within 48 hours.
- Average turn-around time to complete the modifications is 2-3 weeks.
- One-on-one design consultations.

Easy Steps For Fast Service

Visit any MENARDS® Building Materials Desk and request a Custom Change Form.

Simply follow the instructions to receive your quote within two business days.

CUSTOMIZING FACTS

- The average cost for us to customize a house plan is typically less than 1 percent of the building costs — compare that to the national average of 7 percent of building costs.
- The average modification cost for a home is typically $800 to $1,500 (this does not include the cost of the reproducible blueprint, which is required to make plan changes).
- The average cost to modify a project plan is typically between $200-$500.

OTHER HELPFUL INFORMATION

- Feel free to include a sketch, or a specific list of changes you'd like to make.
- One of our designers will contact you within 24 hours with your free estimate.
- Upon accepting the estimate, you will need to purchase the reproducible/PDF set of plans.
- A contract, which includes a specific list of changes and fees will be sent to you for approval.
- Upon approving the contract, our designers will keep you up to date by emailing or faxing sketches throughout the project.
- Plan can be converted to metric.
- Barrier Free Conversion (accommodating a plan for special needs, transferring your living space for everyone).
- Customizing is also available for project plans, such as sheds, garages, apartment garages and more.

MENARDS®

Ranch HOME PLANS

over 200 home plans

Plan #M08-055L-0748 can be found on page 14.

The following pages include a collection of best-selling home plans featuring the ever-popular ranch homes that are still the most widely desired home built today. This collection of one-story homes from some of the nation's leading designers and architects include open floor plans, abundant storage, and space for expansion. Whether you're interested in a cozy cottage or sprawling luxury home, these ranch homes will welcome you and create the perfect atmosphere for quality family living in a timeless setting. We are excited to present this collection designed for gracious ranch living. Whatever your tastes or needs, we invite you to discover the home of your dreams.

Plan #M08-022D-0026 can be found on page 27.

Plan #M08-065L-0041 can be found on page 12.

GRAY SUMMIT

Plan #M08-051L-0187

Photo, above - Stainless steel appliances create a nice contrast against the rich, dark wood cabinets found throughout the kitchen.

Photo, left - The dramatic front entry with a tall ceiling and ornate window treatment offers an inviting feeling when guests arrive.

Photo, above - Step down into the cozy lower level recreation room encompassed by decorative wrought iron railings.

Photo, right - This stunning great room has a formal, yet friendly feel that can only be created when the design uses tall ceilings and open, airy spaces.

Plan #M08-051L-0187

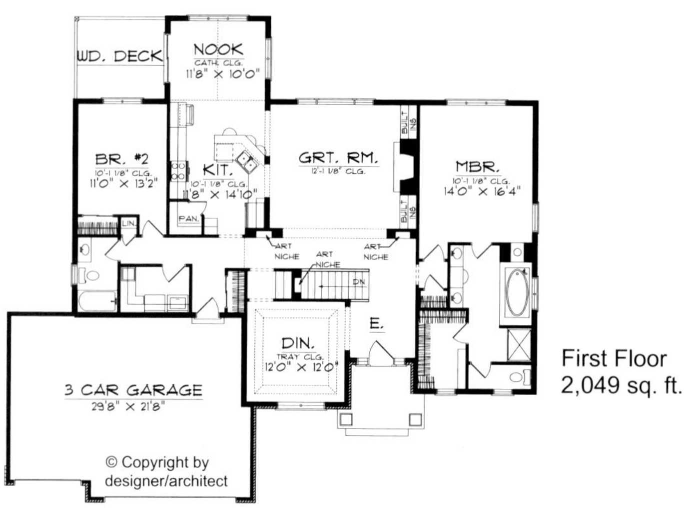

First Floor
2,049 sq. ft.

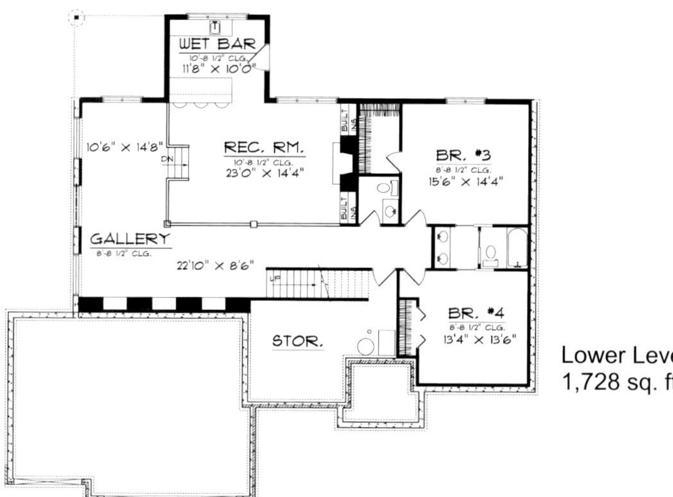

Lower Level
1,728 sq. ft.

TRADITIONAL RANCH

3,777 total square feet of living area

Width: 65'-0" Depth: 58'-0"

4 bedrooms, 3 1/2 baths

3-car garage

Walk-out basement foundation

SPECIAL FEATURES

Energy efficient home with 2" x 6" exterior walls

The master bedroom provides the ultimate relaxation with a deluxe bath and walk-in closet to keep everything organized

A walk-in pantry and snack bar island add efficiency to the kitchen that opens to the great room and cozy nook

The lower level is comprised of two secondary bedrooms, a recreation room, and a wet bar

PRICE CODE P

To order plans, visit the Menards Building Materials Desk or visit www.Menards.com.

HUNGERFORD TRAIL

MENARDS®

Plan #M08-065L-0041

Photo, above - Beautiful columns define the great room and create a lovely entryway from the foyer into the space.

Photo, left - This expansive kitchen has a lengthy peninsula that serves as both a prep and dining surface, while providing a nice view of the nearby great room.

Photo, above - This home's rear deck provides covered outdoor living space ideal for taking in some fresh air whether watching the sunset or enjoying a pleasant rain shower.

Photo, right - Dramatic carpentry offers an extraordinary focal point as seen in this close-up of the great room fireplace.

Plan #M08-065L-0041

OUTDOOR COVERED DECK WARMED BY FIREPLACE

3,171 total square feet of living area

Width: 86'-2" Depth: 63'-8"

3 bedrooms, 2 1/2 baths

3-car side entry garage

Walk-out basement or basement foundation, please specify when ordering

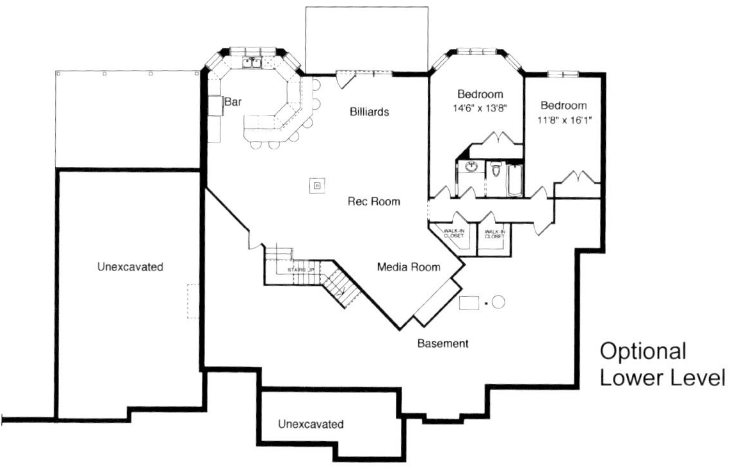

SPECIAL FEATURES

An enormous walk-in closet is located in the master bath and dressing area

The great room, breakfast area and kitchen combine with 12' ceilings to create an open feel

The optional lower level has an additional 1,897 square feet of living area and is designed for entertaining featuring a wet bar with seating, a billiards room, a large media room, two bedrooms, and a full bath

PRICE CODE E

To order plans, visit the Menards Building Materials Desk or visit www.Menards.com.

Plan #M08-055L-0748

Photo, above - Unique contrasts add style and sophistication to the kitchen. With the dark colored stove, richly painted walls and light cabinetry, the feeling of this space is soothing and upscale.

Photo, left - Arched doorways access the bedrooms, while built-ins attract attention in the great room.

Photo, above - The home theater/living room takes you to a whole new dimension of style and ambiance with its rich, chocolate brown walls and mood lighting. Relaxation will never take long as soon as you enter this space.

Photo, right - Full of luxury from end to end, the private master bath enjoys the beauty of inlaid mosaic tile and marble to decorate the tub and floor, while stylish plumbing fixtures and lighting complete the space perfectly.

Plan #M08-055L-0748

EXPANSIVE ONE-STORY DESIGN

2,525 total square feet of living area

Width: 67'-2" Depth: 55'-10"

4 bedrooms, 3 baths

2-car garage

Crawl space or slab foundation, please specify when ordering

SPECIAL FEATURES

Stunning columns frame the foyer that leads into the open great room with fireplace, as well as the home theater/living room

The formal dining room, casual breakfast room and grilling porch with a fireplace provide an abundance of dining opportunities

Three bedrooms and two baths occupy one side of this home, while the master suite is secluded on the other

PRICE CODE E

To order plans, visit the Menards Building Materials Desk or visit www.Menards.com.

ALTAMONT

MENARDS®

Plan #M08-007D-0007

RAMBLING RANCH HAS LUXURIOUS MASTER BEDROOM

2,523 total square feet of living area

Width: 90'-4"   Depth: 48'-4"

3 bedrooms, 2 baths

3-car garage

Basement foundation, drawings also include crawl space and slab foundations

SPECIAL FEATURES

- The entry with a high ceiling leads to a vaulted great room with a wet bar, plant shelf, and a fireplace with a window trio
- The elaborate kitchen with bay and breakfast bar adjoins the morning room with a fireplace-in-a-bay
- The vaulted master bedroom has a fireplace, walk-in closet and double baths

PRICE CODE D

Rear View

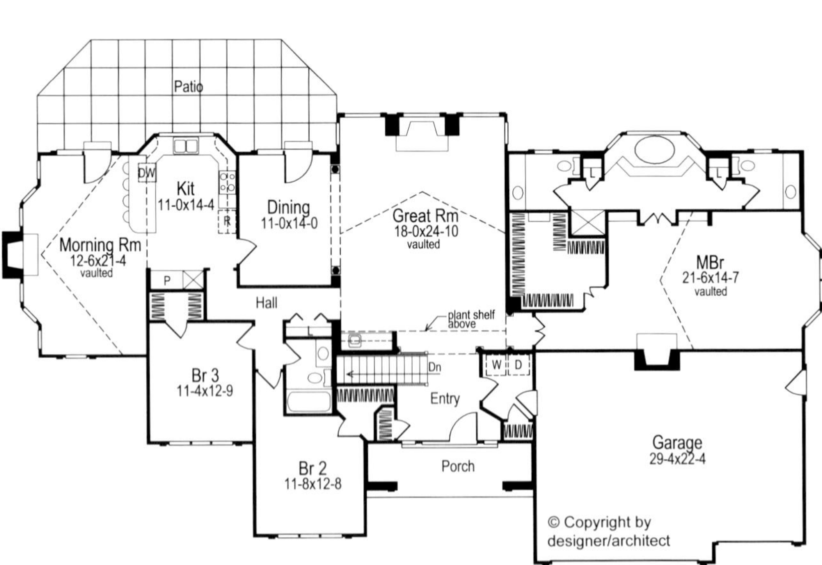

To order plans, visit the Menards Building Materials Desk or visit www.Menards.com.

MENARDS® GREEN ORCHARD

Plan #M08-072L-1108

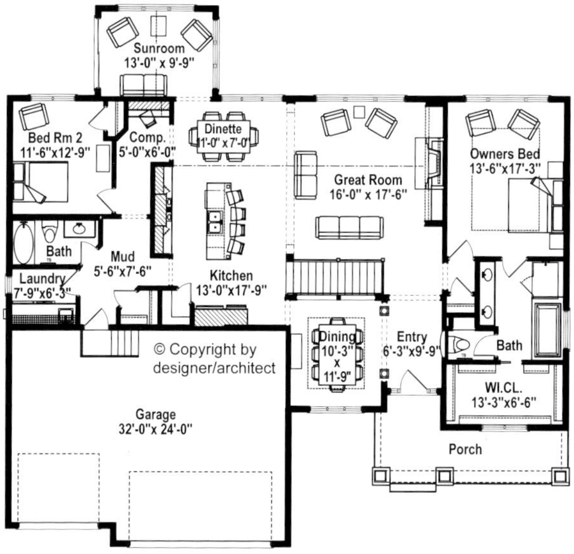

First Floor
2,109 sq. ft.

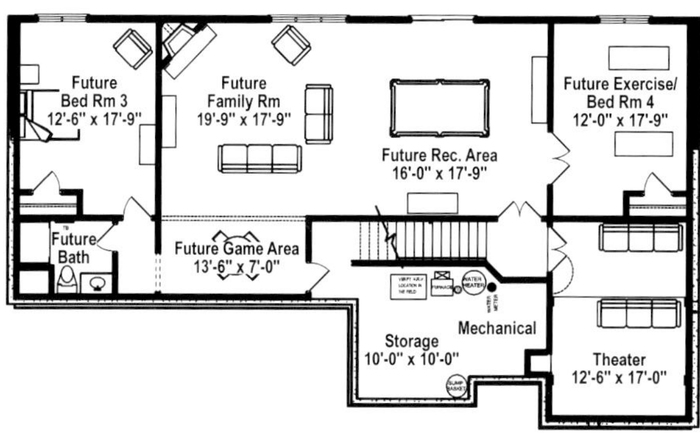

Lower Level
336 sq. ft.

To order plans, visit the Menards Building Materials Desk or visit www.Menards.com.

INVITING FRONT PORCH

2,445 total square feet of living area

Width: 64'-0" Depth: 60'-0"

2 bedrooms, 2 baths

3-car garage

Walk-out basement foundation

SPECIAL FEATURES

Enjoy the spacious great room featuring a beautiful fireplace that creates a dramatic ambiance adding character and flair to this home

The efficient kitchen is quite charming and contains a breakfast island and generous pantry

The attractive sunroom provides a lovely space for relaxing and reading a good book

The optional lower level features an additional 336 square feet of living area

PRICE CODE B

KINGS CROSSING

MENARDS®

Plan #M08-065L-0103

DELIGHTFUL ONE LEVEL HOME

1,860 total square feet of living area

Width: 64'-2"   Depth: 44'-2"

3 bedrooms, 2 baths

2-car garage

Basement or walk-out basement foundation, please specify when ordering

SPECIAL FEATURES

The extended counter in the kitchen offers extra dining space

A bayed breakfast area is open to the great room and kitchen creating a spacious atmosphere

The beautiful corner fireplace in the great room is angled perfectly so it can also be enjoyed from the formal dining room

PRICE CODE C

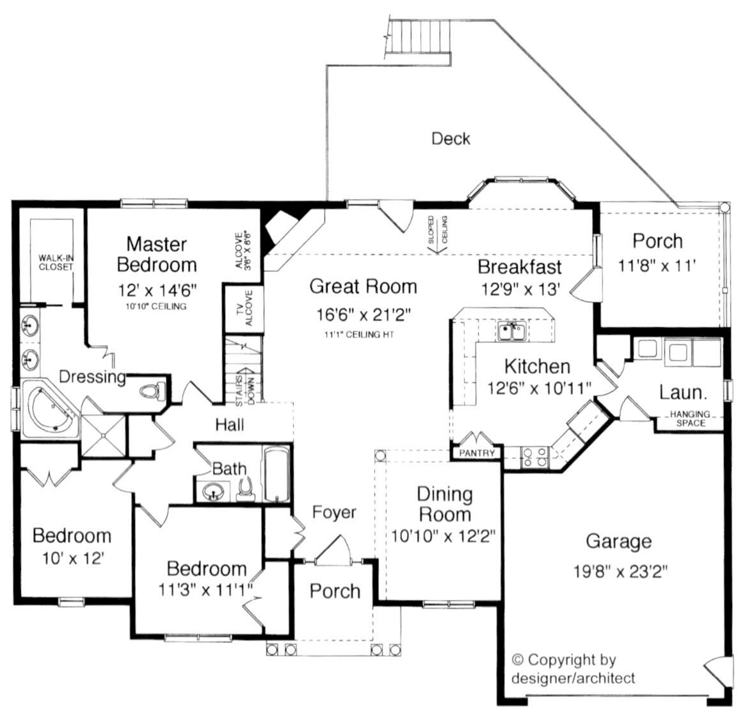

To order plans, visit the Menards Building Materials Desk or visit www.Menards.com.

ELLISPORT

Plan #M08-013L-0015

UNCOMMONLY STYLED RANCH

1,787 total square feet of living area

Width: 55'-8"   Depth: 56'-6"

3 bedrooms, 2 baths

2-car side entry garage

Basement, crawl space or slab foundation, please specify when ordering

SPECIAL FEATURES

Skylights brighten the screen porch that connects to the family room and deck outdoors

The master bedroom features a comfortable sitting area, a large private bath and direct access to the screen porch

The kitchen has a serving bar that extends dining into the family room

The bonus room above the garage has an additional 263 square feet of living area

PRICE CODE B

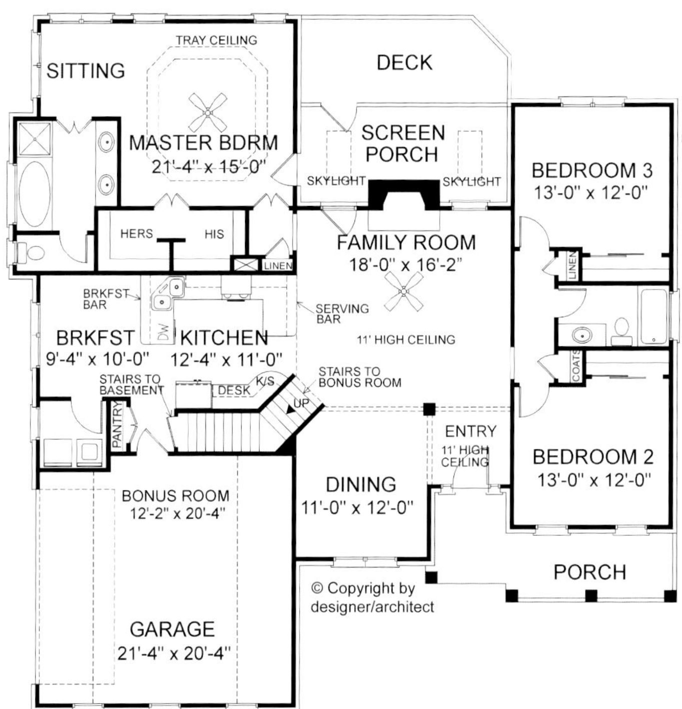

To order plans, visit the Menards Building Materials Desk or visit www.Menards.com.

Plan #M08-021D-0002

CENTRAL FIREPLACE WARMS THIS COZY CONTEMPORARY

1,442 total square feet of living area

Width: 54'-0" Depth: 50'-0"

3 bedrooms, 2 baths

2-car garage

Slab foundation, drawings also include crawl space foundation

SPECIAL FEATURES

The living room has a recessed fireplace

The U-shaped kitchen has an eating bar

The expanded garage offers extra storage

The spacious master bedroom features a sitting area and a large walk-in closet

PRICE CODE B

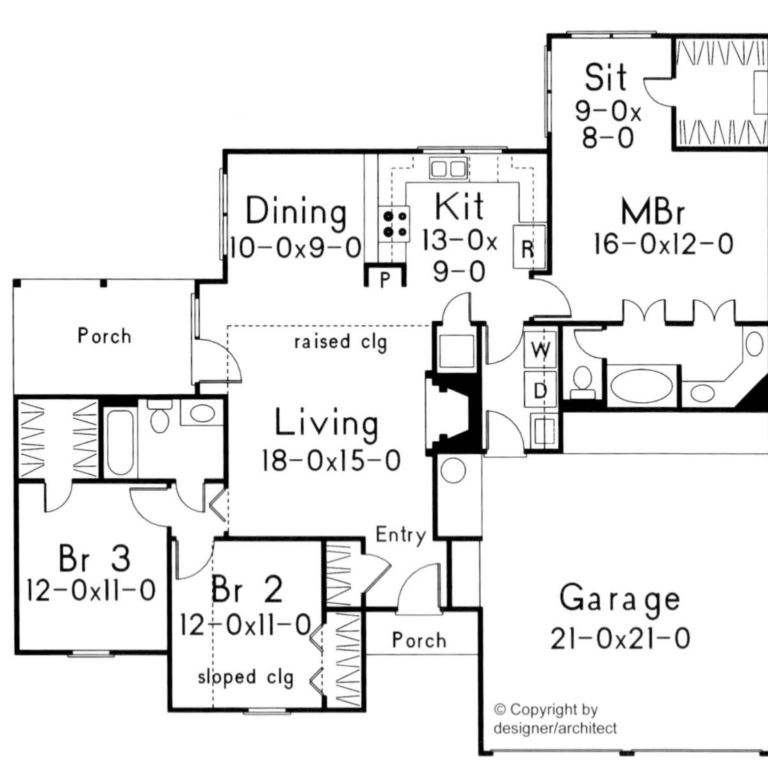

Rear View

To order plans, visit the Menards Building Materials Desk or visit www.Menards.com.

MENARDS®

FOXBURY

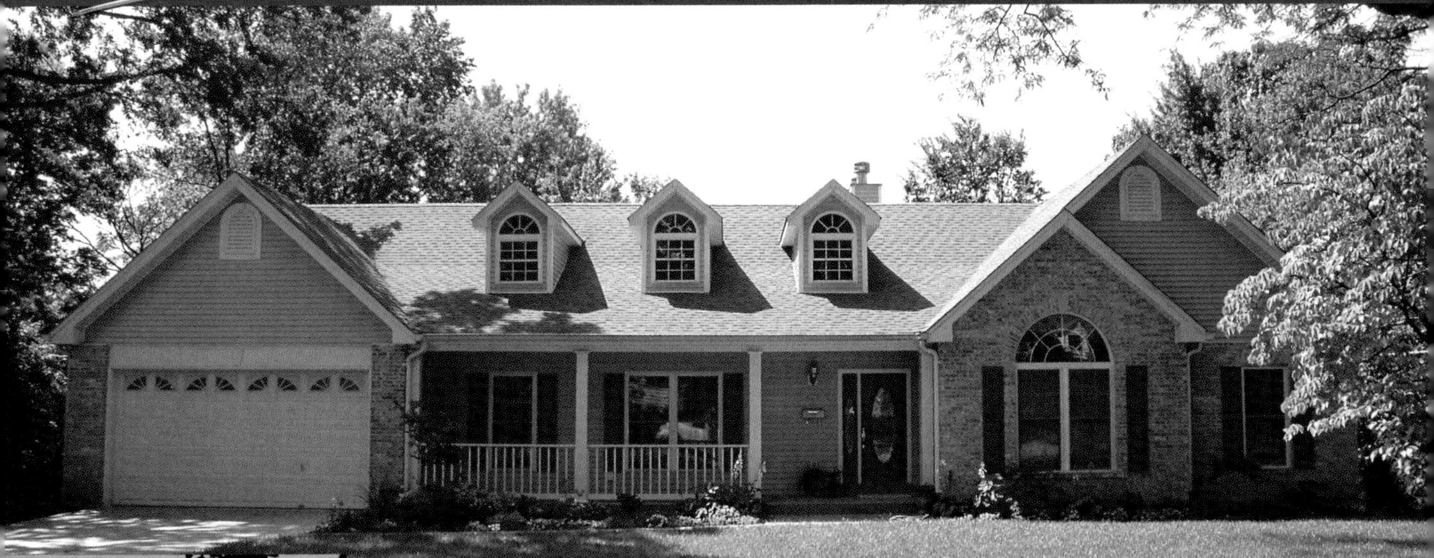

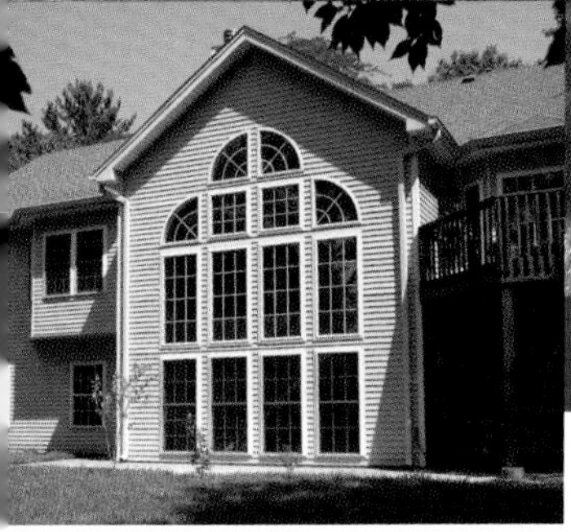

Plan #M08-007D-0010

ATRIUM HAS DRAMATIC AMBIANCE

1,845 total square feet of living area

Width: 83'-0" Depth: 42'-4"

3 bedrooms, 2 baths

3-car garage

Walk-out basement foundation, drawings also include crawl space and slab foundations

SPECIAL FEATURES

The vaulted dining and great rooms are cheerful from an atrium window wall

2" x 6" exterior wall framing available for an additional fee, please specify when ordering

The lower level has an additional 889 square feet of optional living area

PRICE CODE C

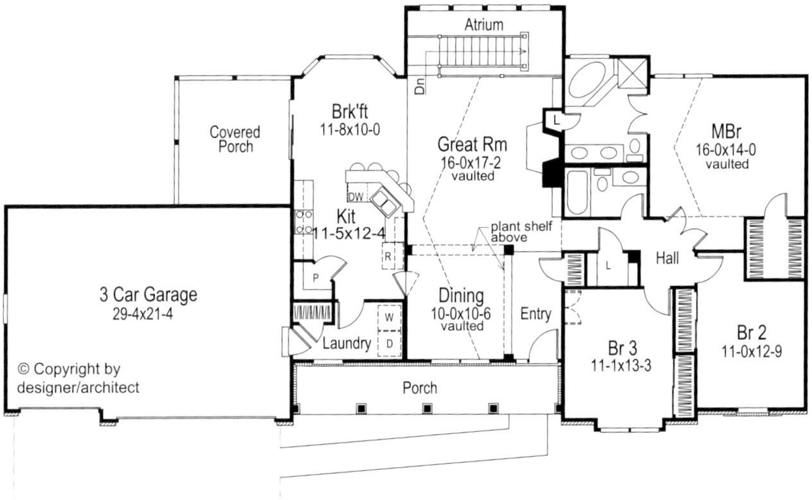

Atrium
Dn
Brk'ft
11-8x10-0
Covered
Porch
Great Rm
16-0x17-2
vaulted
MBr
16-0x14-0
vaulted
L
DW
Kit
11-5x12-4
R
plant shelf
above
P
3 Car Garage
29-4x21-4
Dining
10-0x10-6
vaulted
Entry
L
Hall
W
D
Laundry
Br 3
11-1x13-3
Br 2
11-0x12-9
© Copyright by
designer/architect
Porch

First Floor
1,845 sq. ft.

Atrium
Up
Optional
Family Rm
27-0x15-0
Optional
Br 4
15-4x15-0
Bar
L
Unfinished

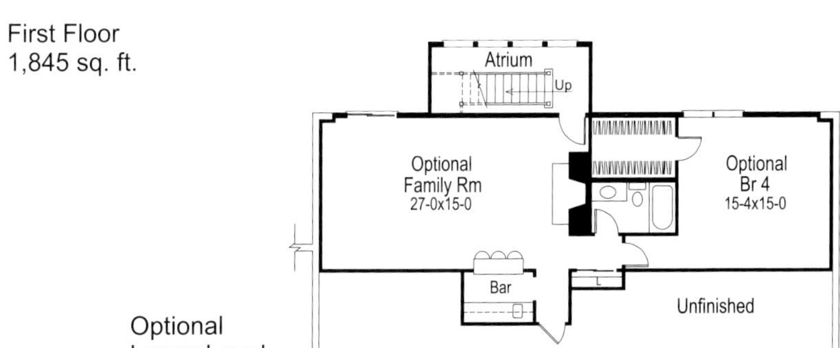

Optional
Lower Level

Rear View

To order plans, visit the Menards Building Materials Desk or visit www.Menards.com.

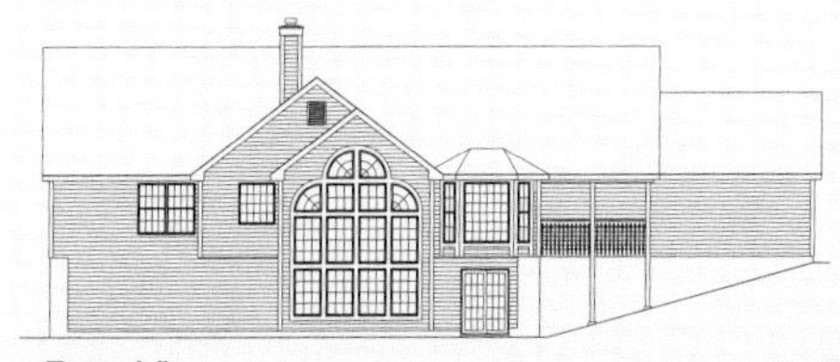

HOLLAND

MENARDS®

Plan #M08-022D-0018

GREAT ROOM WINDOW ADDS CHARACTER INSIDE AND OUT

1,368 total square feet of living area

Width: 48'-0" Depth: 49'-4"

3 bedrooms, 2 baths

2-car garage

Basement foundation

SPECIAL FEATURES

The entry steps down to an open living area that combines the great room and dining area

The vaulted master bedroom has a box-bay window and a bath with a large vanity, a separate tub, and a shower

The cozy breakfast area has direct access to the patio and pass-through kitchen

PRICE CODE A

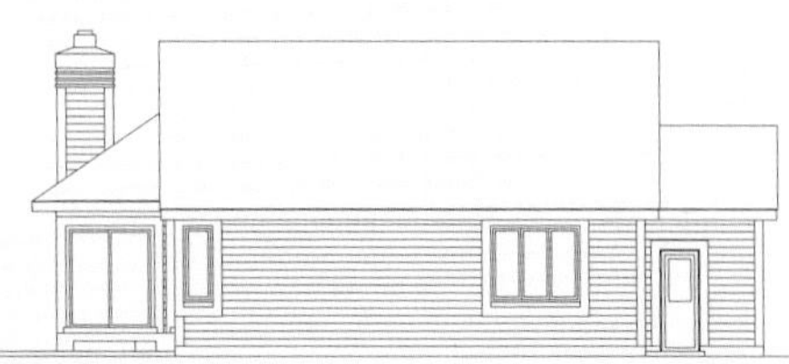

Rear View

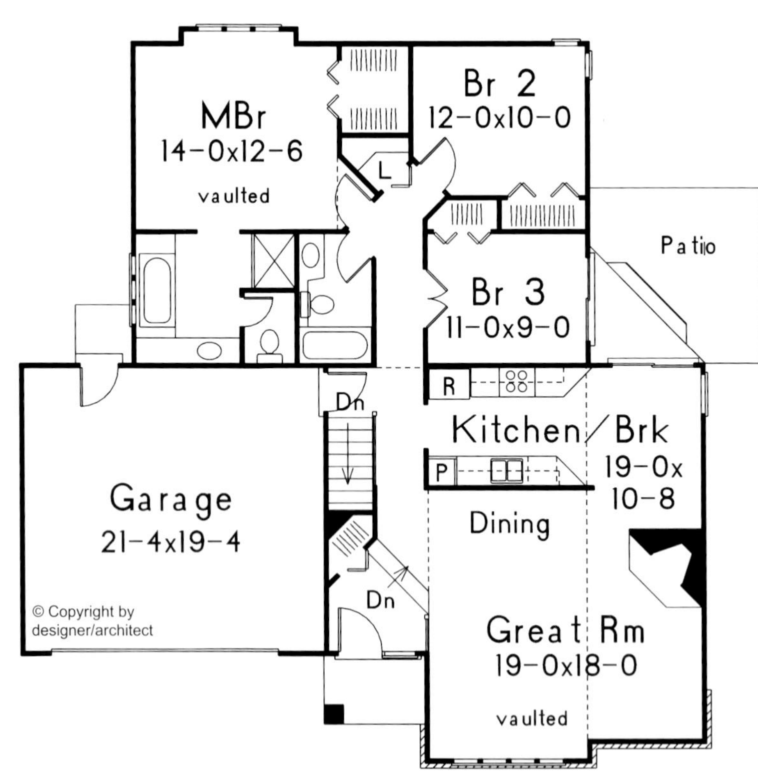

To order plans, visit the Menards Building Materials Desk or visit www.Menards.com.

HUGES HILL

Plan #M08-065L-0170

DECORATIVE ENTRY WELCOMES GUESTS

1,537 total square feet of living area

Width: 59'-8" Depth: 42'-2"

3 bedrooms, 2 baths

2-car garage

Basement foundation

SPECIAL FEATURES

A corner fireplace in the great room is visible from the foyer offering a dramatic first impression

The kitchen island connects to the dining area that features a sloped ceiling and access to the rear porch

The private master bedroom enjoys its own bath, a walk-in closet and access to the rear porch

PRICE CODE B

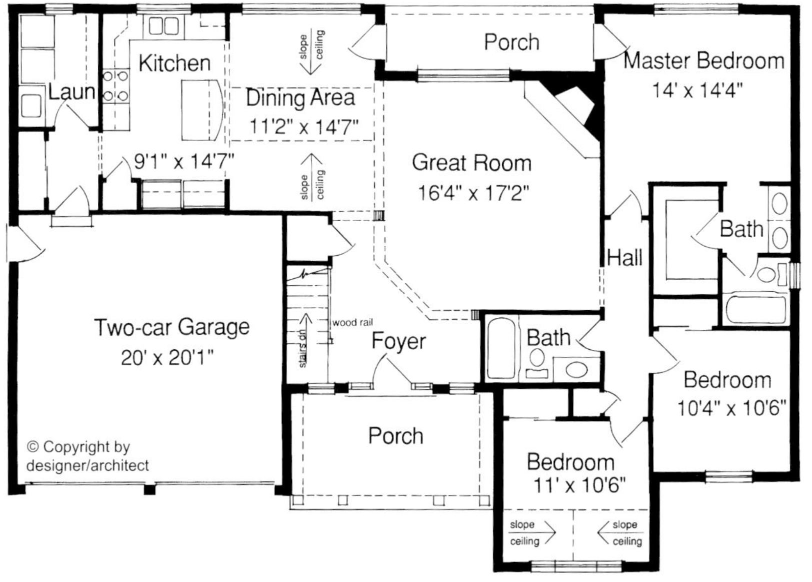

To order plans, visit the Menards Building Materials Desk or visit www.Menards.com.

CEDARWOOD

MENARDS®

Plan #M08-040D-0003

RAMBLING COUNTRY BUNGALOW

1,475 total square feet of living area

Width: 43'-0" Depth: 36'-6"

3 bedrooms, 2 baths

2-car detached side entry garage

Slab foundation, drawings also include crawl space foundation

SPECIAL FEATURES

The family room features a 10' ceiling and a prominent corner fireplace

The kitchen with island counter and garden window makes a convenient connection between the family and dining rooms

A hallway leads to three bedrooms all with large walk-in closets

PRICE CODE B

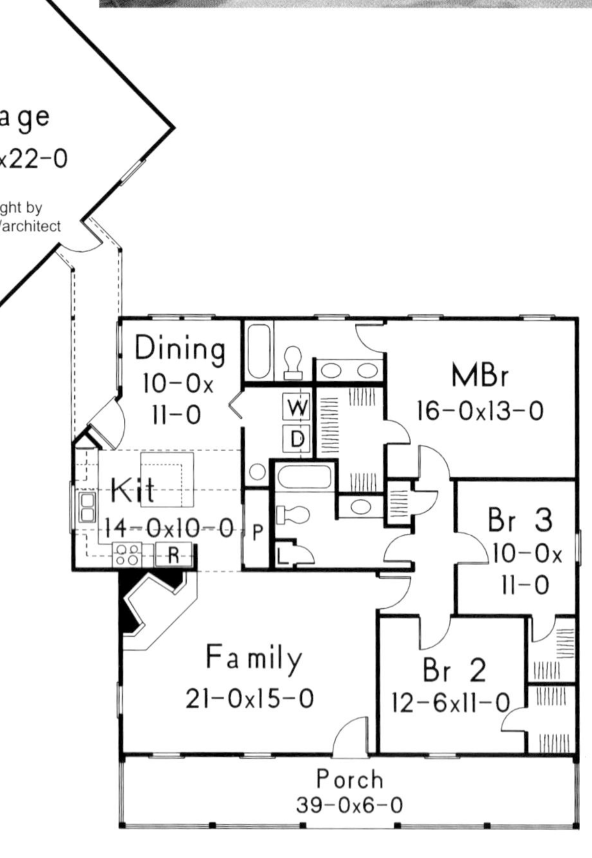

Rear View

To order plans, visit the Menards Building Materials Desk or visit www.Menards.com.

CARLSTON

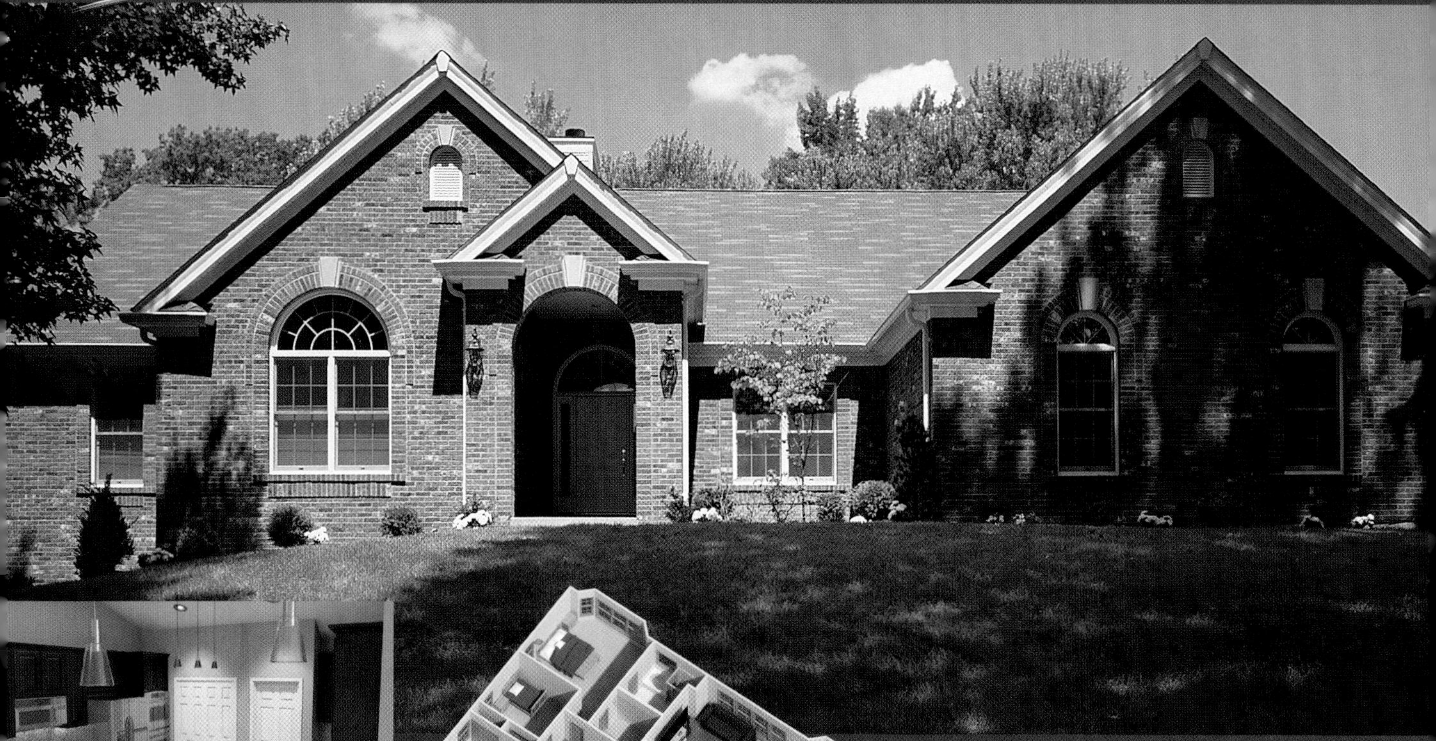

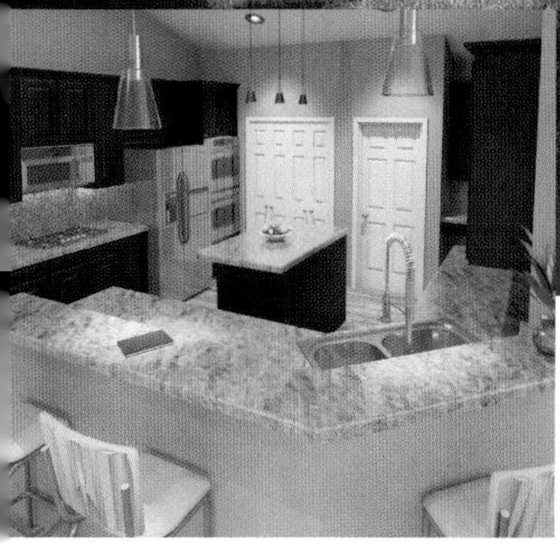

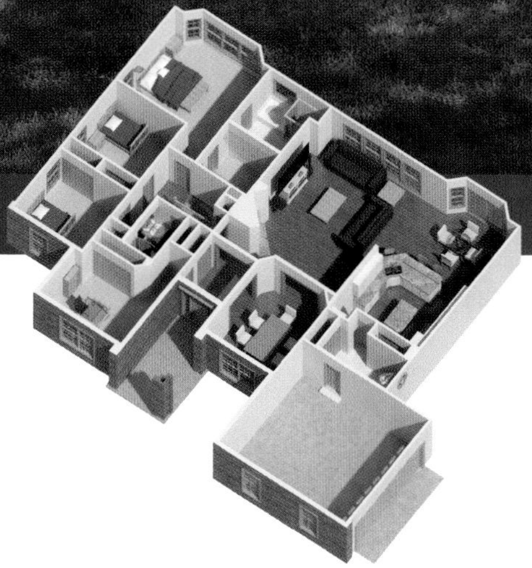

Plan #M08-007D-0062

CLASSIC ELEGANCE

2,483 total square feet of living area

Width: 69'-8" Depth: 56'-0"

3 bedrooms, 2 baths

2-car side entry garage

Basement foundation

SPECIAL FEATURES

A large entry porch with open brick arches and palladian door welcomes guests

The vaulted great room has an entertainment center alcove and the ideal layout for furniture placement

A convenient kitchen with wrap-around counter, menu desk, and pantry opens to the cozy breakfast area

2" x 6" exterior wall framing available for an additional fee, please specify when ordering

PRICE CODE D

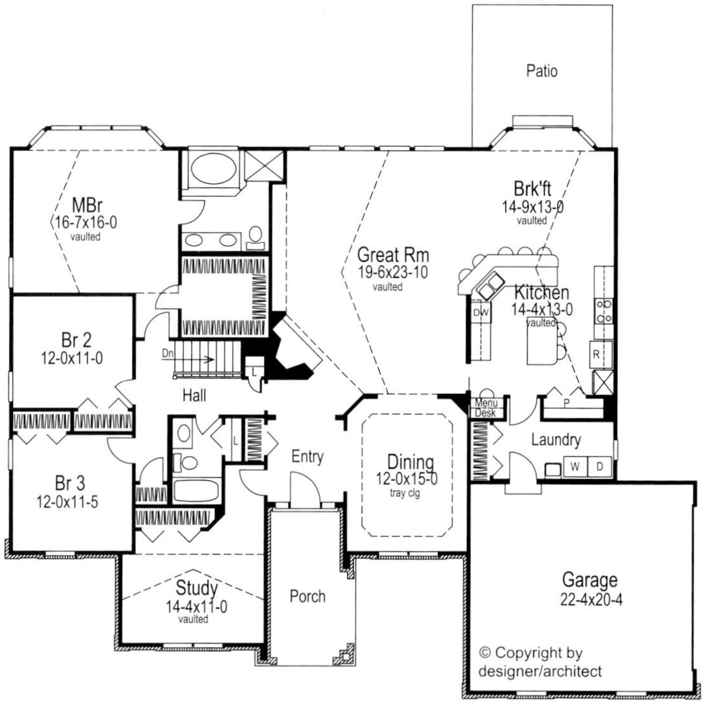

Patio

MBr
16-7x16-0
vaulted

Great Rm
19-6x23-10
vaulted

Brk'ft
14-9x13-0
vaulted

Kitchen
14-4x13-0
vaulted

Br 2
12-0x11-0

Hall

Entry

Dining
12-0x15-0
tray clg

Laundry

Br 3
12-0x11-5

Study
14-4x11-0
vaulted

Porch

Garage
22-4x20-4

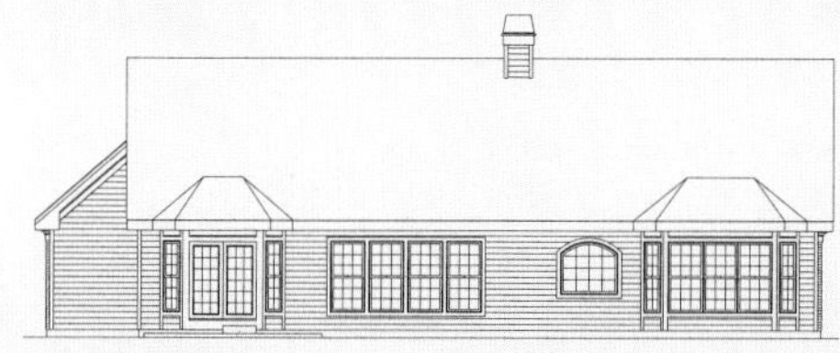

Rear View

To order plans, visit the Menards Building Materials Desk or visit www.Menards.com.

SAVAGE HILL

MENARDS®

Plan #M08-051L-0060

DRAMATIC ROOF LINES CREATE A RANCH WITH STYLE

1,591 total square feet of living area

Width: 64'-8" Depth: 57'-0"

3 bedrooms, 2 baths

3-car garage

Basement foundation

SPECIAL FEATURES

Energy efficient home with 2" x 6" exterior walls

The fireplace in the great room is accented by windows on both sides

The practical kitchen is splendidly designed for organization

The large screen porch is ideal for three-season entertaining

PRICE CODE E

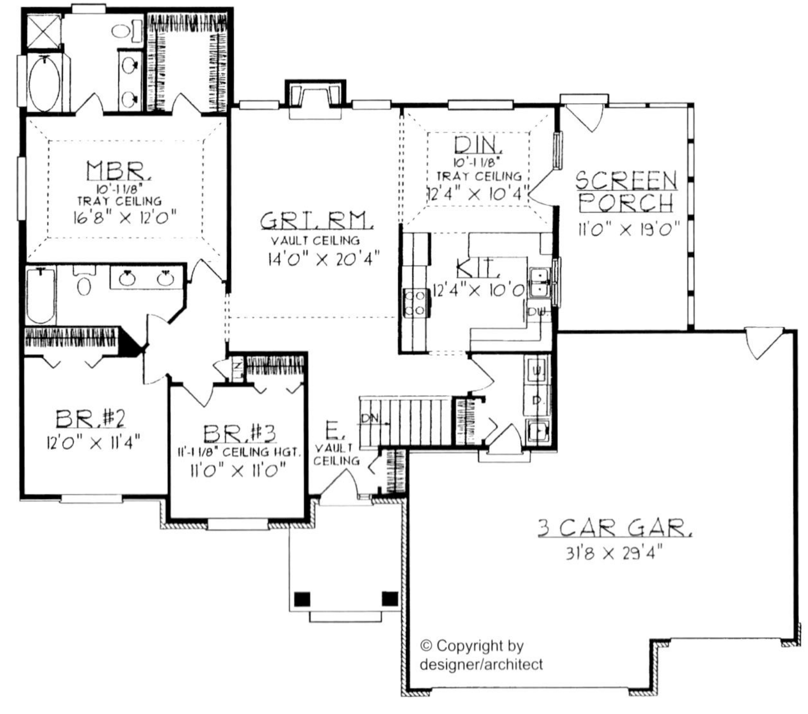

To order plans, visit the Menards Building Materials Desk or visit www.Menards.com.

MENARDS®

KENTLAND

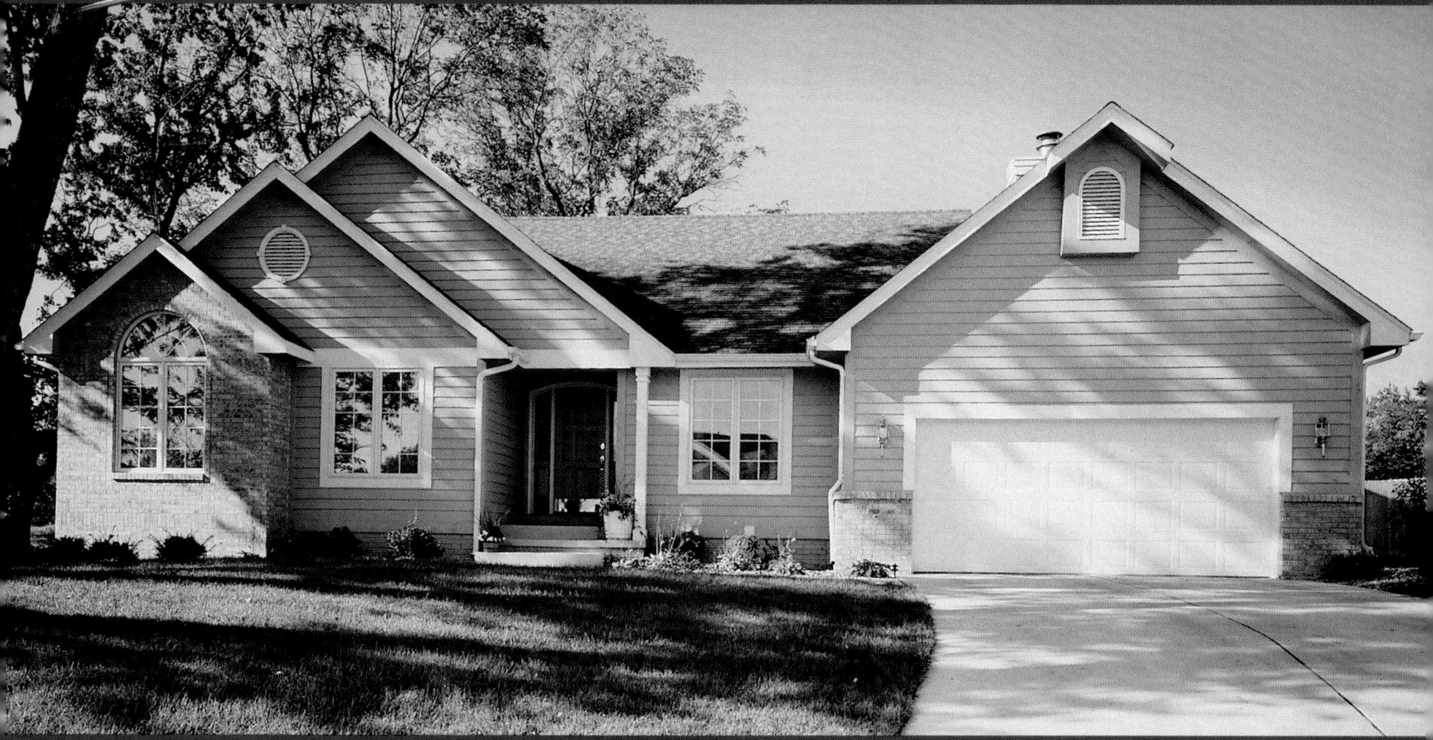

Plan #M08-022D-0026

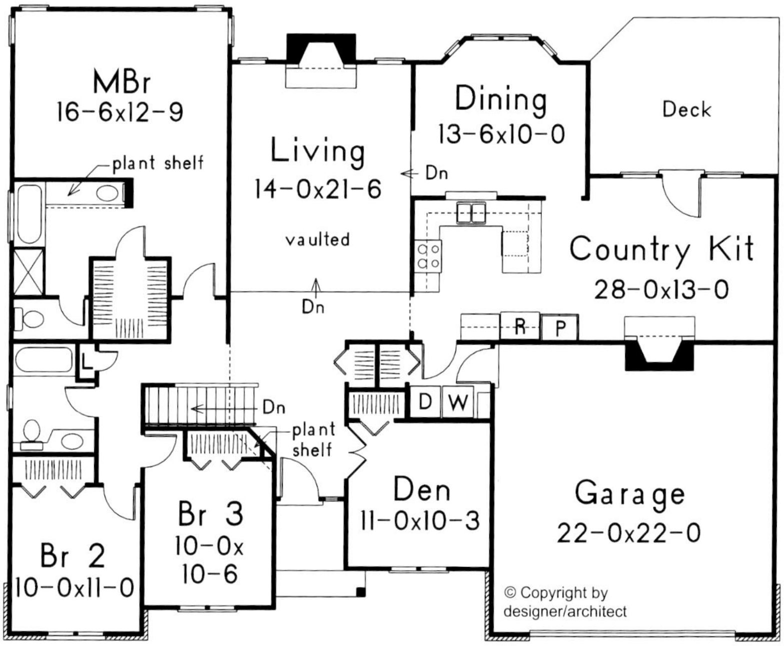

MBr
16-6x12-9
plant shelf
Living
14-0x21-6
vaulted
Dn
Dining
13-6x10-0
Dn
Deck
Country Kit
28-0x13-0
R
P
L
Dn
plant shelf
D
W
Br 2
10-0x11-0
Br 3
10-0x
10-6
Den
11-0x10-3
Garage
22-0x22-0
© Copyright by
designer/architect

To order plans, visit the Menards Building Materials Desk
or visit www.Menards.com.

PROVIDES FAMILY LIVING AT ITS BEST

1,993 total square feet of living area

Width: 60'-0" Depth: 48'-0"

3 bedrooms, 2 baths

2-car garage

Basement foundation

SPECIAL FEATURES

The country kitchen has a cozy fireplace

The formal dining room has a large bay window and leads to the sunken living room

The master bedroom features corner windows, a plant shelf, and a private bath

The entry opens into the vaulted living room with windows flanking the fireplace

PRICE CODE D

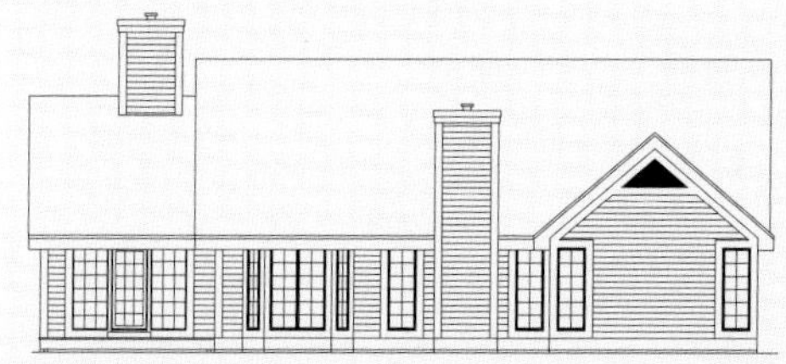

Rear View

SPRINGLAKE

MENARDS®

Plan #M08-065L-0066

CHARMING SIMPLICITY

1,598 total square feet of living area

Width: 59'-4" Depth: 45'-6"

3 bedrooms, 2 baths

2-car garage

Basement foundation

SPECIAL FEATURES

A spacious great room with fireplace and sloped ceiling opens generously to the dining area

Sliding glass doors lead to a covered porch, expanding enjoyment of this home to the outdoors

The spacious kitchen offers an abundance of cabinets and counterspace as well as a peninsula with seating

A master bedroom and two secondary bedrooms make this a great family-sized home

PRICE CODE B

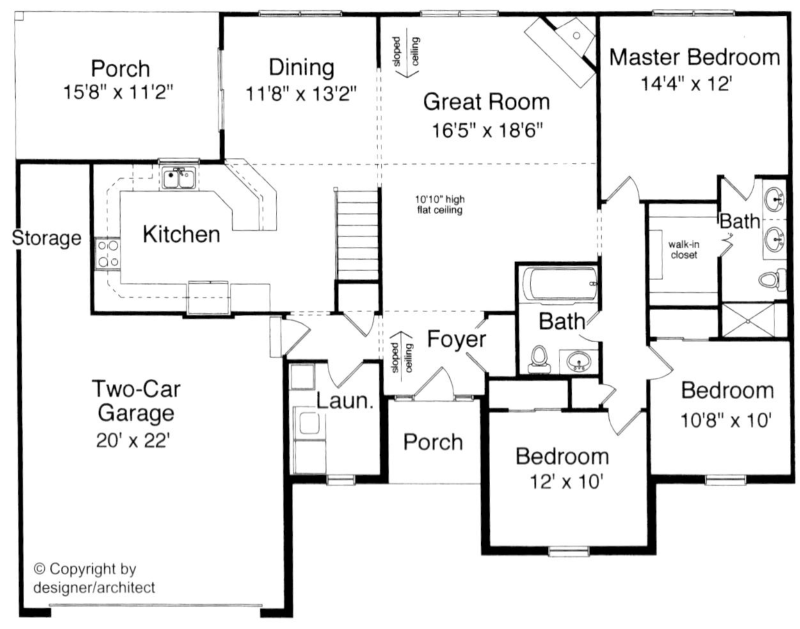

To order plans, visit the Menards Building Materials Desk or visit www.Menards.com.

MENARDS®

SUNFIELD

Plan #M08-021D-0014

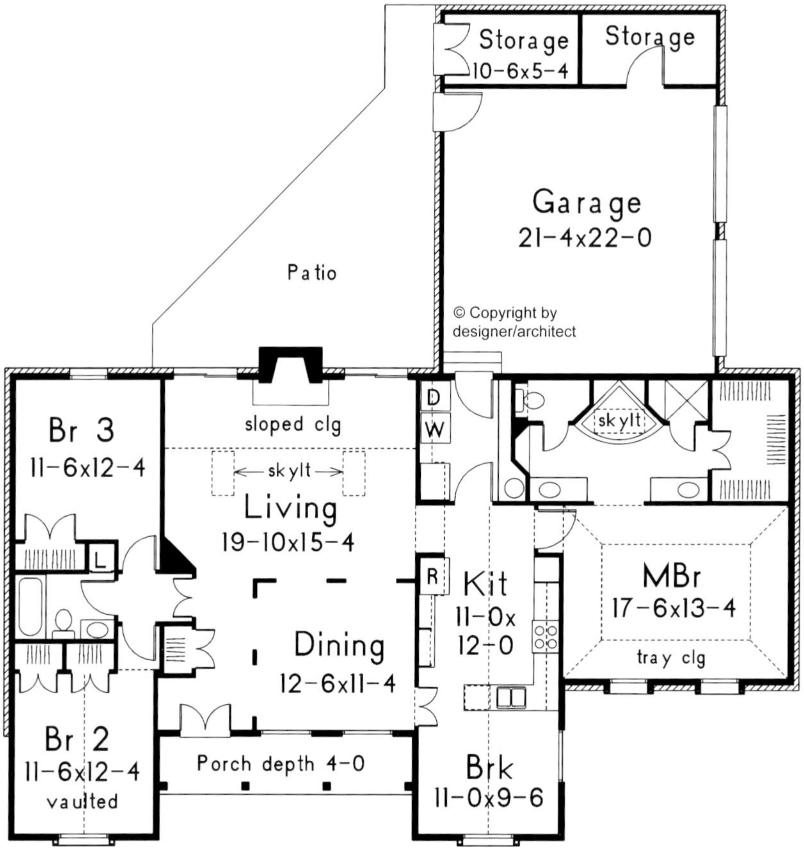

PRIVATE MASTER BEDROOM HAS A GRAND BATH

1,856 total square feet of living area

Width: 62'-0" Depth: 64'-0"

3 bedrooms, 2 baths

2-car side entry garage

Slab foundation, drawings also include crawl space foundation

SPECIAL FEATURES

Energy efficient home with 2" x 6" exterior walls

The living room has a cozy fireplace, a 12' ceiling and skylights

A vaulted ceiling creates an open kitchen and breakfast room

PRICE CODE D

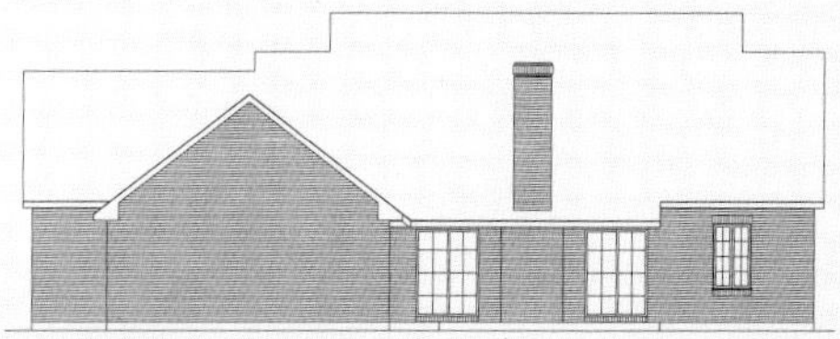

Rear View

To order plans, visit the Menards Building Materials Desk or visit www.Menards.com.

CHELMSFORD TRAIL

MENARDS®

Plan #M08-055L-0030

ATTRACTIVE EXTERIOR

2,107 total square feet of living area

Width: 64'-8" Depth: 62'-1"

4 bedrooms, 2 1/2 baths

2-car garage

Slab or crawl space foundation; basement and walk-out basement foundations available for an additional fee, please specify when ordering

SPECIAL FEATURES

The master bedroom is separated from the other bedrooms for privacy

The spacious breakfast room and kitchen include a center island with eating space

The centralized great room has a fireplace and easy access to any area in the home

PRICE CODE D

To order plans, visit the Menards Building Materials Desk or visit www.Menards.com.

MENARDS® RYEGATE

Plan #M08-077L-0037

SPLIT-BEDROOM DESIGN

1,639 total square feet of living area

Width: 64'-0" Depth: 39'-0"

3 bedrooms, 2 baths

2-car side entry garage

Slab or crawl space foundation, please specify when ordering

SPECIAL FEATURES

The great room has a tray ceiling and a welcoming fireplace

The kitchen is designed for efficiency with plenty of counterspace and a conveniently placed pantry and refrigerator

The eating area opens onto the back covered porch through beautiful French doors

PRICE CODE E

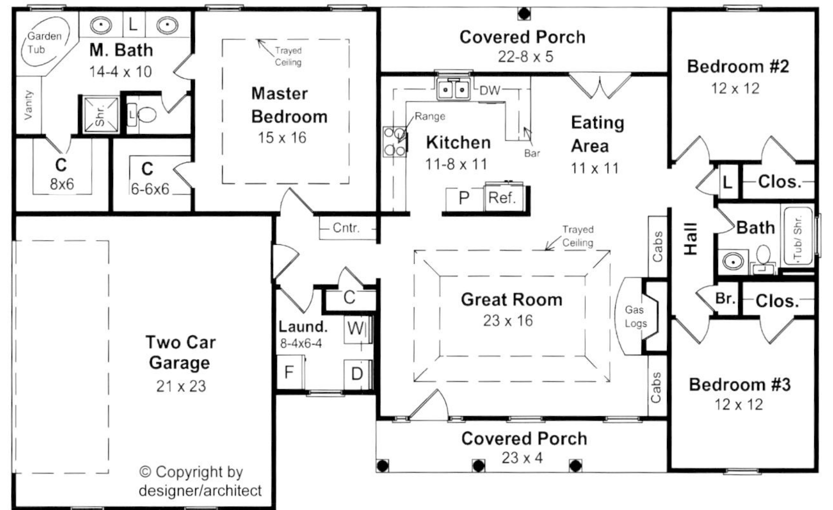

To order plans, visit the Menards Building Materials Desk or visit www.Menards.com.

Plan #M08-013L-0053

BRIGHT, CHEERFUL WINDOWS

2,461 total square feet of living area

Width: 71'-4" Depth: 74'-8"

3 bedrooms, 3 1/2 baths

3-car side entry garage

Basement foundation

SPECIAL FEATURES

The cooktop island in the kitchen has ample counterspace for easy food preparation and connects to the cozy hearth room

The luxurious master suite has a large closet with conveniently separated hanging areas

The covered deck/screened porch with vaulted ceiling creates a great outdoor gathering area

The optional second floor has an additional 518 square feet of living area

PRICE CODE D

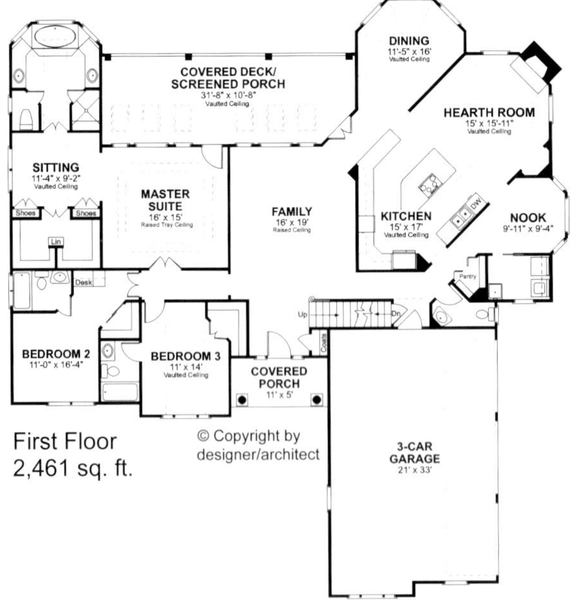

First Floor
2,461 sq. ft.

© Copyright by
designer/architect

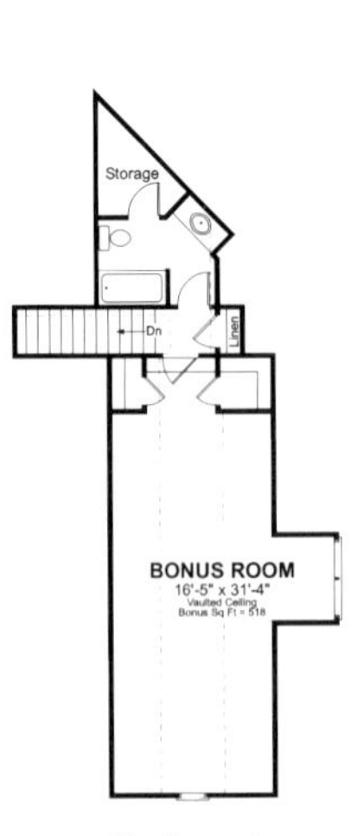

Optional
Second Floor

To order plans, visit the Menards Building Materials Desk
or visit www.Menards.com.

MENARDS®

CATALINA PLACE

Plan #M08-065L-0250

BEAUTIFUL ONE-LEVEL HOME

2,959 total square feet of living area

Width: 76'-0" Depth: 68'-1"

3 bedrooms, 2 1/2 baths

3-car side entry garage

Walk-out basement foundation

SPECIAL FEATURES

A beamed ceiling tops the great room and a fireplace with built-ins decorate one wall

A breakfast area, sitting area, and stylish kitchen create a family center perfect for casual gatherings

A library with built-in shelving and angled walls provides an area dedicated for organized work at home

PRICE CODE E

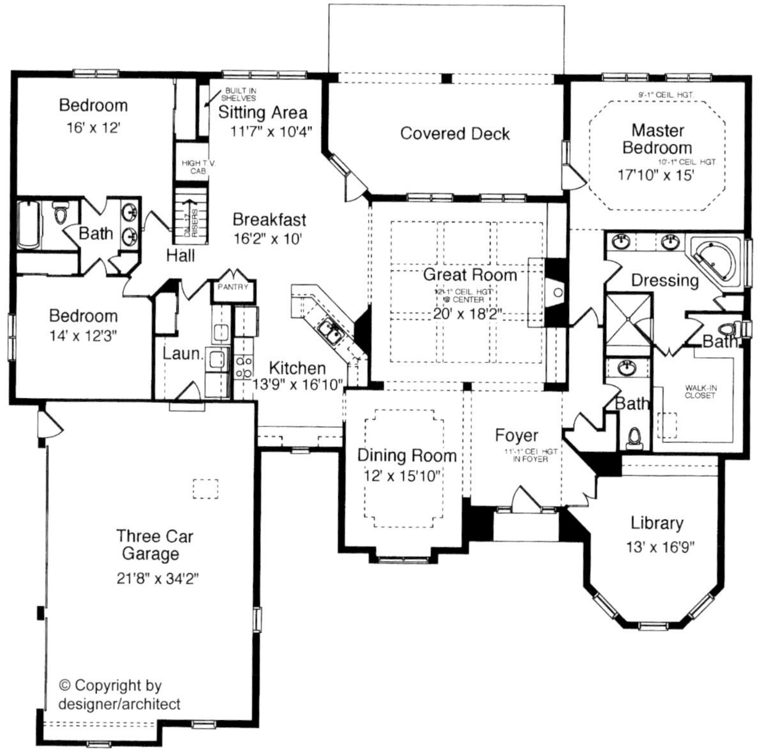

To order plans, visit the Menards Building Materials Desk or visit www.Menards.com.

Plan #M08-077L-0002

FRONT AND REAR COVERED PORCHES ADD CHARM

1,855 total square feet of living area

Width: 72'-8" Depth: 51'-0"

3 bedrooms, 2 1/2 baths

2-car side entry garage

Basement, crawl space or slab foundation, please specify when ordering

SPECIAL FEATURES

The great room boasts a 12' ceiling and a corner fireplace

The bayed breakfast area adjoins the kitchen that features a a walk-in pantry

The relaxing master bedroom includes a private bath with a walk-in closet and a garden tub

The optional second floor has an additional 352 square feet of living area

PRICE CODE E

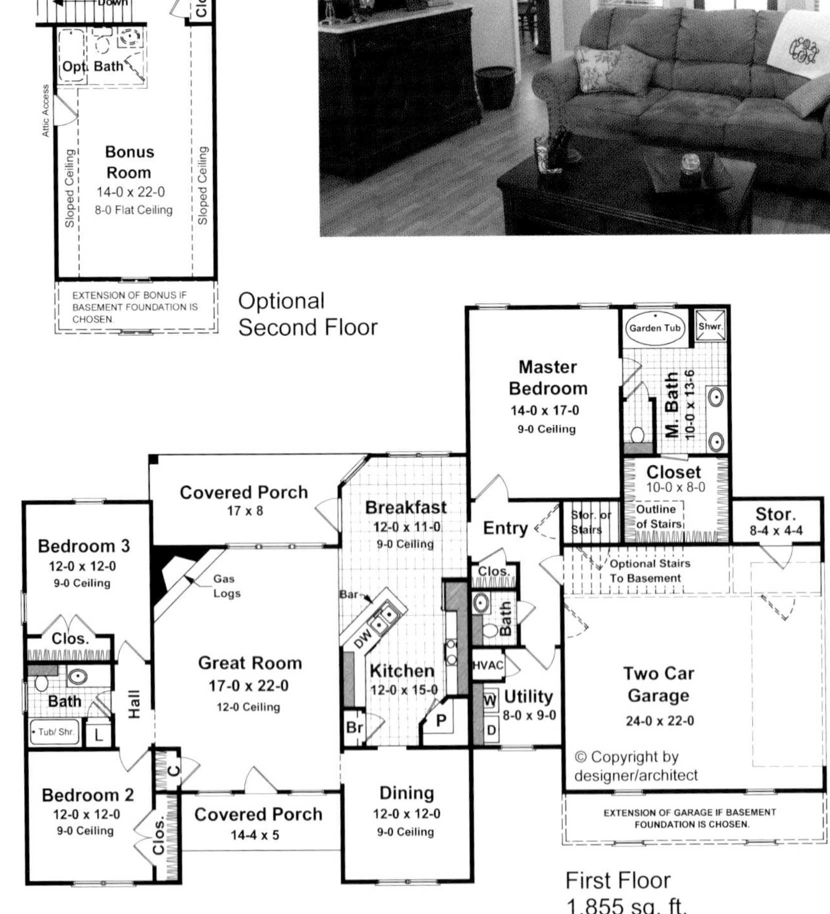

To order plans, visit the Menards Building Materials Desk or visit www.Menards.com.

MENARDS®

EVERGREEN

Plan #M08-027D-0006

GREAT ROOM FORMS CORE OF THIS HOME

2,076 total square feet of living area

Width: 63'-0" Depth: 57'-8"

3 bedrooms, 2 baths

2-car garage

Basement foundation, drawings also include walk-out basement foundation

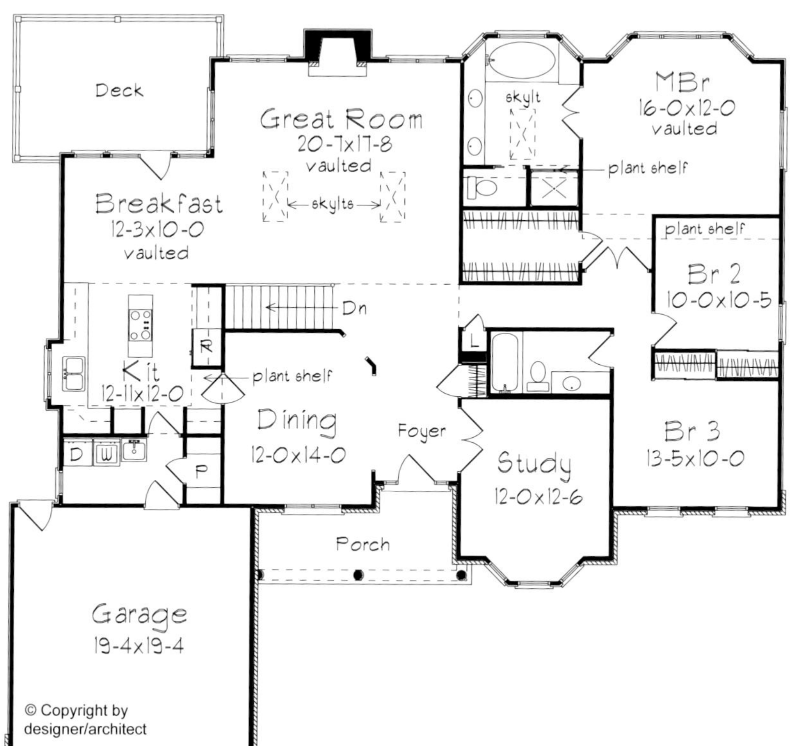

SPECIAL FEATURES

The vaulted great room has a fireplace flanked by windows and skylights

The kitchen leads to the vaulted breakfast room and rear deck

The study, located off of the foyer, provides a great location for a home office

Large bay windows grace the master bedroom and bath

PRICE CODE C

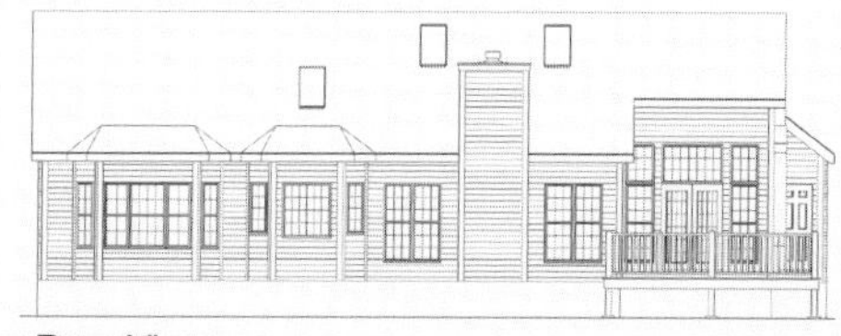
Rear View

To order plans, visit the Menards Building Materials Desk or visit www.Menards.com.

WILLOWHILL

MENARDS®

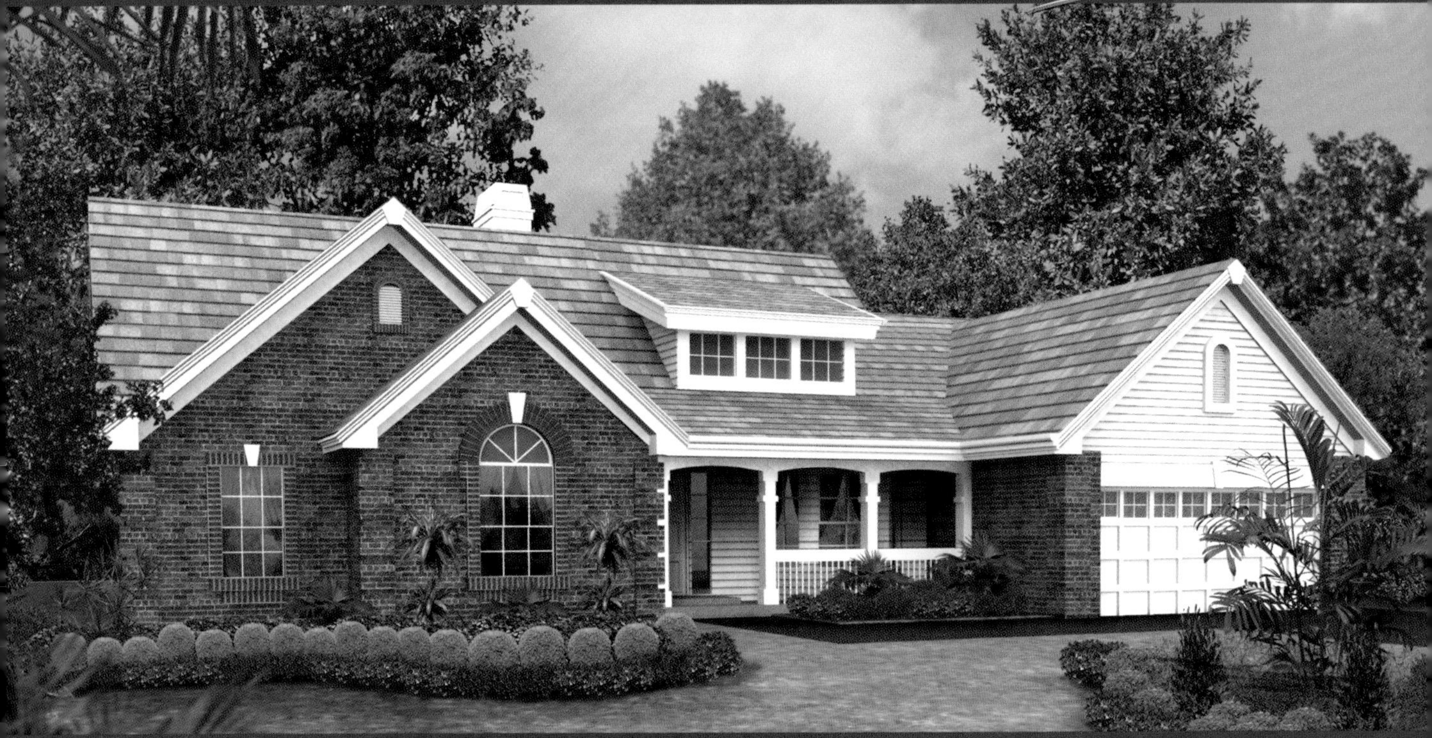

Plan #M08-007D-0157

INVITING RANCH

1,599 total square feet of living area

Width: 65'-4" Depth: 46'-4"

4 bedrooms, 2 1/2 baths

2-car garage

Basement foundation

SPECIAL FEATURES

The spacious entry leads to the great room featuring a vaulted ceiling, a fireplace, and an octagon-shaped dining area with views

The kitchen has a snack counter open to the dining area, a breakfast area with bay window, and a built-in pantry

The master bedroom has a sitting area, a large walk-in closet, and a luxury bath

The laundry room has a half bath and access to the garage with storage area

PRICE CODE B

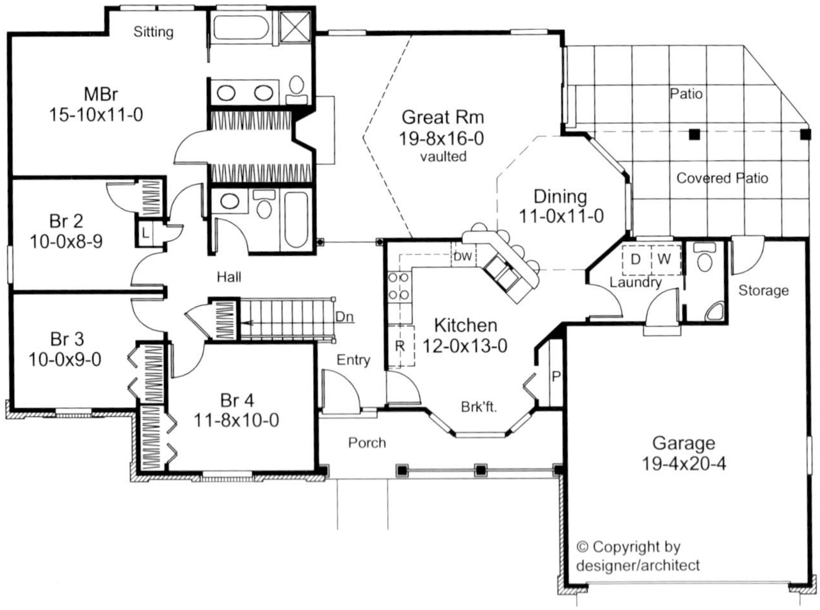

Sitting
MBr
15-10x11-0
Great Rm
19-8x16-0
vaulted
Patio
Covered Patio
Dining
11-0x11-0
Br 2
10-0x8-9
L
DW
D
W
Laundry
Storage
Hall
Dn
Br 3
10-0x9-0
Kitchen
12-0x13-0
R
Entry
P
Br 4
11-8x10-0
Brk'ft.
Porch
Garage
19-4x20-4
© Copyright by
designer/architect

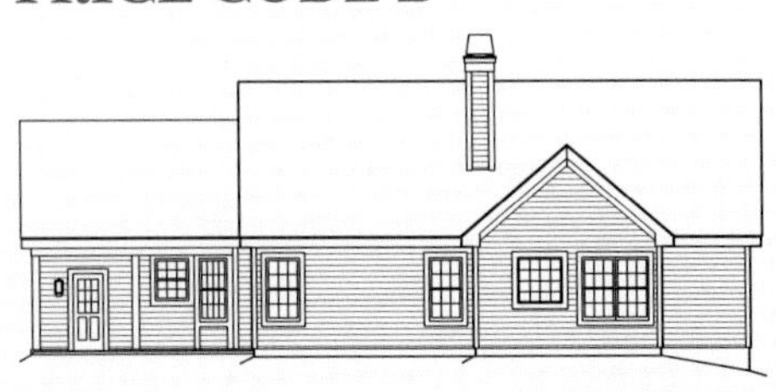

Rear View

To order plans, visit the Menards Building Materials Desk
or visit www.Menards.com.

MENARDS®

SUNRIDGE

Plan #M08-048D-0011

VAULTED CEILINGS ADD SPACIOUSNESS

1,550 total square feet of living area

Width: 43'-0" Depth: 59'-0"

3 bedrooms, 2 baths

2-car garage

Slab foundation

SPECIAL FEATURES

An alcove in the family room can be used as a corner fireplace or as a media center

The master bedroom has a large walk-in closet, and a bath with a skylight, a separate tub, and a shower

The kitchen with pantry and breakfast bar connects to the family room

The family room and master bedroom access the covered patio

PRICE CODE B

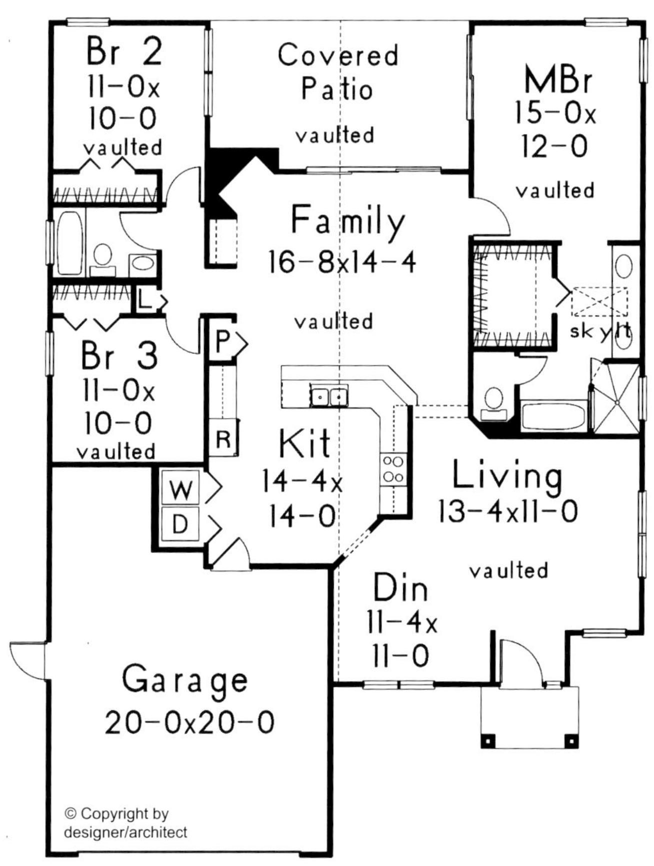

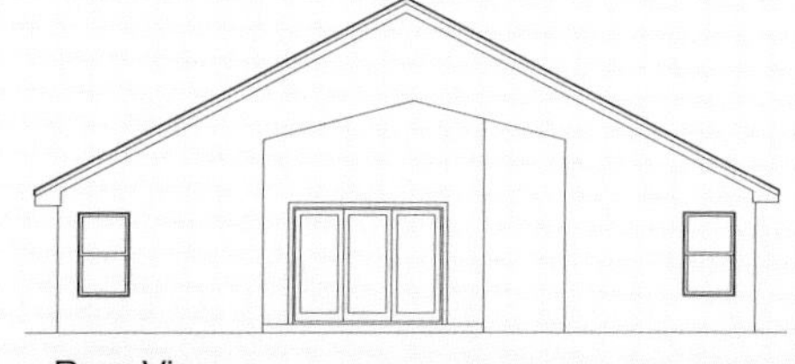

Rear View

To order plans, visit the Menards Building Materials Desk or visit www.Menards.com.

ROBERTA

MENARDS®

Plan #M08-065L-0022

SPACIOUS FOYER WELCOMES GUESTS

1,593 total square feet of living area

Width: 60'-0" Depth: 48'-10"

3 bedrooms, 2 baths

2-car garage

Basement foundation

SPECIAL FEATURES

This home is designed with an insulated foundation system featuring pre-mounted insulation on concrete walls providing a drier, warmer and smarter structure

The rear covered porch is a pleasant surprise and perfect for enjoying the outdoors

The great room is filled with extras such as a corner fireplace, a sloping ceiling, and a lovely view to the outdoors

A large island with seating separates the kitchen from the dining area

PRICE CODE B

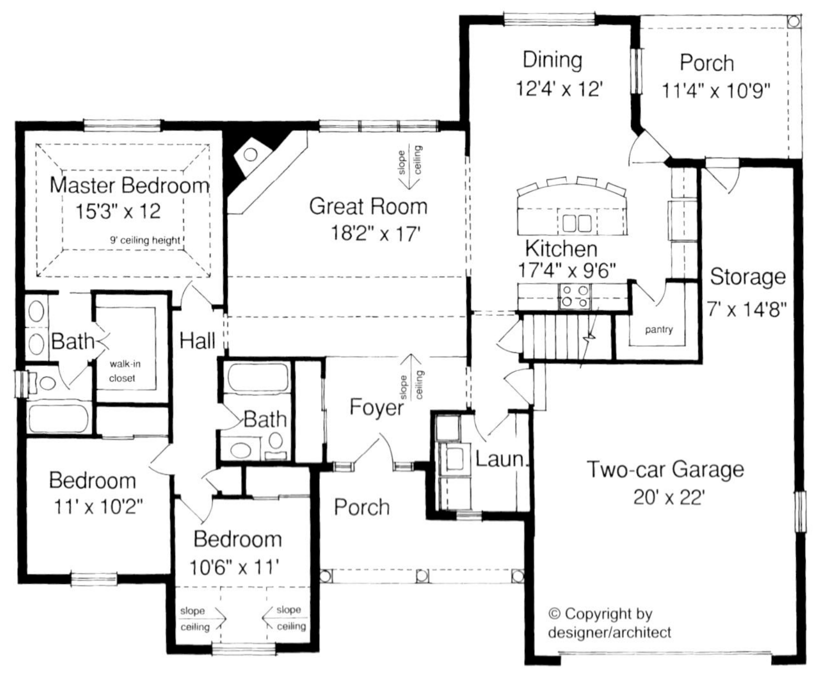

To order plans, visit the Menards Building Materials Desk or visit www.Menards.com.

PRINCETON RIDGE

Plan #M08-055L-0211

FIREPLACES WARM CHARMING RANCH

2,405 total square feet of living area

Width: 66'-4" Depth: 67'-2"

4 bedrooms, 3 baths

3-car side entry garage

Slab or crawl space foundation, please specify when ordering

SPECIAL FEATURES

The grilling and covered porches combine for a relaxing outdoor living area

The master suite enjoys a bayed sitting room and a luxurious bath with a large walk-in closet

The kitchen, breakfast and hearth rooms combine for a cozy family living area

The optional second floor has an additional 358 square feet of living area

PRICE CODE E

BREAKFAST ROOM 11'-0" X 9'-0"
GRILLING PORCH 10'-4" X 7'-8"
COVERED PORCH 18'-0" X 11'-8"
GAS FIREPLACE
HEARTH ROOM 11'-0" X 14'-0"
KITCHEN 10'-4" X 15'-0"
COMPUTER CENTER
LAU. 8'-4" X 6'-6"
PANTRY
FRENCH DOORS
MEDIA CENTER
GREAT ROOM 10' CEILING 18'-0" X 17'-4"
8" COLUMNS
DINING ROOM 10' CEILING 11'-0" X 12'-6"
FOYER 10' CEILING 7'-0" X 12'-6"
PORCH 11' CEILING 18'-0" X 5'-0"
GARAGE 21'-4" X 34'-4"
WHP TUB
GLASS SHWR
SITTING ROOM 9'-4" X 9'-4"
MASTER SUITE 13'-6" X 15'-3"
M.BATH 11'-8" X 22'-0"
LIN.
BEDROOM 4 11'-4" X 10'-8"
BEDROOM 3 11'-4" X 10'-11"
OPT. DOOR
BEDROOM 2/ STUDY 14'-0" X 12'-0"
BOOK SHELVES
BATH

First Floor
2,405 sq. ft.

BONUS ROOM 11'-8" X 29'-0"
3' WALLS
6' 8" LINE

Optional Second Floor

To order plans, visit the Menards Building Materials Desk or visit www.Menards.com.

MOYLAN

MENARDS®

Plan #M08-055L-0105

WELCOMING COVERED PORCH

1,023 total square feet of living area

Width: 45'-0" Depth: 41'-0"

3 bedrooms, 2 baths

2-car garage

Crawl space or slab foundation, please specify when ordering

SPECIAL FEATURES

The kitchen includes a snack bar and is open to the great room and the breakfast room

The master suite features a private bath

The laundry area is centrally located near all of the bedrooms for convenience

PRICE CODE B

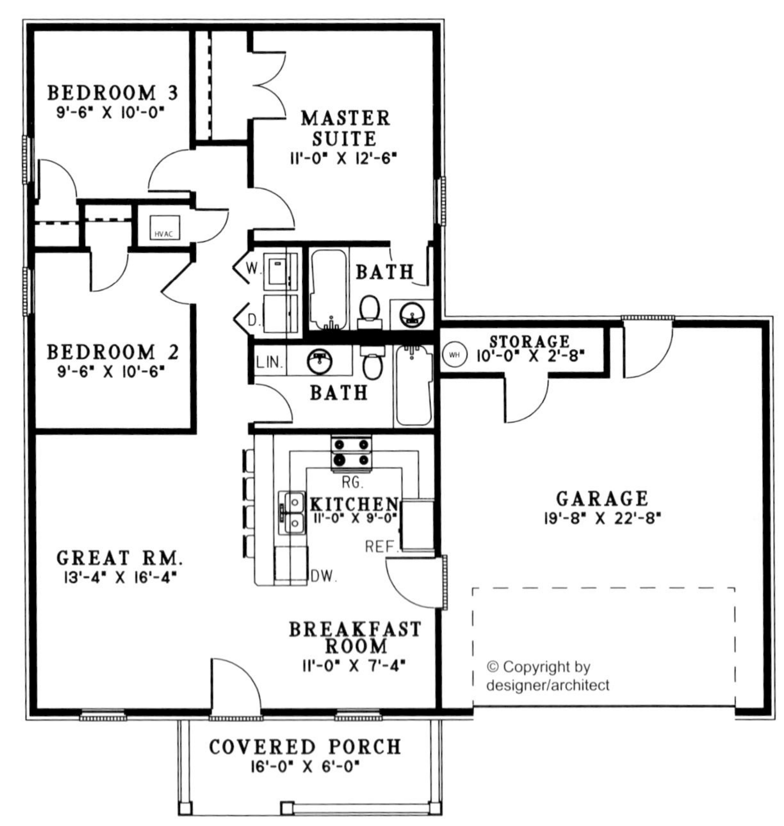

To order plans, visit the Menards Building Materials Desk or visit www.Menards.com.

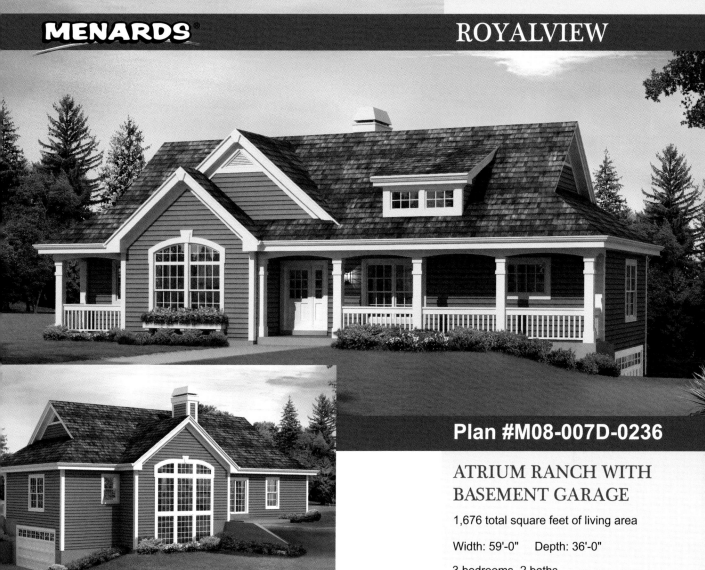

ROYALVIEW

Plan #M08-007D-0236

ATRIUM RANCH WITH BASEMENT GARAGE

1,676 total square feet of living area

Width: 59'-0" Depth: 36'-0"

3 bedrooms, 2 baths

2-car drive under side entry garage

Basement foundation

SPECIAL FEATURES

The vaulted great room features a fireplace and an atrium staircase with arched window wall

A walk-in pantry, laundry room, and breakfast area are featured in the well-planned kitchen with center island

The vaulted master bedroom has an arched window with a planter box on the exterior, two walk-in closets, and a luxury bath

The lower level atrium has 85 square feet of living area which is included in the total square footage

PRICE CODE B

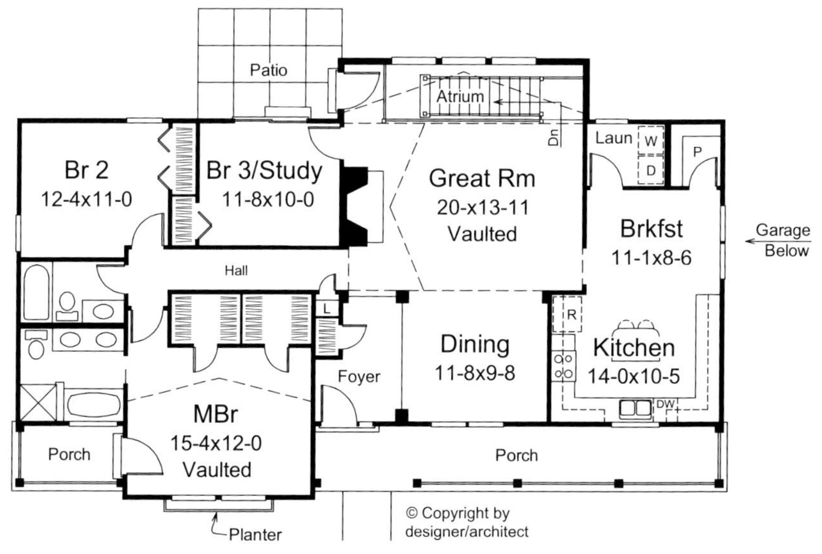

To order plans, visit the Menards Building Materials Desk or visit www.Menards.com.

FRUITLAND

MENARDS®

Plan #M08-013L-0025

INVITING VAULTED ENTRY

2,097 total square feet of living area

Width: 70'-2" Depth: 59'-0"

3 bedrooms, 3 baths

3-car side entry garage

Basement, crawl space or slab foundation, please specify when ordering

SPECIAL FEATURES

The country kitchen, family room and dining area add interest to this home

The family room includes a TV niche making this a cozy place to relax

The sumptuous master bedroom includes a sitting area, a walk-in closet, and a full bath with double vanities

The bonus room above garage has an additional 452 square feet of living space

PRICE CODE D

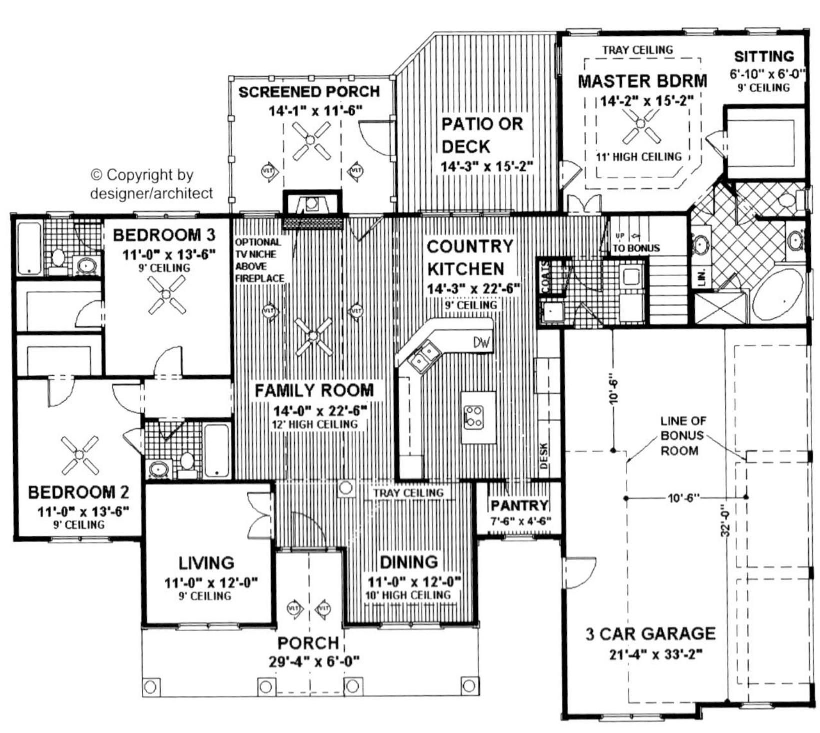

To order plans, visit the Menards Building Materials Desk or visit www.Menards.com.

MENARDS®

SHARITA

Plan #M08-077L-0007

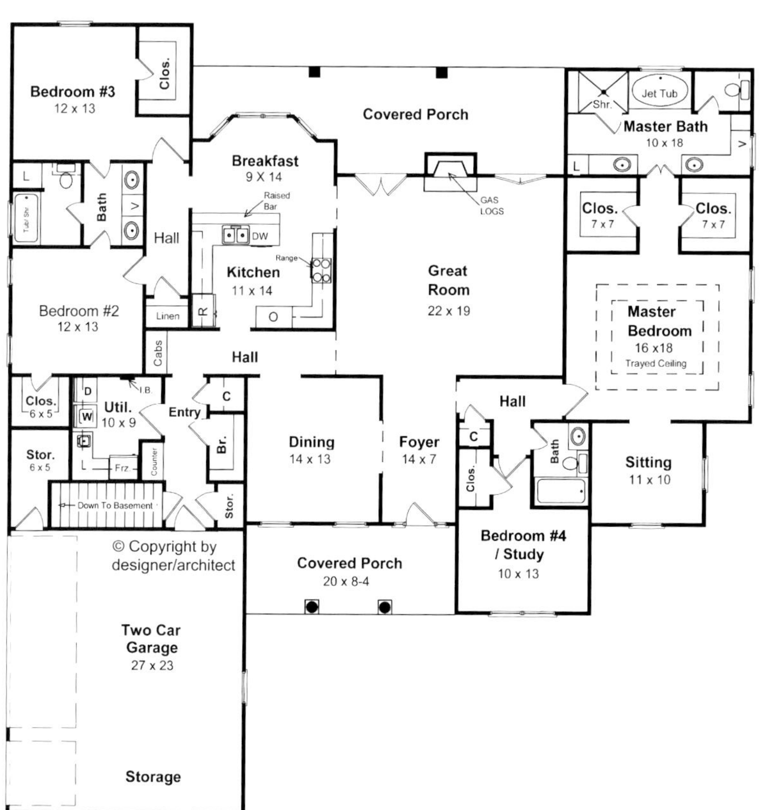

LUXURIOUS MASTER BEDROOM

2,805 total square feet of living area

Width: 71'-4" Depth: 70'-2"

4 bedrooms, 3 baths

2-car side entry garage

Basement, crawl space or slab foundation, please specify when ordering

SPECIAL FEATURES

The wrap-around counter in the kitchen opens to a bayed breakfast area

The great room features a grand fireplace flanked by two sets of double doors that access the rear covered porch

Bedrooms #2 and #3 enjoy walk-in closets

The extra-large utility room offers an abundance of workspace

PRICE CODE F

To order plans, visit the Menards Building Materials Desk or visit www.Menards.com.

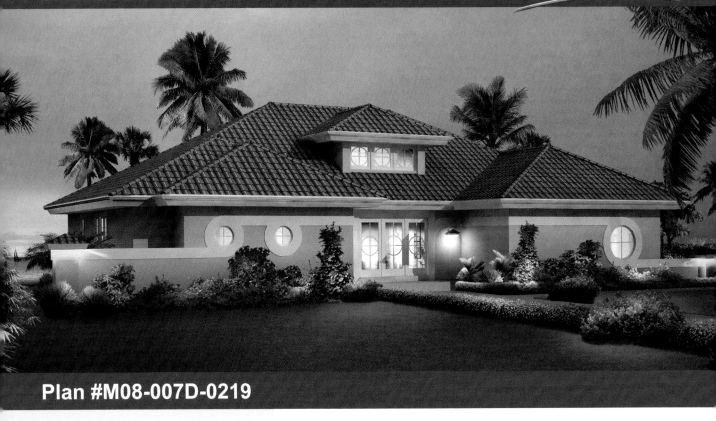

TAMPA SPRINGS

MENARDS®

Plan #M08-007D-0219

IDEAL SUNBELT DESIGN

1,939 total square feet of living area

Width: 62'-0" Depth: 48'-0"

2 bedrooms, 2 baths

2-car side entry garage

Crawl space foundation

SPECIAL FEATURES

A grand entry has unique curved walls and flanking coat closets leading down a few steps into an enormous sunken great room

The spacious kitchen with cabinets galore has a built-in pantry, a functional island/snack bar, and a dining area

A laundry room, plus mechanical and coat closets are conveniently situated between the kitchen and the garage

The huge master bedroom features a luxury bath with separate shower, a large walk-in closet, and a private covered patio

PRICE CODE B

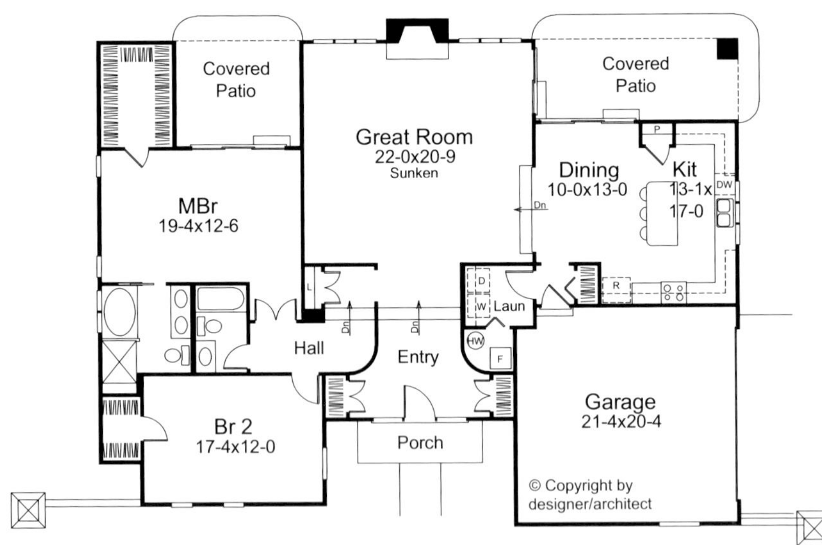

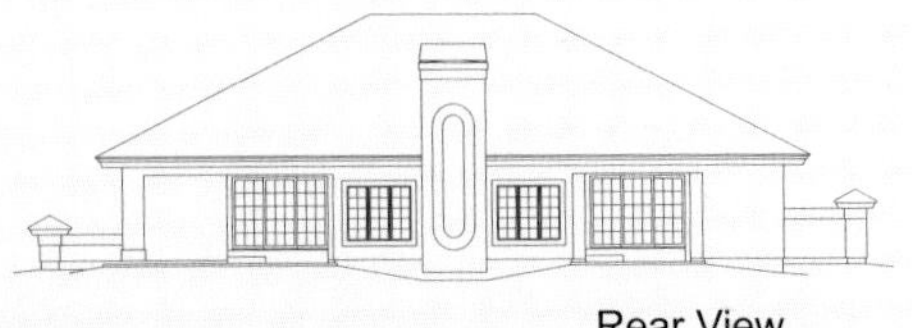
Rear View

To order plans, visit the Menards Building Materials Desk
or visit www.Menards.com.

MENARDS®

ELMSDALE

Plan #M08-017D-0004

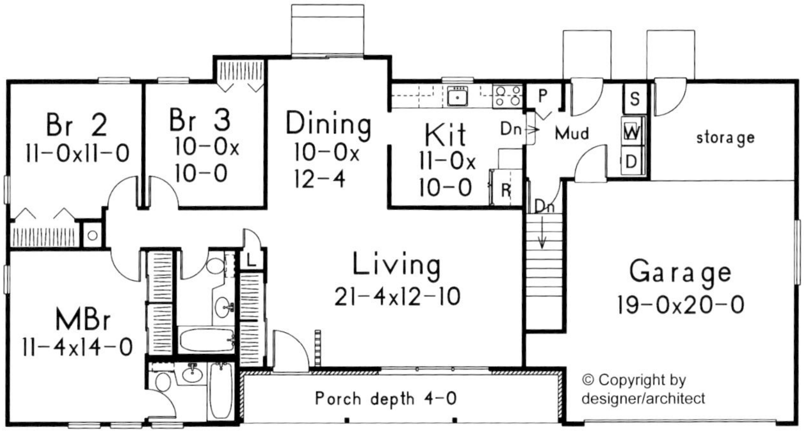

SWEEPING RANCH WITH HIP ROOF

1,315 total square feet of living area

Width: 66'-4" Depth: 30'-4"

3 bedrooms, 2 baths

2-car garage

Basement foundation, drawings also include slab foundation

SPECIAL FEATURES

The dining room has sliding glass doors to the rear patio

There is a large storage space in the garage

The kitchen has a cozy eating area and access to the mud room

The large living room has double closets for storage and coats

PRICE CODE B

To order plans, visit the Menards Building Materials Desk or visit www.Menards.com.

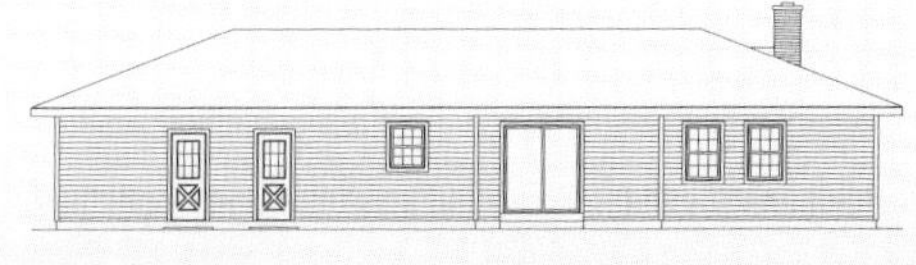

Rear View

RYLAND

MENARDS®

Plan #M08-005D-0001

CLASSIC RANCH HAS GRAND APPEAL WITH EXPANSIVE PORCH

1,400 total square feet of living area

Width: 72'-0" Depth: 34'-4"

3 bedrooms, 2 baths

2-car garage

Basement foundation, drawings also include crawl space foundation

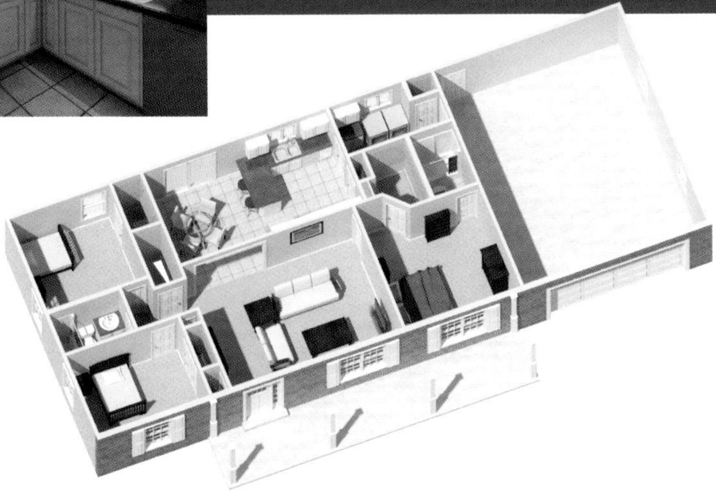

SPECIAL FEATURES

The master bedroom is secluded for privacy

The large utility room has additional cabinet space

The covered porch provides an outdoor seating area

The living room and master bedroom feature vaulted ceilings

PRICE CODE B

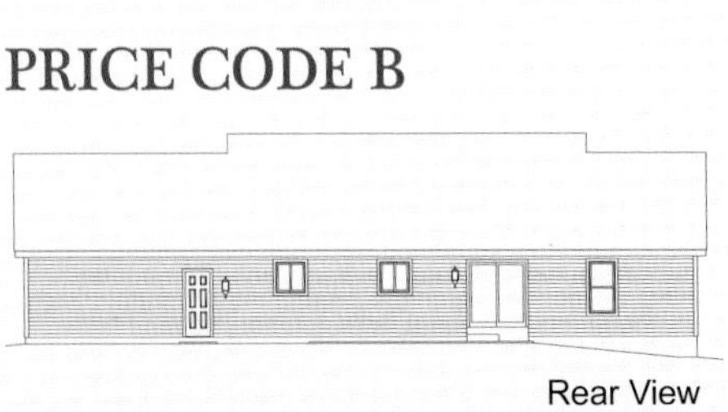

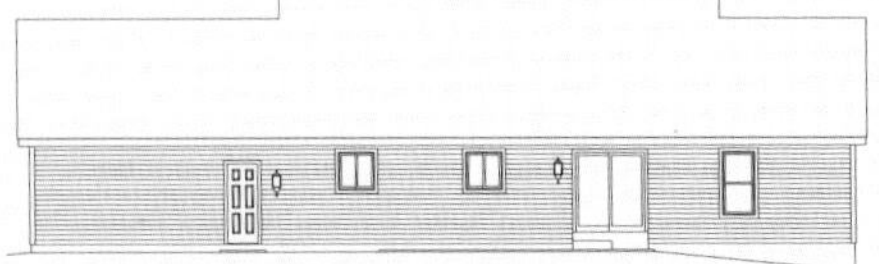

Rear View

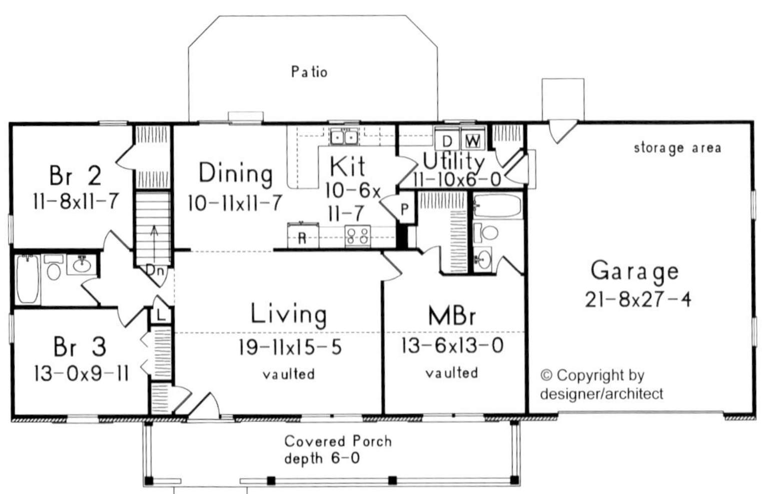

To order plans, visit the Menards Building Materials Desk or visit www.Menards.com.

MENARDS®

ROCHELLE BAY

Plan #M08-007D-0204

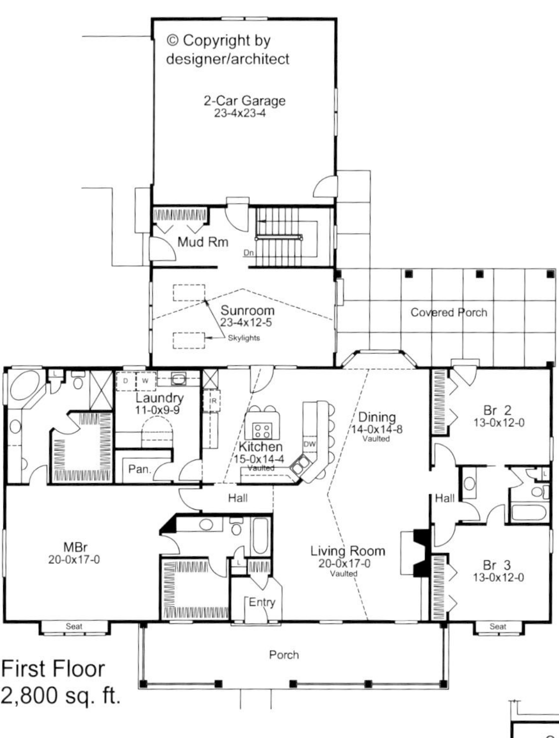

First Floor
2,800 sq. ft.

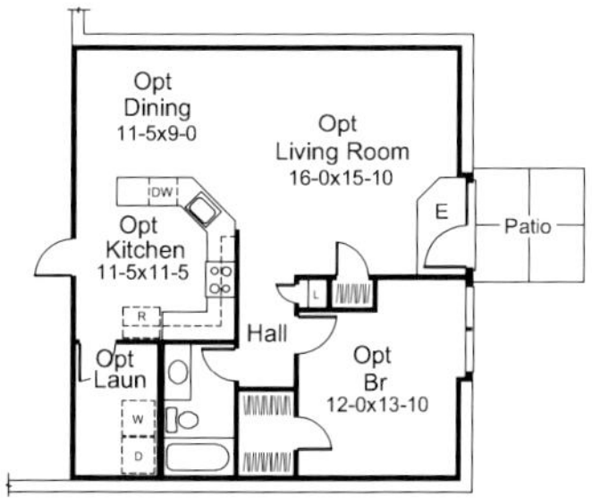

Opt Dining 11-5x9-0
Opt Living Room 16-0x15-10
Opt Kitchen 11-5x11-5
Patio
Hall
Opt Laun
Opt Br 12-0x13-10

Optional Lower Level

To order plans, visit the Menards Building Materials Desk or visit www.Menards.com.

SUNROOM AND TWO COVERED PORCHES

2,800 total square feet of living area

Width: 71'-0" Depth: 84'-4"

3 bedrooms, 3 baths

2-car side entry garage

Walk-out basement foundation

SPECIAL FEATURES

The vaulted living and dining rooms have a fireplace and a bay window with views of the rear covered porch

The spacious master bedroom with coffered ceiling has both his and hers baths with large walk-in closets

A sunroom is near the rear covered porch

The optional lower level basement apartment has an additional 932 square feet of living area

PRICE CODE D

Rear View

ROCKWOOD

MENARDS®

Plan #M08-006D-0003

SCULPTURED ROOF LINE AND FACADE ADD CHARM

1,674 total square feet of living area

Width: 78'-4" Depth: 50'-0"

3 bedrooms, 2 baths

2-car garage

Basement foundation, drawings also include crawl space and slab foundations

SPECIAL FEATURES

The vaulted great room, dining area and kitchen all enjoy a central fireplace

The convenient laundry/mud room connects to the garage and has a handy stairs to the basement

The master bedroom features a full bath with a tub, a separate shower, and a walk-in closet

PRICE CODE B

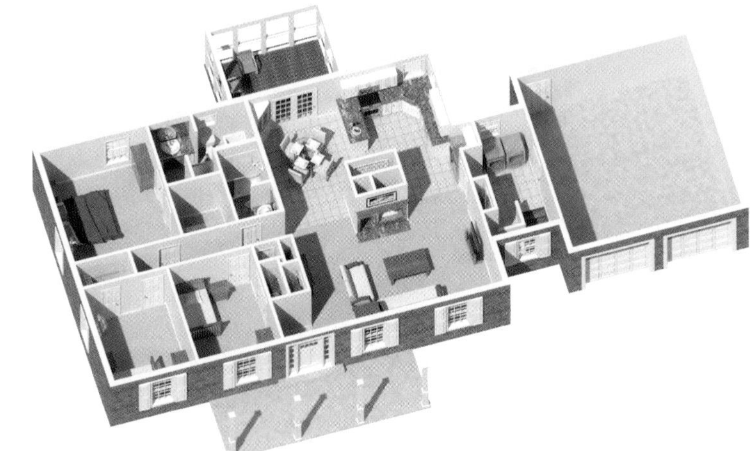

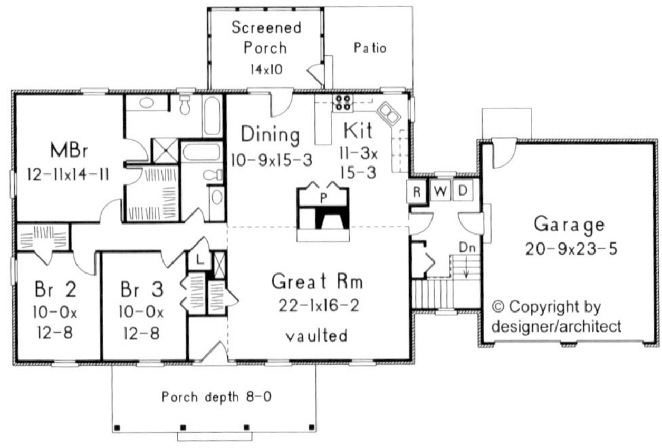

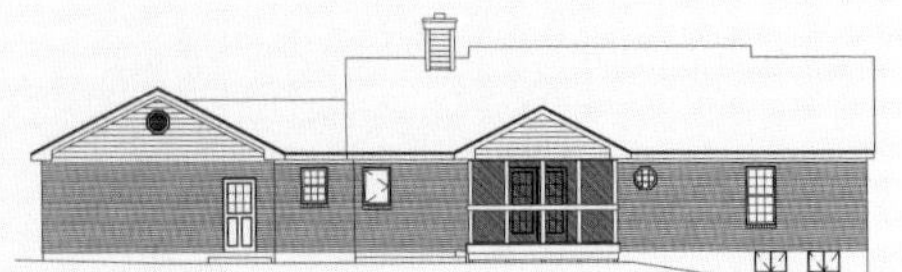

Rear View

To order plans, visit the Menards Building Materials Desk or visit www.Menards.com.

MENARDS®

YATES

Plan #M08-013L-0051

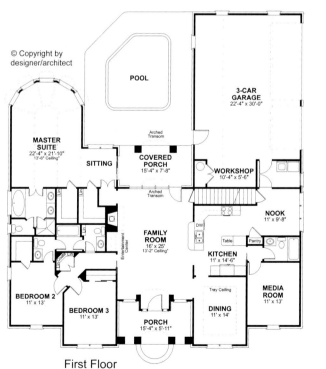

BEAUTIFUL BRICK EXTERIOR

2,260 total square feet of living area

Width: 62'-0" Depth: 69'-2"

3 bedrooms, 3 baths

3-car side entry garage

Basement or crawl space foundation, please specify when ordering

SPECIAL FEATURES

The master suite has a bayed window wall with a view of the backyard and pool

The large kitchen includes a useful table in the middle

The entertainment center and fireplace create a focal point in the family room

The optional second floor has an additional 404 square feet of living space

PRICE CODE D

POOL

3-CAR GARAGE 22'-4" x 30'-0"

MASTER SUITE 22'-4" x 21'-10" 13'-0" Ceiling

SITTING

Arched Transom

COVERED PORCH 15'-4" x 7'-8"

WORKSHOP 10'-4" x 5'-6"

Arched Transom

NOOK 11' x 9'-8"

FAMILY ROOM 16' x 25' 13'-2" Ceiling

Entertainment Center

DW

Table

Pantry

KITCHEN 11' x 14'-6"

Lin

Coats

Tray Ceiling

MEDIA ROOM 11' x 13'

BEDROOM 2 11' x 13'

BEDROOM 3 11' x 13'

PORCH 15'-4" x 5'-11"

DINING 11' x 14'

First Floor
2,260 sq. ft.

BONUS ROOM 10'-6" x 30'-10" 404 Sq. Ft.

Optional
Second Floor

To order plans, visit the Menards Building Materials Desk or visit www.Menards.com.

TRISTA

MENARDS®

Plan #M08-051L-0174

IMPRESSIVE ENTRY SETS TONE OF HOME

1,817 total square feet of living area

Width: 57'-0" Depth: 56'-0"

3 bedrooms, 2 baths

2-car garage

Basement foundation

SPECIAL FEATURES

Energy efficient home with 2" x 6" exterior walls

12' ceilings grace the entry and great room

The formal dining room boasts a 12' ceiling and a wall of windows bringing in warm natural light

The bayed nook accesses the outdoors

The master bedroom has two closets and a private bath

PRICE CODE E

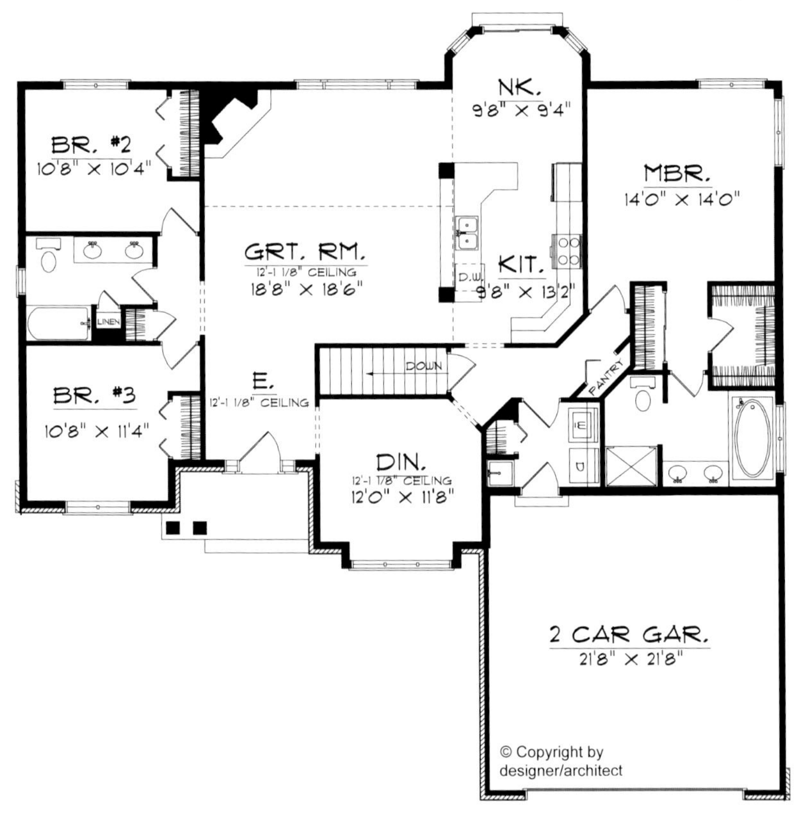

Rear View

To order plans, visit the Menards Building Materials Desk or visit www.Menards.com.

MENARDS®

BAKERSPORT

Plan #M08-058D-0060

TRADITIONAL RANCH HOME

2,015 total square feet of living area

Width: 59'-0" Depth: 56'-0"

3 bedrooms, 2 1/2 baths

3-car side entry garage

Basement foundation

SPECIAL FEATURES

The foyer opens into the spacious vaulted great room

The open kitchen/breakfast area includes an island with space for seating, a pantry, and a built-in desk

The bedrooms remain private from the living areas

PRICE CODE C

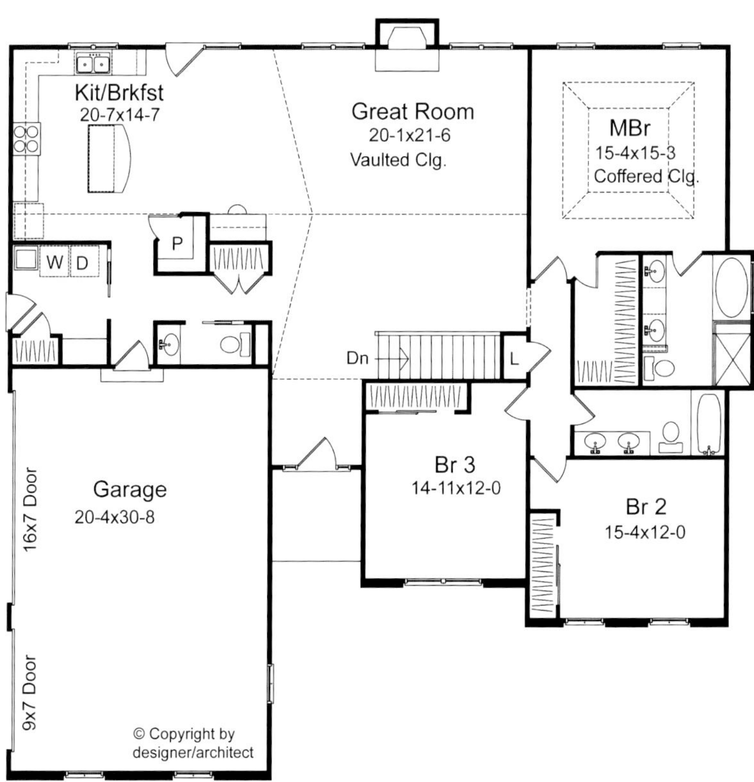

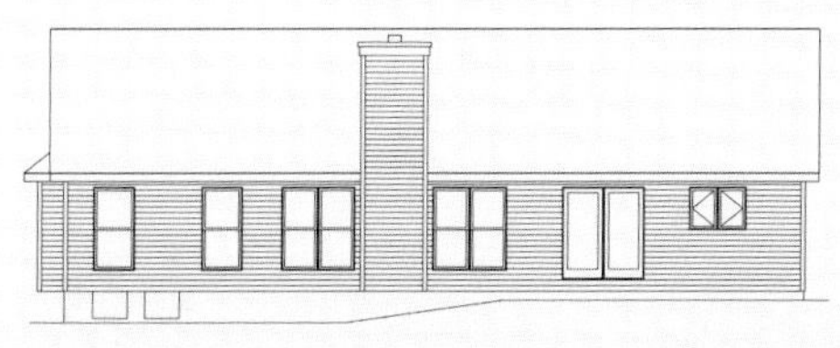

Rear View

To order plans, visit the Menards Building Materials Desk or visit www.Menards.com.

HILLSHIRE

MENARDS®

Plan #M08-057D-0010

SPLIT-BEDROOM FLOOR PLAN

1,242 total square feet of living area

Width: 58'-0" Depth: 48'-0"

3 bedrooms, 2 baths

2-car garage

Basement foundation

SPECIAL FEATURES

Energy efficient home with 2" x 6" exterior walls

The wide foyer opens to the living room for a spacious atmosphere and a grand first impression

The centrally located kitchen easily serves the large dining and living rooms

The split-bedroom design allows privacy for the homeowners who will love spending time in their master bedroom retreat

PRICE CODE A

To order plans, visit the Menards Building Materials Desk or visit www.Menards.com.

MENARDS®

SHADYVIEW

Plan #M08-007D-0124

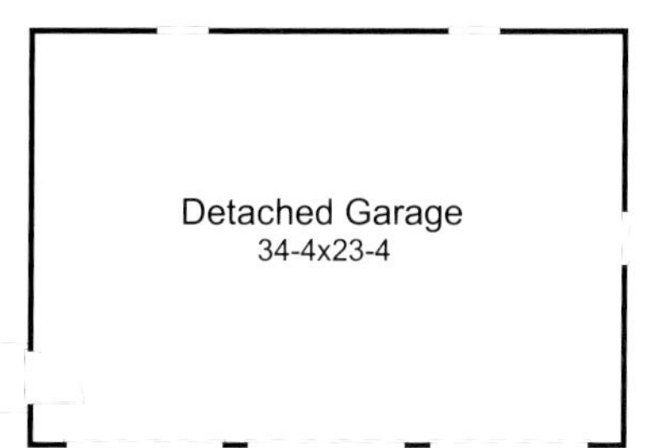

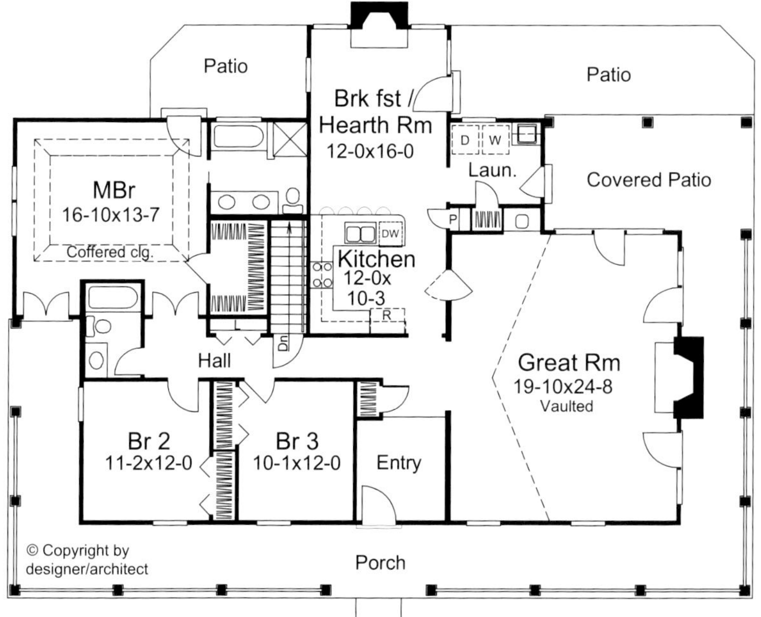

To order plans, visit the Menards Building Materials Desk or visit www.Menards.com.

COUNTRY RANCH HOME

1,944 total square feet of living area

Width: 65'-0" Depth: 51'-0"

3 bedrooms, 2 baths

3-car detached garage

Basement foundation

SPECIAL FEATURES

The entry leads to a spacious vaulted great room featuring a fireplace, a wet bar, and porch access through three doors

The U-shaped kitchen is open to the breakfast/hearth room and enjoys a snack bar, a fireplace, and patio access

A luxury bath, walk-in closet and porch access are amenities of the master bedroom

PRICE CODE C

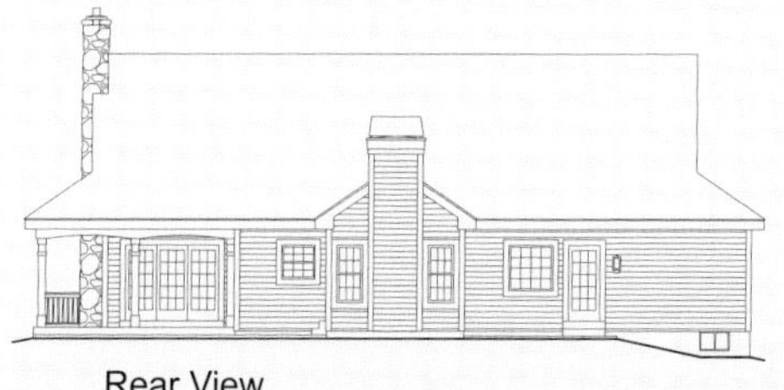

Rear View

SUNDERLAND MANOR

MENARDS®

Plan #M08-077L-0184

LUXURY INSIDE AND OUT

2,400 total square feet of living area

Width: 73'-6"   Depth: 62'-0"

4 bedrooms, 2 1/2 baths

2-car side entry garage

Slab or crawl space foundation, please specify when ordering

SPECIAL FEATURES

All of the bedrooms feature walk-in closets for extra organization

The master bedroom with private bath and two walk-in closets is separated from the other bedrooms for privacy

The flex space is a versatile room that can adapt to your needs whether it be an office or formal dining room

The unfinished bonus room has an additional 452 square feet of living area

PRICE CODE F

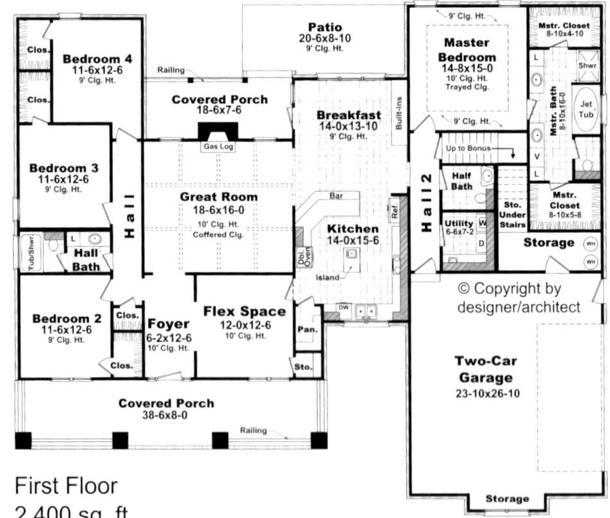

First Floor
2,400 sq. ft.

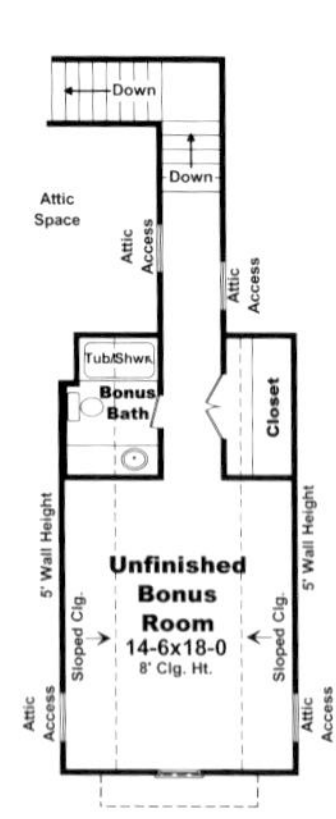

Optional
Second Floor

To order plans, visit the Menards Building Materials Desk or visit www.Menards.com.

MENARDS®

SAXONY II

Plan #M08-001D-0053

MBr
12-3x12-3
Family/Din
15-2x12-3
Kit
11-3x
12-3
Garage
23-8x21-5
Furn W D P
L
© Copyright by
designer/architect
Br 2
11-3x10-1
Br 3
10-1x11-6
Living
23-1x11-6
Porch depth 5-0

STYLISH RANCH WITH RUSTIC CHARM

1,344 total square feet of living area

Width: 72'-0" Depth: 33'-0"

3 bedrooms, 2 baths

2-car garage

Crawl space foundation, drawings also include basement and slab foundations

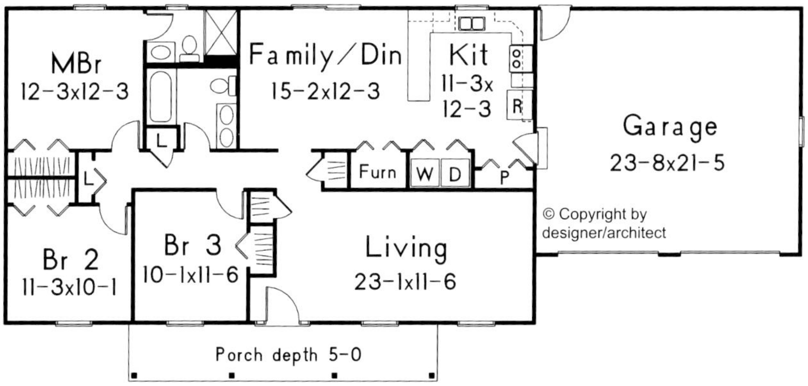

SPECIAL FEATURES

The family/dining room has sliding glass doors to the outdoors

The master bedroom has a private bath

The hall bath includes a double-bowl vanity for added convenience

The U-shaped kitchen features a large pantry and laundry area

2" x 6" exterior wall framing available for an additional fee, please specify when ordering

PRICE CODE A

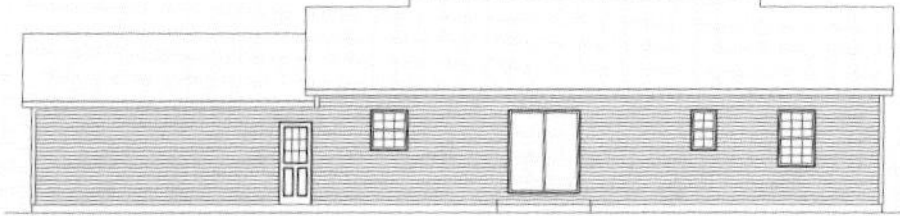

Rear View

To order plans, visit the Menards Building Materials Desk or visit www.Menards.com.

ALYSSA

MENARDS®

Plan #M08-121D-0028

COUNTRY-STYLE COTTAGE

1,433 total square feet of living area

Width: 36'-0" Depth: 54'-0"

2 bedrooms, 2 baths

2-car garage

Basement foundation

SPECIAL FEATURES

The vaulted dining area enjoys access to the rear patio

The kitchen boasts a corner island and flows into the vaulted great room

There are many amenities in the master bedroom including a private bath and a walk-in closet

PRICE CODE AA

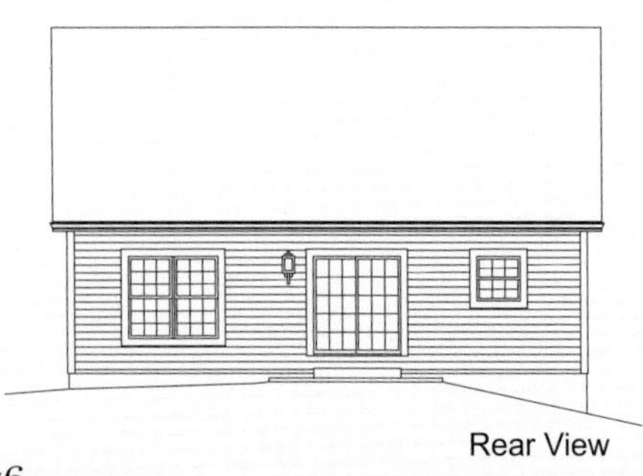

Rear View

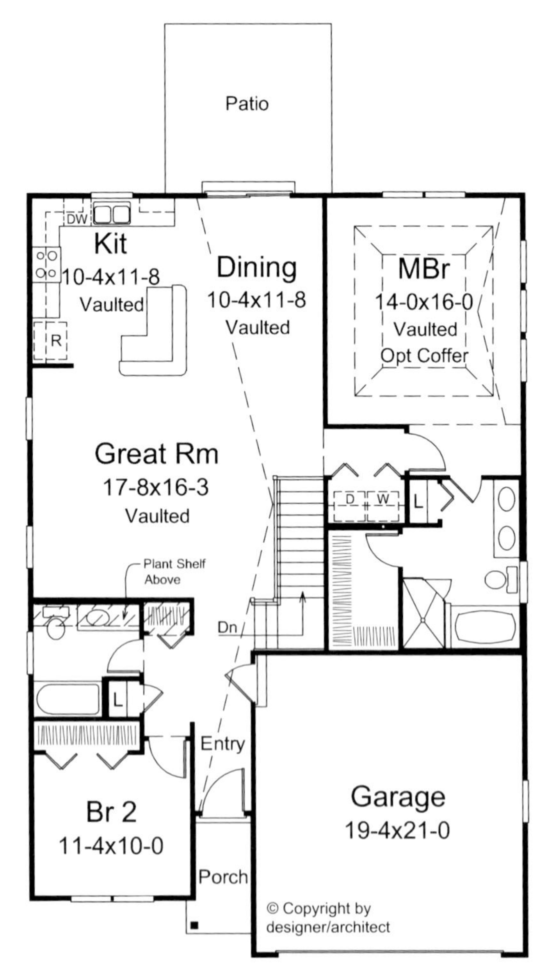

To order plans, visit the Menards Building Materials Desk or visit www.Menards.com.

MENARDS®

DAYTON TERRACE

Plan #M08-041D-0004

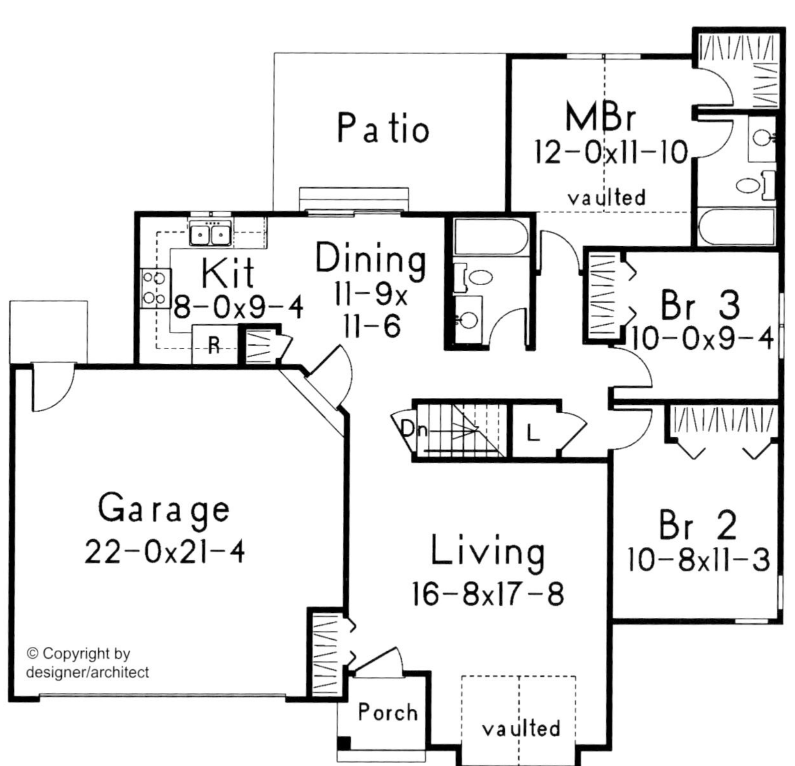

To order plans, visit the Menards Building Materials Desk or visit www.Menards.com.

A VAULTED CEILING FRAMES CIRCLE-TOP WINDOW

1,195 total square feet of living area

Width: 50'-0" Depth: 47'-0"

3 bedrooms, 2 baths

2-car garage

Basement foundation

SPECIAL FEATURES

- The dining room opens onto the patio
- The master bedroom features a vaulted ceiling, a private bath, and a walk-in closet
- The coat closets are located by both of the entrances
- A convenient secondary entrance is located at the back of the garage

PRICE CODE AA

Rear View

Plan #M08-007D-0230

OPEN FLOOR PLAN

1,923 total square feet of living area

Width: 76'-4" Depth: 46'-4"

3 bedrooms, 2 baths

2-car side entry garage

Slab foundation

SPECIAL FEATURES

A spacious entrance invites you into the grand-sized great room with fireplace, a bar area open to the kitchen with glass sliding doors to the rear patio, and the adjacent dining room

The smartly designed bay-shaped kitchen features cabinet and counter space galore with a 7' wide window above the sink for taking in the views

A luxury bath with double entry doors, a walk-in closet, and 9' wide glass sliding doors to the rear patio, are special features of the master bedroom

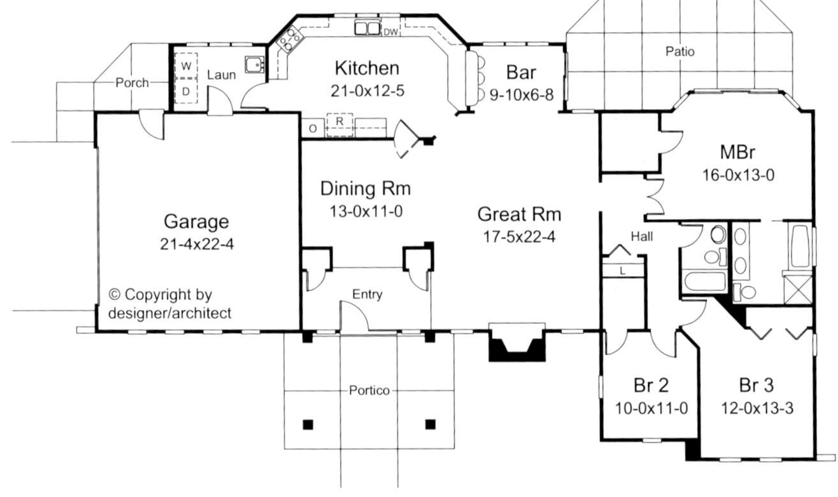

PRICE CODE D

Rear View

To order plans, visit the Menards Building Materials Desk or visit www.Menards.com.

MENARDS®

KINSLEY

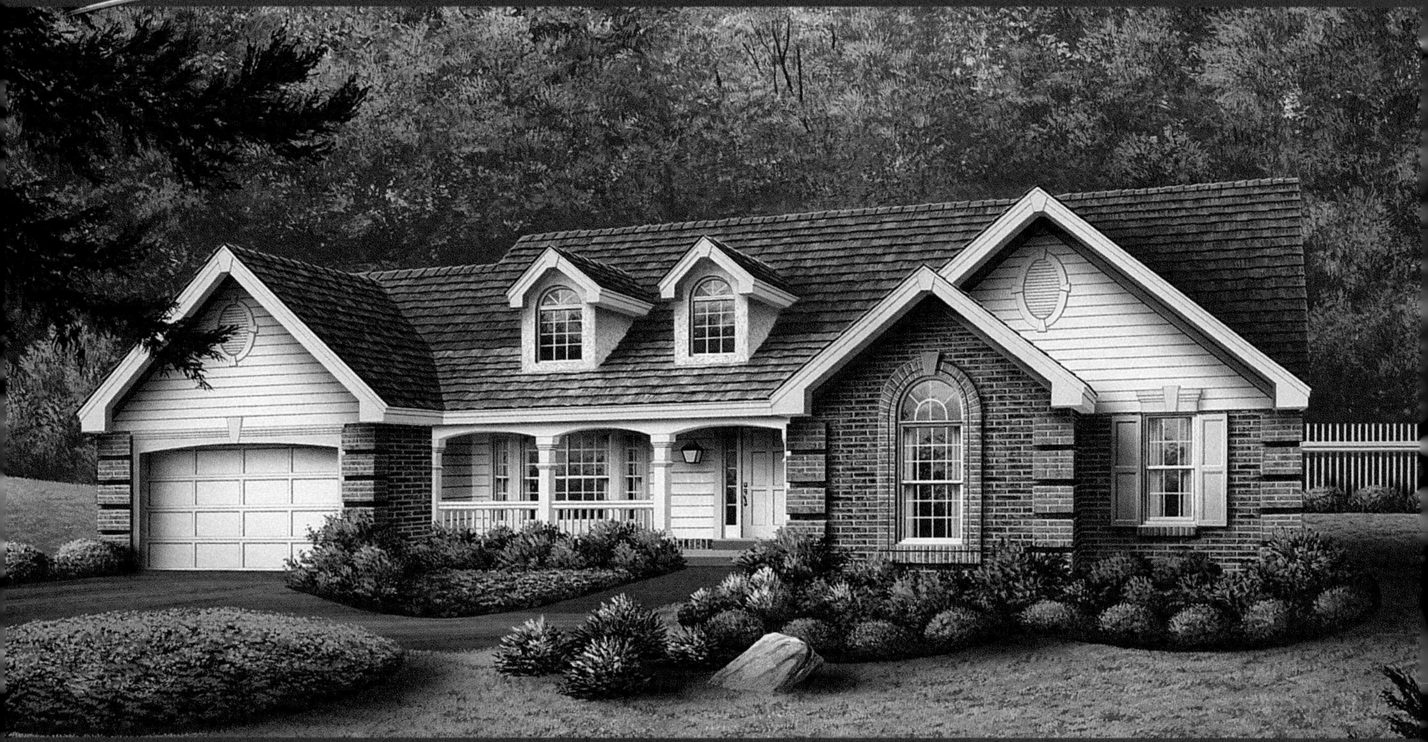

Plan #M08-007D-0049

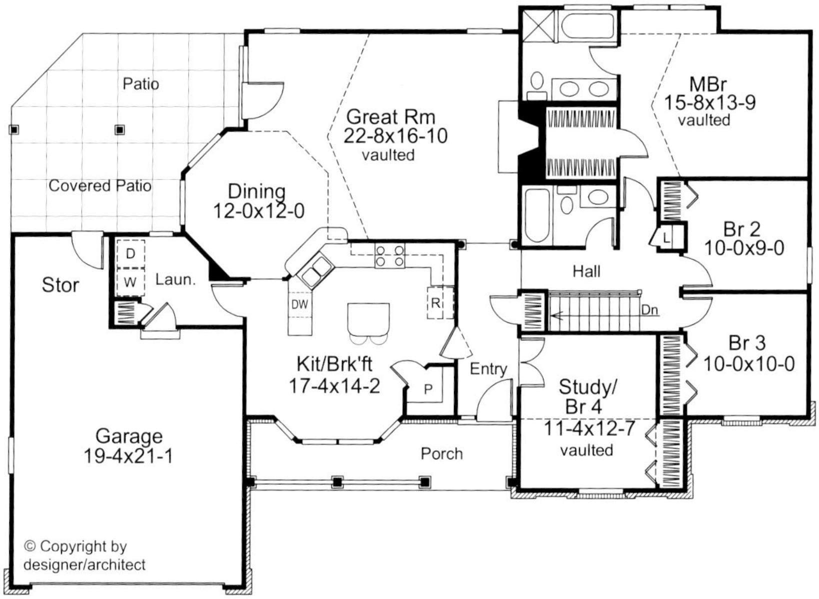

Patio
Covered Patio
Great Rm
22-8x16-10
vaulted
Dining
12-0x12-0
MBr
15-8x13-9
vaulted
Br 2
10-0x9-0
Hall
Dn
Stor
D
W
Laun.
DW
R
Kit/Brk'ft
17-4x14-2
P
Entry
Br 3
10-0x10-0
Study/
Br 4
11-4x12-7
vaulted
Garage
19-4x21-1
Porch
L

CLASSIC EXTERIOR AND INNOVATIVE INTERIOR

1,791 total square feet of living area

Width: 68'-0"   Depth: 48'-4"

4 bedrooms, 2 baths

2-car garage

Basement foundation, drawings also include crawl space and slab foundations

SPECIAL FEATURES

The vaulted great room and octagon dining area have patio views

The kitchen/breakfast area has dining space, an island, and a walk-in pantry

The master bedroom enjoys a vaulted ceiling and a sitting area

2" x 6" exterior wall framing available for an additional fee, please specify when ordering

PRICE CODE C

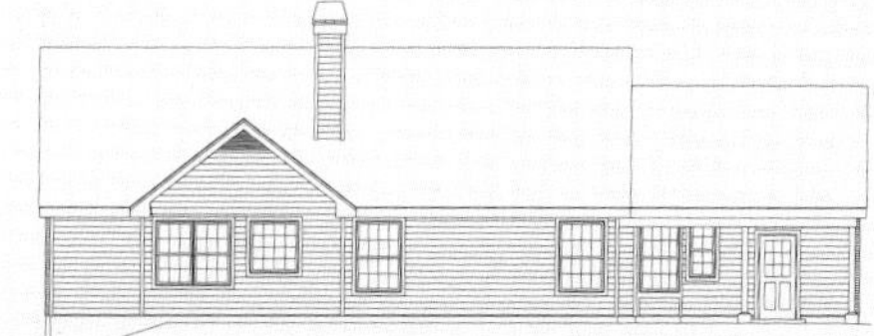

Rear View

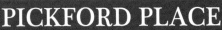

PICKFORD PLACE

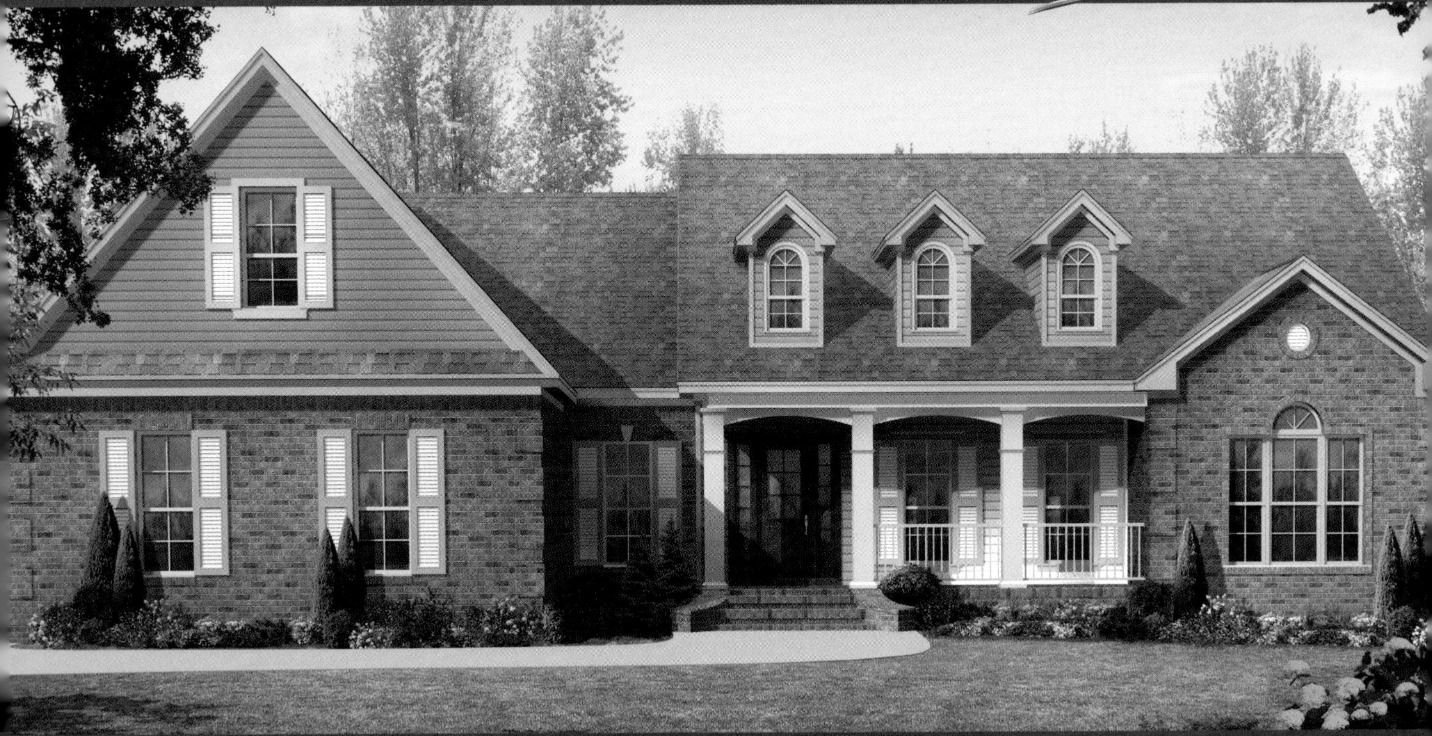

Plan #M08-077L-0131

FASHIONABLE FAMILY HOME

2,021 total square feet of living area

Width: 69'-0" Depth: 59'-10"

3 bedrooms, 2 1/2 baths

2-car side entry garage

Basement, slab or crawl space foundation, please specify when ordering

SPECIAL FEATURES

A corner garden tub in the private master bath becomes the ultimate retreat from the stresses of everyday life

A large eating area extends off of the kitchen featuring a center island and access to the covered porch with outdoor kitchen

A media/hobby room can be found through double doors in the large great room

The unfinished bonus room has an additional 354 square feet of living area

PRICE CODE F

To order plans, visit the Menards Building Materials Desk or visit www.Menards.com.

MENARDS®

KEMPTON PLACE

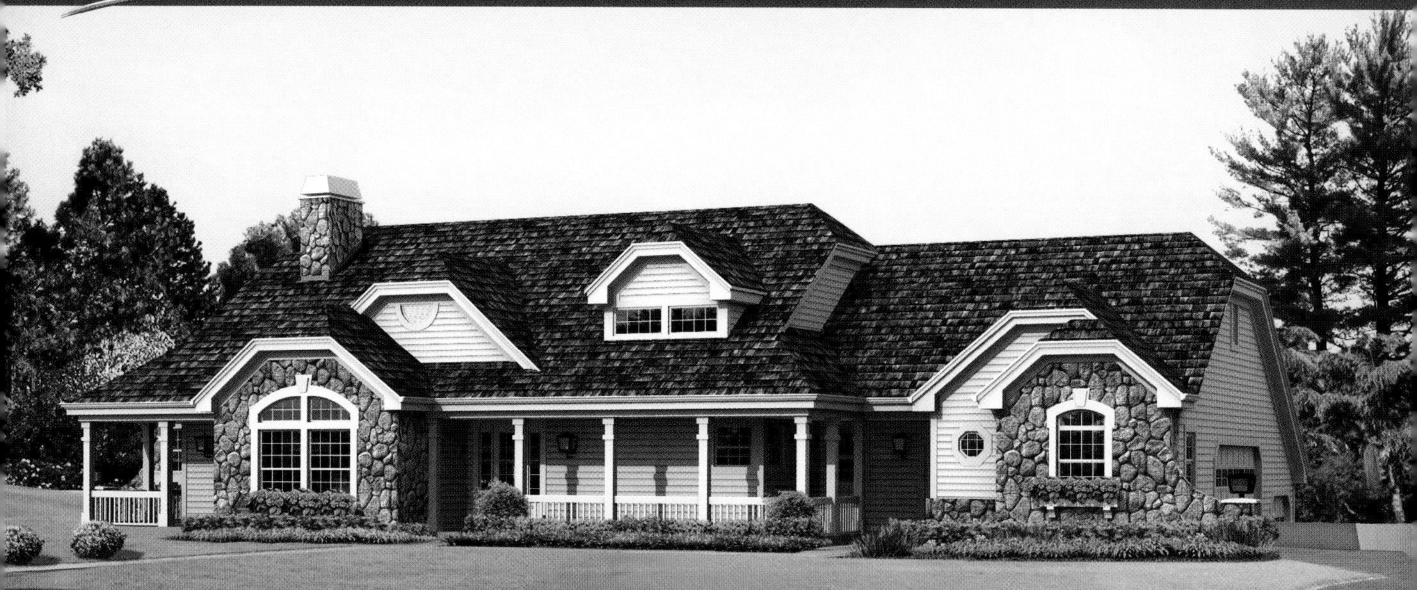

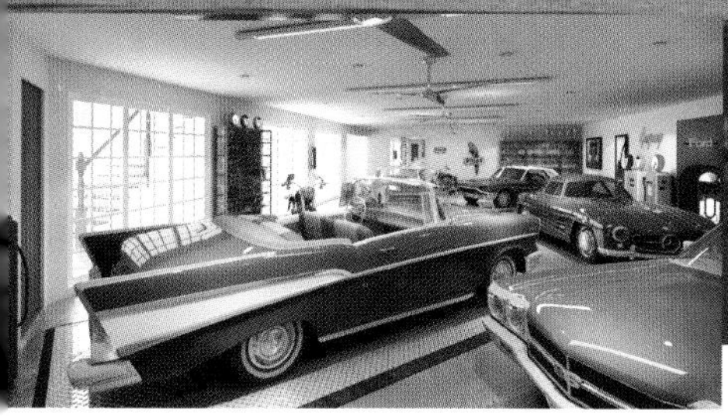

Plan #M08-007D-0234

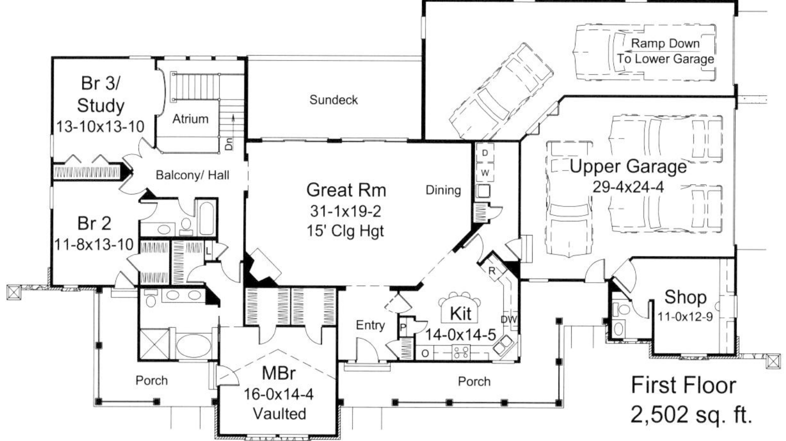

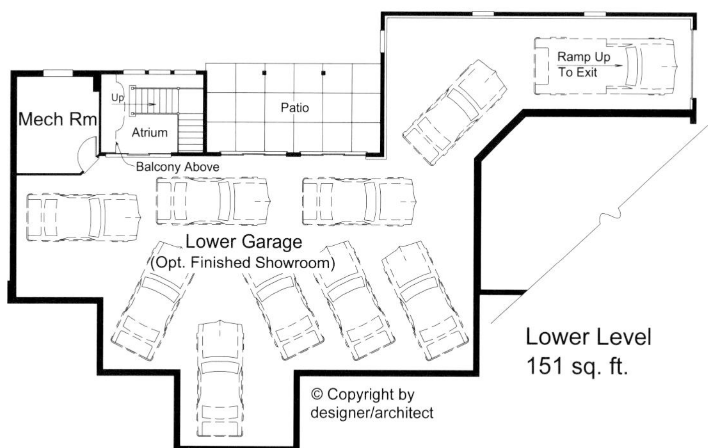

To order plans, visit the Menards Building Materials Desk or visit www.Menards.com.

CAR LOVER'S HOME STORES 12 CARS AND RV

2,653 total square feet of living area

Width: 95'-0" Depth: 59'-4"

3 bedrooms, 2 1/2 baths

12-car garage, 1-RV garage

Walk-out basement foundation

SPECIAL FEATURES

This home appears to have only a 3-car garage, but it will store/display 12 autos plus a small RV in the lower and upper garages accessible from the driveway

The upper garage has a workshop with half bath, while the lower garage handles car maneuvering and placement plus three 9' glass sliding doors

The mechanical room on the lower level is 151 square feet

PRICE CODE E

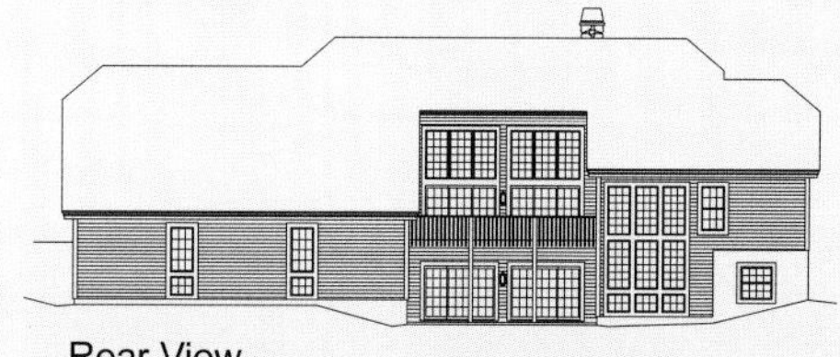

Rear View

SAVANNAH

MENARDS®

Plan #M08-001D-0080

DOUBLE GABLES FRAME FRONT PORCH

1,832 total square feet of living area

Width: 56'-0" Depth: 44'-0"

3 bedrooms, 2 baths

2-car detached garage

Crawl space foundation, drawings also include basement and slab foundations

SPECIAL FEATURES

The master bedroom is enhanced by skylights and a bath with a garden tub, a separate shower, and a walk-in closet

The U-shaped kitchen has a pantry, a laundry area, and view of the breakfast room

2" x 6" exterior wall framing available for an additional fee, please specify when ordering

PRICE CODE C

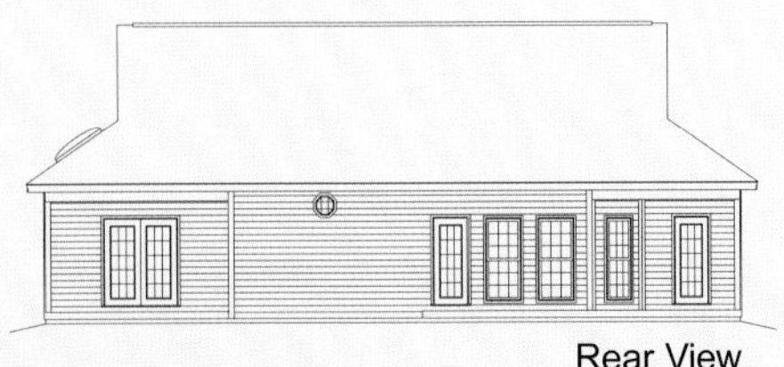
Rear View

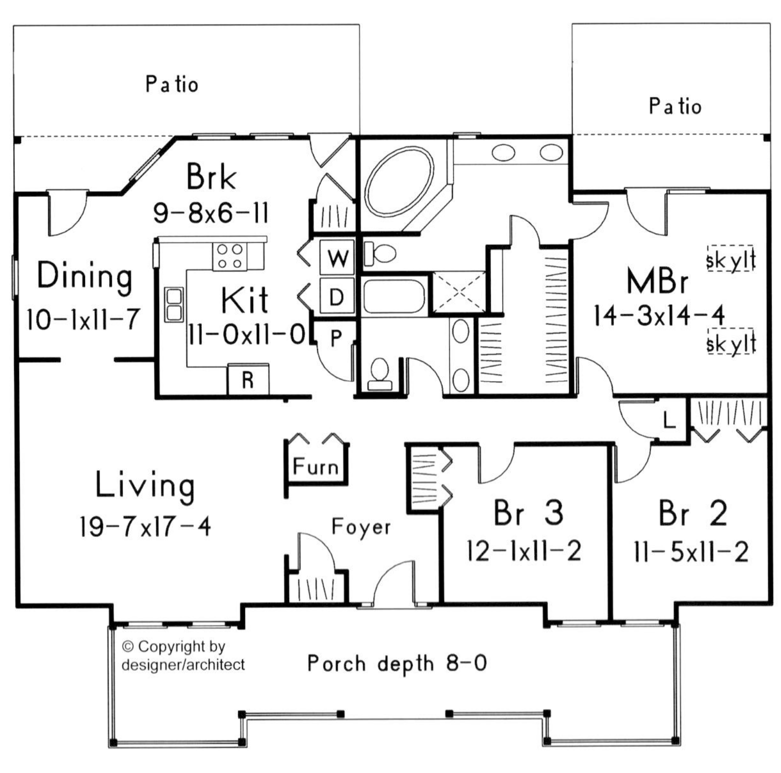

To order plans, visit the Menards Building Materials Desk or visit www.Menards.com.

MENARDS® FERNLEAF

Plan #M08-055L-0205

COLUMNS DEFINE DINING ROOM

1,989 total square feet of living area

Width: 64'-2" Depth: 49'-0"

4 bedrooms, 3 baths

2-car side entry garage

Slab, crawl space, basement or walk-out basement foundation, please specify when ordering

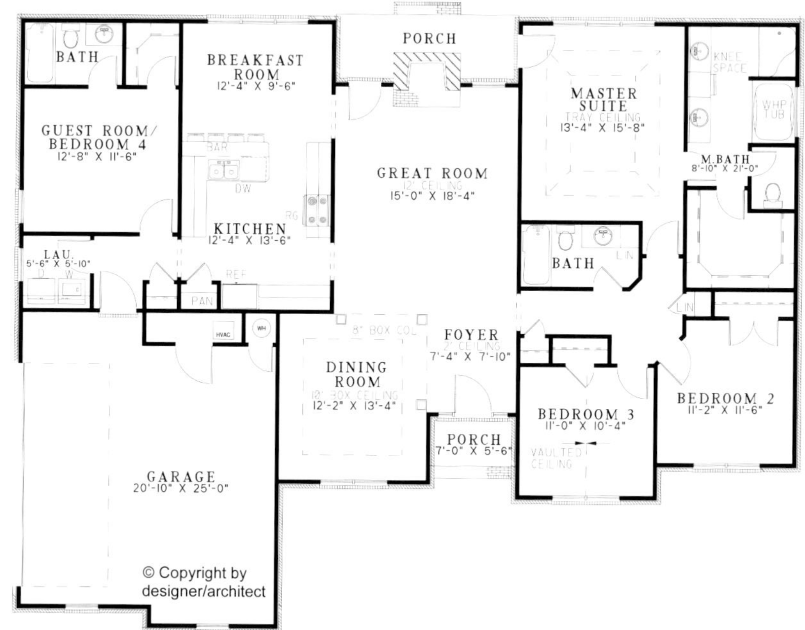

SPECIAL FEATURES

The kitchen includes a counter with seating that opens to the charming breakfast room

The guest bedroom is privately located and includes a bath and a walk-in closet

A tray ceiling, deluxe bath, and a massive walk-in closet enhance the master suite

PRICE CODE D

To order plans, visit the Menards Building Materials Desk or visit www.Menards.com.

EVELYN

MENARDS®

Plan #M08-121D-0013

CHARMING HOME WITH ATRIUM

2,100 total square feet of living area

Width: 56'-8"   Depth: 59'-0"

3 bedrooms, 2 baths

2-car garage

Walk-out basement foundation

SPECIAL FEATURES

The vaulted great room has a fireplace and a staircase to the atrium below

The efficient kitchen has seating for quick and easy meals next to the sunny breakfast area

A bay window, a private bath, and a walk-in closet are all amenities of the master bedroom

PRICE CODE B

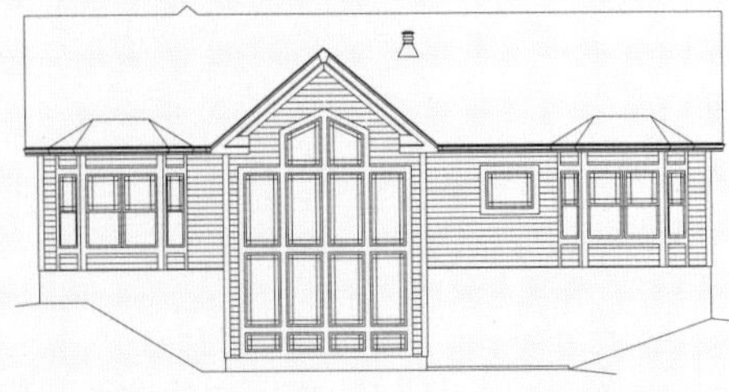

Rear View

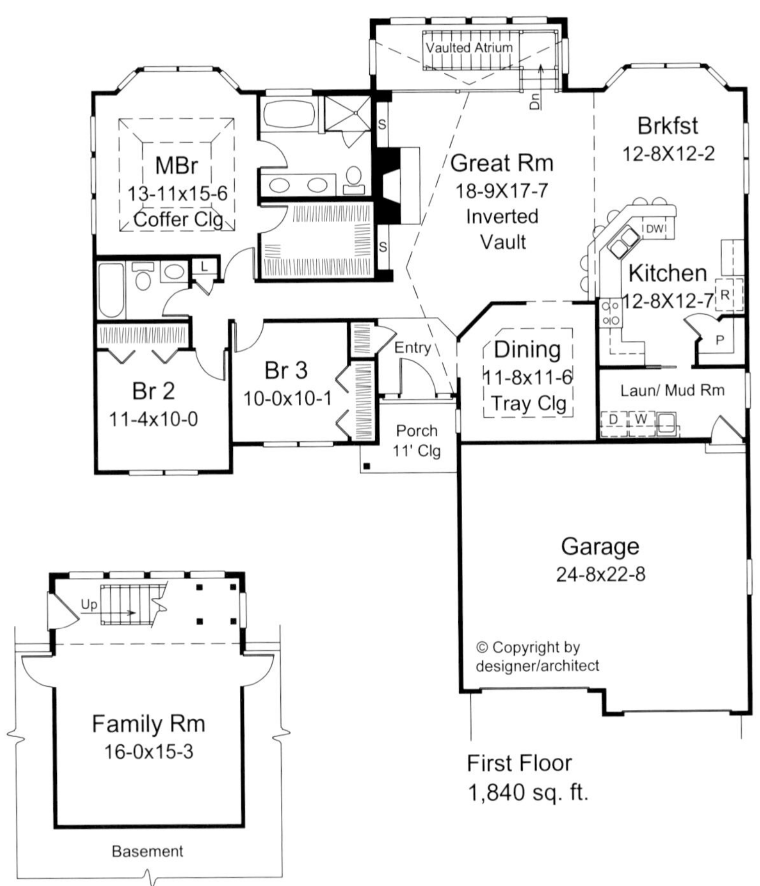

First Floor
1,840 sq. ft.

Lower Level
260 sq. ft.

To order plans, visit the Menards Building Materials Desk
or visit www.Menards.com.

MENARDS®

SPRING HILL

Plan #M08-068D-0010

BEDROOMS SEPARATE FROM REST OF HOME

1,849 total square feet of living area

Width: 74'-6" Depth: 43'-0"

3 bedrooms, 2 1/2 baths

2-car side entry garage

Slab foundation, drawings also include crawl space foundation

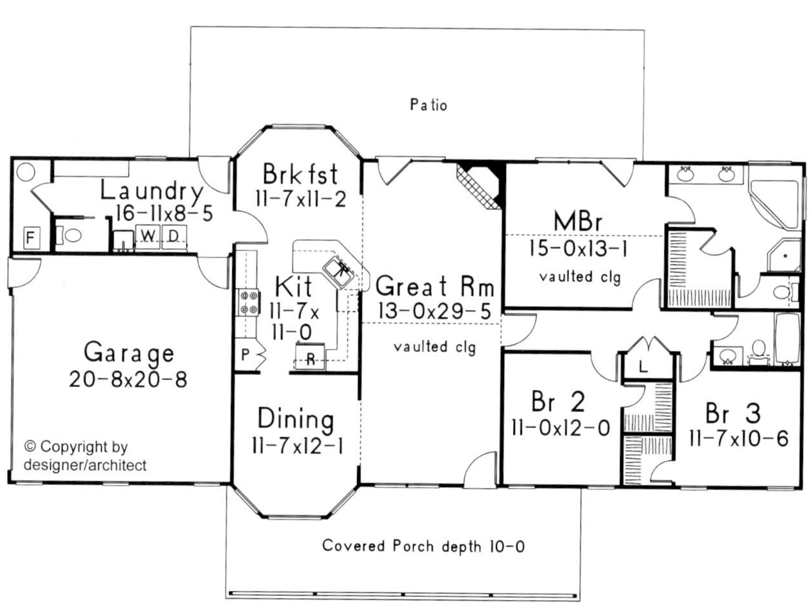

SPECIAL FEATURES

The large laundry room has many extras including a storage area and a half bath

The master bath has a corner whirlpool tub, a double-bowl vanity, a separate shower, and a walk-in closet

The secondary bedrooms include walk-in closets

The kitchen has an eating counter and is adjacent to the dining and breakfast rooms

PRICE CODE C

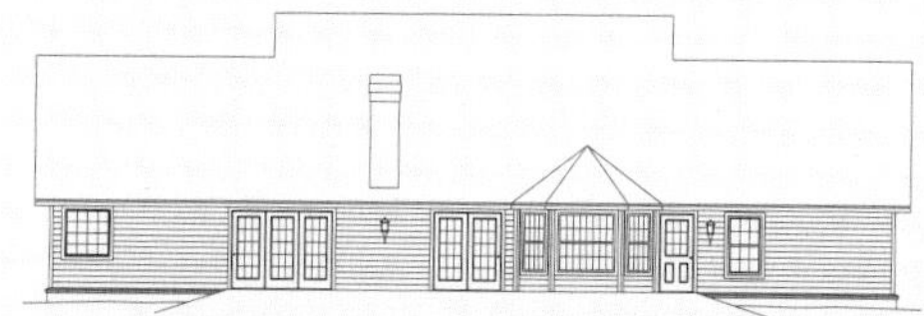

Rear View

To order plans, visit the Menards Building Materials Desk or visit www.Menards.com.

MOUNTAINMILL

MENARDS®

Plan #M08-008D-0004

CHARMING COUNTRY FACADE

1,643 total square feet of living area

Width: 70'-0" Depth: 34'-0"

3 bedrooms, 2 baths

2-car garage

Basement foundation, drawings also include crawl space and slab foundations

SPECIAL FEATURES

An attractive front entry porch gives this ranch a country accent

The spacious family room is the focal point of this design

The kitchen and hobby/laundry room are conveniently located near the gathering areas

The formal living room in the front of the home provides an area for quiet and privacy

The master bedroom has access to a private bath and a generous walk-in closet

PRICE CODE B

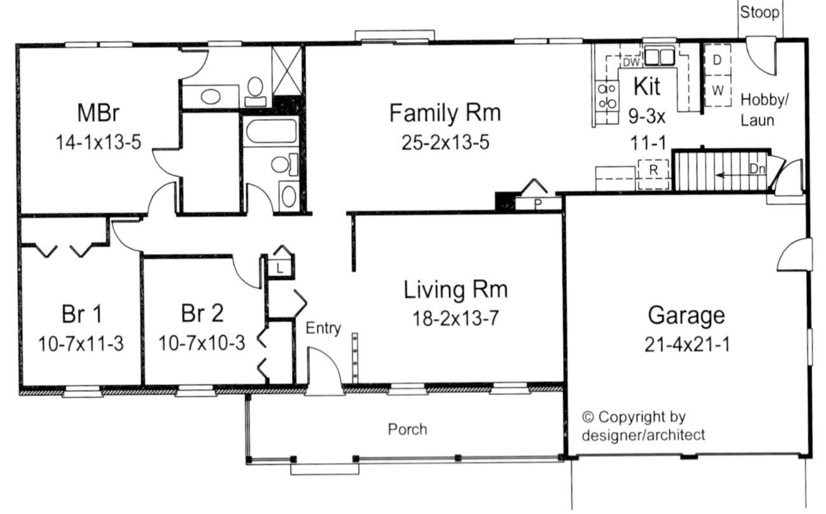

To order plans, visit the Menards Building Materials Desk or visit www.Menards.com.

MENARDS

LAKE ARGYLE

Plan #M08-007D-0214

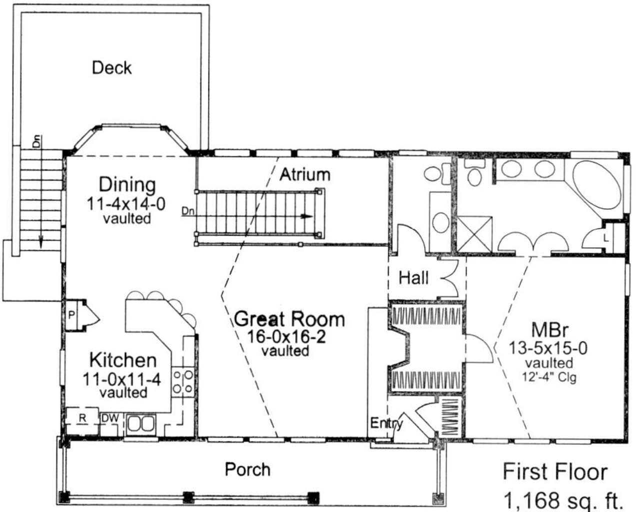

First Floor
1,168 sq. ft.

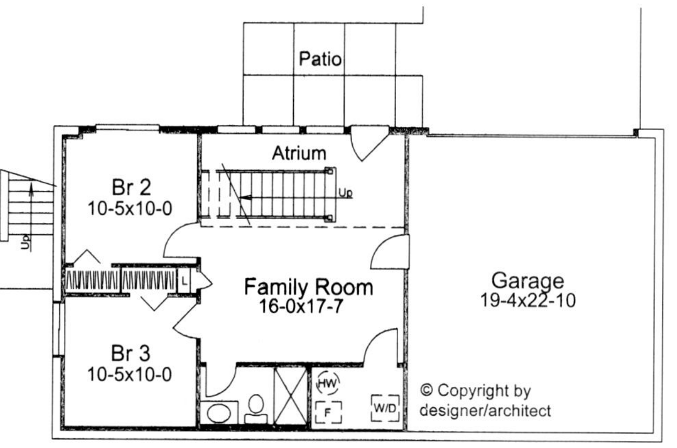

Lower Level
512 sq. ft.

To order plans, visit the Menards Building Materials Desk
or visit www.Menards.com.

TERRIFIC LAKE HOUSE

1,680 total square feet of living area

Width: 48'-0" Depth: 31'-0"

3 bedrooms, 2 1/2 baths

2-car drive under rear entry garage

Walk-out basement foundation

SPECIAL FEATURES

The vaulted great room, dining area, and kitchen enjoy sunlight from the atrium

A vaulted ceiling, double entry doors, a luxury bath, and a large walk-in closet are all features of the master bedroom

The lower level consists of a family room/atrium, two secondary bedrooms, a full bath, a mechanical closet/laundry and a two-car rear entry garage

PRICE CODE B

Rear View

LOCKWOOD

MENARDS®

Plan #M08-007D-0050

PRESTIGE ABOUNDS IN A CLASSIC RANCH

2,723 total square feet of living area

Width: 79'-4" Depth: 66'-6"

3 bedrooms, 2 1/2 baths

3-car side entry garage

Basement foundation

SPECIAL FEATURES

A large porch invites you into an elegant foyer that accesses a vaulted study with private hall and coat closet

The great room is second to none, comprised of a fireplace, built-in shelves, a vaulted ceiling and a 1 1/2 story window wall

A spectacular hearth room with vaulted ceiling and masonry fireplace opens to an elaborate kitchen featuring two snack bars, a cooking island, and a walk-in pantry

PRICE CODE E

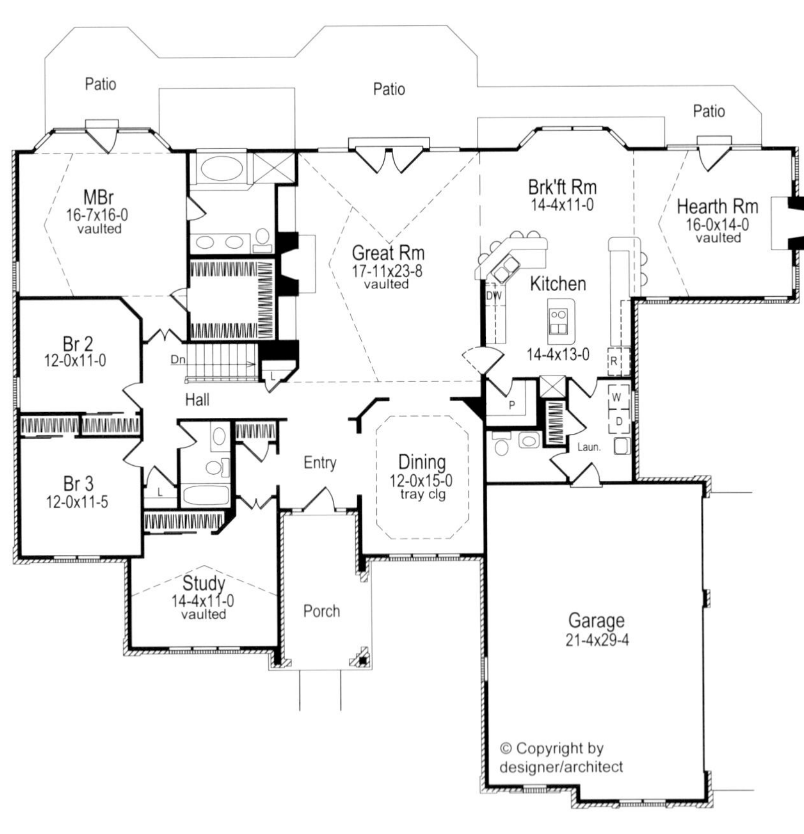

Rear View

To order plans, visit the Menards Building Materials Desk
or visit www.Menards.com.

MENARDS®

BRISBANE BAY

Plan #M08-055L-0026

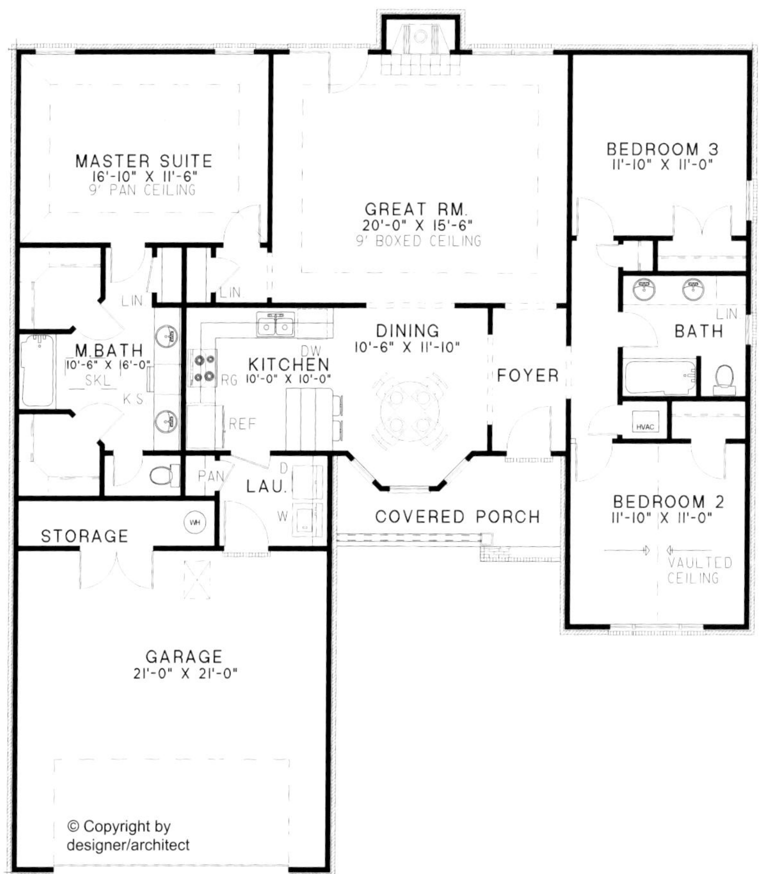

BAYED DINING ROOM

1,538 total square feet of living area

Width: 50'-0"   Depth: 56'-0"

3 bedrooms, 2 baths

2-car garage

Slab, walk-out basement, basement, or crawl space foundation, please specify when ordering

SPECIAL FEATURES

Energy efficient home with 2" x 6" exterior walls

The dining and great rooms and their openness are highlighted in this design

The master suite has many amenities including double walk-in closets in the private bath

The Traditional ranch facade looks great in any neighborhood

PRICE CODE C

To order plans, visit the Menards Building Materials Desk or visit www.Menards.com.

BARRON

MENARDS

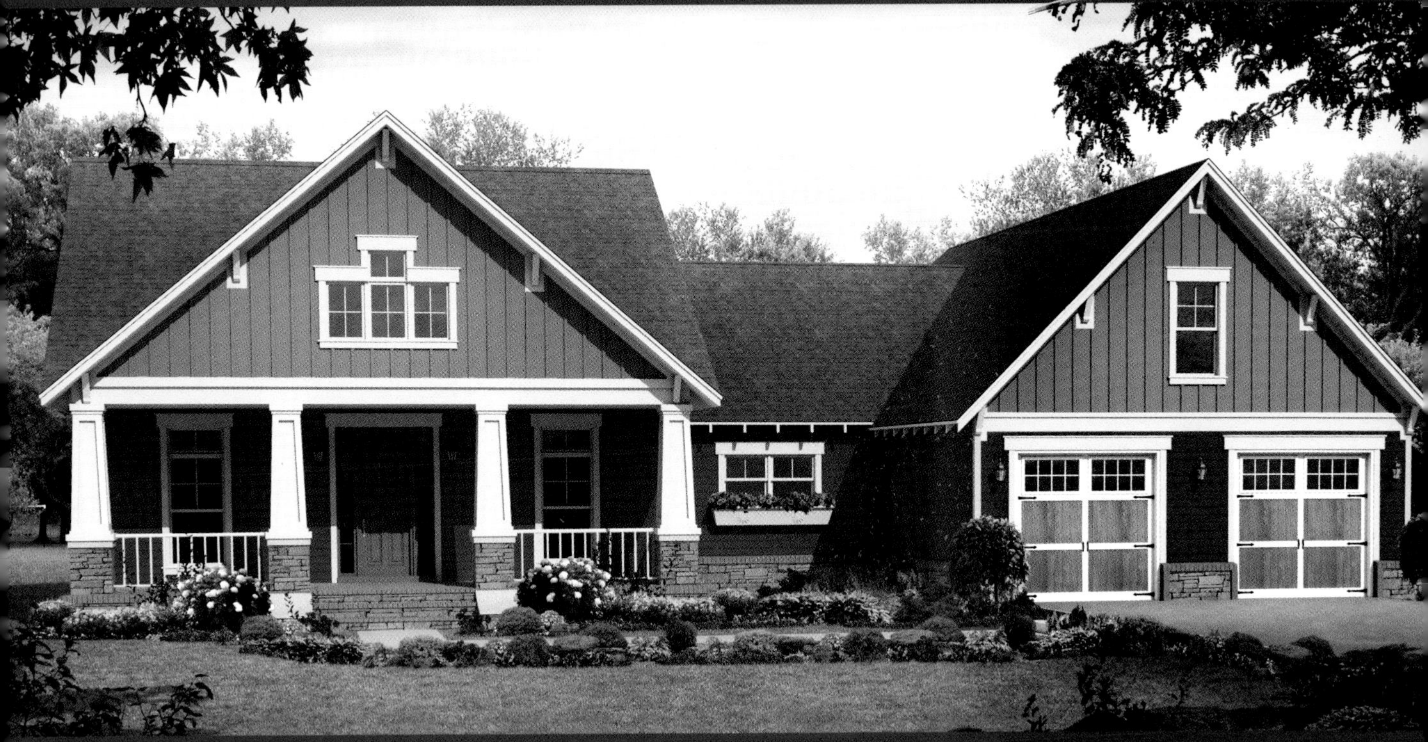

Plan #M08-077L-0142

MAJESTIC, CENTRAL GREAT ROOM

2,067 total square feet of living area

Width: 70'-0" Depth: 56'-0"

3 bedrooms, 2 1/2 baths

2-car garage

Slab or crawl space foundation, please specify when ordering

SPECIAL FEATURES

An enormous master bath has separate vanities, a whirlpool tub, and a walk-in closet on each end

The flex space would make an excellent formal dining room or home office space

The rear covered porch is a fantastic outdoor retreat and leads onto the open patio

The unfinished bonus room has an additional 379 square feet of living area

PRICE CODE F

Optional Second Floor

First Floor
2,067 sq. ft.

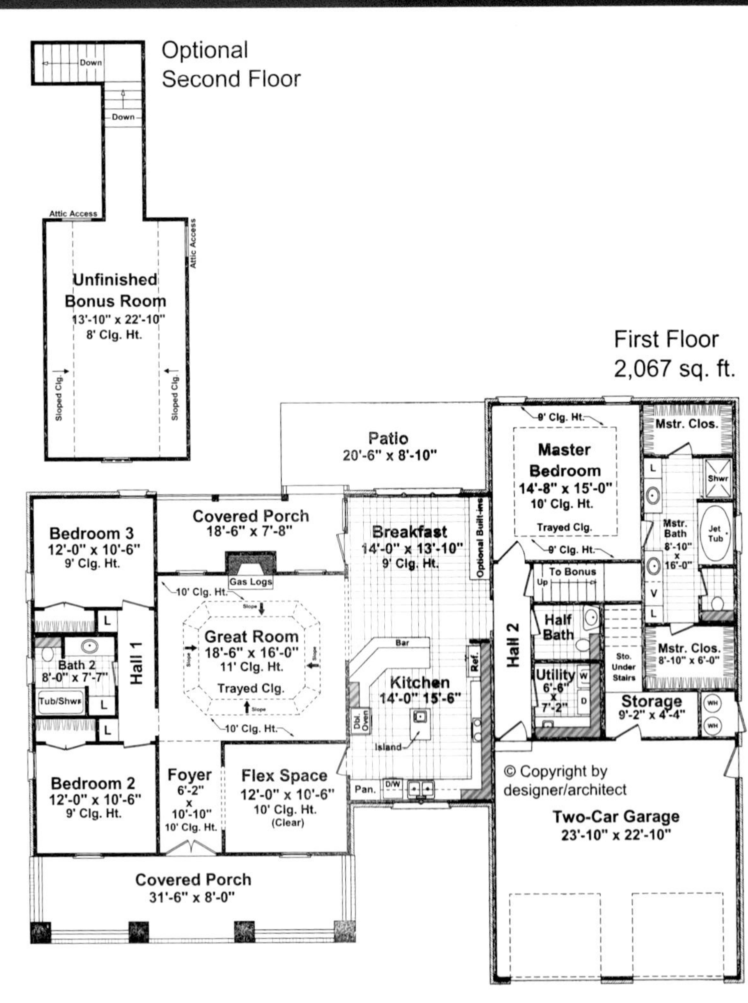

To order plans, visit the Menards Building Materials Desk or visit www.Menards.com.

MENARDS®

SALINAS

Plan #M08-039L-0026

MULTIPLE WALK-IN CLOSETS

1,542 total square feet of living area

Width: 58'-4"   Depth: 48'-4"

3 bedrooms, 2 baths

2-car garage

Crawl space or slab foundation, please specify when ordering

SPECIAL FEATURES

Varied ceiling heights throughout this home help create a distinctive interior

The master suite encourages privacy and contains a full bath and a roomy walk-in closet

The kitchen island incorporates the cooktop creating more functional counterspace

PRICE CODE C

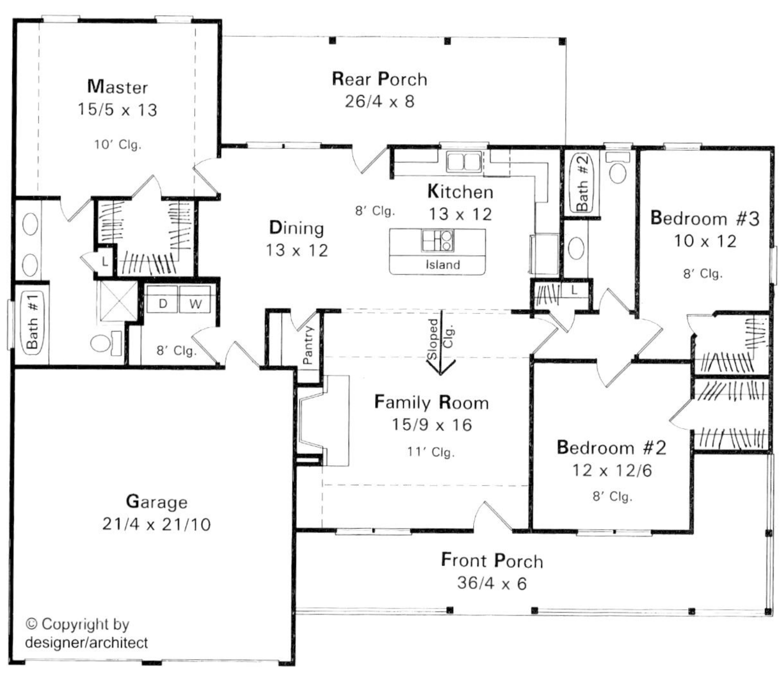

To order plans, visit the Menards Building Materials Desk or visit www.Menards.com.

WYANDOTTE TRAIL

MENARDS®

Plan #M08-065L-0030

PERFECT FOR A CASUAL LIFESTYLE

1,860 total square feet of living area

Width: 64'-2"   Depth: 44'-6"

3 bedrooms, 2 baths

2-car side entry garage

Walk-out basement foundation

SPECIAL FEATURES

French doors invite the outdoors in to become a part of the great room and the breakfast area

The comfortable master bedroom has a deluxe bath, a large walk-in closet, and a secluded alcove

A convenient snack bar is arranged to offer views to both the breakfast area with angled walls and the great room with a cozy fireplace

PRICE CODE C

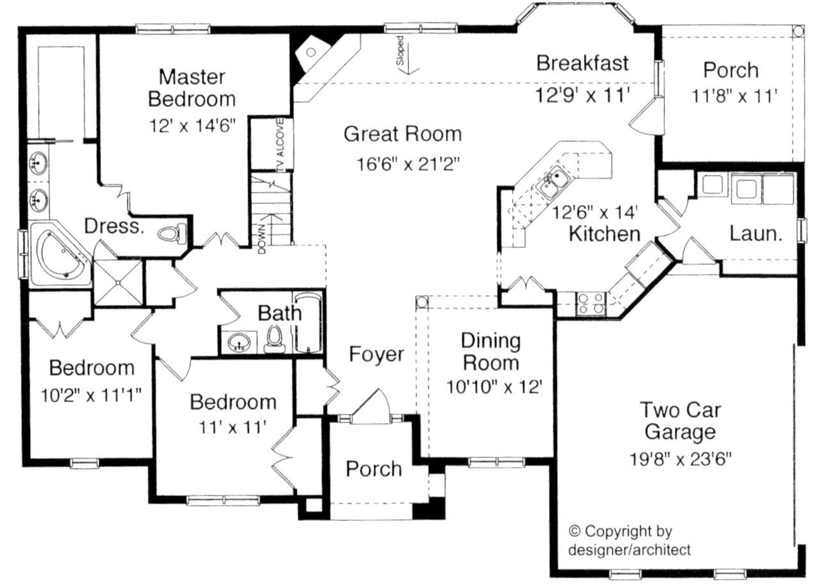

To order plans, visit the Menards Building Materials Desk or visit www.Menards.com.

CHESHIRE HILLS

Plan #M08-007D-0207

WHEELCHAIR FRIENDLY AND ENERGY EFFICIENT

2,884 total square feet of living area

Width: 79'-4" Depth: 61'-4"

3 bedrooms, 2 1/2 baths

2-car side entry garage

Walk-out basement foundation

SPECIAL FEATURES

Designed for energy efficiency, this home has R68 ceiling insulation, 2x6 wall construction with R33 insulated vinyl siding, triple-glazed insulated wood windows and doors and a cedar shake roof

The entire home is wheelchair accessible

The great room has a fireplace with shelves, space for an optional elevator, and is open to an atrium on the lower level with an additional 100 square feet

PRICE CODE D

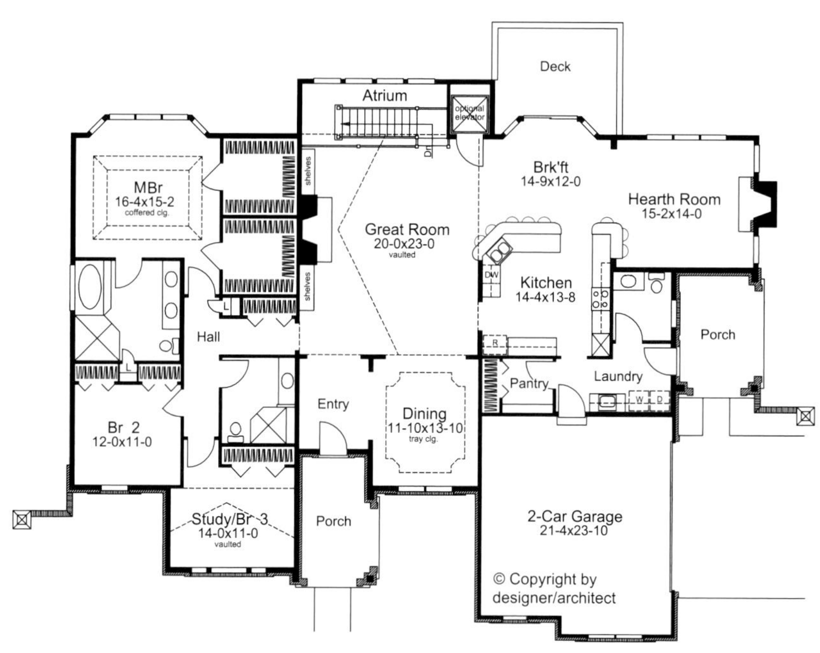

Rear View

To order plans, visit the Menards Building Materials Desk or visit www.Menards.com.

EASTWOOD HILL

MENARDS®

Plan #M08-055L-0017

BUILT-IN COMPUTER DESK

1,525 total square feet of living area

Width: 51'-6" Depth: 49'-10"

3 bedrooms, 2 baths

2-car garage

Slab, basement, walk-out basement or crawl space foundation, please specify when ordering

SPECIAL FEATURES

A cozy corner fireplace is highlighted in the great room

A unique glass block window over the whirlpool tub in the master bath brightens the interior

An open bar overlooks both the kitchen and the great room

The breakfast room leads to an outdoor grilling and covered porch

PRICE CODE D

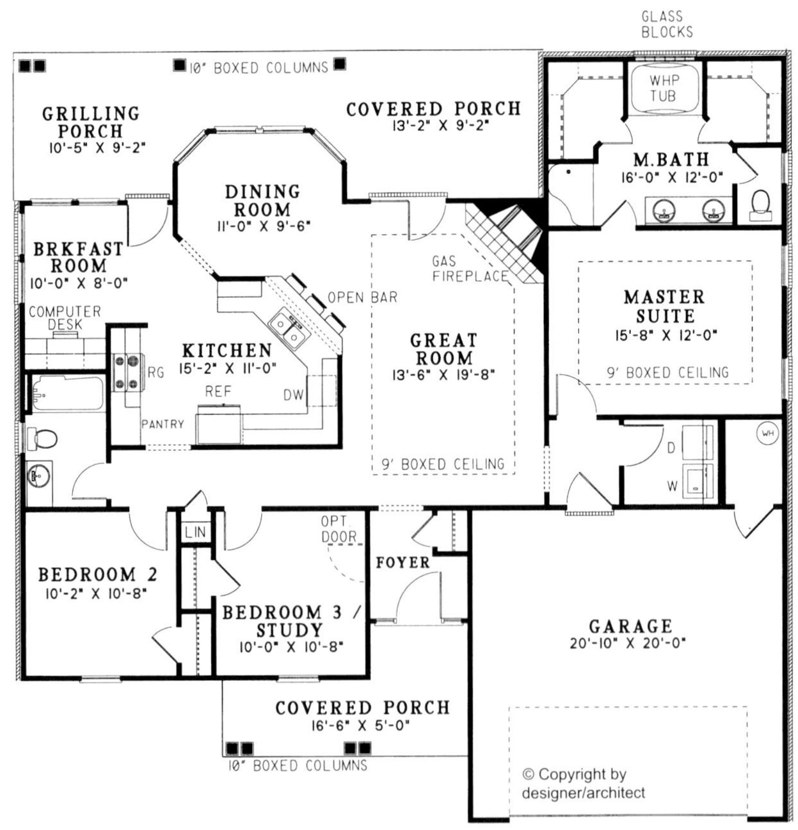

To order plans, visit the Menards Building Materials Desk or visit www.Menards.com.

MENARDS®

HAILEY

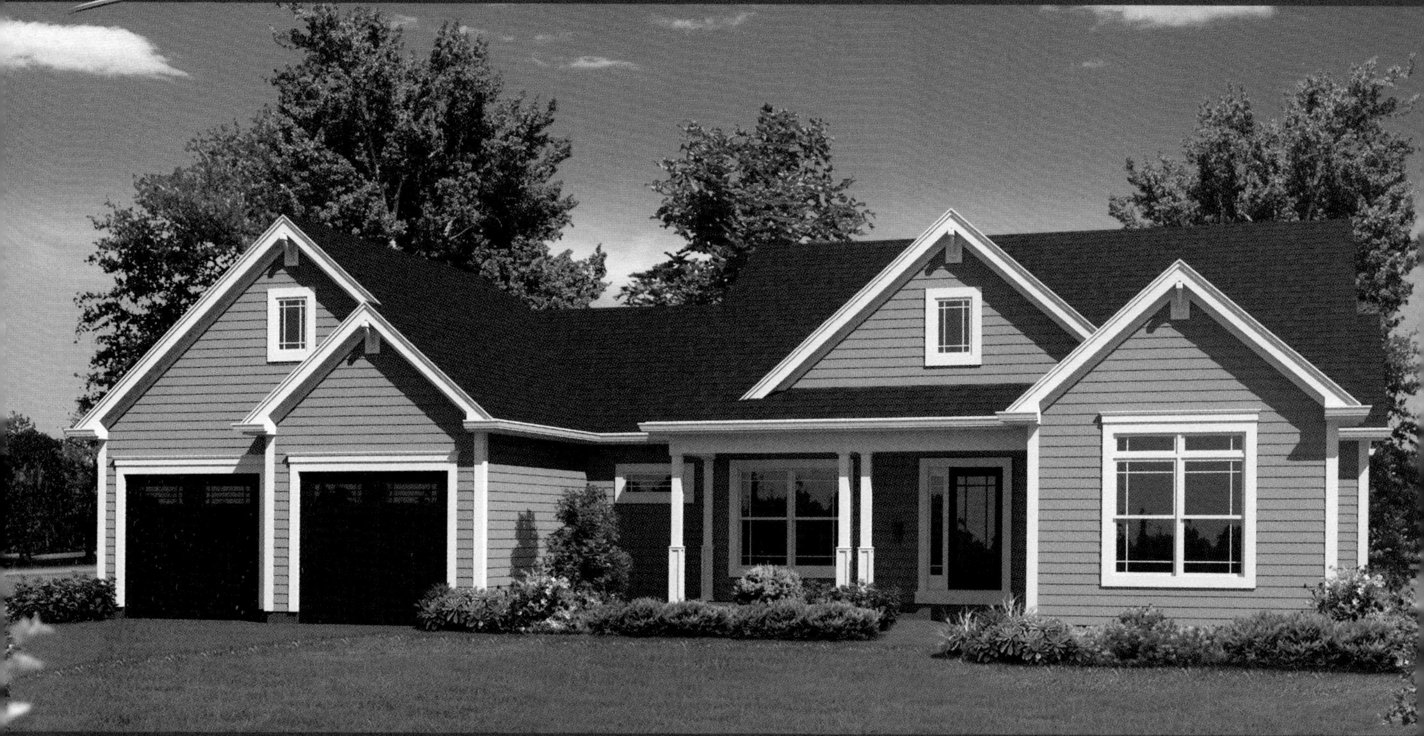

Plan #M08-121D-0020

Patio
MBr
17-7x15-3
Std Coffer
Opt Vault
L
Great Rm
16-7x19-7
Vault Clg
Kit/ Brkfst
19-4x15-4
Vaulted
DW
Desk
R
P
Storage
9-0x7-4
LOCKERS
Laun/
Mud Rm
W
D
Dining
12-1x13-8
Vault Clg
Foyer
Dn
Br 3
10-0x10-0
L
Garage
24-8x22-0
Porch
Br 2
13-8x11-10
© Copyright by
designer/architect

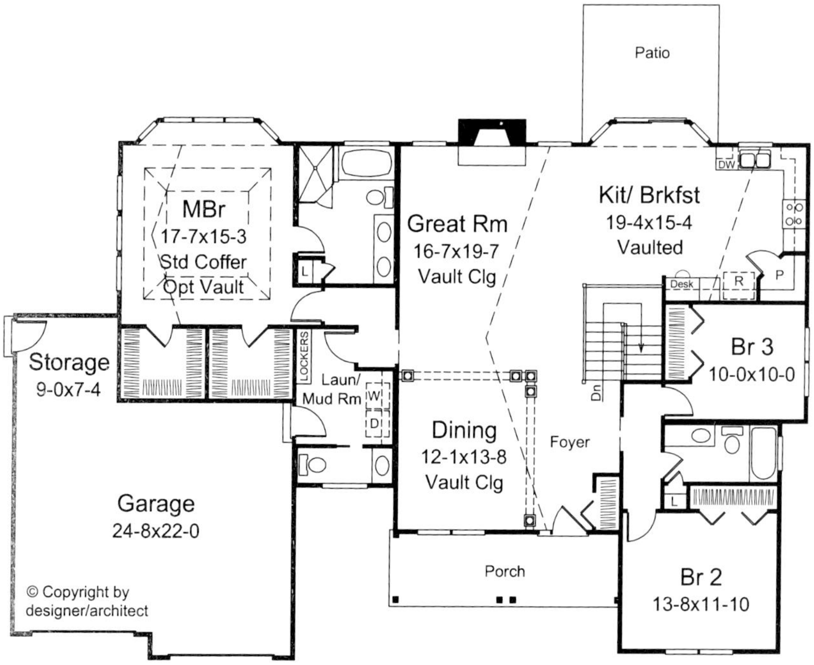

VAULTED CEILINGS ADD CHARISMA

2,037 total square feet of living area

Width: 70'-8" Depth: 47'-0"

3 bedrooms, 2 1/2 baths

2-car garage

Basement foundation

SPECIAL FEATURES

The vaulted kitchen/breakfast area enjoys a walk-in pantry and a sunny bay window with access to the rear patio

There is extra storage space in the garage that has access to the outdoors

Two spacious walk-in closets and a private bath are some of the amenities of the master bedroom

PRICE CODE B

Rear View

To order plans, visit the Menards Building Materials Desk or visit www.Menards.com.

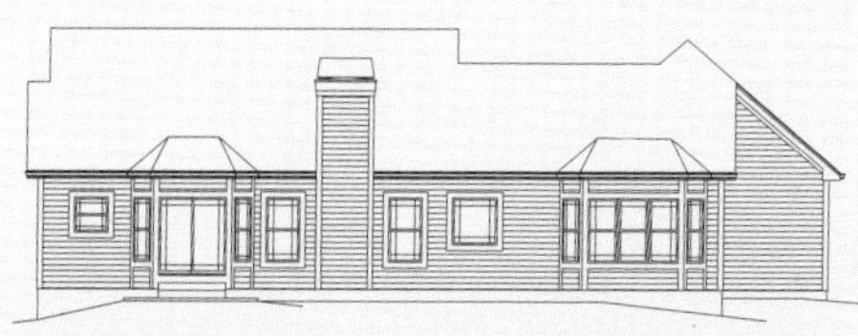

BOYLAN HEIGHTS

MENARDS®

Plan #M08-077L-0181

WELCOMING PORCH

1,919 total square feet of living area

Width: 69'-0" Depth: 59'-8"

3 bedrooms, 2 1/2 baths

2-car side entry garage

Basement foundation

SPECIAL FEATURES

A raised bar in the kitchen provides excellent serving space

The dining/office is a versatile space that can adapt to your needs

The master bedroom with private bath and walk-in closets is separated from the other bedrooms for privacy

The bonus room above the garage has an additional 338 square feet of living area

PRICE CODE E

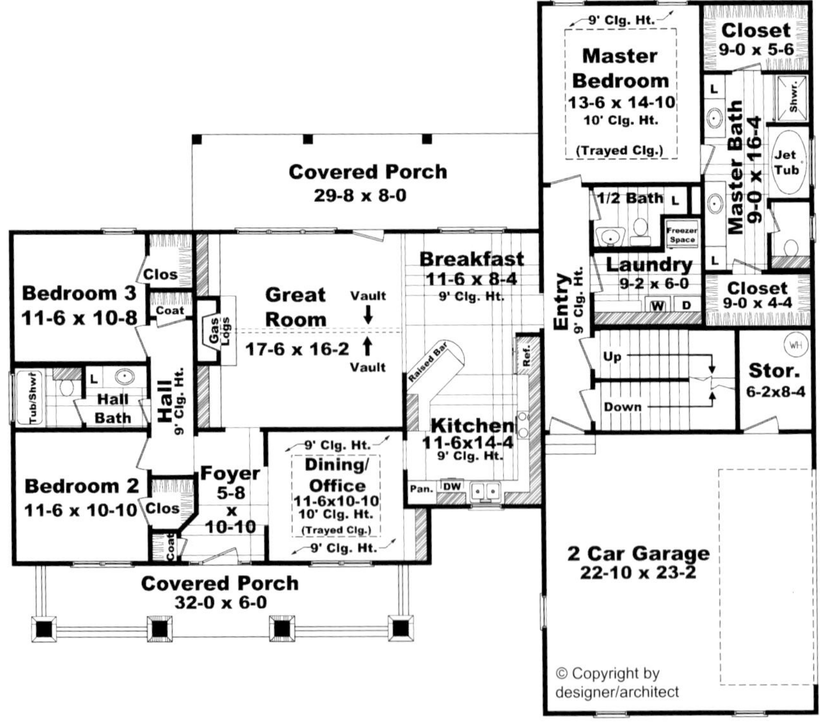

To order plans, visit the Menards Building Materials Desk or visit www.Menards.com.

WARREN CLIFF

Plan #M08-013L-0046

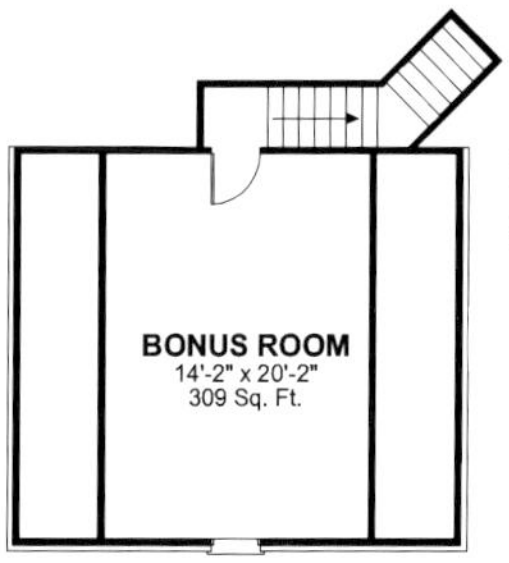

BONUS ROOM
14'-2" x 20'-2"
309 Sq. Ft.

Optional
Second Floor

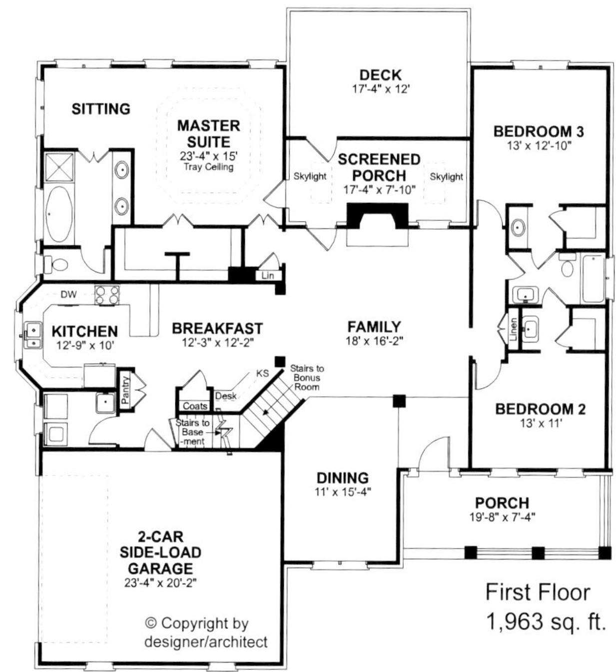

First Floor
1,963 sq. ft.

FAMILY FRIENDLY HOME

1,963 total square feet of living area

Width: 57'-8" Depth: 57'-6"

3 bedrooms, 2 baths

2-car side entry garage

Basement foundation

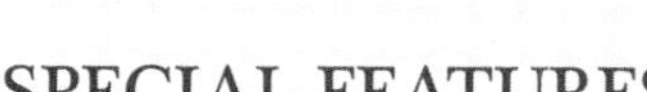

SPECIAL FEATURES

An efficient U-shaped kitchen has counterspace on all sides

The spacious master suite with sunny sitting area makes a quiet retreat

The centrally located family room between all bedroom areas provides a true family gathering area

The screened porch with skylights is well lit, yet sheltered

The second floor bonus room has an additional 309 square feet of living space

PRICE CODE C

To order plans, visit the Menards Building Materials Desk or visit www.Menards.com.

COMPTON PLACE

Plan #M08-007D-0213

SPLIT BEDROOM HOME OFFERS PRIVACY ZONES

2,394 total square feet of living area

Width: 72'-8" Depth: 35'-4"

3 bedrooms, 2 baths

3-car drive under rear entry garage

Walk-out basement foundation

SPECIAL FEATURES

The vaulted living room has an arched window and a 14' see-through fireplace

A large bay window, a walk-in pantry, and a snack bar all help to define the kitchen

Two large bedrooms with walk-in closets share a Jack and Jill bath

The staircase leads to the laundry room, walk-out basement, and three-car garage

PRICE CODE C

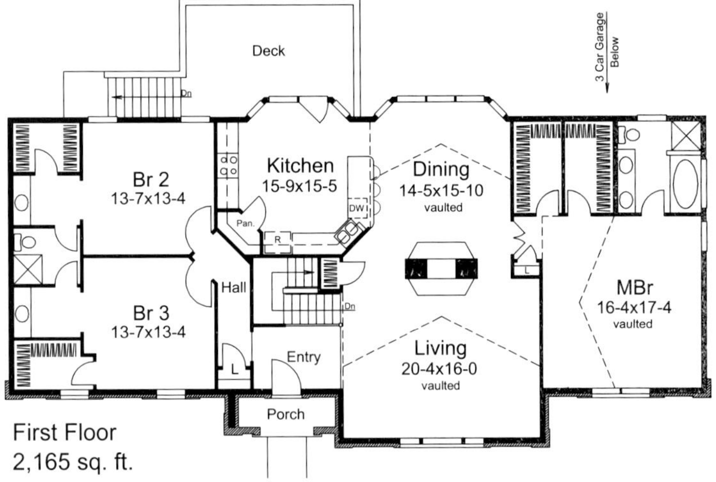

First Floor
2,165 sq. ft.

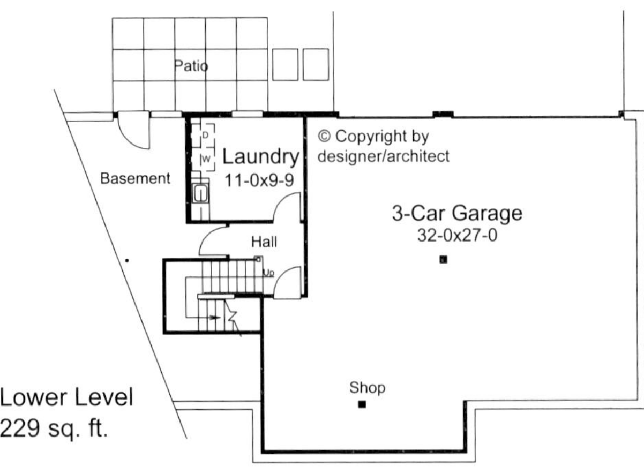

Lower Level
229 sq. ft.

Rear View

To order plans, visit the Menards Building Materials Desk or visit www.Menards.com.

MENARDS®

SANTA JENITA

Plan #M08-007D-0066

First Floor
2,408 sq. ft.

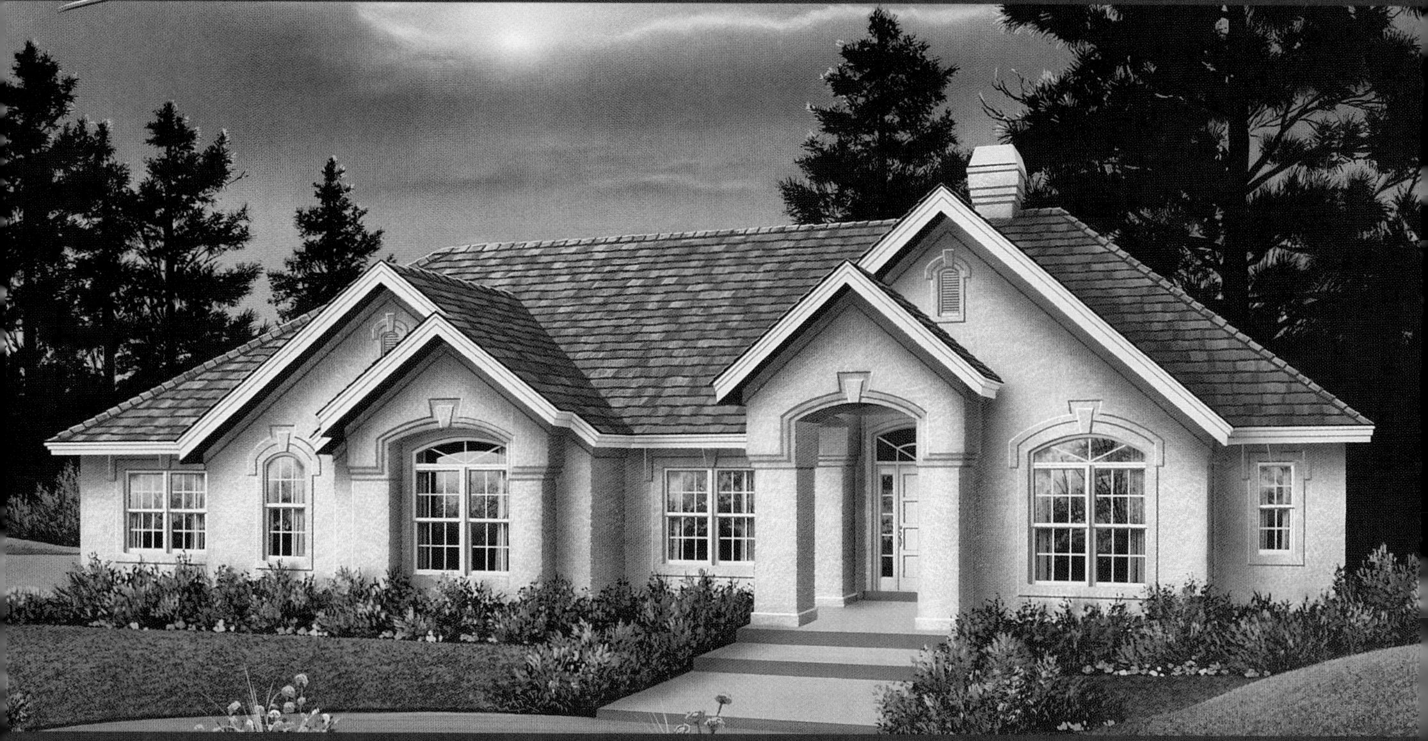

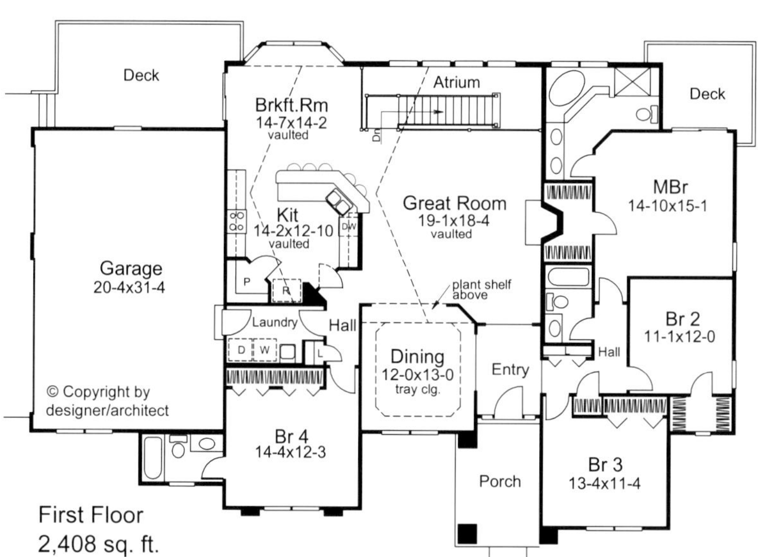

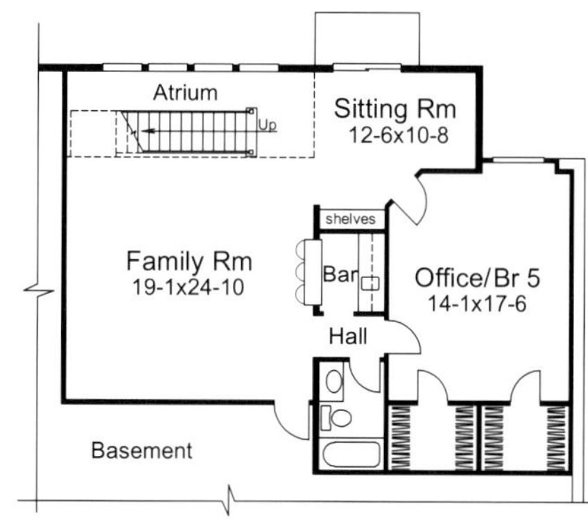

Lower Level
934 sq. ft.

To order plans, visit the Menards Building Materials Desk
or visit www.Menards.com.

FLORIDIAN ARCHITECTURE WITH MOTHER-IN-LAW SUITE

3,342 total square feet of living area

Width: 75'-8" Depth: 52'-6"

5 bedrooms, 4 baths

3-car side entry garage

Walk-out basement foundation

SPECIAL FEATURES

Stylish Floridian architecture

The vaulted great room overlooks an atrium window wall and joins the dining room, breakfast area, and the kitchen

Bedroom #4 is perfect for an in-law suite, children home from college and has a private bath

PRICE CODE D

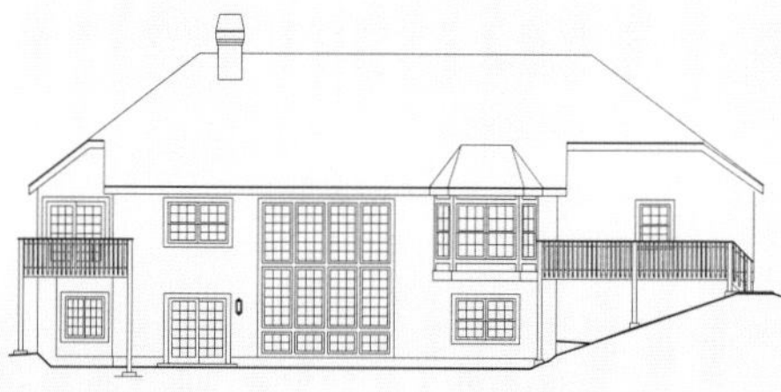

Rear View

Plan #M08-021D-0006

CHARMING COUNTRY STYLING IN THIS RANCH

1,600 total square feet of living area

Width: 75'-0" Depth: 37'-0"

3 bedrooms, 2 baths

2-car side entry garage

Slab foundation, drawings also include crawl space and basement foundations

SPECIAL FEATURES

Energy efficient home with 2" x 6" exterior walls

The sunken living room features a massive stone fireplace and a 16' vaulted ceiling

The dining room is conveniently located next to the kitchen and divided for privacy

Special amenities include a sewing area, and a large utility area

PRICE CODE D

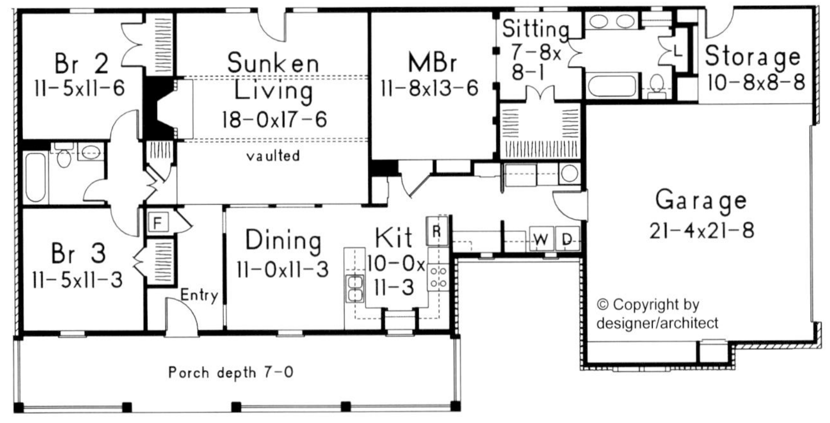

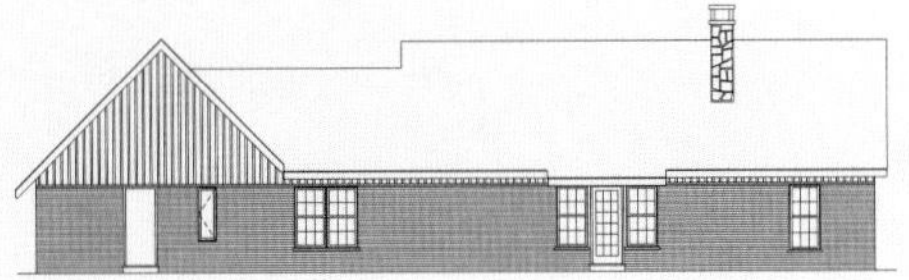
Rear View

To order plans, visit the Menards Building Materials Desk or visit www.Menards.com.

MENARDS®

TAMPA BAY

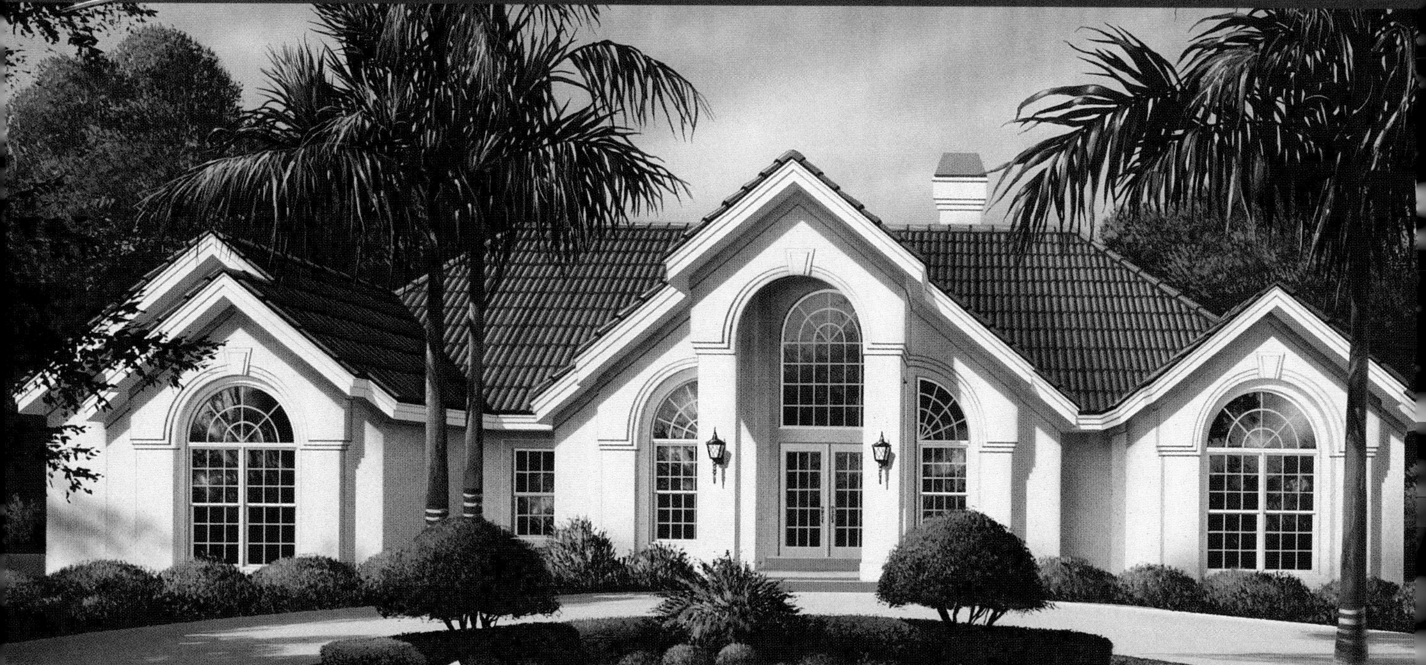

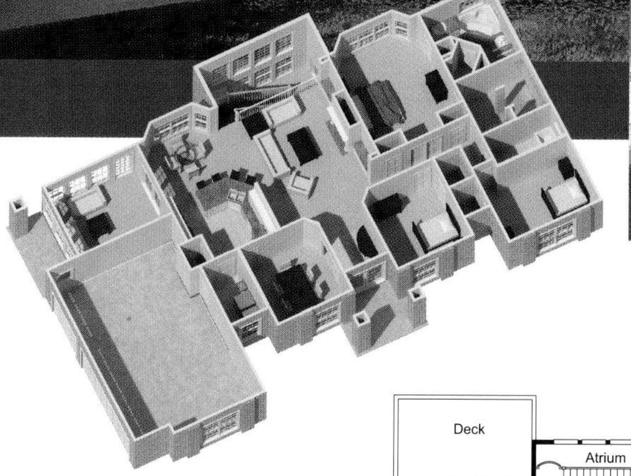

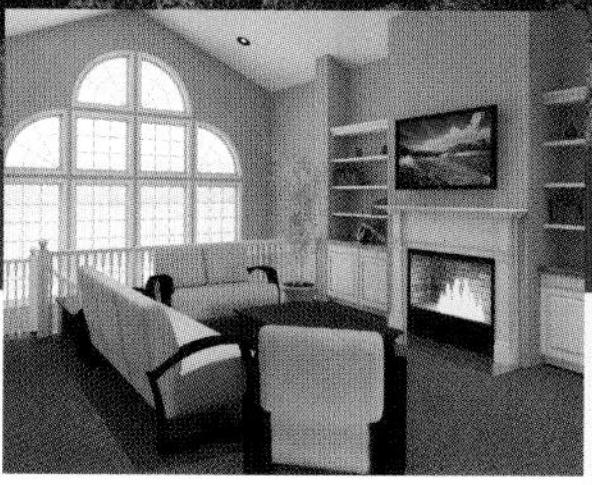

Plan #M08-007D-0098

ATRIUM RANCH WITH TRUE PIZZAZZ

2,398 total square feet of living area

Width: 78'-8" Depth: 51'-0"

3 bedrooms, 2 baths

3-car side entry garage

Walk-out basement foundation

Deck
Atrium
Dn
Porch
Sunroom
15-0x11-8
Brk'ft
13-2x11-0
Great Room
18-6x21-4
vaulted
shelves
MBr
14-6x17-0
Kitchen
12-8x12-0
DW
P
R
plant shelf
above
Hall
Garage
20-4x30-10
Laun
W
D
Dining
12-0x13-0
vaulted
Entry
Br 3
12-0x13-0
vaulted
Br 2
14-8x11-0
vaulted
Porch
© Copyright by
designer/architect
vaulted

First Floor
2,398 sq. ft.

Atrium
Up
Patio
Opt Family Rm
18-0x21-4
Opt Br 4
14-6x15-7
Hall
shelves
shelves
Basement

Optional
Lower Level

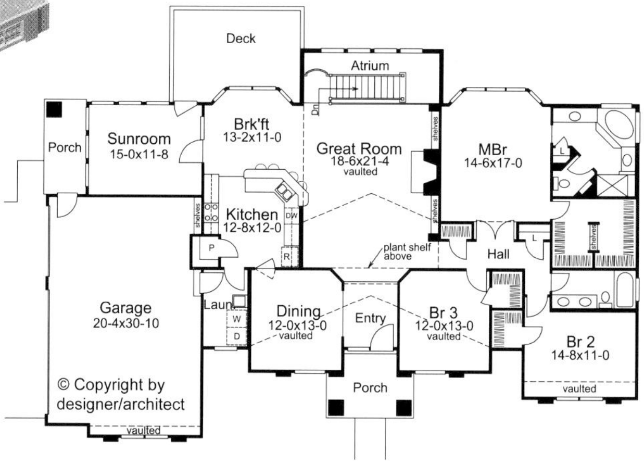

SPECIAL FEATURES

A grand entry porch leads to a dramatic vaulted entry foyer with a plant shelf

The great room enjoys a 12' vaulted ceiling

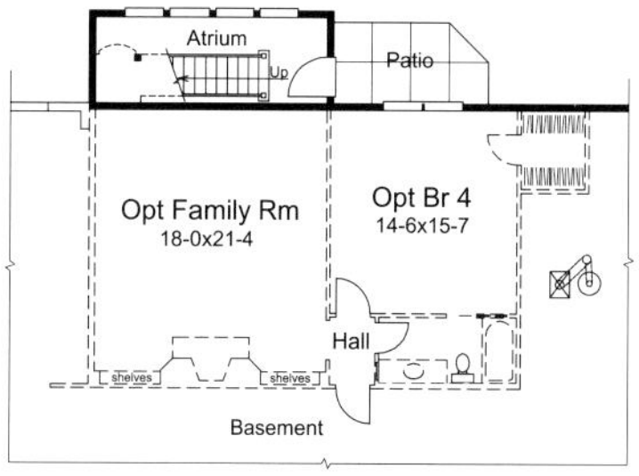

A conveniently located sunroom and side porch adjoin the breakfast room and garage

763 square feet of optional living area on the lower level

2" x 6" exterior wall framing available for an additional fee, please specify when ordering

PRICE CODE D

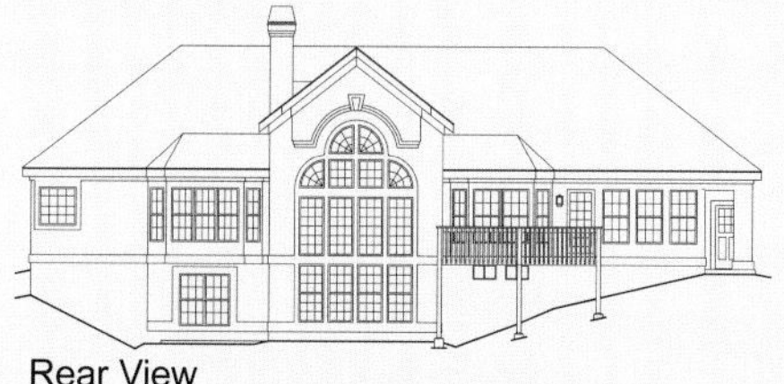

Rear View

To order plans, visit the Menards Building Materials Desk or visit www.Menards.com.

CHERRY SPRING

MENARDS®

Plan #M08-055L-0158

OPEN LIVING AREAS

1,636 total square feet of living area

Width: 53'-0"   Depth: 59'-10"

3 bedrooms, 2 baths

2-car garage

Slab or crawl space foundation, please specify when ordering

SPECIAL FEATURES

The covered grilling porch is large enough for outdoor cooking and entertaining

The bar with seating in the kitchen is great for serving snacks or casual meals

Columns separate the dining room from the rest of the house without enclosing it

PRICE CODE C

To order plans, visit the Menards Building Materials Desk or visit www.Menards.com.

MENARDS®

SANDRA

Plan #M08-121D-0008

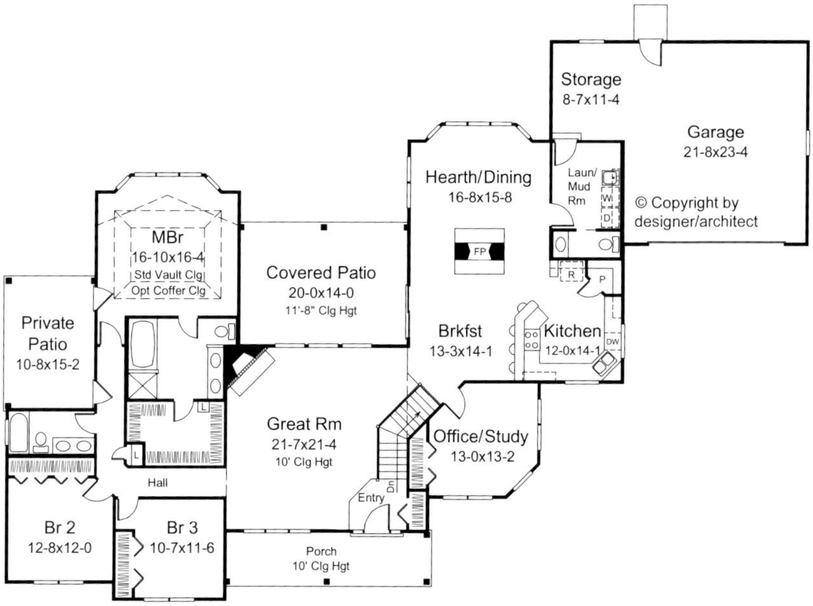

GREAT COVERED PATIO FOR OUTDOOR LIVING

2,487 total square feet of living area

Width: 96'-2" Depth: 65'-8"

3 bedrooms, 2 1/2 baths

2-car garage

Basement foundation

Storage 8-7x11-4
Garage 21-8x23-4
Hearth/Dining 16-8x15-8
Laun/ Mud Rm
© Copyright by designer/architect
MBr 16-10x16-4 Std Vault Clg Opt Coffer Clg
Covered Patio 20-0x14-0 11'-8" Clg Hgt
Private Patio 10-8x15-2
Brkfst 13-3x14-1
Kitchen 12-0x14-1
Great Rm 21-7x21-4 10' Clg Hgt
Office/Study 13-0x13-2
Hall
Entry
Br 2 12-8x12-0
Br 3 10-7x11-6
Porch 10' Clg Hgt

SPECIAL FEATURES

The beautiful vaulted master bedroom features a spacious bath and direct access to a private covered patio

A see-through fireplace illuminates both the hearth/dining area and the breakfast room, while acting as the main focal point in both spaces

A trio of windows, a 10' ceiling height, and a corner fireplace create a pleasant atmosphere in the great room

PRICE CODE C

To order plans, visit the Menards Building Materials Desk or visit www.Menards.com.

Rear View

NATALIE

Plan #M08-121D-0024

CHARMING COUNTRY CRAFTSMAN HOME

1,994 total square feet of living area

Width: 62'-2" Depth: 56'-0"

3 bedrooms, 2 baths

2-car garage

Basement foundation

SPECIAL FEATURES

The vaulted entry flows into the spacious great room with corner fireplace and a wall of windows

A large walk-in closet and private bath with double-bowl vanity are some of the amenities of the master bedroom

The kitchen has a walk-in pantry and eating bar that has lovely views of the sunny breakfast area

PRICE CODE B

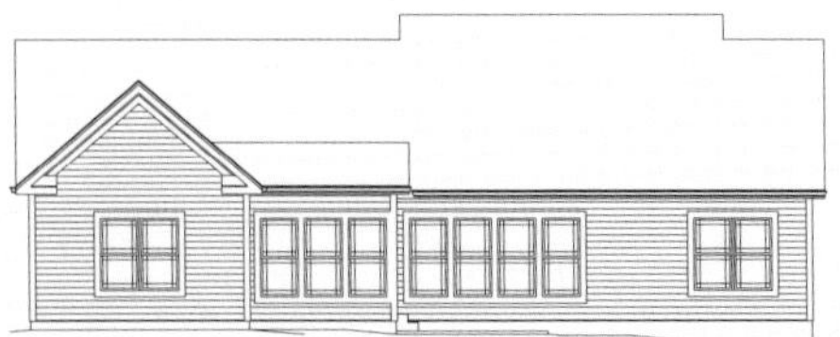

Rear View

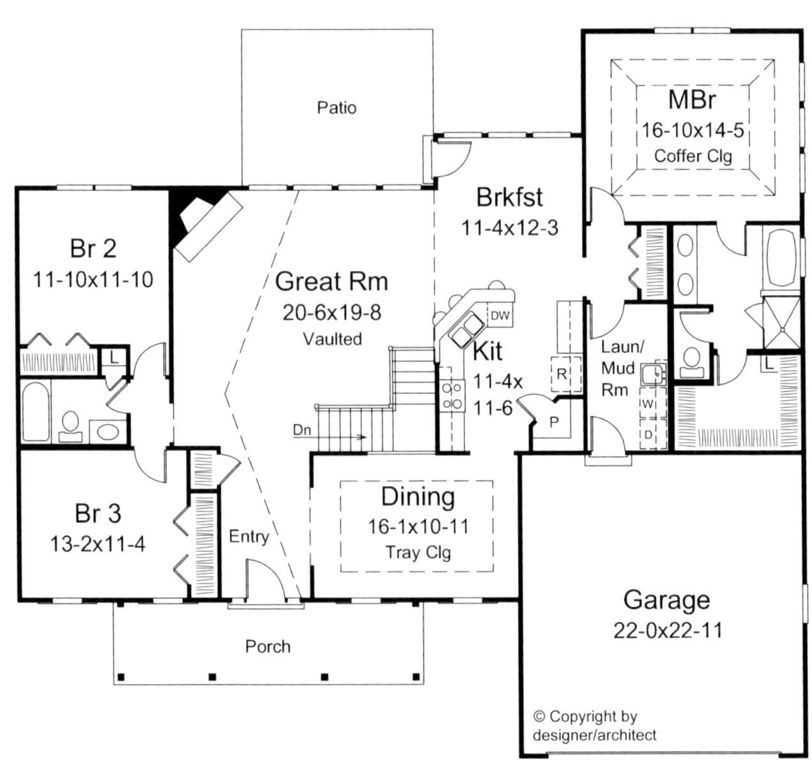

To order plans, visit the Menards Building Materials Desk or visit www.Menards.com.

GREENSAVER ATRIUM

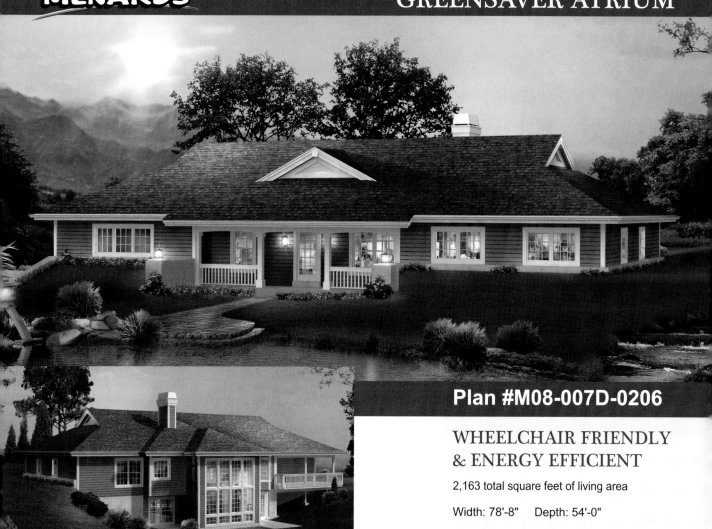

Plan #M08-007D-0206

WHEELCHAIR FRIENDLY & ENERGY EFFICIENT

2,163 total square feet of living area

Width: 78'-8" Depth: 54'-0"

3 bedrooms, 2 baths

3-car side entry garage

Walk-out basement foundation

SPECIAL FEATURES

Plan includes 2" x 6" and 2" x 8" wall construction and insulated vinyl siding with triple-glazed insulated windows and doors

The basement has insulated walls and a natural cooling system created by a 40' buried pipe that has a constant 55-degree earth temperature to help cool the house

The vaulted great room and atrium with two-story window wall provide southern views and warmth from the sun

PRICE CODE C

Covered Deck
3-Car Garage 22-4x29-4
Brk'ft 12-2x13-0
Kitchen 11-5x14-4
Pan.
Laundry
Atrium
Great Room 16-8x20-8
plant shelf above
Dining 12-0x12-4
Entry
Porch Patio
Mbr 15-2x15-8
Hall
Br 3 11-0x13-1
Br 2 11-3x13-1

Rear View

CARR CREEK

MENARDS®

Plan #M08-055L-0203

CENTRALLY LOCATED KITCHEN

2,388 total square feet of living area

Width: 68'-0" Depth: 74'-0"

4 bedrooms, 2 1/2 baths

2-car side entry garage

Slab or crawl space foundation, please specify when ordering

SPECIAL FEATURES

The foyer opens into the great room that features a gas fireplace, a media center, and access to the rear covered porch

The formal dining room, breakfast room with access to the porch, and kitchen counter with seating all provide plenty of dining space

The master suite enjoys two walk-in closets and a deluxe bath with twin vanities and a whirlpool tub

PRICE CODE D

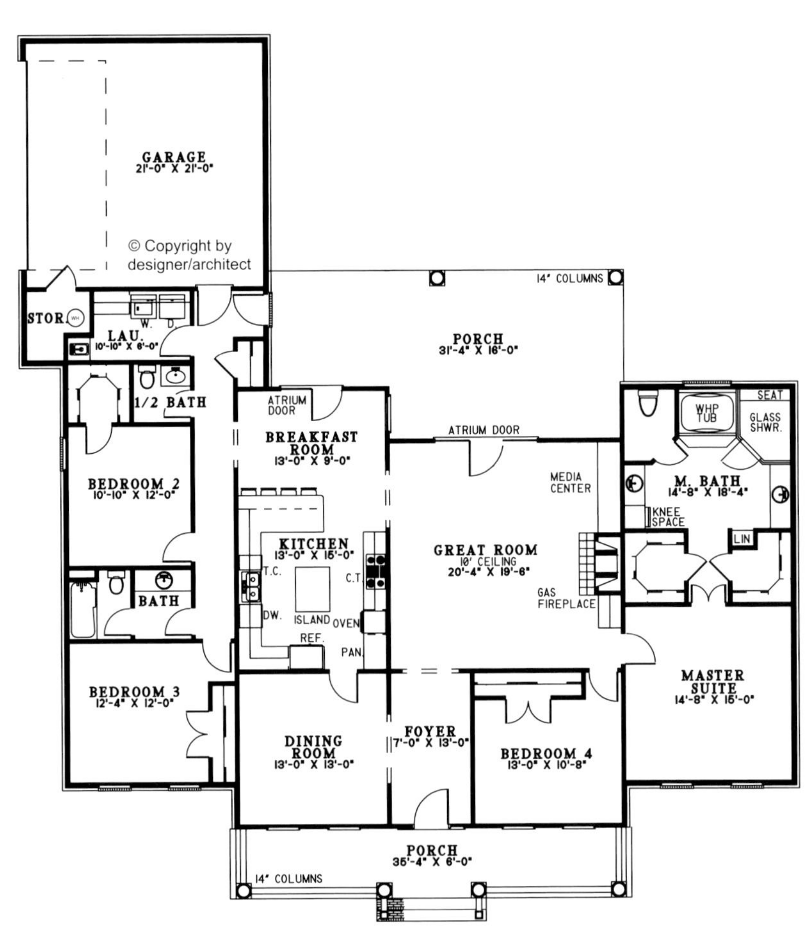

To order plans, visit the Menards Building Materials Desk or visit www.Menards.com.

MENARDS® Luxury HOME PLANS

MENARDS® Luxury Home Plan collection will help you envision your dream home as it comes to life. Browse through this distinguished collection of home plans and discover a variety of architectural styles from tasteful to glamorous. Surround yourself with luxury and build a dream home like you never could imagine.

Plan #M08-055L-0817 can be found on page 95.

Plan #M08-051L-0246 can be found on page 92.

Plan #M08-065L-0024 can be found on page 90.

CHARLEVOIX CREEK

Plan #M08-055L-0215

Photo, above - The kitchen is infused with a rustic feel thanks to the wood plank flooring that fills the space and leads into the breakfast room.

Photo, left - Rustic wood beams top the enchanting great room that features a center stone fireplace with flat screen television above.

Photo, above - Just beyond the porch, you'll discover this ever-popular outdoor fireplace designed for comfortable gathering in the colder months.

Photo, right - Elevated to new heights, the master suite enjoys a specially designed beamed ceiling treatment drawing the eye upward.

Plan #M08-055L-0215

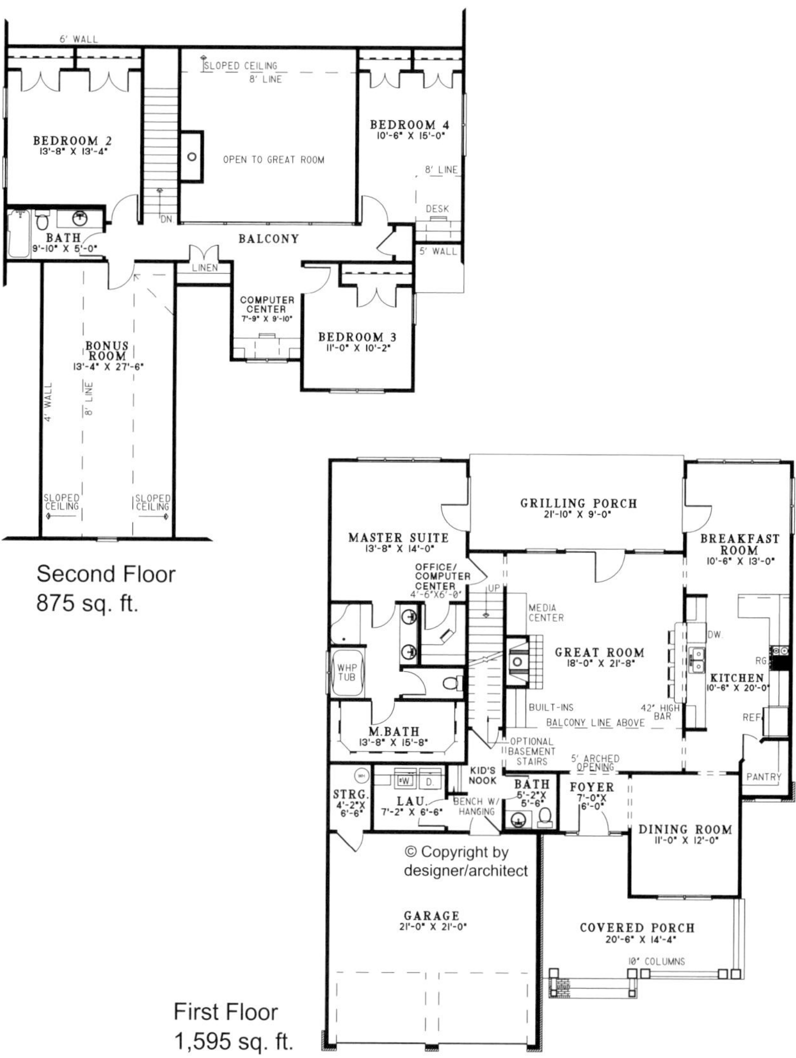

To order plans, visit the Menards Building Materials Desk
or visit www.Menards.com.

EXQUISITE CRAFTSMAN STYLE

2,470 total square feet of living area

Width: 47'-4" Depth: 58'-8"

4 bedrooms, 2 1/2 baths

2-car garage

Slab or crawl space foundation, please specify when ordering

SPECIAL FEATURES

An extended counter in the kitchen has enough dining space for four people to gather around and enjoy a meal comfortably

A media center is designed next to the fireplace in the cozy great room

Rustic shutters and shingle siding add a great custom feel to the exterior of this home

The bonus room above the garage offers an additional 389 square feet of future living area

PRICE CODE E

WAINBRIDGE

Plan #M08-065L-0024

Photo, above - It is no surprise that the kitchen opens to the hearth room, as both are favorite gathering spots for family and friends. The stone fireplace in the hearth room off of the kitchen adds something special to the family's favorite gathering place. With drinks in the under counter wine cooler and a crackling fire nearby, memories are ready to be made.

Photo, left - The ample space above the mantle can be used to showcase collected works of art, family pictures, or your favorite flat screen television. With the two-story ceiling this already spacious great room is magnificent.

Photo, above - The foyer is the first impression many guests receive. The intricate glass door framed securely with warm wood allows natural light to flood the entryway, while beckoning guests into the home.

Photo, right - The spacious formal dining room is ideally located. Double doors allow guests to gather after dinner on the porch, enjoying the fresh air and one another's company.

Plan #M08-065L-0024

STATELY COLONIAL ENTRY

4,652 total square feet of living area

Width: 90'-6" Depth: 78'-9"

4 bedrooms, 3 1/2 baths

3-car side entry garage

Walk-out basement foundation

SPECIAL FEATURES

A grand foyer introduces a formal dining room and a library with a beamed ceiling and built-ins

Covered porches at the rear of the home offer splendid views

A magnificent master bedroom has a 10' ceiling, a private sitting area, and a luxurious dressing room with walk-in closet

The secondary bedrooms have window seats, large closets and private bath access

PRICE CODE G

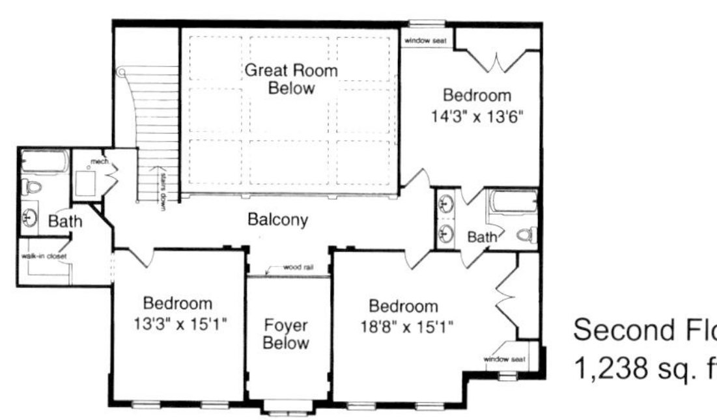

Second Floor 1,238 sq. ft.

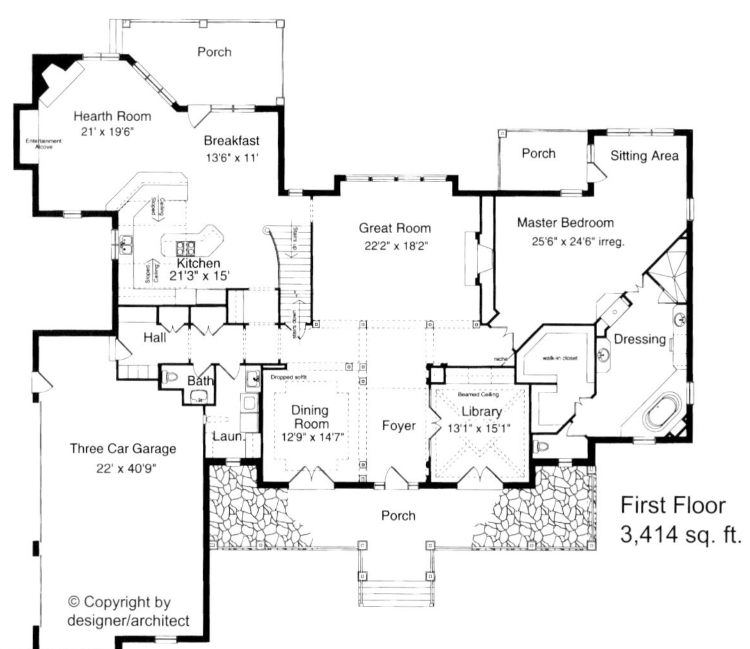

First Floor 3,414 sq. ft.

To order plans, visit the Menards Building Materials Desk or visit www.Menards.com.

NORTHAIRE

Plan #M08-051L-0246

Photo, above - This spectacular kitchen will lift any mood. Conveniences include a cooktop island and snack bar counter. And, the adjoining breakfast nook/sun room is surrounded in light, keeping the area bright and cheerful.

Photo, left - The living room offers a more formal place to entertain or relax with family and friends.

Photo, right - Comfortable and cozy, the family room provides warmth around the fireplace and plenty of places to store family collectibles.

BR.#3
13'0" x 13'0"
BR.#2
12'6" x 13'6"
LOFT
DOWN
LINEN
LIN
PLANT LEDGE
OPEN TO E.
BR.#4
11'4" x 15'0"

Second Floor
956 sq. ft.

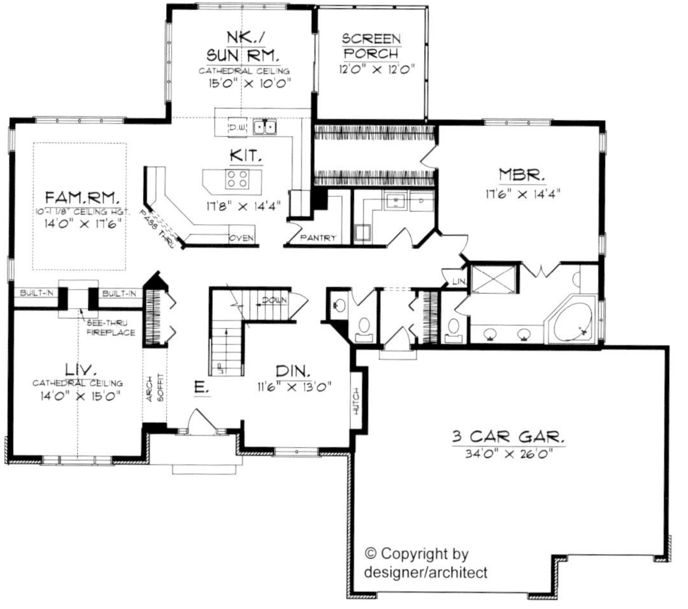

First Floor
2,143 sq. ft.

Plan #M08-051L-0246

EVERY BEDROOM HAS A WALK-IN CLOSET

3,099 total square feet of living area

Width: 71'-0" Depth: 62'-0"

4 bedrooms, 2 1/2 baths

3-car garage

Basement foundation

SPECIAL FEATURES

Energy efficient home with 2" x 6" exterior walls

A see-through fireplace warms both the formal living room and casual family room

The chef of the family will love this gourmet kitchen complete with an abundance of counterspace, a stovetop island, and a walk-in pantry

The breakfast nook/sun room with access to a screen porch allows the family to enjoy the great outdoors all year long

PRICE CODE G

To order plans, visit the Menards Building Materials Desk or visit www.Menards.com.

TENNILLE

MENARDS®

Luxury Plans

Plan #M08-013L-0039

SPRAWLING FAMILY FARMHOUSE

2,972 total square feet of living area

Width: 93'-10"   Depth: 61'-2"

4 bedrooms, 3 1/2 baths

3-car side entry garage

Walk-out basement, crawl space or slab foundation, please specify when ordering

SPECIAL FEATURES

Extra storage is available beyond bedroom #2 on the second floor

An angled staircase in the entry adds architectural interest

A charming screened porch is accessible from the breakfast area

The bonus room above the garage has an additional 396 square feet of living area

PRICE CODE E

Second Floor
986 sq. ft.

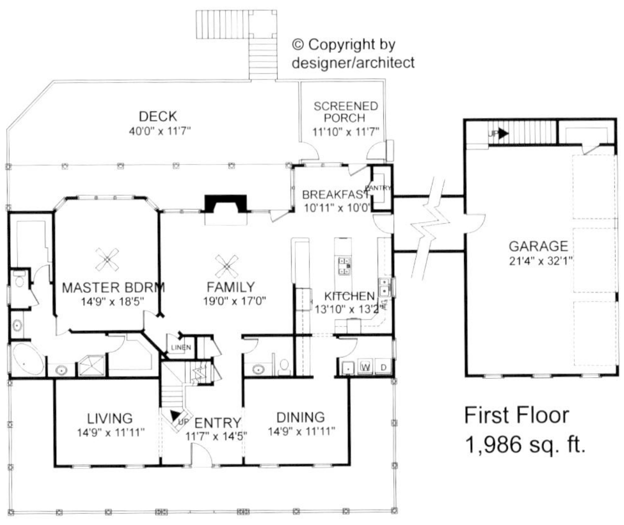

First Floor
1,986 sq. ft.

To order plans, visit the Menards Building Materials Desk or visit www.Menards.com.

MENARDS®

BERGAMO MANOR

Plan #M08-055L-0817

EUROPEAN LUXURY

2,889 total square feet of living area

Width: 42'-0" Depth: 79'-6"

4 bedrooms, 2 1/2 baths

2-car garage

Crawl space or slab foundation, please specify when ordering

SPECIAL FEATURES

Stone, a striking turret, and decorative roof lines accent this home and give it a European flair

The luxurious first floor offers a massive great room, a plush master suite, a quiet office, and access to the outdoor living porch furnished with a stone hearth fireplace

The second floor consists of three bedrooms, a shared bath, and a handy computer center

The second floor bonus room has an additional 378 square feet of living area

PRICE CODE E

MASTER SUITE 14'-8" X 17'-0" 10' BOXED CEILING
M.BATH 10'-4"x 17'-4"
WHP TUB
SHWR
OFFICE 12'-0" X 10'-0"
LAU. 5'-6"x 6'-6"
STRG 5'-6"x 3'-6"
1/2 B 4'-10"x 6'-10"
OPTIONAL BASEMENT STAIRS
GREAT ROOM 14'-8" X 23'-10"
STONE HEARTH
ARCHED OPENING
FIREPLACE W/ STONE HEARTH
OUTDOOR LIVING PORCH 26'-8" X 12'-0"
BREAKFAST ROOM 11'-0" X 9'-0"
KITCHEN 11'-0" X 12'-8"
FOYER 8'-0"x 8'-4"
OPEN TO ABOVE
ENTRY PRCH 8'-0"x 4'-8"
DINING ROOM 19'-4" X 11'-0"
14' CEILING
GARAGE 21'-4" X 22'-6"

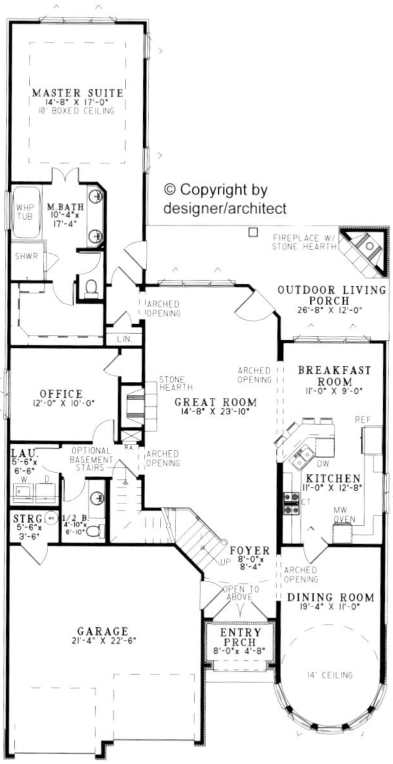

First Floor
1,819 sq. ft.

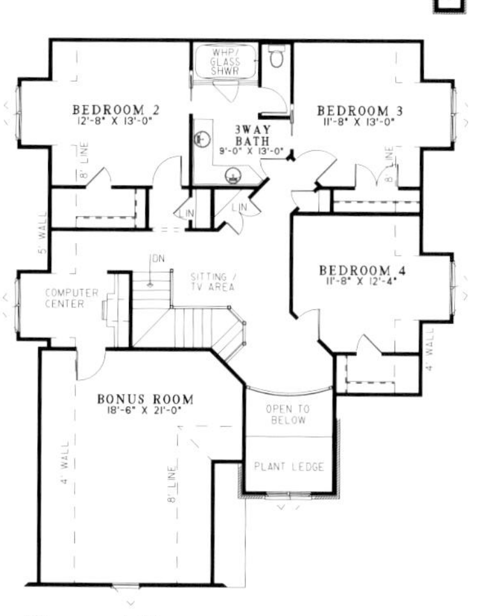

Second Floor
1,070 sq. ft.

To order plans, visit the Menards Building Materials Desk or visit www.Menards.com.

Luxury Plans

OXFORD PARK

MENARDS®

Plan #M08-072L-1123

STYLISH CRAFTSMAN SYMMETRY

2,715 total square feet of living area

Width: 78'-0"   Depth: 54'-0"

4 bedrooms, 2 1/2 baths

4-car garage

Walk-out basement or basement foundation, please specify when ordering

SPECIAL FEATURES

Energy efficient home with 2" x 6" exterior walls

The cheerful kitchen has a double-bowl sink in the island, a large corner pantry, and opens up to the cheerful dining area

Double doors off of the entry hall lead to a sophisticated study with access to the front covered wrap-around porch

The owner's suite has an optional fireplace and offers a generous closet and a private bath with a double-bowl vanity, an amazing walk-in shower, and a whirlpool tub

PRICE CODE D

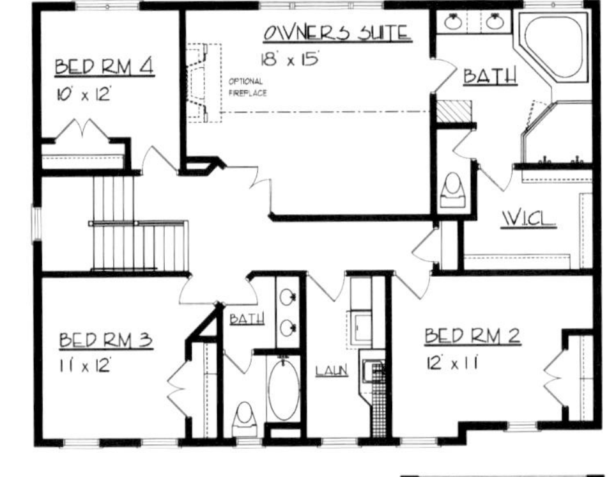

Second Floor
1,337 sq. ft.

First Floor
1,378 sq. ft.

To order plans, visit the Menards Building Materials Desk or visit www.Menards.com.

MENARDS®

MACKENZIE

Plan #M08-121D-0040

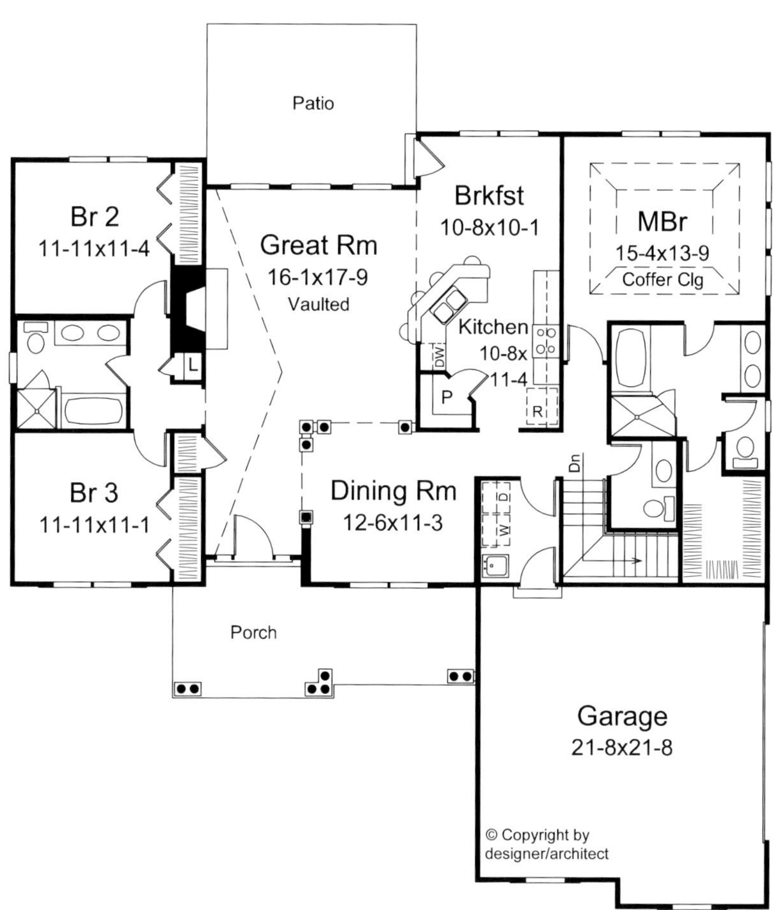

To order plans, visit the Menards Building Materials Desk
or visit www.Menards.com.

AMENITY-FILLED MASTER BEDROOM AND BATH

1,863 total square feet of living area

Width: 58'-0" Depth: 58'-0"

3 bedrooms, 2 1/2 baths

2-car side entry garage

Basement foundation

SPECIAL FEATURES

A vaulted ceiling spans from the foyer to the great room, creating an open feel

The centrally located kitchen easily serves both the formal dining room as well as the more casual breakfast area

The beautiful private master bedroom enjoys its own well appointed bath and walk-in closet

PRICE CODE B

Rear View

GIANCARLO

MENARDS®

Plan #M08-055L-0174

EXCITING GAME ROOM

2,755 total square feet of living area

Width: 69'-0" Depth: 69'-10"

3 bedrooms, 4 1/2 baths

3-car side entry garage

Slab, crawl space, basement or walk-out basement foundation, please specify when ordering

SPECIAL FEATURES

The breakfast room boasts a two-story vaulted ceiling

Each bedroom has a private bath

The 10' covered porch has plenty of space for eating outdoors or just relaxing

PRICE CODE E

Second Floor
349 sq. ft.

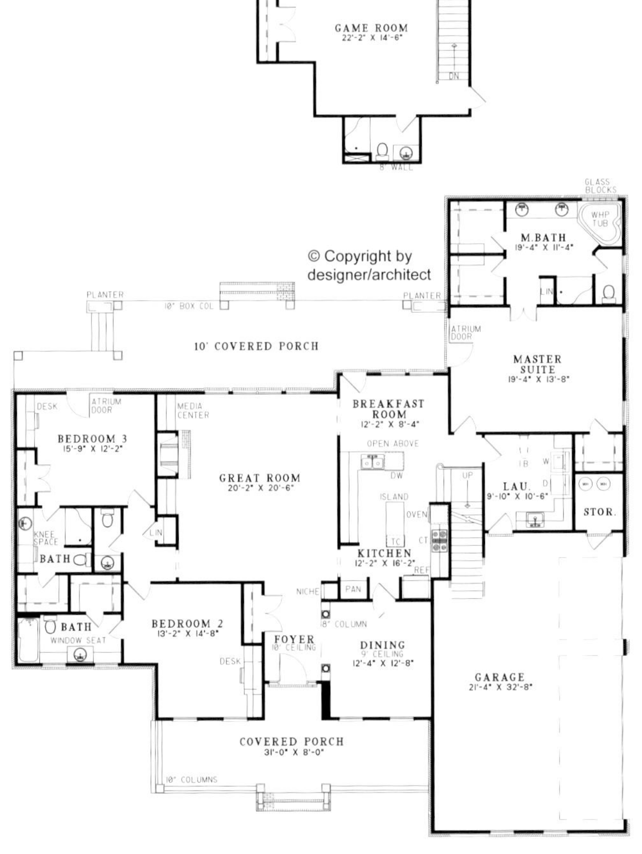

First Floor
2,406 sq. ft.

To order plans, visit the Menards Building Materials Desk or visit www.Menards.com.

MENARDS®

KELBY HILL

Luxury Plans

Plan #M08-065L-0012

Second Floor
823 sq. ft.

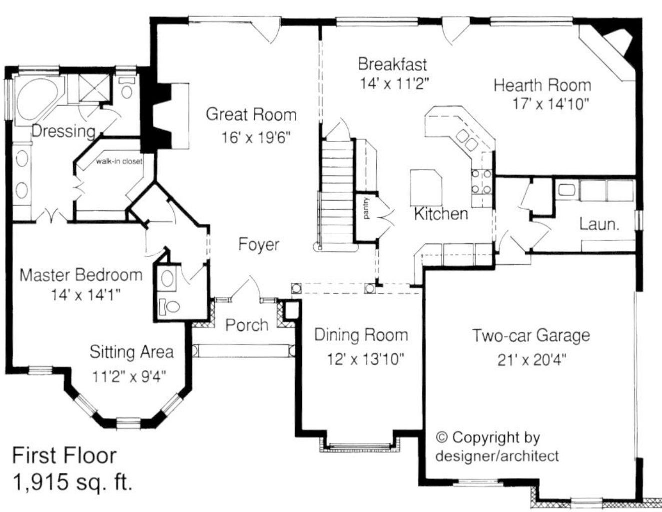

First Floor
1,915 sq. ft.

MANY WONDERFIL FEATURES

2,738 total square feet of living area

Width: 63'-4" Depth: 48'-0"

4 bedrooms, 3 1/2 baths

2-car side entry garage

Basement foundation

SPECIAL FEATURES

An open entrance offers a spectacular view of the windowed rear wall and fireplace in the great room

The kitchen, breakfast and hearth rooms combine to offer an open and comfortable gathering place

The master bedroom is topped with an 11' ceiling and features a sitting alcove and deluxe bath

PRICE CODE E

To order plans, visit the Menards Building Materials Desk or visit www.Menards.com.

ALYSON

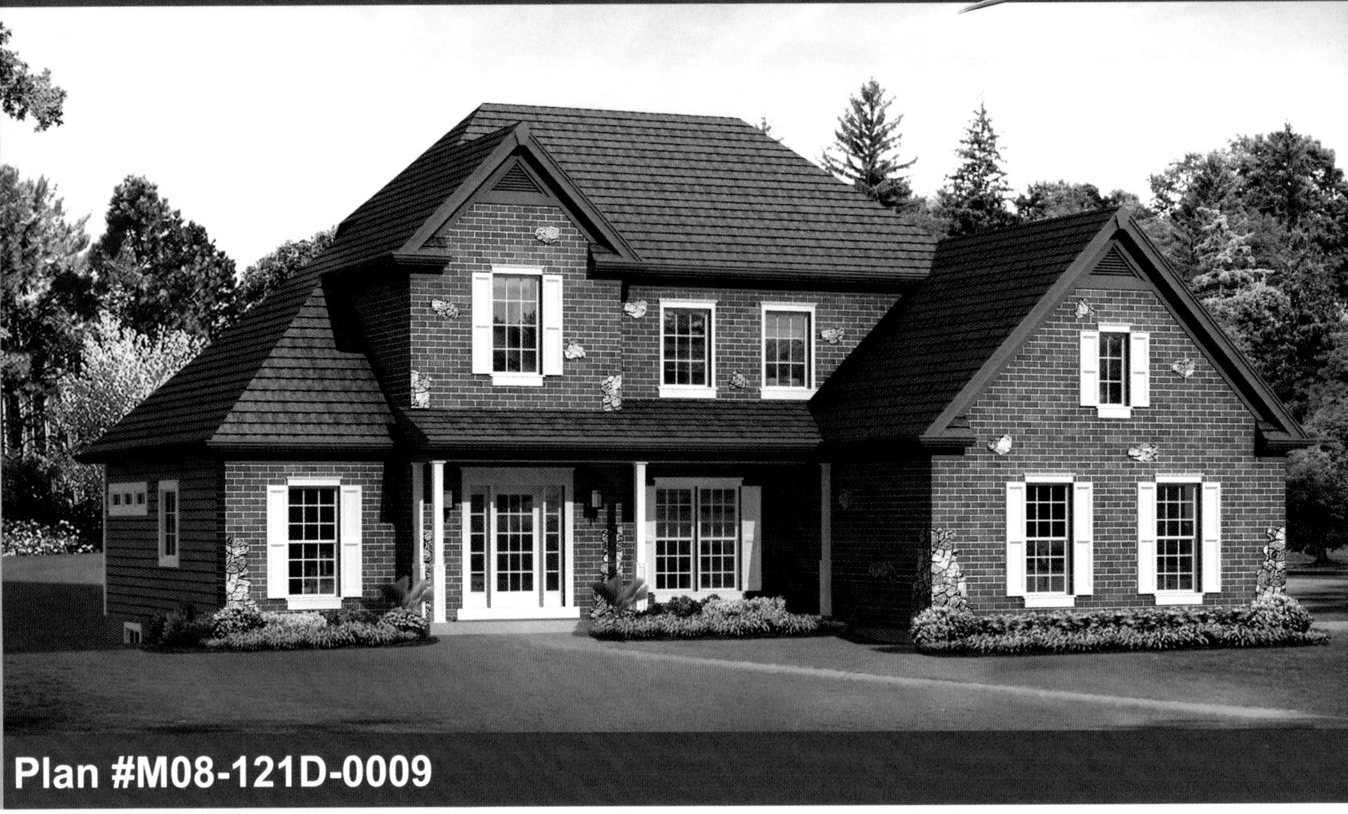

Plan #M08-121D-0009

VAULTED TWO-STORY GREAT ROOM

2,240 total square feet of living area

Width: 56'-8" Depth: 57'-4"

3 bedrooms, 2 1/2 baths

2-car side entry garage

Basement foundation

SPECIAL FEATURES

The master bedroom enjoys a private first floor location along with an amenity-filled bath and a walk-in closet

A flexible loft space can be found on the second floor perfect for a home office or children's play area

The functional kitchen has an eating bar and a corner walk-in pantry

PRICE CODE C

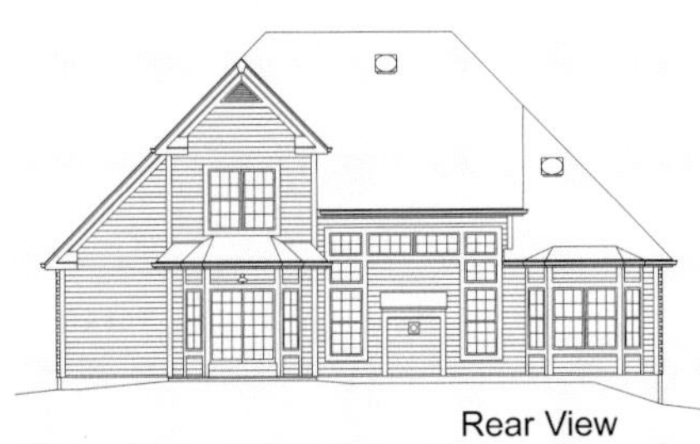

Rear View

Second Floor
630 sq. ft.

First Floor
1,610 sq. ft.

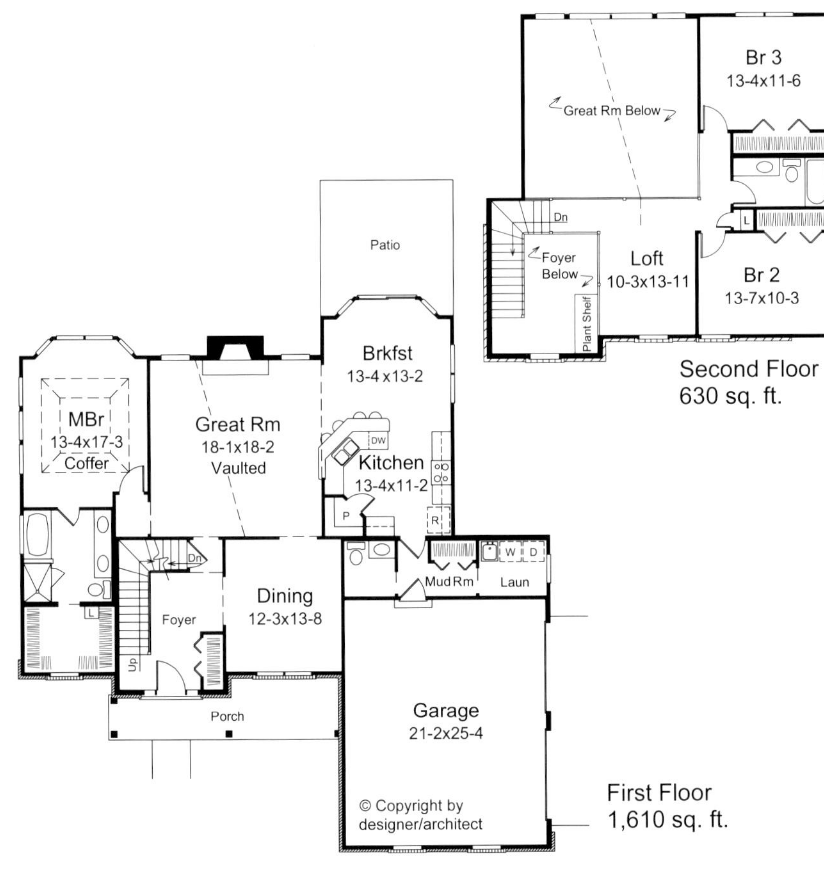

To order plans, visit the Menards Building Materials Desk or visit www.Menards.com.

MENARDS®

BERNICE FARM

Plan #M08-051L-0155

Second Floor
1,173 sq. ft.

First Floor
2,108 sq. ft.

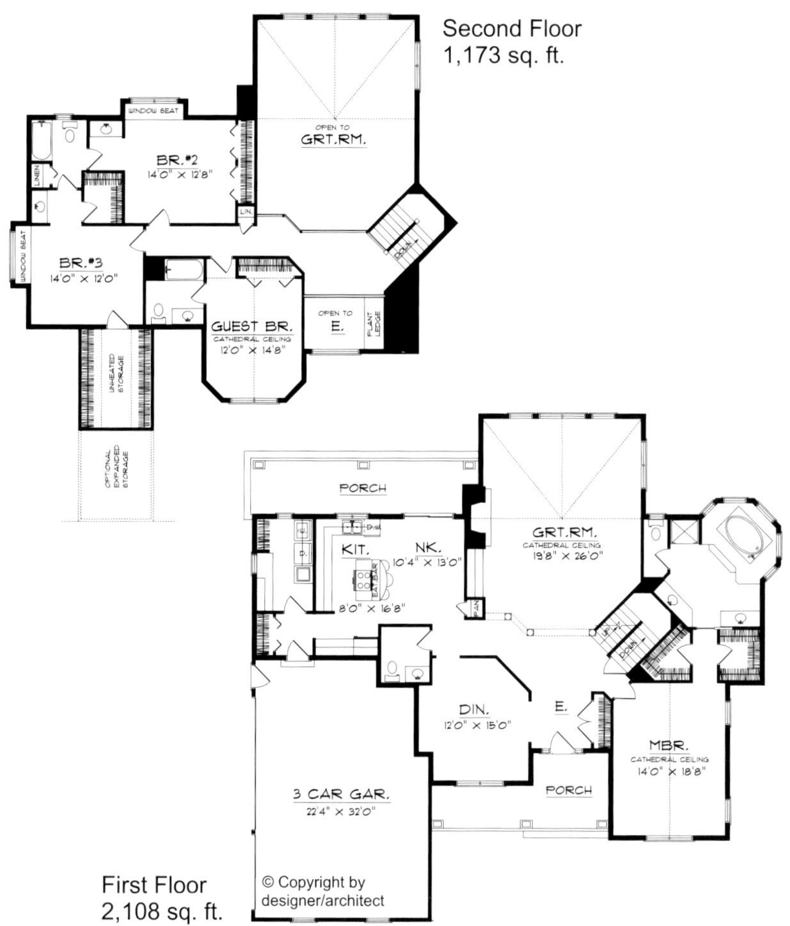

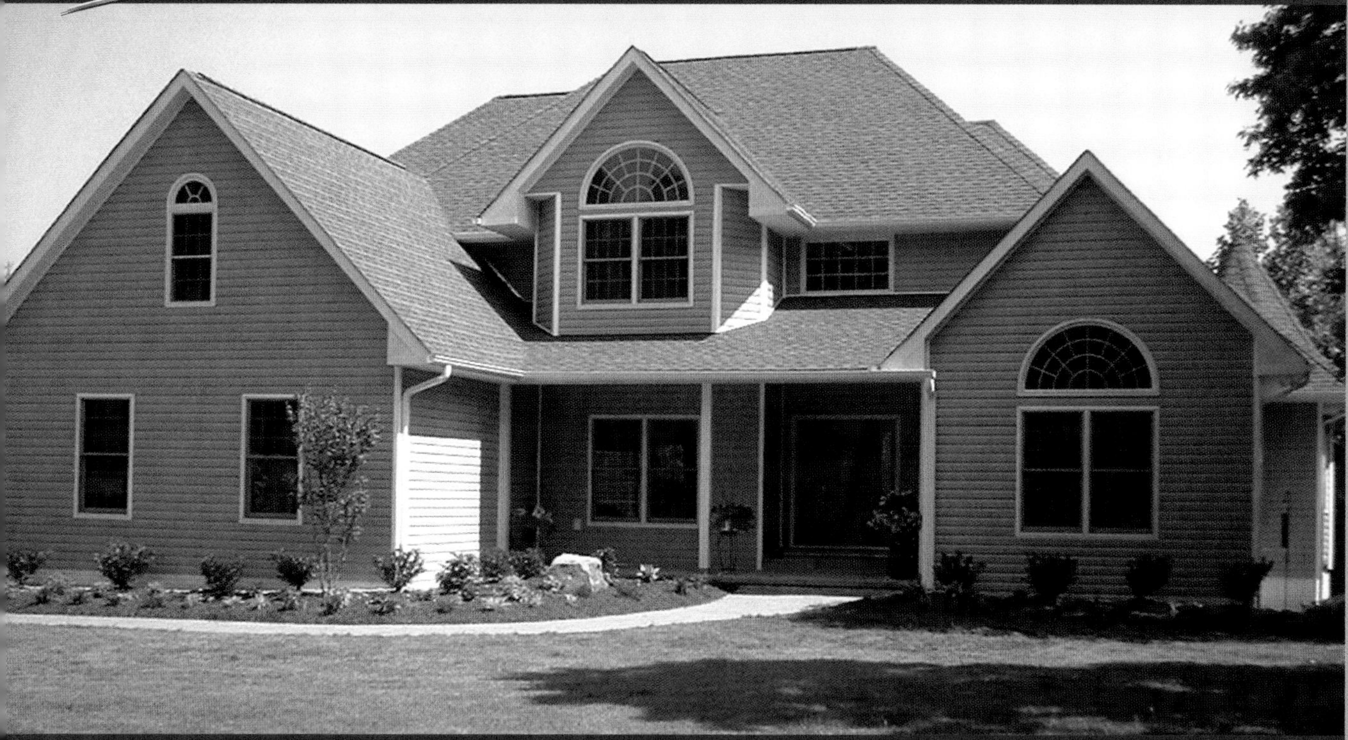

ELEGANT COUNTRY HOME

3,281 total square feet of living area

Width: 66'-0" Depth: 62'-0"

4 bedrooms, 3 1/2 baths

3-car side entry garage

Basement foundation

SPECIAL FEATURES

Energy efficient home with 2" x 6" exterior walls

The luxury master bedroom has two walk-in closets and a deluxe bath

The kitchen has a cooktop island with eating bar and opens to the nook

Bedrooms #2 and #3 each feature a cozy window seat and share a Jack and Jill bath

PRICE CODE G

Rear View

To order plans, visit the Menards Building Materials Desk or visit www.Menards.com.

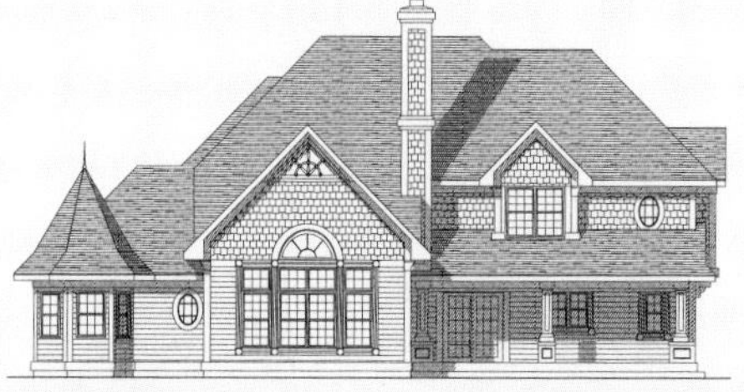

PELHAM PARK

Plan #M08-013L-0031

PEACEFUL SCREENED PORCH FOR RELAXING

2,253 total square feet of living area

Width: 57'-0"   Depth: 51'-0"

4 bedrooms, 3 baths

2-car side entry garage

Walk-out basement, crawl space or slab foundation, please specify when ordering

SPECIAL FEATURES

Two bedrooms on the second floor share a bath

Two walk-in closets, a private bath, and a sitting area leading to an outdoor deck are all amenities of the master suite

The bonus room on the second floor has an additional 247 square feet of living area

PRICE CODE D

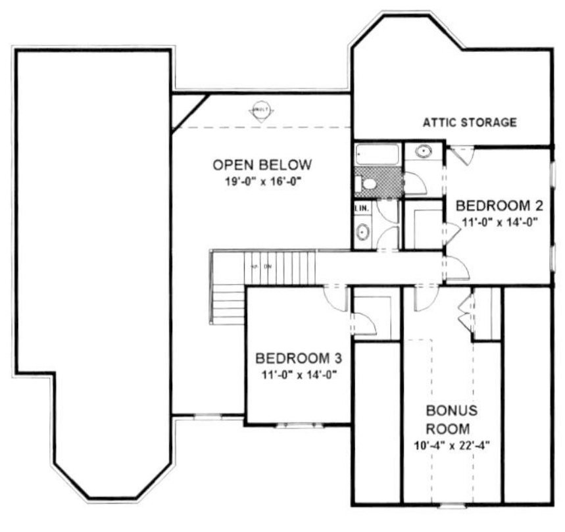

Second Floor
534 sq. ft.

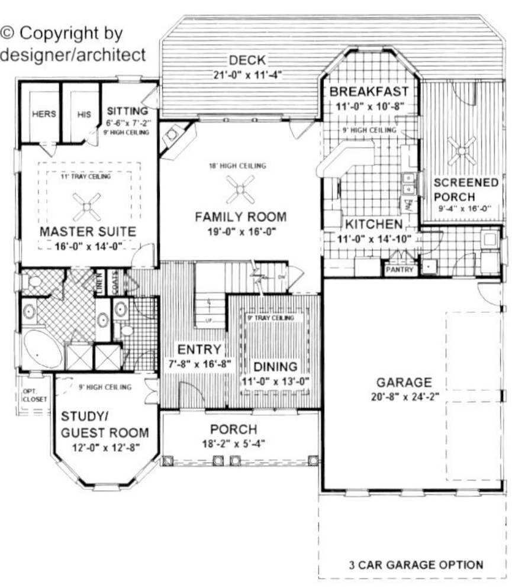

First Floor
1,719 sq. ft.

To order plans, visit the Menards Building Materials Desk or visit www.Menards.com.

MENARDS®

OLIVIA

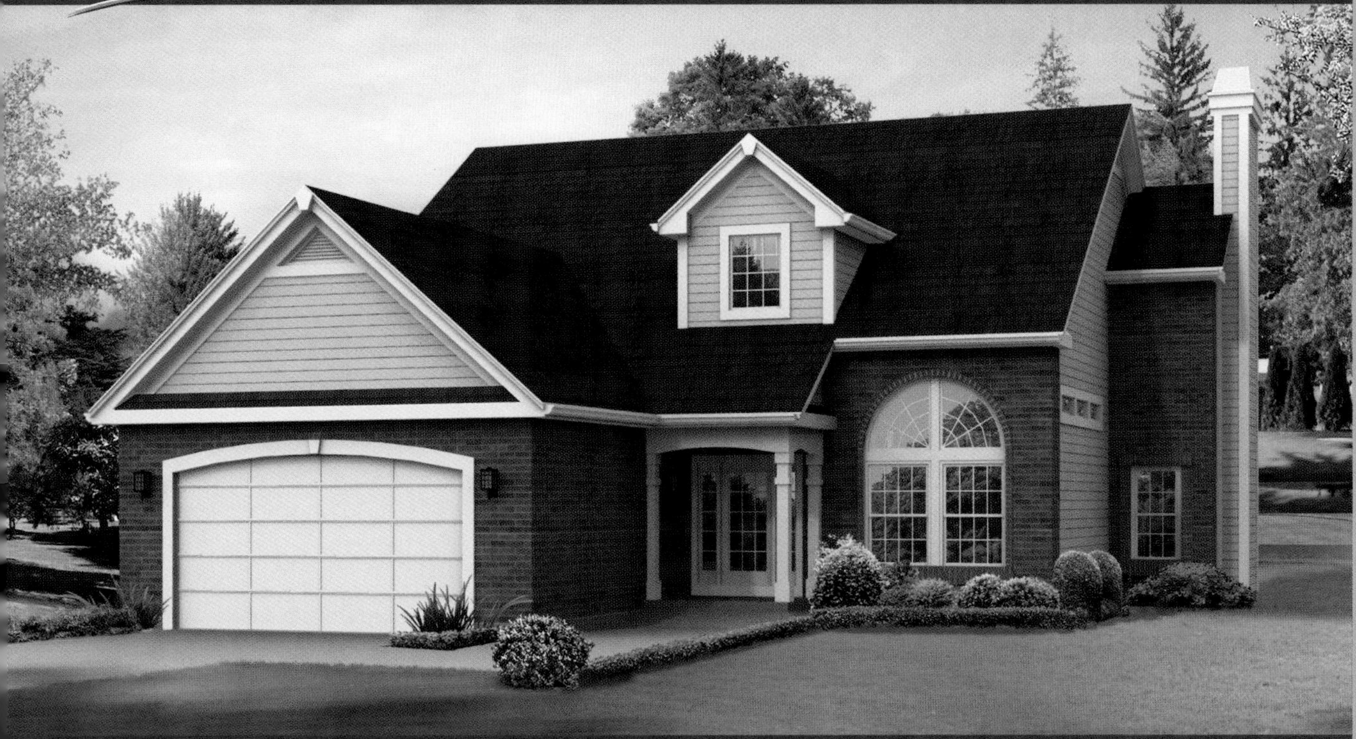

Luxury Plans

Plan #M08-121D-0001

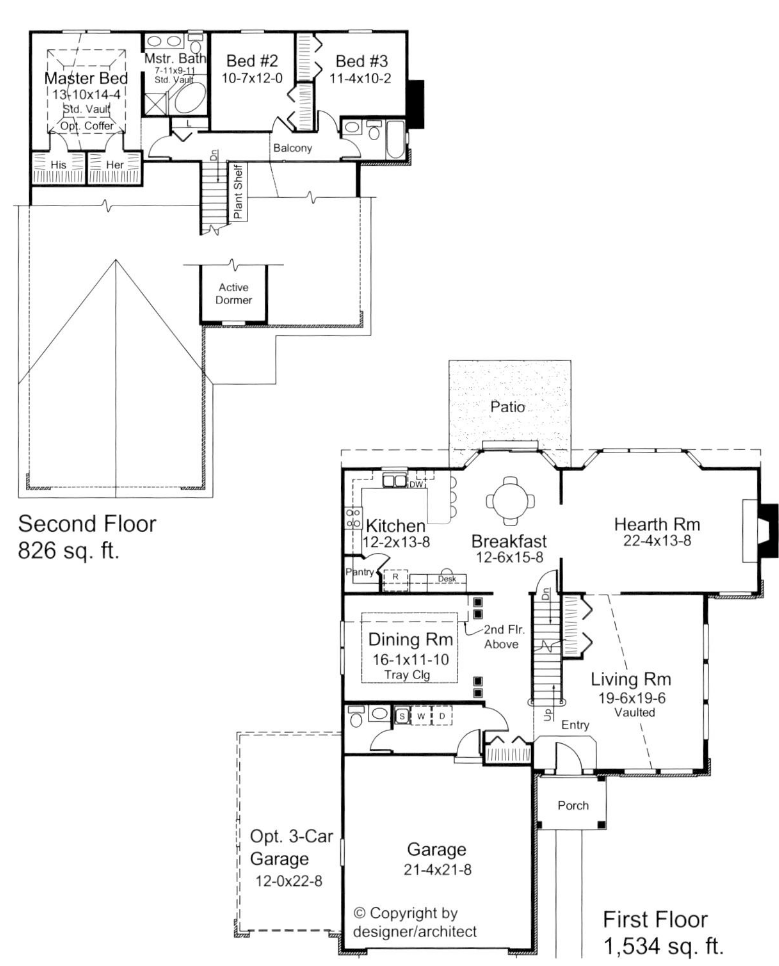

To order plans, visit the Menards Building Materials Desk or visit www.Menards.com.

ARCHED WINDOW ADDS CURB APPEAL

2,360 total square feet of living area

Width: 50'-4" Depth: 56'-8"

3 bedrooms, 2 1/2 baths

2-car garage

Basement foundation

SPECIAL FEATURES

The U-shaped kitchen has a large walk-in pantry, a desk, and extra counterspace

Luxury can be found in the second floor master bedroom including his and her walk-in closets and a private bath

2" x 6" exterior wall framing available for an additional fee, please specify when ordering

PRICE CODE C

Rear View

FOREST PARK

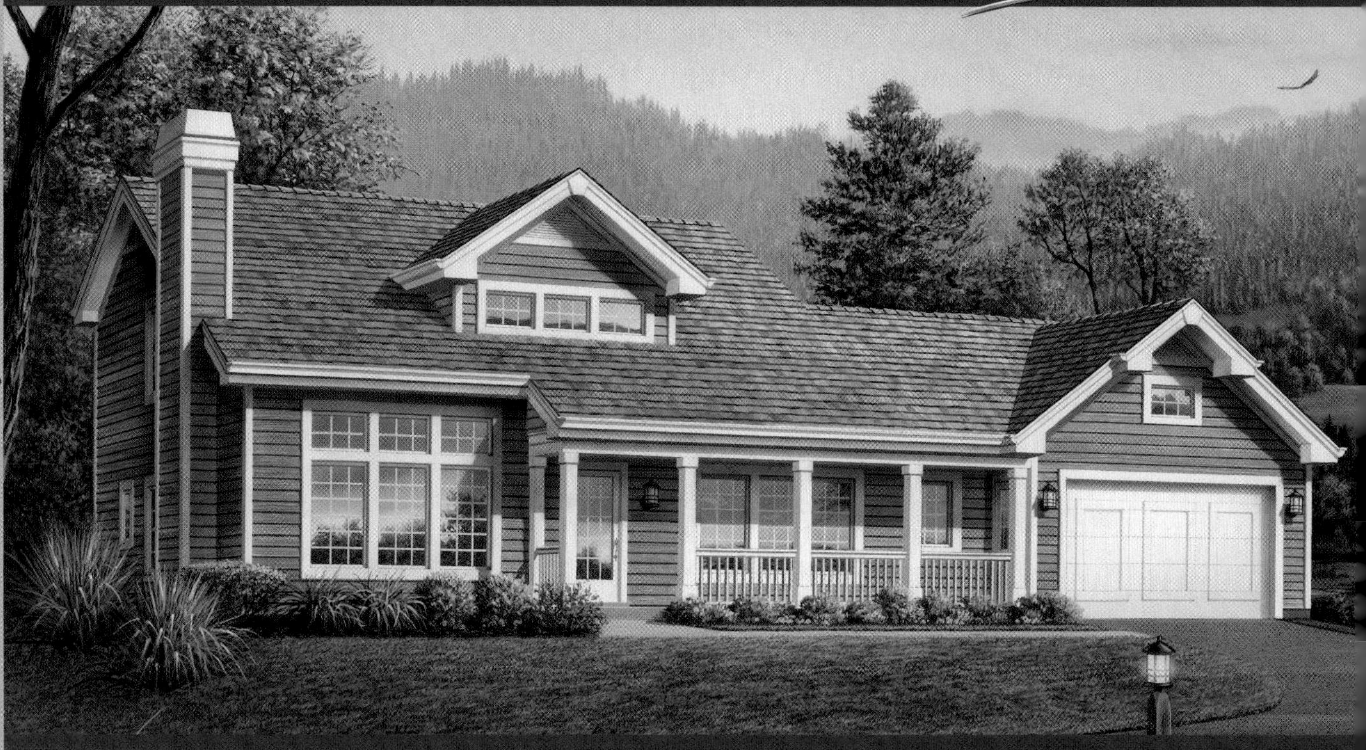

Plan #M08-007D-0209

COVERED PATIO WITH BAR AND SAUNA

2,365 total square feet of living area

Width: 67'-0" Depth: 44'-0"

4 bedrooms, 3 1/2 baths

2-car garage

Crawl space foundation

SPECIAL FEATURES

A winding staircase leading to the second floor's spacious bedrooms is central to this home's carefully designed interior

Both the kitchen and breakfast area view the covered and uncovered rear patios that include skylights, a vaulted ceiling, a walk-in bar and sauna room

The first floor features a private study or guest bedroom with bath and closet

PRICE CODE C

Rear View

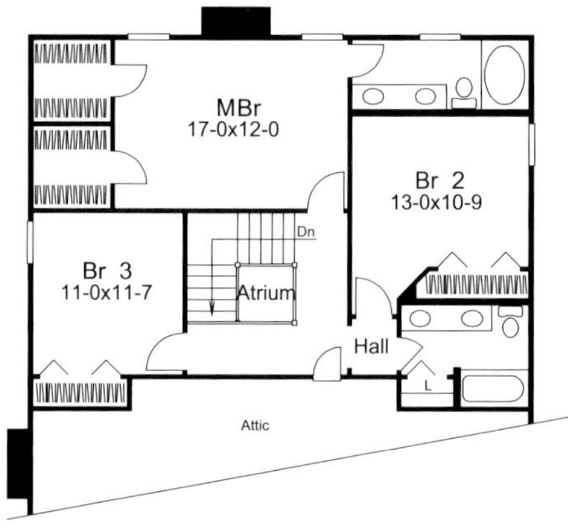

Second Floor
888 sq. ft.

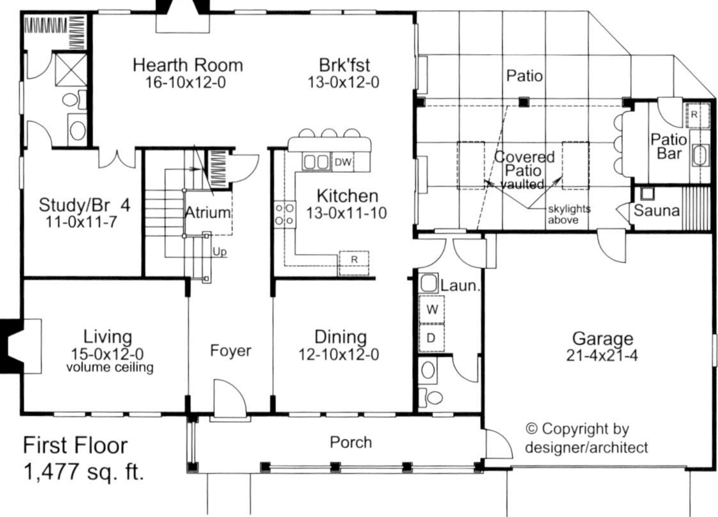

First Floor
1,477 sq. ft.

MARIANNA PARK

MENARDS®

Luxury Plans

Plan #M08-013L-0116

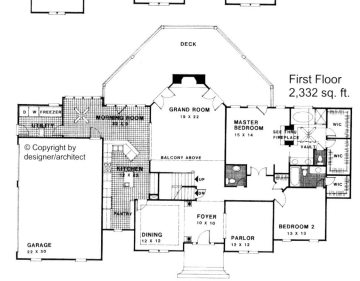

Second Floor
939 sq. ft.

First Floor
2,332 sq. ft.

UPPER GRAND ROOM
BEDROOM 3 12 X 14
VAULT
BALCONY
DN
TREY CEILING
UPPER FOYER
BONUS BEDROOM 5 13 X 25
STUDY 12 X 12
BEDROOM 4 12 X 13

DECK
GRAND ROOM 19 X 22
MASTER BEDROOM 15 X 14
SEE THRU FIREPLACE
WIC
VAULT
D W FREEZER
UTILITY
MORNING ROOM
KITCHEN
BALCONY ABOVE
UP
DN
PANTRY
FOYER 10 X 10
DINING 12 X 12
PARLOR 12 X 12
BEDROOM 2 13 X 13
GARAGE 22 X 30

LARGE OPEN DECK

3,271 total square feet of living area

Width: 85'-0" Depth: 46'-0"

4 bedrooms, 4 1/2 baths

3-car side entry garage

Walk-out basement foundation

SPECIAL FEATURES

The grand room features a handsome fireplace framed by French doors on both sides leading out to the deck

The see-through fireplace gives the master bedroom a natural focal point

The second floor balcony overlooks the grand room

A bonus room/bedroom #5 above the garage allows for an additional 412 square feet of living area

PRICE CODE E

To order plans, visit the Menards Building Materials Desk or visit www.Menards.com.

DUNGATE

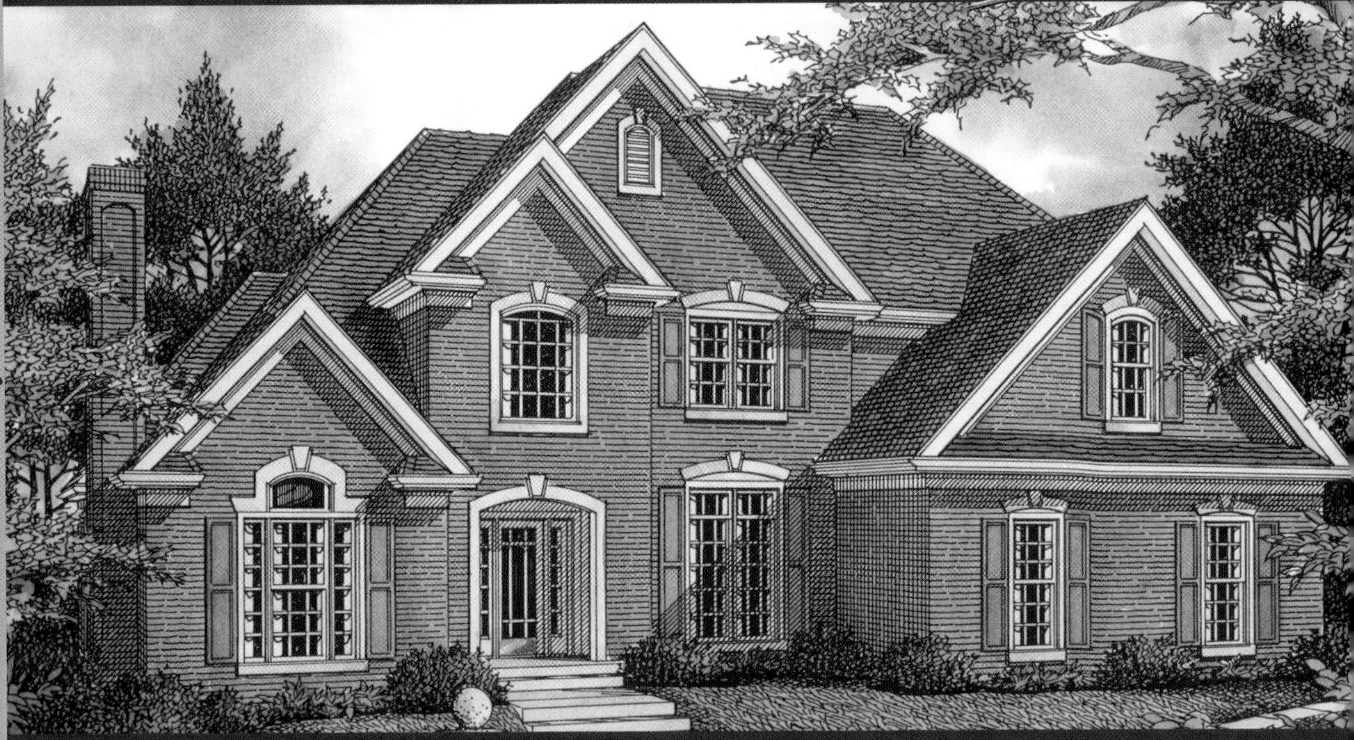

MENARDS®

Plan #M08-013L-0038

IMPRESSIVE BRICK TWO-STORY

2,954 total square feet of living area

Width: 60'-6" Depth: 55'-2"

4 bedrooms, 3 1/2 baths

2-car side entry garage

Basement or crawl space foundation, please specify when ordering

SPECIAL FEATURES

The master bedroom has a double-door entry into the luxurious bath

A private study has direct access into the master bedroom

The vaulted ceiling and bay window add light and dimension to the breakfast room

PRICE CODE E

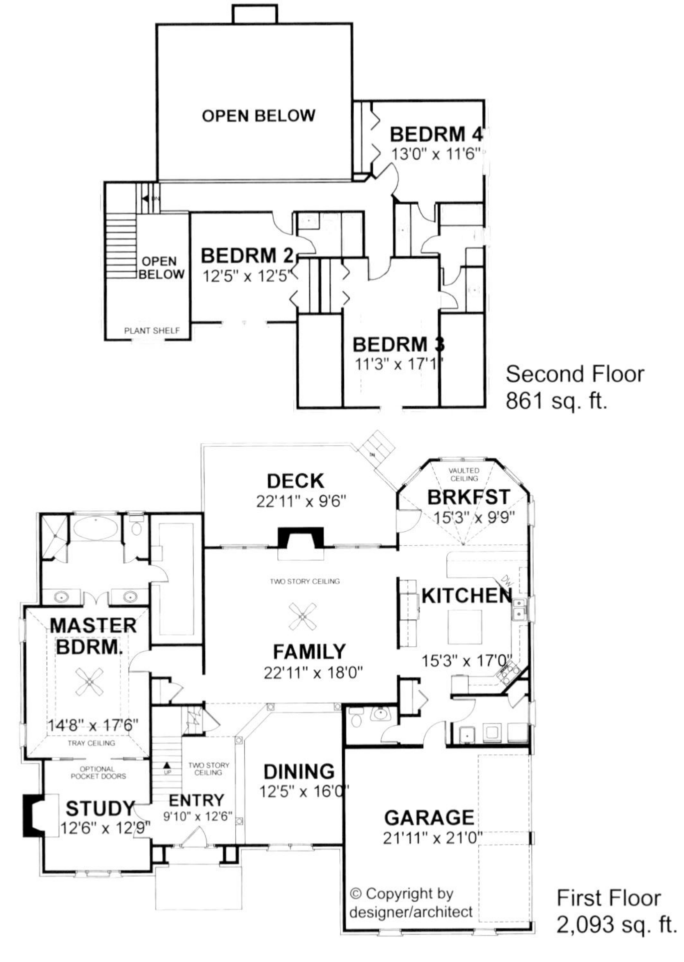

To order plans, visit the Menards Building Materials Desk or visit www.Menards.com.

FOREST FALLS

Luxury Plans

Plan #M08-007D-0211

PRIVATE APARTMENT WITHIN A HOME

3,346 total square feet of living area

Width: 74'-8" Depth: 58'-0"

5 bedrooms, 4 full baths, 2 half baths

2-car side entry garage

Walk-out basement foundation

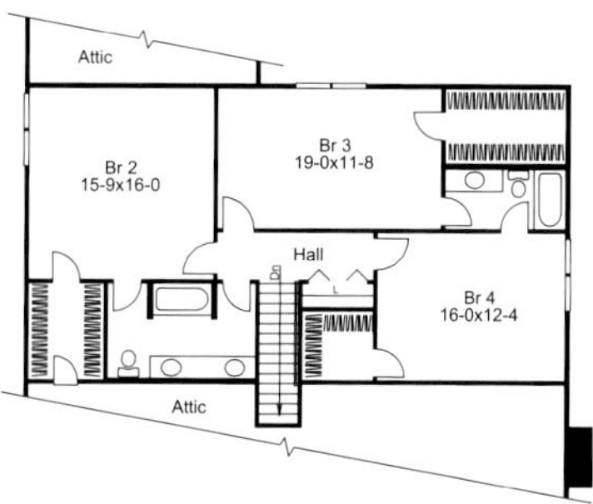

Second Floor
1,170 sq. ft.

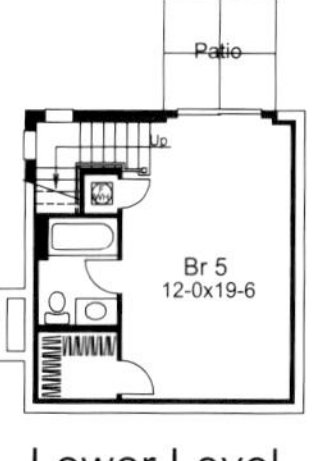

Lower Level
380 sq. ft.

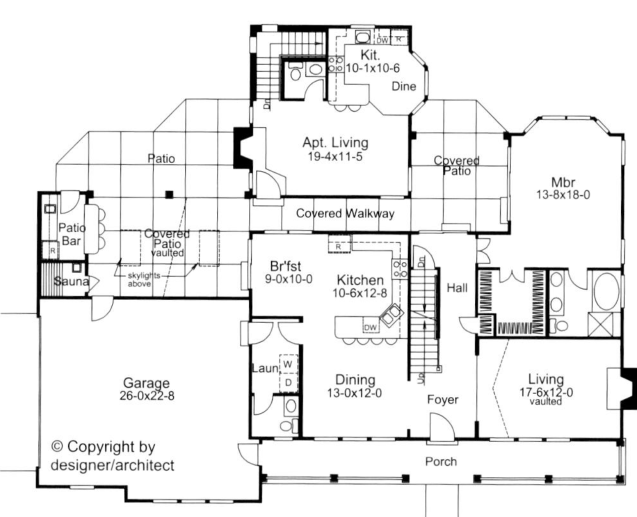

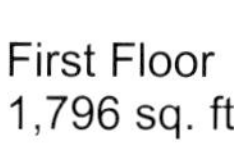

First Floor
1,796 sq. ft.

To order plans, visit the Menards Building Materials Desk or visit www.Menards.com.

SPECIAL FEATURES

The kitchen is open to the dining and breakfast areas

A covered patio, luxury bath, and walk-in closet are amenities of the master bedroom

In addition to the bedrooms on the second floor, an apartment that has 432 square feet that is included in the total square footage is located to the rear of the home

PRICE CODE E

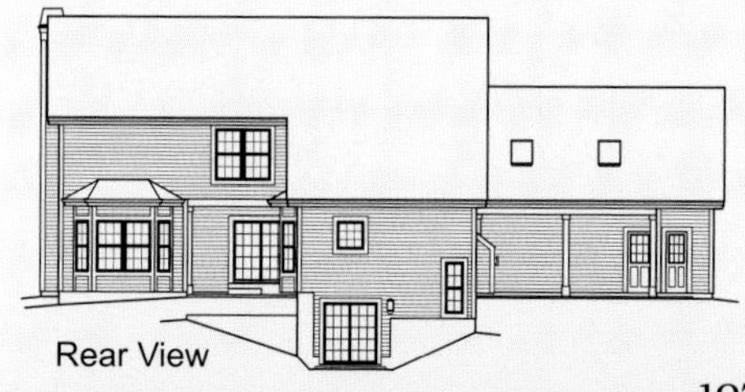

Rear View

WESTMINSTER HEIGHTS

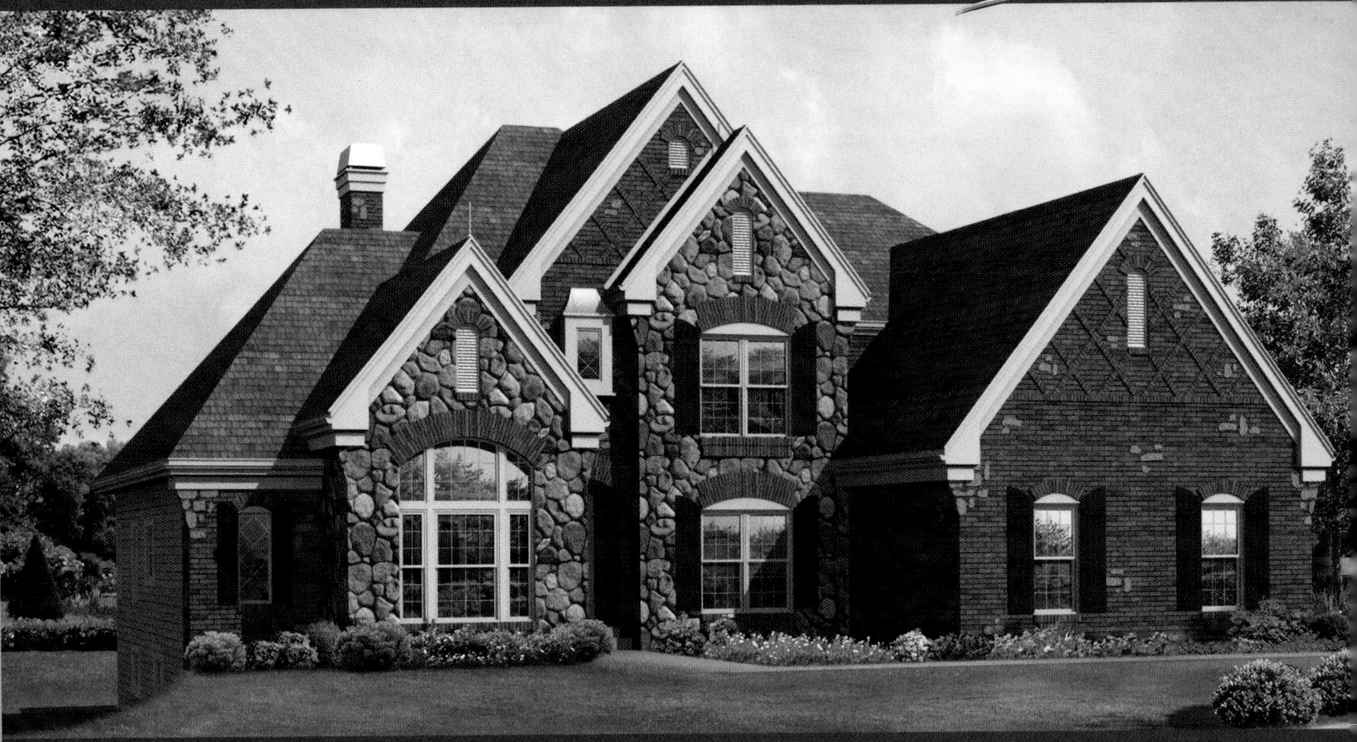

Plan #M08-007D-0203

TUDOR STYLE HOME

4,409 total square feet of living area

Width: 75'-8" Depth: 70'-0"

4 bedrooms, 3 1/2 baths

3-car side entry garage

Walk-out basement foundation

SPECIAL FEATURES

A melody of stone, brick, batten shutters and steep roof gables successfully recreate a timeless "Old World" look

A vaulted study, large dining room with tray ceiling, and a two-story great room with gallery all adjoin the two-story foyer

The kitchen has state-of-the-art features including an island snack bar for six

PRICE CODE F

Second Floor
1,394 sq. ft.

First Floor
3,015 sq. ft.

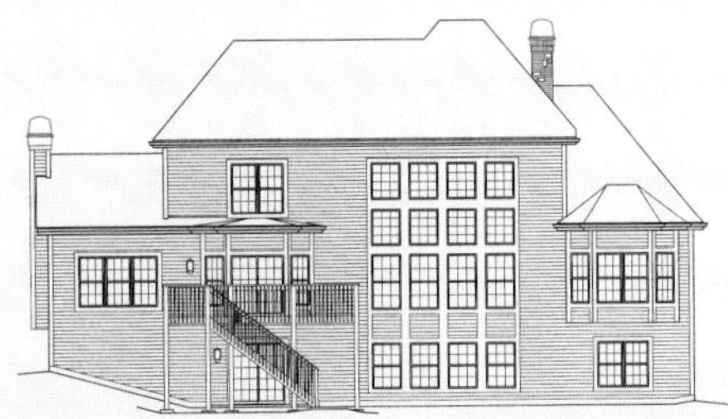

Rear View

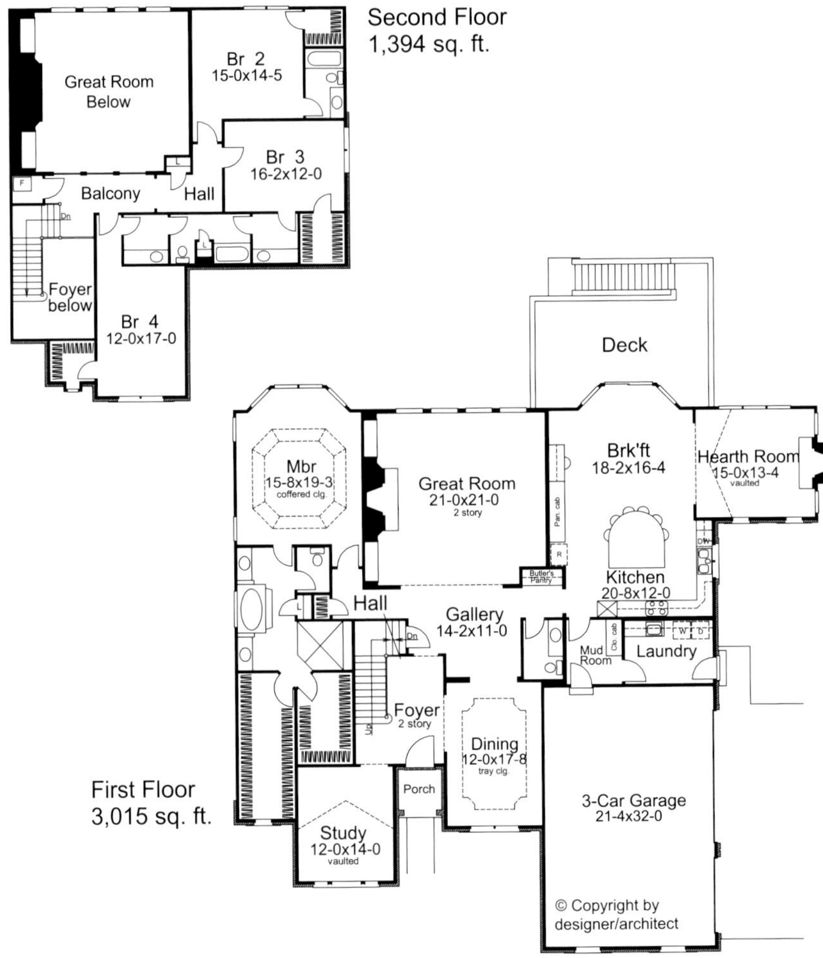

To order plans, visit the Menards Building Materials Desk
or visit www.Menards.com.

MENARDS®

AUTUMN

Plan #M08-121D-0014

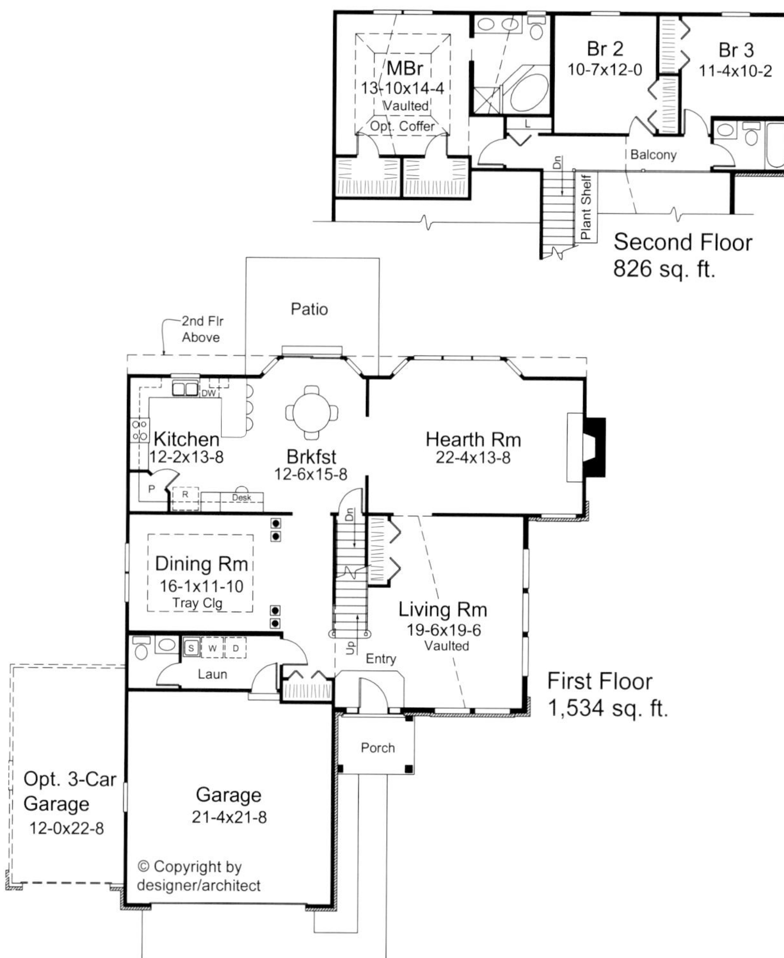

To order plans, visit the Menards Building Materials Desk or visit www.Menards.com.

ATTRACTIVE STONE EXTERIOR

2,360 total square feet of living area

Width: 50'-4" Depth: 56'-8"

3 bedrooms, 2 1/2 baths

2-car garage

Basement foundation

SPECIAL FEATURES

The hearth room is graced with a fireplace

The vaulted master bedroom has a bath with whirlpool tub, separate shower, and a double-bowl vanity

2" x 6" exterior wall framing available for an additional fee, please specify when ordering

PRICE CODE C

Rear View

SHAMROCK PLACE

MENARDS®

Plan #M08-007D-0197

LUXURY LIVING DEFINED

2,764 total square feet of living area

Width: 52'-4" Depth: 42'-4"

4 bedrooms, 2 1/2 baths

2-car garage

Basement foundation

SPECIAL FEATURES

The exterior has brick, stone, multiple gables, a porch, and cedar shake siding

A grand-sized entry accesses a private parlor with double doors, a dining room with tray ceiling, and a powder room

The kitchen enjoys a center island, a huge walk-in pantry, a built-in double oven, and also features a 50' vista through the breakfast and family rooms

PRICE CODE E

Rear View

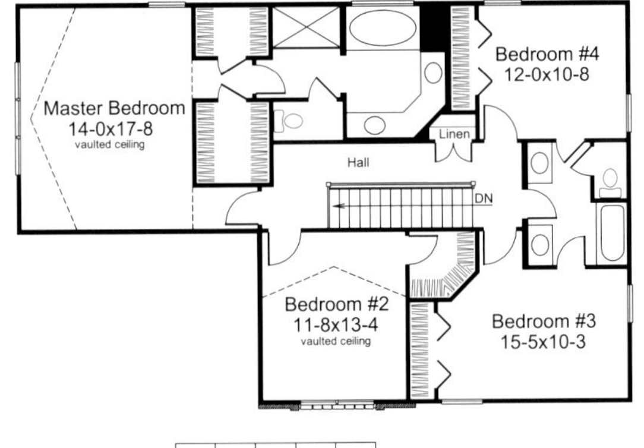

Second Floor
1,332 sq. ft.

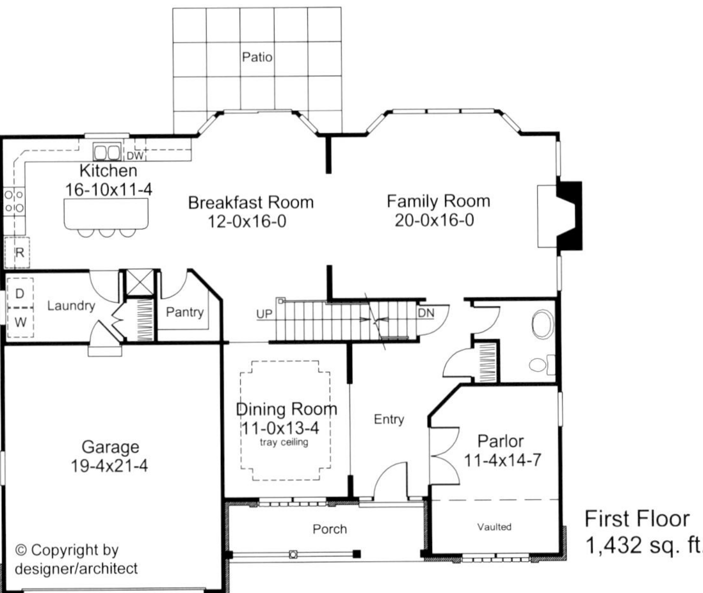

First Floor
1,432 sq. ft.

To order plans, visit the Menards Building Materials Desk or visit www.Menards.com.

MENARDS®

FOREST LAKE

Luxury Plans

Plan #M08-007D-0208

MBr 18-0x13-0

Br 2 13-0x12-0

Br 3 13-0x13-1

Atrium vaulted

Dn

Hall

Attic

plant shelf w/clerestory windows above

Second Floor
1,149 sq. ft.

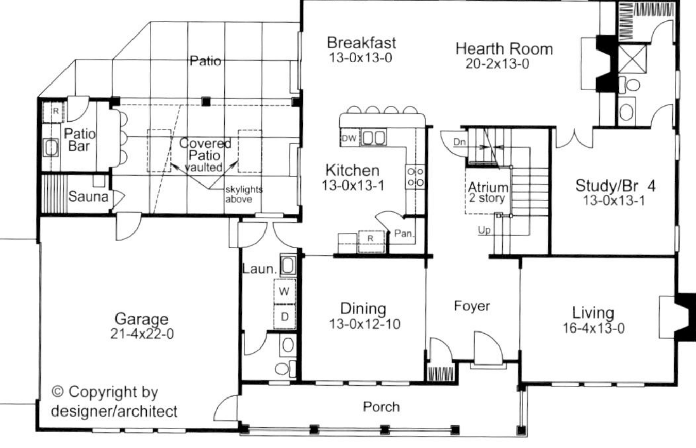

First Floor
1,724 sq. ft.

LOVELY COUNTRY HOME

2,873 total square feet of living area

Width: 70'-4" Depth: 45'-4"

4 bedrooms, 3 1/2 baths

2-car side entry garage

Basement foundation

SPECIAL FEATURES

The foyer leads into a two-story atrium with a winding staircase

The hearth and breakfast rooms offer a 31' vista with adjacent study or private fourth bedroom boasting its own bath and walk-in closet, ideal for guests or a live-in mother-in-law

The large covered rear patio includes a vaulted ceiling with skylights, a walk-in wet bar with serving counter, and a sauna room, perfect for entertaining

PRICE CODE D

Rear View

To order plans, visit the Menards Building Materials Desk or visit www.Menards.com.

ROXBURY

MENARDS®

Plan #M08-007D-0065

ATRIUM RANCH HOME

3,261 total square feet of living area

Width: 59'-8" Depth: 59'-0"

6 bedrooms, 3 baths

2-car garage

Walk-out basement foundation

SPECIAL FEATURES

The vaulted great room has an arched colonnade entry, bay windowed atrium with staircase, and a fireplace

The vaulted kitchen enjoys bay doors to the deck and a pass-through breakfast bar

The breakfast area offers a bay window and snack bar open to the kitchen with a large laundry room nearby

PRICE CODE D

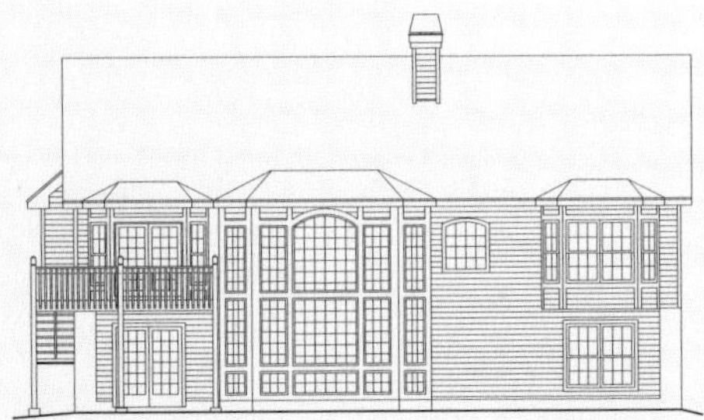

Rear View

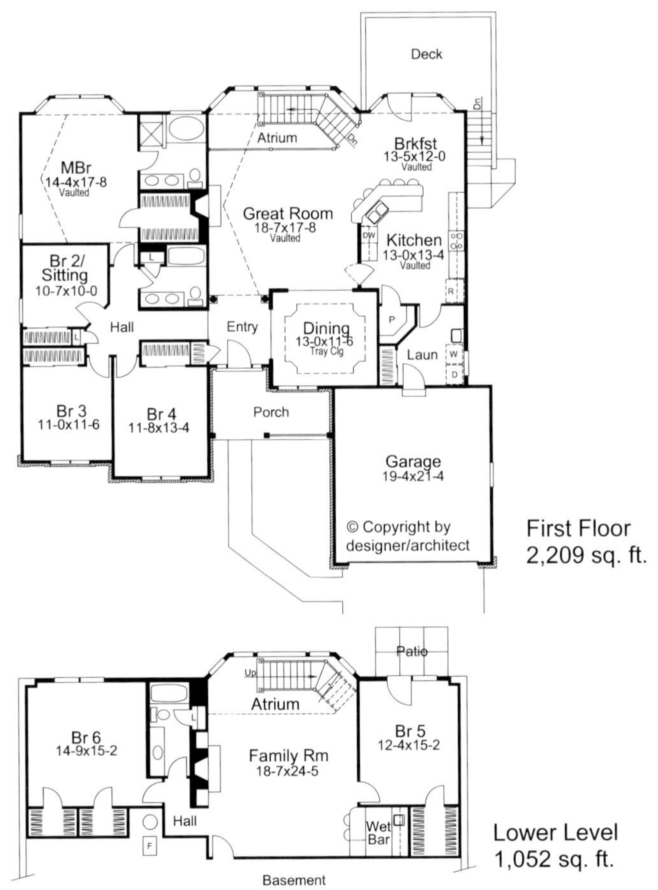

First Floor
2,209 sq. ft.

Lower Level
1,052 sq. ft.

To order plans, visit the Menards Building Materials Desk or visit www.Menards.com.

MENARDS®

GREENSAVER I

Luxury Plans

Plan #M08-007D-0205

Second Floor
902 sq. ft.

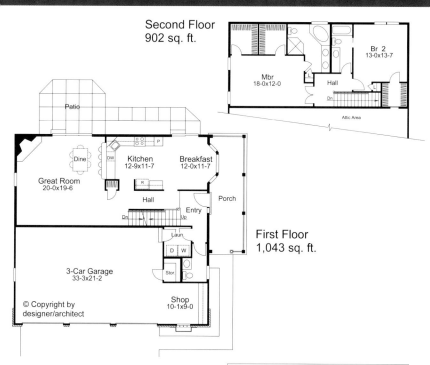

Mbr
18-0x12-0

Br 2
13-0x13-7

Hall

Dn

Attic Area

Patio

Dine

DW

Kitchen
12-9x11-7

Breakfast
12-0x11-7

Great Room
20-0x19-6

R

P

Hall

Entry

Porch

Dn

Up

Laun.

D W

3-Car Garage
33-3x21-2

Stor

Shop
10-1x9-0

© Copyright by
designer/architect

First Floor
1,043 sq. ft.

Secret Closet

Projector Above

8' screen

Bookcase Door

Family/Theater
18-6x15-5

WH F

Br 3/Office
12-0x13-0

Bar R

Hall

Up

Exercise
8-6x11-4

Lower Level
937 sq. ft.

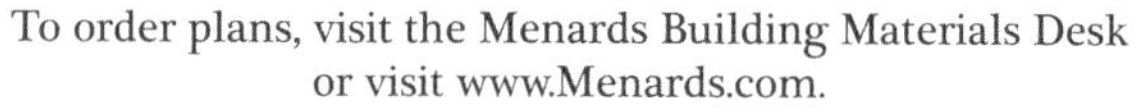

To order plans, visit the Menards Building Materials Desk
or visit www.Menards.com.

CAREFULLY DESIGNED FOR EFFICIENCY

2,882 total square feet of living area

Width: 52'-0" Depth: 42'-4"

3 bedrooms, 3 1/2 baths

3-car garage

Basement foundation

SPECIAL FEATURES

The garage roof deflects wind and acts as a thermal barrier to the home's finished spaces, and triple-glazed insulated wood windows and doors are also used

2" x 6" walls with multiple insulating materials create an approximate value of R34 with R70 in the attic

The basement has insulated walls and a natural cooling system with a buried pipe

PRICE CODE D

Rear View

LACERNE PLACE

MENARDS®

Luxury Plans

Plan #M08-007D-0250

MASTER BEDROOM IS SECOND TO NONE

4,465 total square feet of living area

Width: 81'-8" Depth: 54'-8"

4 bedrooms, 3 1/2 baths

3-car side entry garage

Walk-out basement foundation

SPECIAL FEATURES

Arched double doors lead you into a foyer with a stately staircase

The kitchen/breakfast room has a center island, snack bar, menu desk, cabinet pantries, and a bayed breakfast area

The master bedroom has a coffered ceiling, double-entry doors, two walk-in closets and a bath

PRICE CODE G

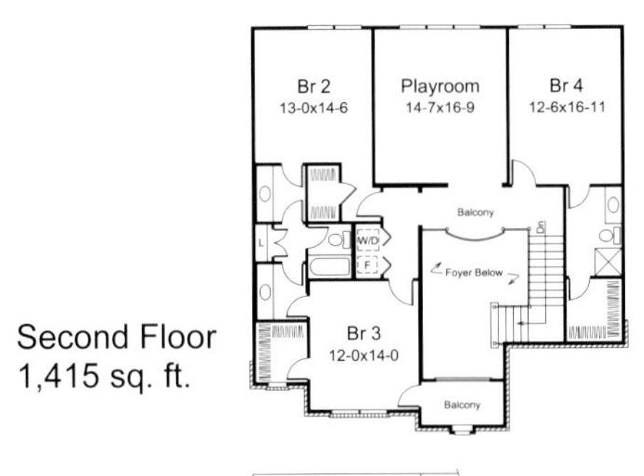

Second Floor
1,415 sq. ft.

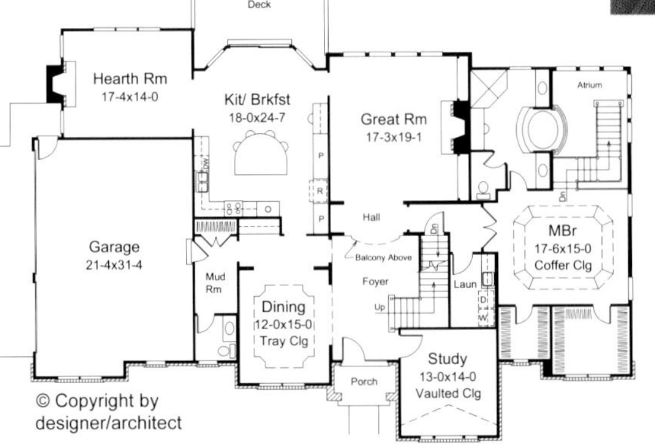

© Copyright by designer/architect

First Floor
2,850 sq. ft.

Lower Level
200 sq. ft.

Rear View

To order plans, visit the Menards Building Materials Desk or visit www.Menards.com.

SAMANTHA

Plan #M08-121D-0004

COUNTRY KITCHEN GREAT FOR GATHERING

3,782 total square feet of living area

Width: 101'-0" Depth: 50'-0"

4 bedrooms, 3 1/2 baths

2-car garage

Basement foundation

SPECIAL FEATURES

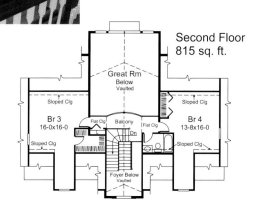

A stylish foyer staircase ascends to the second floor balcony

The lower level includes a media/theater room with built-in bookshelves

The formal dining room is decorated with a tray ceiling drawing the eye upward

A massive 42" direct vent fireplace and window wall helps bring the outdoors in

2" x 6" exterior wall framing available for an additional fee, please specify when ordering

PRICE CODE E

Second Floor
815 sq. ft.

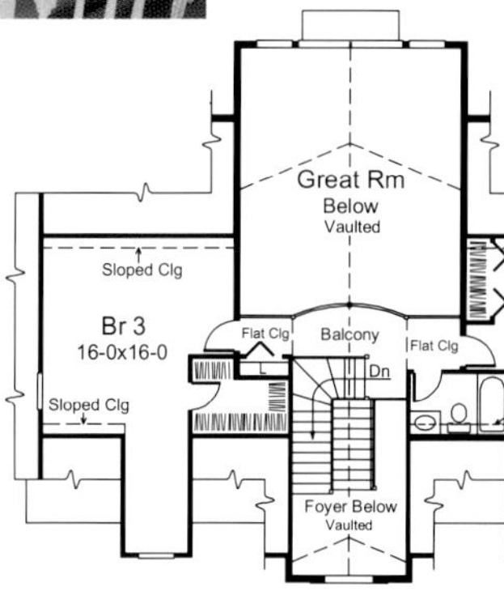

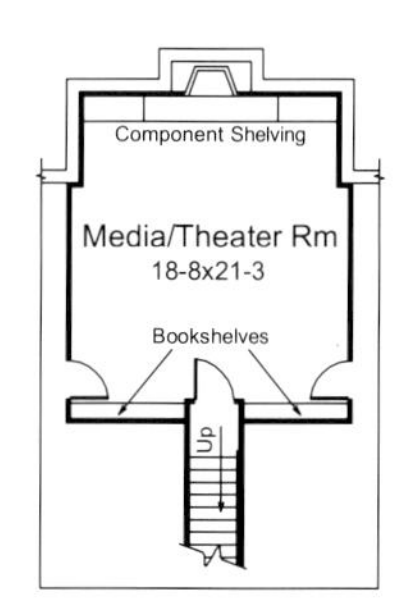

Lower Level
396 sq. ft.

First Floor
2,571 sq. ft.

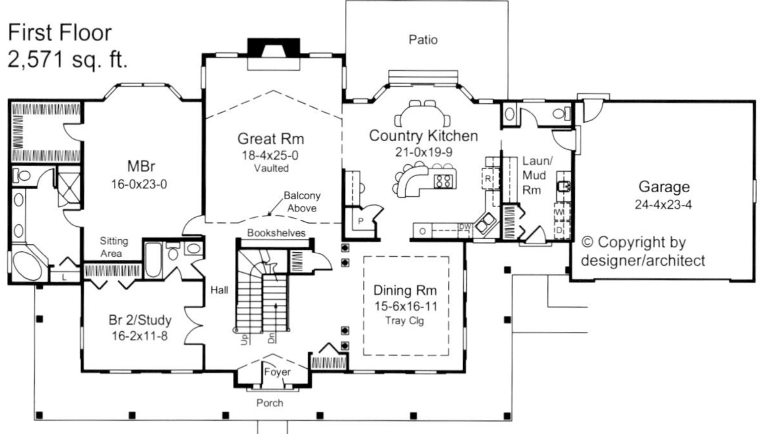

Rear View

To order plans, visit the Menards Building Materials Desk or visit www.Menards.com.

WESTERSHIRE PLACE

MENARDS®

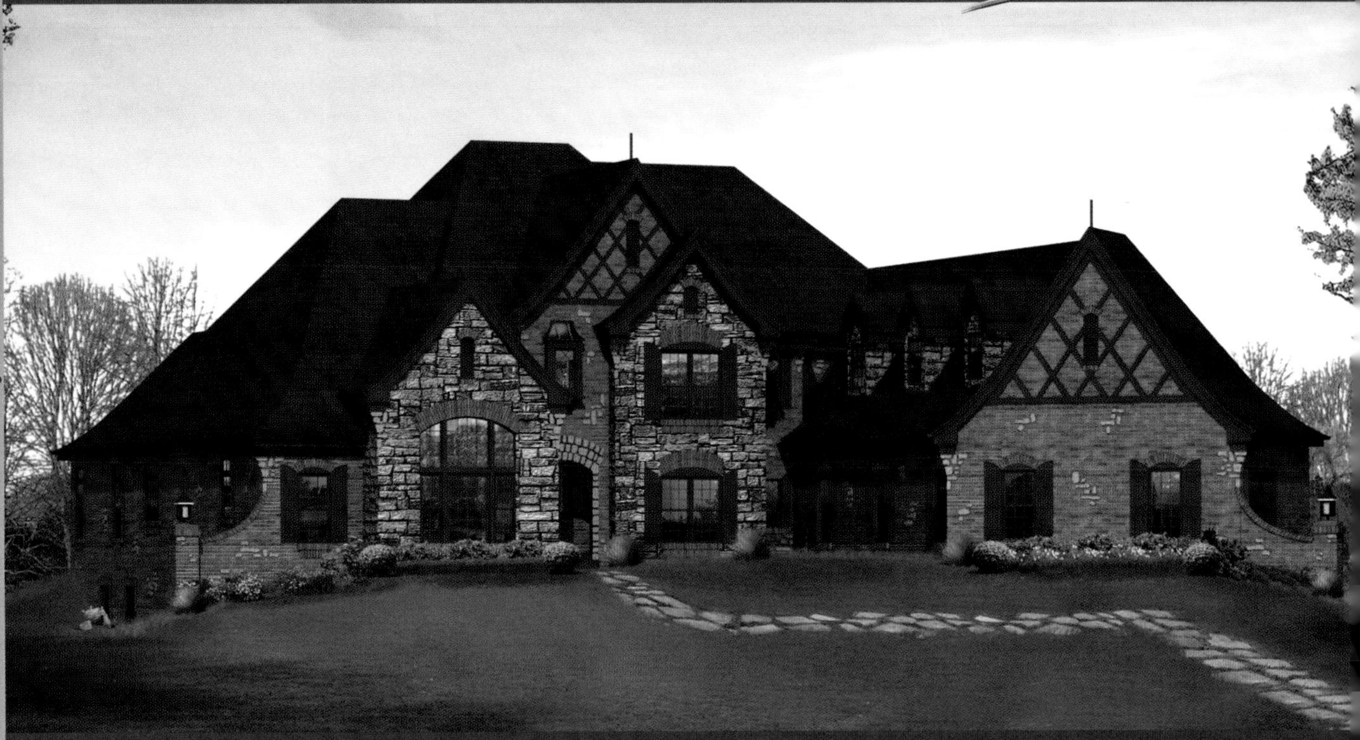

Plan #M08-007D-0202

OLD ENGLISH LUXURY

6,088 total square feet of living area

Width: 84'-8"   Depth: 125'-3"

4 bedrooms, 4 full baths, 2 half baths

5-car side entry garage

Basement foundation

SPECIAL FEATURES

The two-story foyer invites guests into the grand scale great room

The kitchen includes a 9' island with seating, octagon-shaped breakfast area, a vaulted hearth room with fireplace, and a covered porch

The master bedroom has a bay window, a coffered ceiling, and a huge bath with a sauna, whirlpool tub, and two walk-in closets

PRICE CODE H

First Floor
4,294 sq. ft.

Second Floor
1,794 sq. ft.

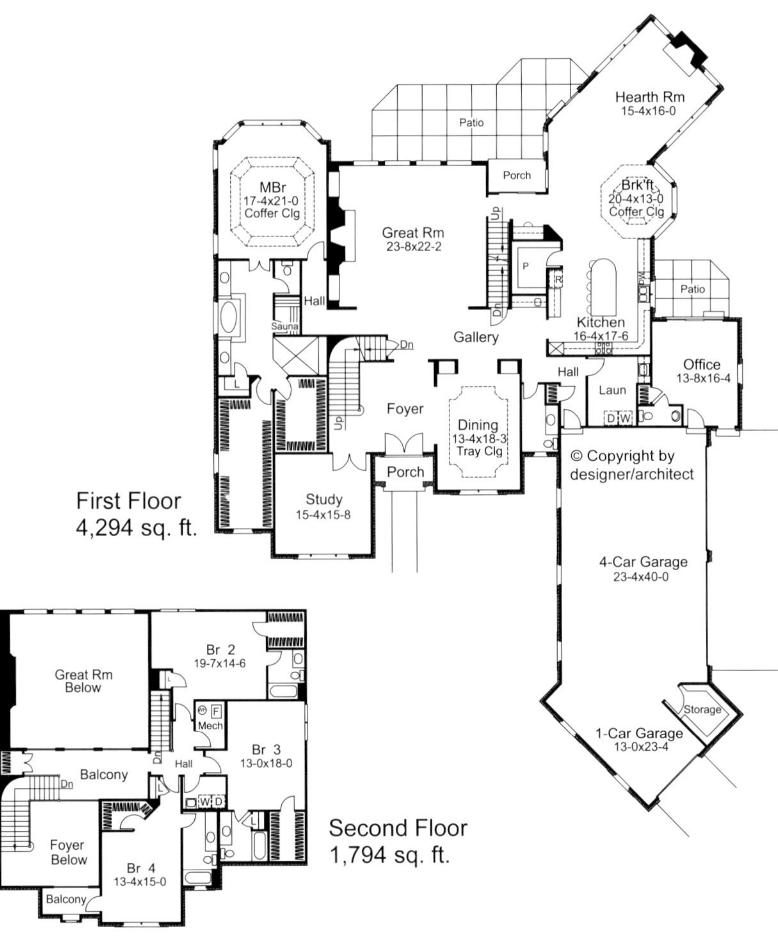

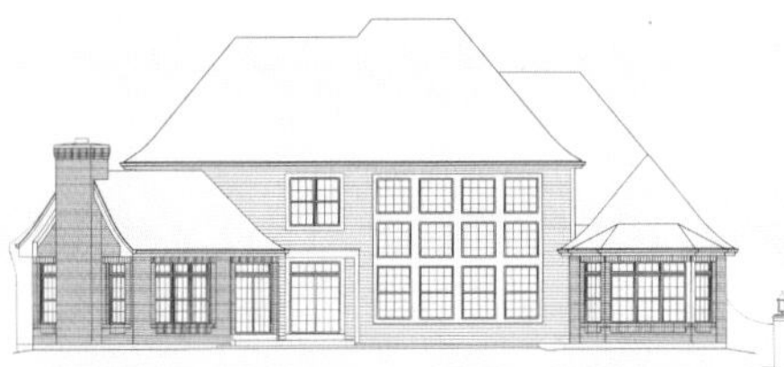

Rear View

To order plans, visit the Menards Building Materials Desk
or visit www.Menards.com.

Second Floor
445 sq. ft.

First Floor
2,530 sq. ft.

PRIVATE MASTER SUITE

2,975 total square feet of living area

Width: 59'-6" Depth: 70'-10"

5 bedrooms, 4 baths

2-car side entry garage

Crawl space or slab foundation, please specify when ordering

SPECIAL FEATURES

The dining room has a 12' ceiling and butler's pantry nearby

The second floor bedroom, or "teenage room," has access to a computer center making it an ideal space for a school-aged child, or as a home office area

The bonus room has an additional 425 square feet of living area

PRICE CODE E

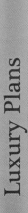

ENGLEWOOD

MENARDS®

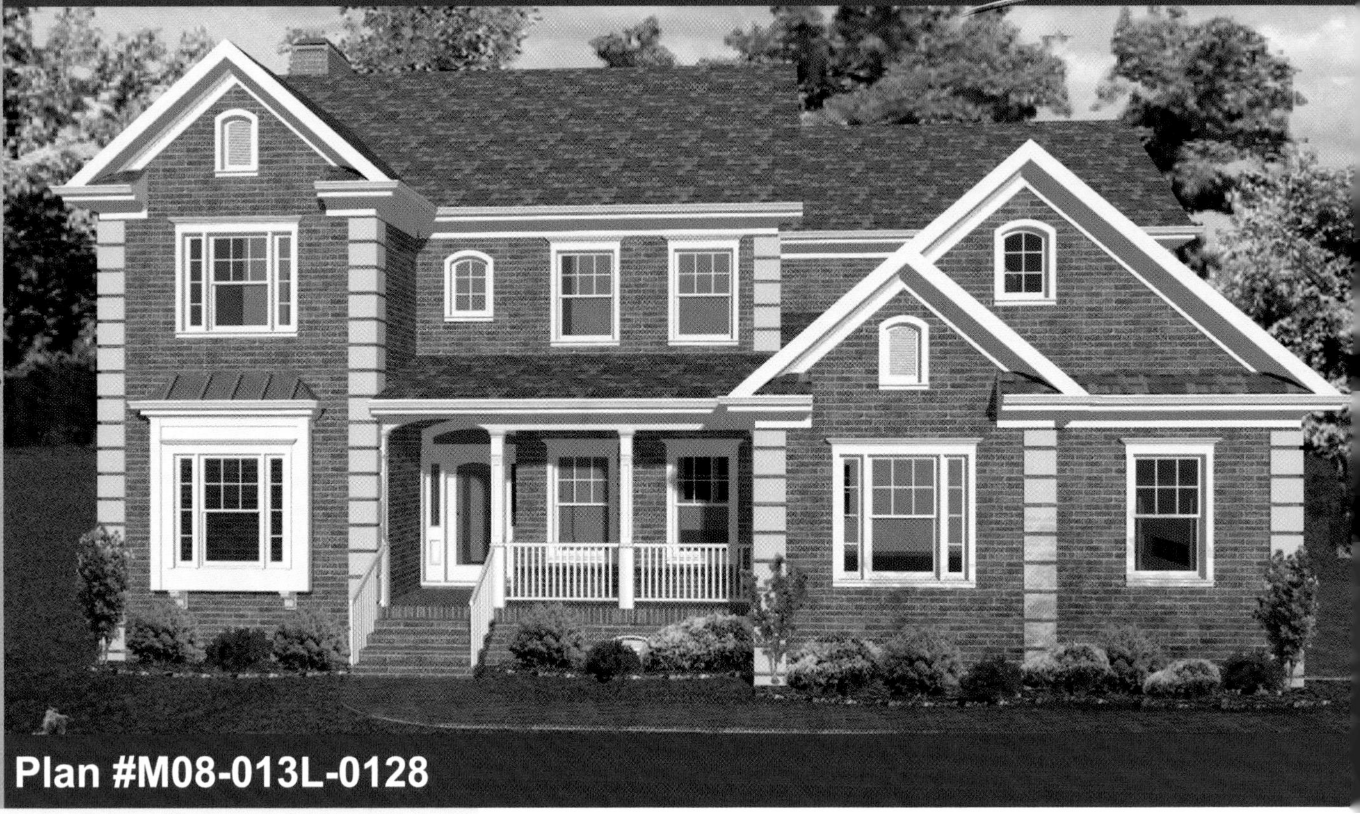

Plan #M08-013L-0128

CORNER QUOINS ADD ELEGANCE TO EXTERIOR

2,760 total square feet of living area

Width: 53'-2" Depth: 51'-8"

4 bedrooms, 4 baths

3 1/2-car side entry garage

Basement foundation

SPECIAL FEATURES

Both secondary bedrooms on the second floor have their own full baths and large activity areas

The screened porch off of the family room offers a place for outdoor relaxation

A box-bay window adds charm and character to guest bedroom #4

PRICE CODE G

Second Floor
1,460 sq. ft.

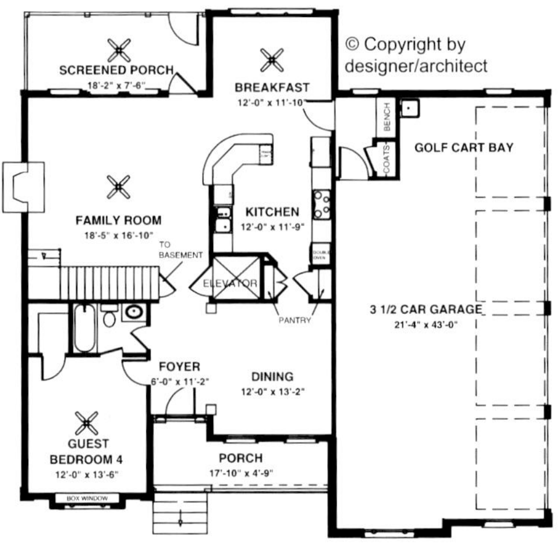

First Floor
1,300 sq. ft.

WELLINGTON MANOR

Plan #M08-055L-0199

GRAND LIVING AREAS

2,951 total square feet of living area

Width: 73'-6"   Depth: 80'-6"

4 bedrooms, 3 baths

3-car side entry garage

Slab, crawl space, basement or walk-out basement foundation, please specify when ordering

SPECIAL FEATURES

The master suite is luxurious with a see-through fireplace, two walk-in closets, a deluxe bath, and a sitting room with access to the lanai

The great room features a 12' ceiling, a wet bar, built-in cabinets, and a fireplace that also warms the adjoining kitchen and breakfast area

The secondary bedrooms enjoy direct access to the baths

PRICE CODE F

To order plans, visit the Menards Building Materials Desk or visit www.Menards.com.

JILLIAN

MENARDS®

Plan #M08-121D-0005

COZY CORNER FIREPLACE IN THE GREAT ROOM

1,562 total square feet of living area

Width: 65'-0" Depth: 46'-4"

3 bedrooms, 2 baths

2-car garage

Basement foundation

SPECIAL FEATURES

The formal vaulted dining room is graced with decorative corner columns

The breakfast bar has seating for five and overlooks the large great room

All of the bedrooms are located near each other for convenient family living

2" x 6" exterior wall framing available for an additional fee, please specify when ordering

PRICE CODE A

Rear View

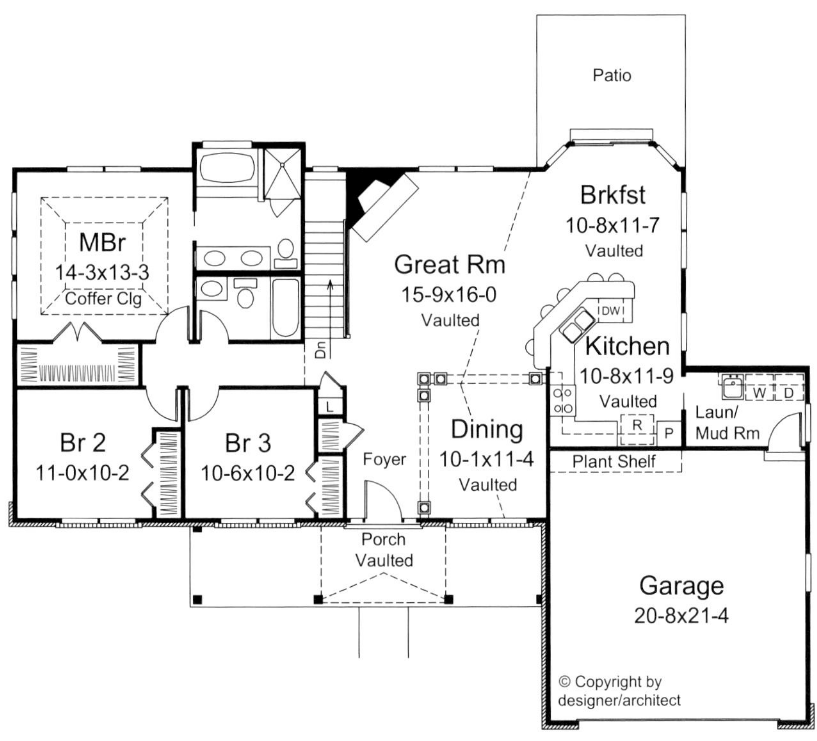

To order plans, visit the Menards Building Materials Desk or visit www.Menards.com.

MENARDS®

MARYLAND MANOR

Plan #M08-007D-0232

COUNTRY HOME WITH CHARM AND GREAT PLANNING

1,915 total square feet of living area

Width: 76'-0" Depth: 50'-8"

3 bedrooms, 2 1/2 baths

3-car side entry garage

Slab foundation

SPECIAL FEATURES

The great room has a large dining area, a corner fireplace, and awesome views of the rear veranda

Several corner windows brighten the sink area in the kitchen

The vaulted master bedroom has two walk-in closets, a bath, and a private porch

The oversized garage includes a coat closet, a half bath, and a workbench

PRICE CODE D

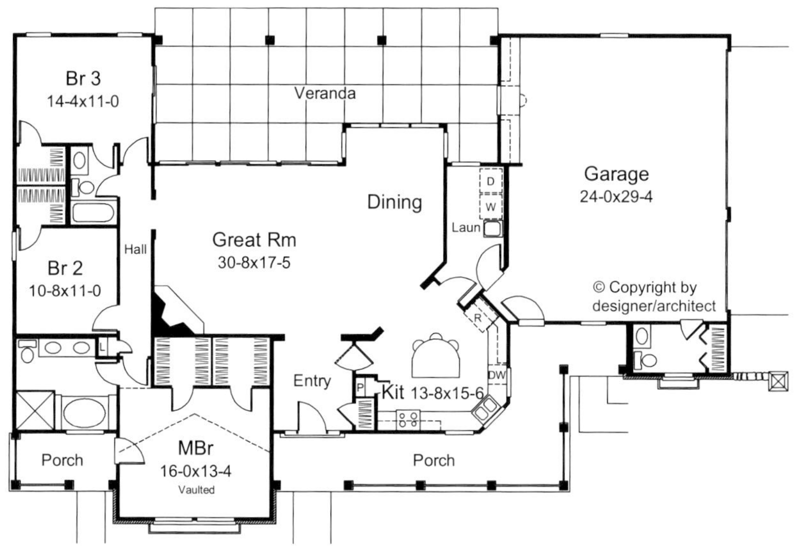

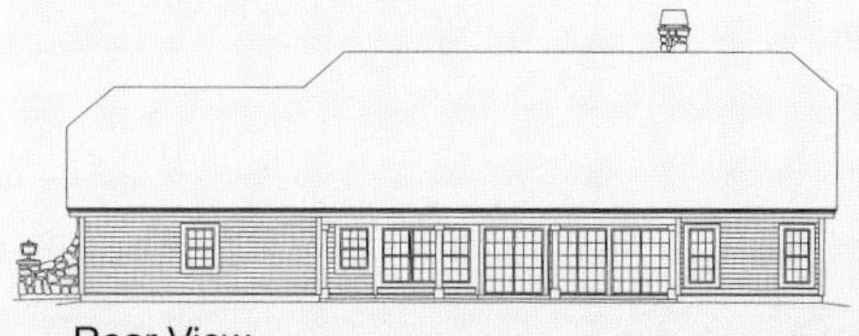
Rear View

To order plans, visit the Menards Building Materials Desk
or visit www.Menards.com.

STELLAVILLE

Plan #M08-013L-0027

SPACIOUS COUNTRY KITCHEN

2,184 total square feet of living area

Width: 71'-2"   Depth: 58'-1"

3 bedrooms, 3 baths

2-car side entry garage

Basement, crawl space or slab foundation, please specify when ordering

SPECIAL FEATURES

The delightful family room has access to the screened porch for enjoyable outdoor living

The secluded master suite is complete with a sitting area and luxurious bath

The formal living room has a double-door entry easily converting it to a study or home office

Two secondary bedrooms have their own baths

The bonus room above the garage has an additional 379 square feet of living space

PRICE CODE D

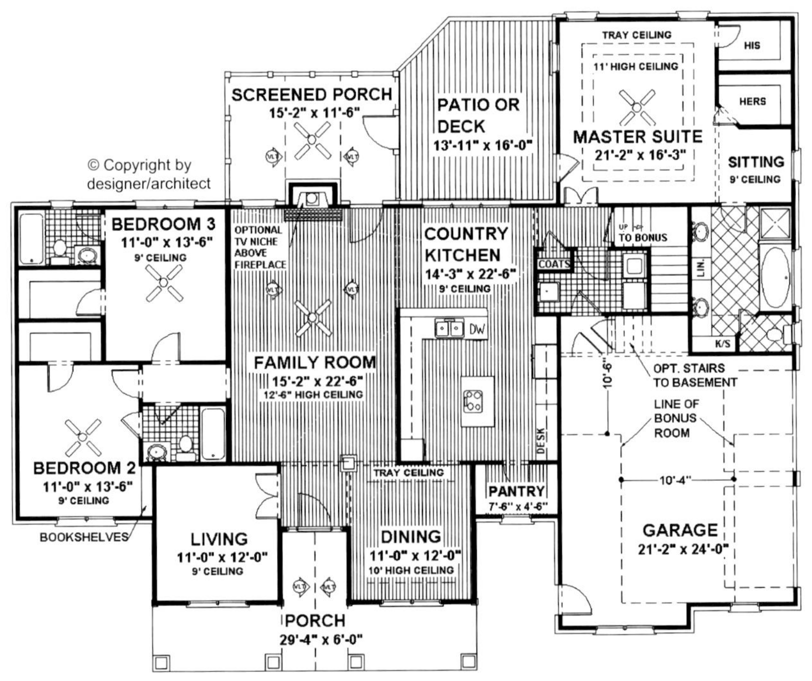

To order plans, visit the Menards Building Materials Desk or visit www.Menards.com.

MENARDS®

GABRIELLA

Plan #M08-121D-0019

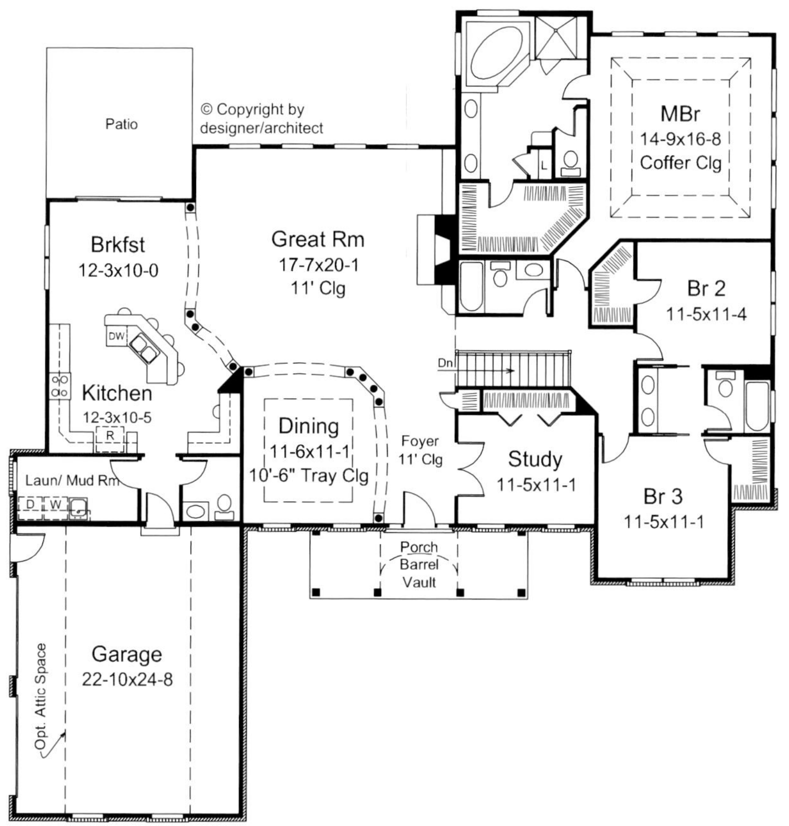

To order plans, visit the Menards Building Materials Desk or visit www.Menards.com.

COLUMNS HIGHLIGHT THE FRONT PORCH

2,814 total square feet of living area

Width: 73'-0" Depth: 75'-4"

3 bedrooms, 3 1/2 baths

2-car side entry garage

Basement foundation

SPECIAL FEATURES

The spacious great room has a fireplace and is brightened by multiple windows

The kitchen features a center island with an eating bar for causal meals and a planning center

An amazing private bath with corner whirlpool tub and spacious closet completes the master bedroom

The study could easily be converted to a fourth bedroom

PRICE CODE D

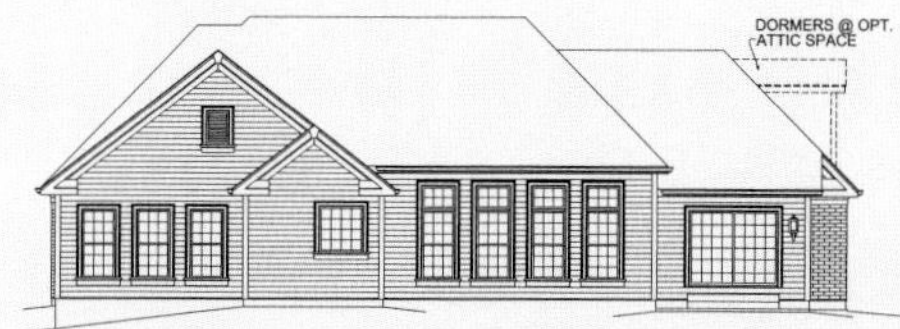

Rear View

STONECROFT

MENARDS®

Plan #M08-077L-0053

CLASSIC COUNTRY HOME

1,852 total square feet of living area

Width: 78'-0" Depth: 49'-6"

3 bedrooms, 2 1/2 baths

2-car garage

Basement, crawl space or slab foundation, please specify when ordering

SPECIAL FEATURES

The stately great room features a vaulted ceiling and a corner gas fireplace

The covered or screened-in porch is a great place to relax and enjoy the outdoors

The future bonus room on the second floor has an additional 370 square feet of living space

PRICE CODE E

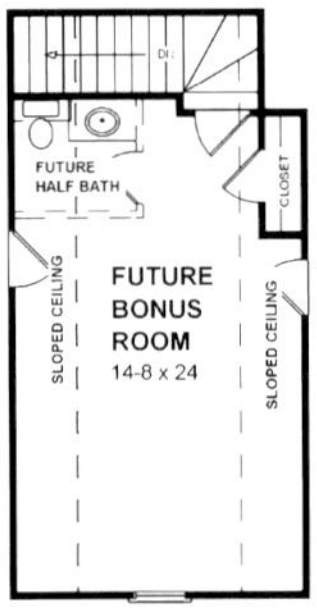

FUTURE HALF BATH
CLOSET
SLOPED CEILING
FUTURE BONUS ROOM 14-8 x 24

Optional Second Floor

First Floor
1,852 sq. ft.

To order plans, visit the Menards Building Materials Desk or visit www.Menards.com.

MENARDS®

WOODFIELD MANOR

Plan #M08-007D-0212

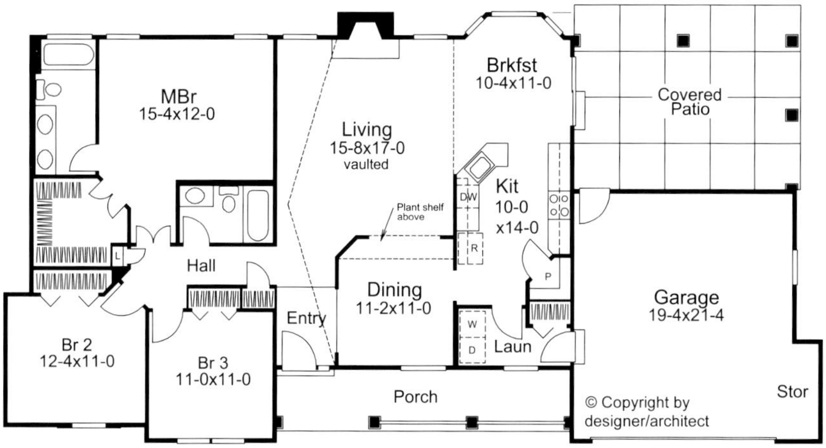

MBr
15-4x12-0
Living
15-8x17-0
vaulted
Brkfst
10-4x11-0
Covered
Patio
Plant shelf
above
DW
Kit
10-0
x14-0
R
P
Hall
L
Dining
11-2x11-0
Entry
W
D
Laun
Garage
19-4x21-4
Br 2
12-4x11-0
Br 3
11-0x11-0
Porch
Stor
© Copyright by
designer/architect

COUNTRY RANCH WITH COVERED PATIO

1,568 total square feet of living area

Width: 72'-8"   Depth: 37'-4"

3 bedrooms, 2 baths

2-car garage

Crawl space foundation, drawings also include slab foundation

SPECIAL FEATURES

Classic gables, dormers and decorative circular windows combine to create this stylish facade

A walk-in pantry is featured in the well-designed kitchen and is adjacent to a convenient laundry room

The master bedroom with double entry doors is nicely appointed with an over sized bath and large walk-in closet

PRICE CODE A

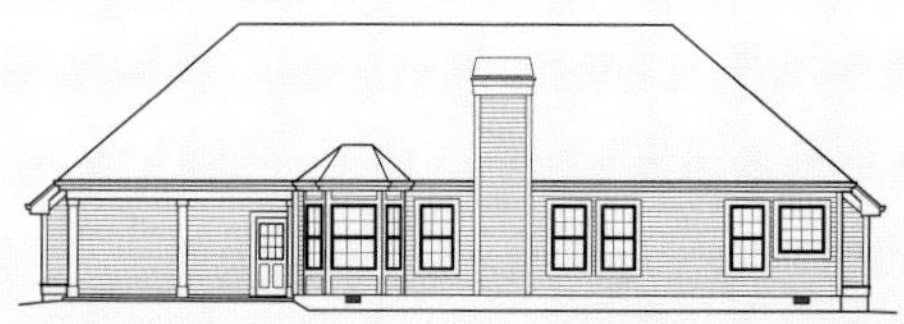

Rear View

To order plans, visit the Menards Building Materials Desk or visit www.Menards.com.

WOOSTOCK

MENARDS®

Plan #M08-013L-0155

MAGNIFICENT ONE-LEVEL LIVING

1,800 total square feet of living area

Width: 63'-0" Depth: 73'-0"

3 bedrooms, 3 baths

3-car side entry garage

Crawl space foundation

SPECIAL FEATURES

The wonderful family room boasts a 10' ceiling and opens nicely to the eating area and spacious kitchen

The chef of the family is sure to love this cheerful kitchen equipped with a unique shaped island, plenty of counterspace and a functional pass-thru to the formal dining room

The luxurious master suite includes two closets, a separate shower, a double-bowl vanity and access to the screen porch

The optional bonus room above the garage has an additional 503 square feet of living area

PRICE CODE B

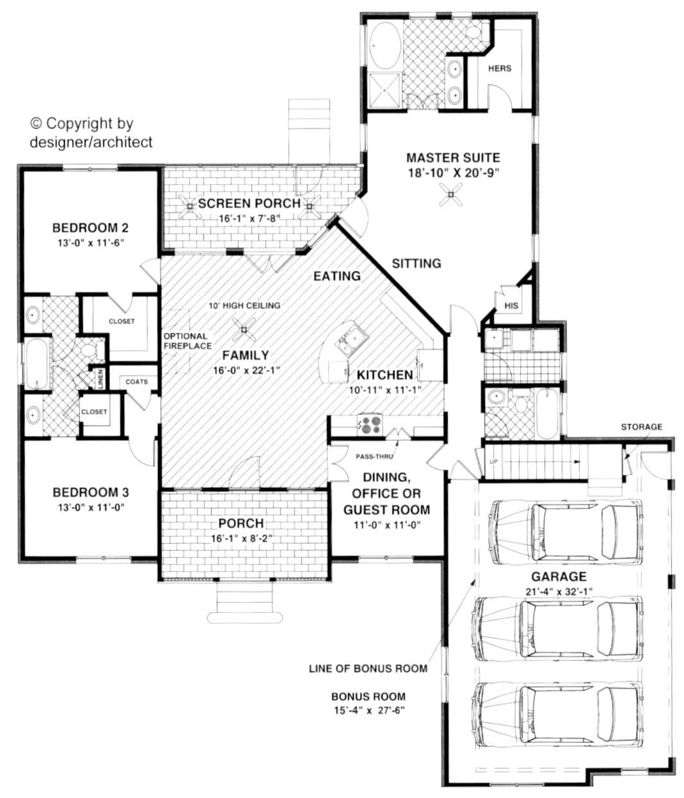

To order plans, visit the Menards Building Materials Desk or visit www.Menards.com.

MENARDS®

ABIGAIL

Plan #M08-121D-0011

LOVELY SEE-THROUGH FIREPLACE

2,241 total square feet of living area

Width: 68'-4"   Depth: 56'-0"

4 bedrooms, 2 1/2 baths

2-car side entry garage

Basement foundation

SPECIAL FEATURES

11' ceilings can be found in the entry, great room, kitchen and dining area

The kitchen island with breakfast bar has an extension with space for up to seven

The elegant master bedroom enjoys two walk-in closets and a private bath

2" x 6" exterior wall framing available for an additional fee, please specify when ordering

PRICE CODE C

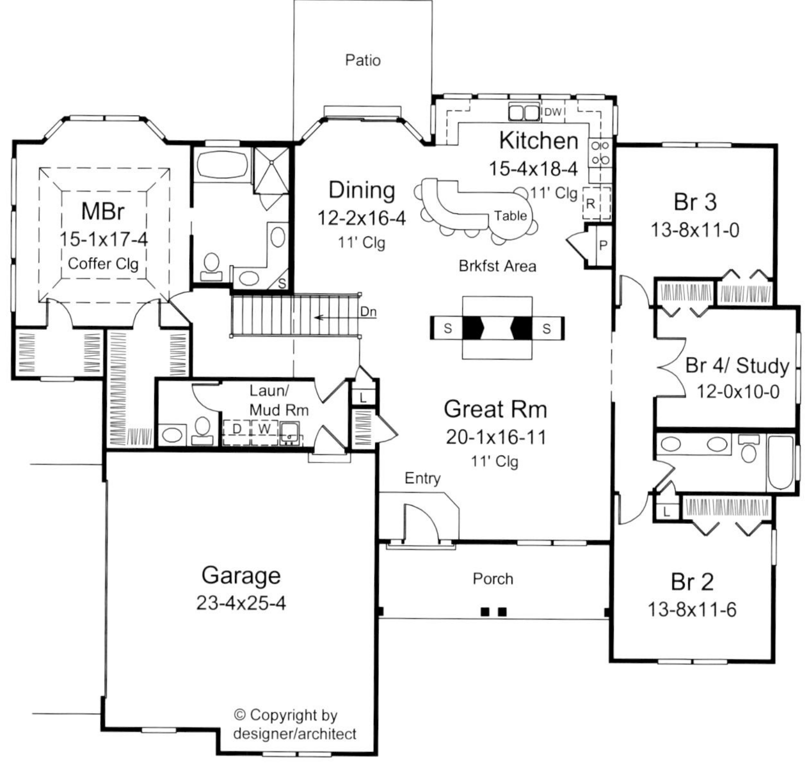

To order plans, visit the Menards Building Materials Desk or visit www.Menards.com.

Rear View

FLORENCE

Plan #M08-017D-0005

COMFORTABLE ONE-STORY HOME

1,367 total square feet of living area

Width: 71'-4" Depth: 35'-10"

3 bedrooms, 2 baths

2-car garage

Basement foundation, drawings also include slab foundation

SPECIAL FEATURES

Energy efficient home with 2" x 6" exterior walls

The dining room has a full wall of windows and convenient storage area

The breakfast area leads to the rear terrace through sliding doors

The large living room features a high ceiling, skylight and fireplace

PRICE CODE B

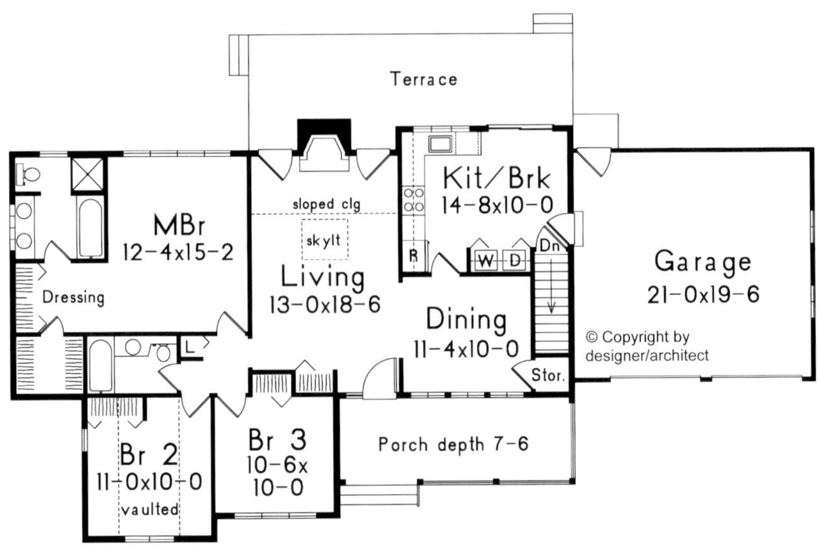

Rear View

To order plans, visit the Menards Building Materials Desk or visit www.Menards.com.

MENARDS

STONEFIELD

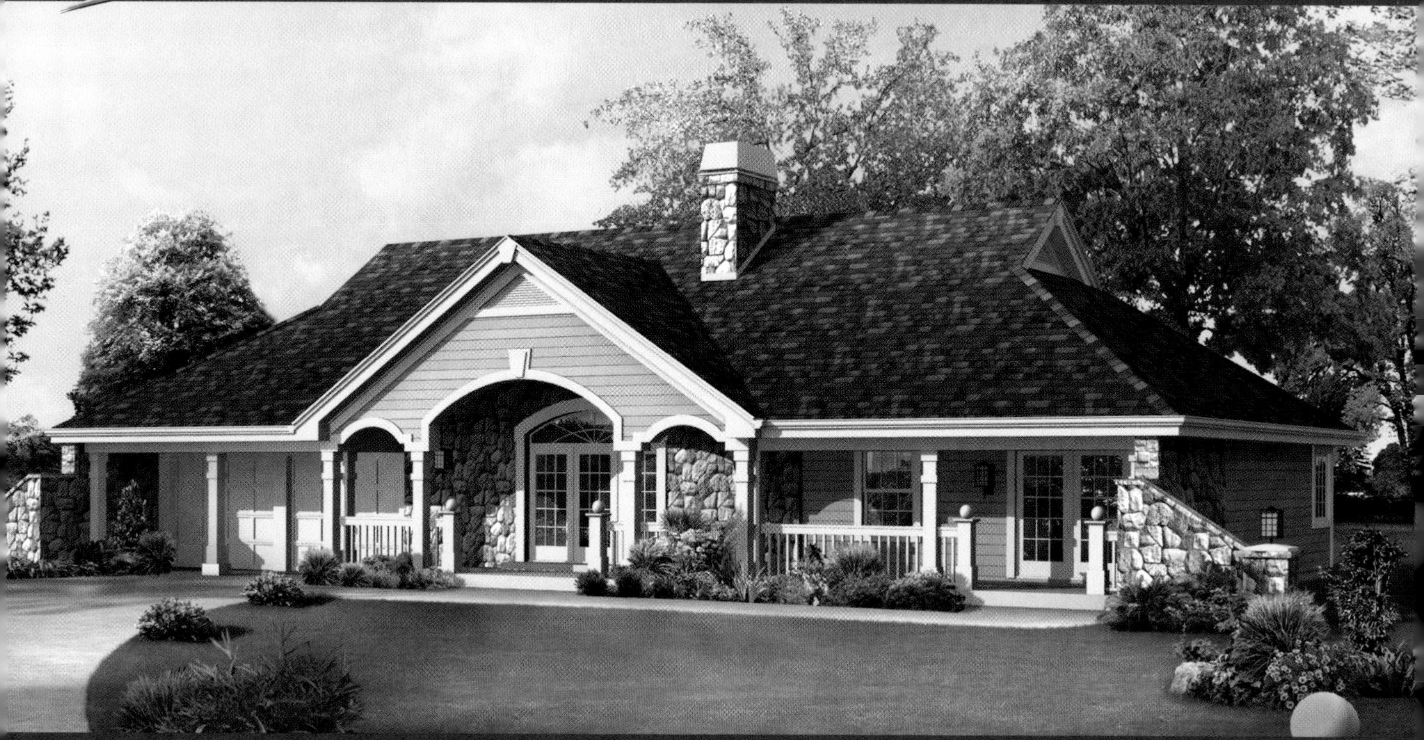

Plan #M08-007D-0216

Patio
Storage 10-8x6-8
D W
Laun
Dining 10-1x13-8 Vaulted
R Pantry
Kit 9-0x13-8
DW
Br 3 10-0x11-9
L
Hall
Garage 21-1x22-0
HW F
Living Rm 18-0x15-0 Vaulted
Br 2 10-5x11-4
MBr 13-5x15-0

Porch

COUNTRY RANCH HOME

1,510 total square feet of living area

Width: 70'-0" Depth: 36'-10"

3 bedrooms, 2 baths

2-car garage

Slab foundation, drawings also include crawl space foundation

SPECIAL FEATURES

Energy efficient home with 2" x 6" exterior walls

Open living room and dining area feature vaulted ceilings, a fireplace, and French doors to the rear patio

The well-planned kitchen has a large built-in corner pantry and a snack counter, all open to the living room

Convenient to the kitchen is a nice-sized laundry room with a sink

PRICE CODE A

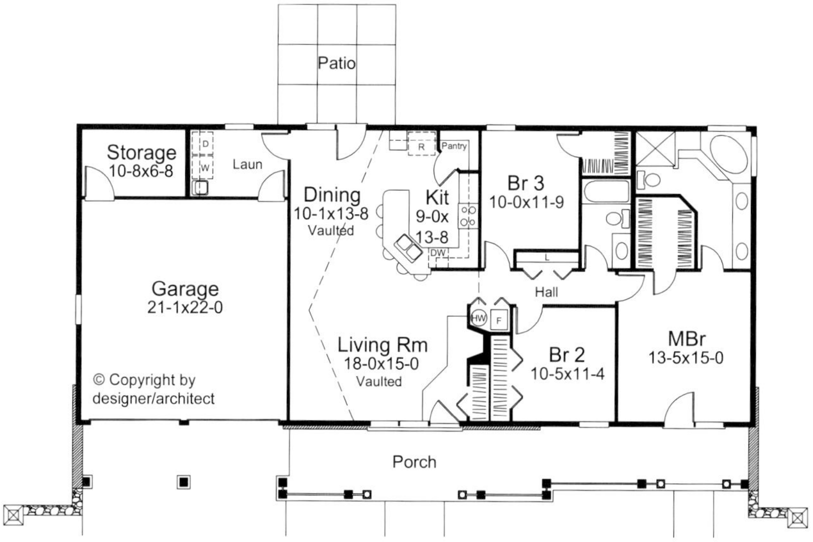

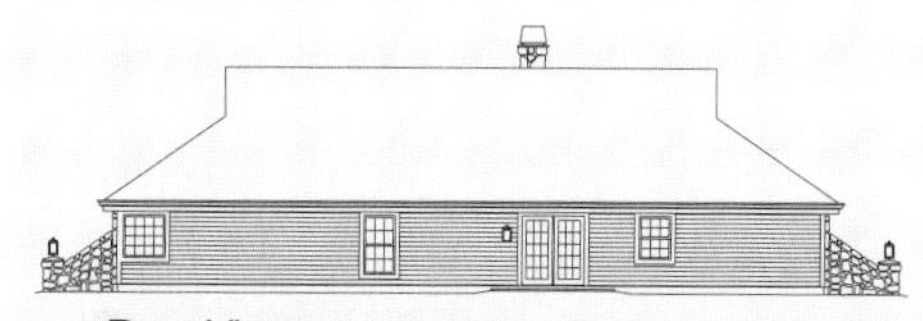

Rear View

MANOR GROVE

MENARDS®

Plan #M08-007D-0120

A DESIGN FOR PRIVACY AND FLEXIBILITY

1,914 total square feet of living area

Width: 63'-8" Depth: 55'-4"

4 bedrooms, 3 baths

2-car garage

Basement foundation

SPECIAL FEATURES

The vaulted great room has a dining area, a corner fireplace, and doors to the rear patio

The secondary bedrooms offer walk-in closets and share a Jack and Jill bath

A multi-purpose room has a laundry alcove and can easily be used as a hobby room, sewing room, or a small office

The bedroom #4/study could open to the master bedroom and be an office/nursery

PRICE CODE C

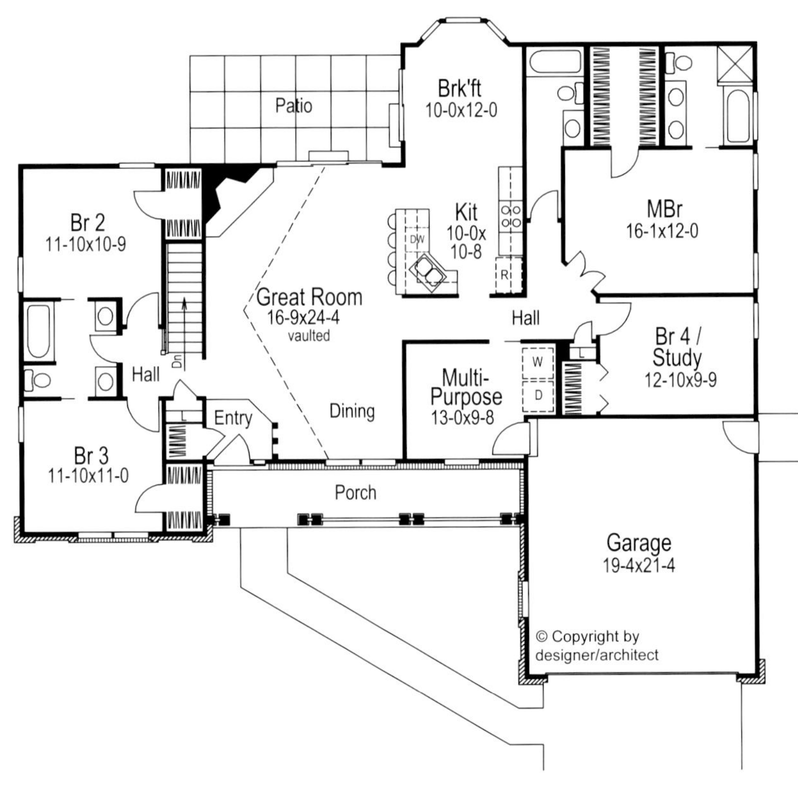

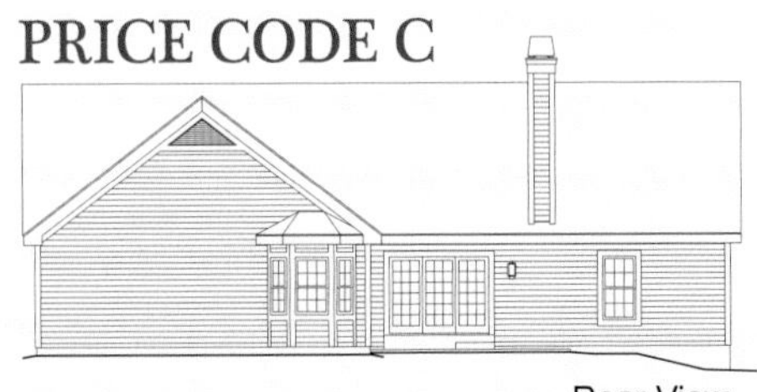

Rear View

To order plans, visit the Menards Building Materials Desk or visit www.Menards.com.

GRANDTREE

Plan #M08-058D-0061

OPEN LIVING AREAS

1,642 total square feet of living area

Width: 66'-0" Depth: 44'-0"

3 bedrooms, 2 baths

3-car garage

Basement foundation

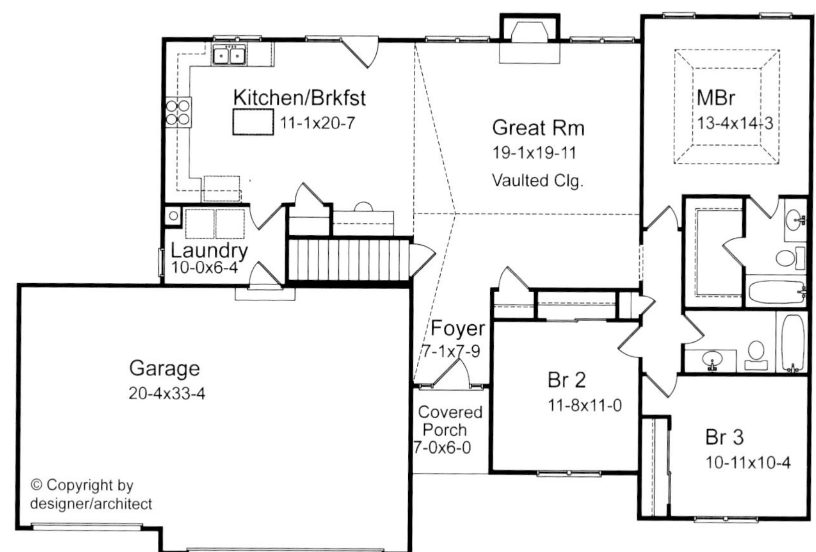

SPECIAL FEATURES

The bedrooms are separated from the main living areas for privacy

The vaulted great room is warmed by a grand fireplace

Family activities are sure to be a breeze with this spacious floor plan

A convenient laundry area is located at the garage entrance

PRICE CODE B

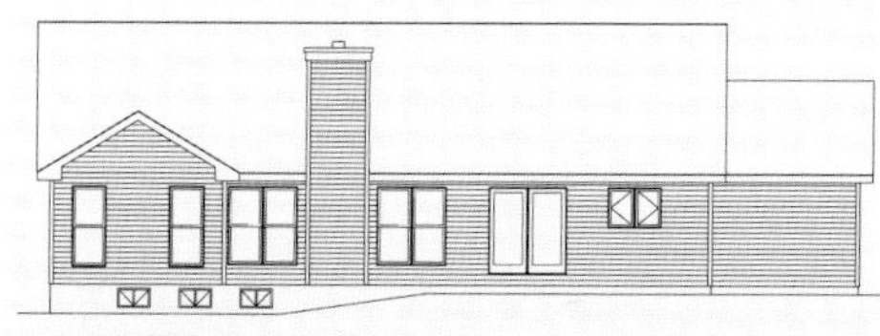

Rear View

To order plans, visit the Menards Building Materials Desk
or visit www.Menards.com.

PIEDMONT PARK

MENARDS®

Plan #M08-077L-0065

INVITING FRONT PORCH

2,138 total square feet of living area

Width: 79'-4" Depth: 57'-6"

3 bedrooms, 3 baths

2-car garage

Basement, crawl space or slab foundation, please specify when ordering

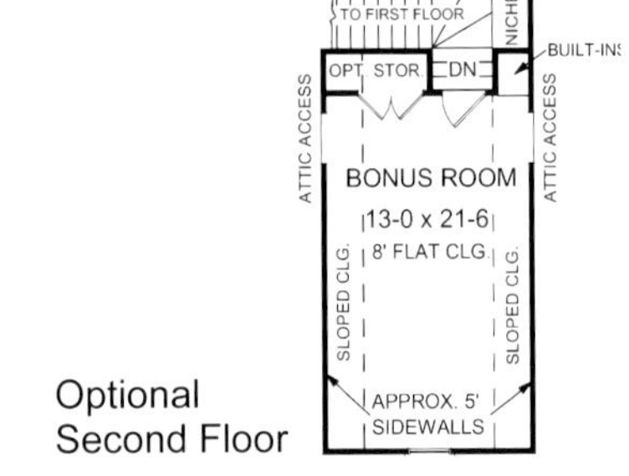

Optional Second Floor

SPECIAL FEATURES

The vaulted sunroom is an enchanting space to dine and it accesses two covered porches

The master bedroom enjoys his and her baths and walk-in closets as well as access to one rear porch and an optional storage, lounge, or office space

The bonus room on the second floor has an additional 302 square feet of living space

PRICE CODE F

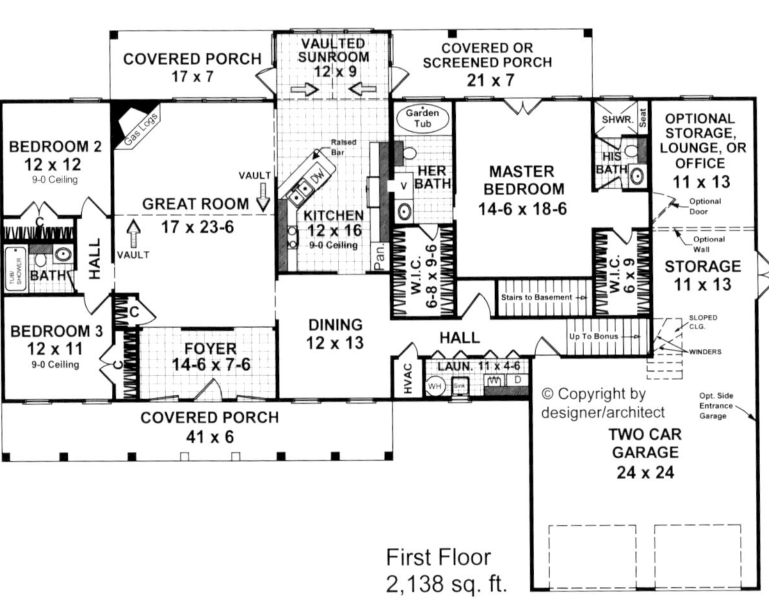

First Floor
2,138 sq. ft.

To order plans, visit the Menards Building Materials Desk or visit www.Menards.com.

MENARDS®

ADRIANNA

Plan #M08-055L-0210

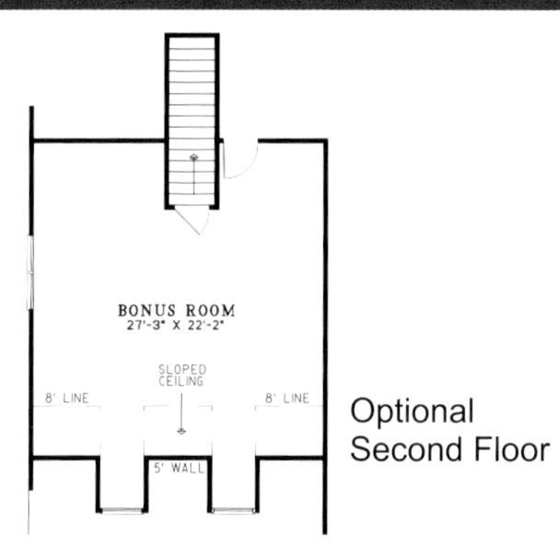

Optional Second Floor

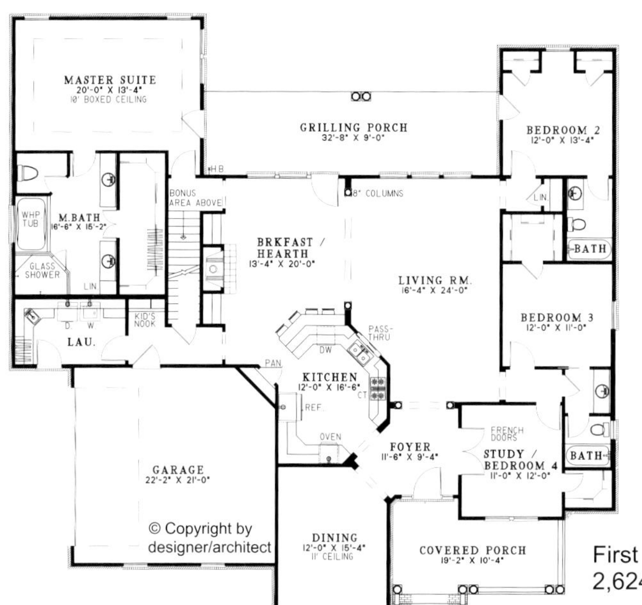

First Floor
2,624 sq. ft.

To order plans, visit the Menards Building Materials Desk
or visit www.Menards.com.

ENCHANTING RANCH

2,624 total square feet of living area

Width: 66'-4" Depth: 64'-0"

4 bedrooms, 3 baths

2-car side entry garage

Slab or crawl space foundation, please specify when ordering

SPECIAL FEATURES

Bedroom #2 is secluded and includes a private bath making it ideal for a guest suite

The master suite features a 10' ceiling, porch access and a deluxe bath with two vanities and an extra-large walk-in closet

The large laundry room has a separate entrance

The optional second floor has an additional 561 square feet of living space

PRICE CODE F

CRANDALL CLIFF

MENARDS®

Plan #M08-013L-0130

EXCITING ONE-LEVEL HOME

1,798 total square feet of living area

Width: 54'-0" Depth: 56'-2"

3 bedrooms, 2 1/2 baths

2-car side entry garage

Slab foundation, basement and crawl space foundations available for an additional fee

SPECIAL FEATURES

A gourmet kitchen, a casual dining room, and a rear covered porch overlooking the pool make this home a delight for entertaining

The generous master suite features a sitting area and large walk-in closet with separate his and her sections

The front home office can easily become a guest bedroom with its walk-in closet and private bath access

The bonus room above the garage has an additional 328 square feet of living area

PRICE CODE E

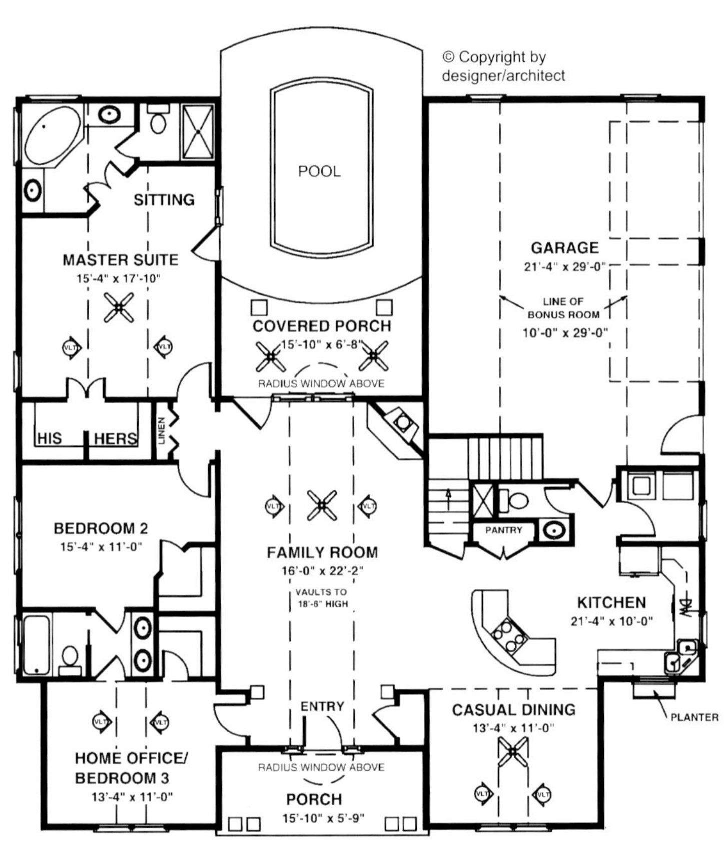

To order plans, visit the Menards Building Materials Desk or visit www.Menards.com.

MENARDS

BETHANY

Plan #M08-068D-0007

COLOSSAL GREAT ROOM

1,599 total square feet of living area

Width: 62'-0" Depth: 40'-0"

4 bedrooms, 2 baths

2-car garage

Basement foundation, drawings also include crawl space and slab foundations

SPECIAL FEATURES

The kitchen is designed for efficiency with a large pantry and easy access to the laundry room

Bedroom #3 has a charming window seat

The master bedroom has a full bath and large walk-in closet

PRICE CODE B

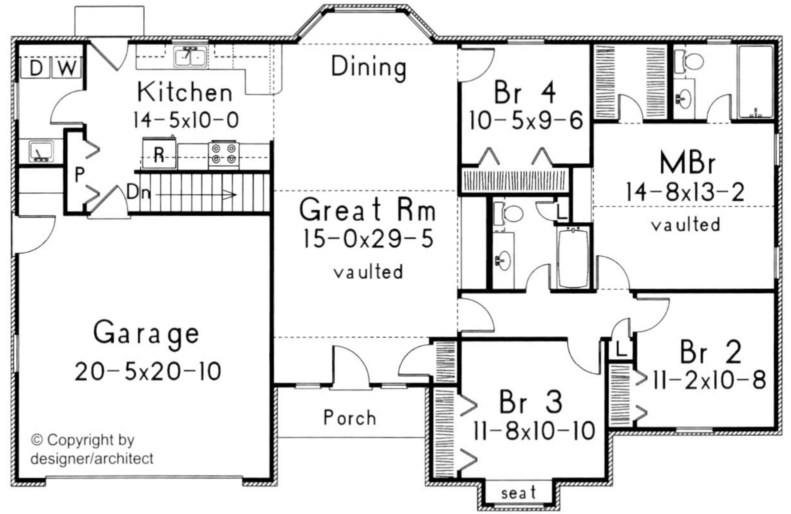

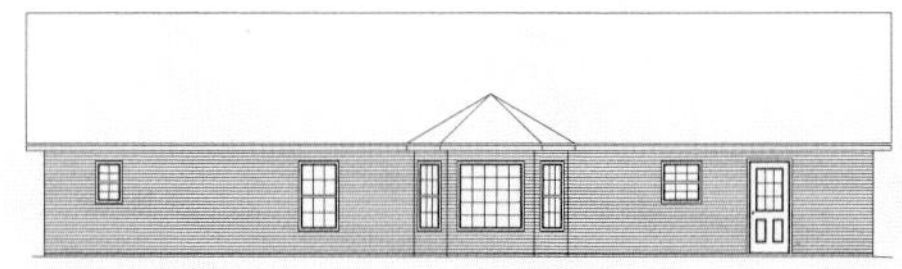

Rear View

To order plans, visit the Menards Building Materials Desk or visit www.Menards.com.

MOSS LANDING

MENARDS®

Plan #M08-039L-0007

PRIVATE BEDROOM AREA

1,550 total square feet of living area

Width: 68'-3"   Depth: 73'-8"

3 bedrooms, 2 baths

2-car detached side entry garage

Slab or crawl space foundation, please specify when ordering

SPECIAL FEATURES

The wrap-around front porch is an ideal gathering place

A handy snack bar is positioned so the kitchen flows into the family room

The master bedroom has many amenities including a private bath and a spacious walk-in closet

PRICE CODE B

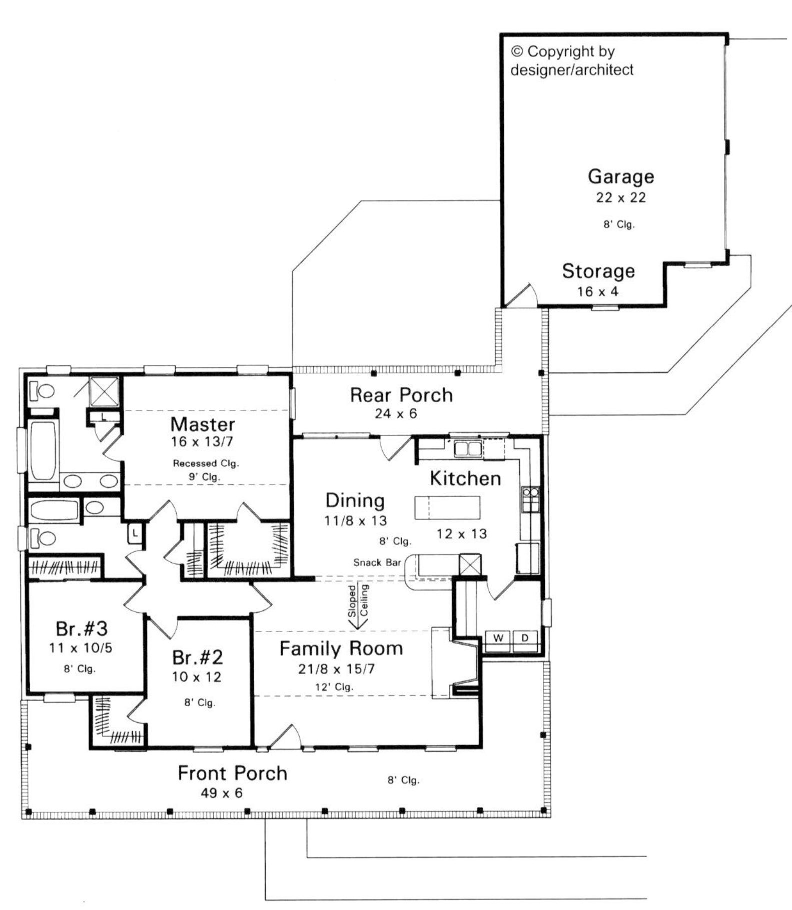

To order plans, visit the Menards Building Materials Desk or visit www.Menards.com.

MENARDS®

WELSBERG

Plan #M08-055L-0213

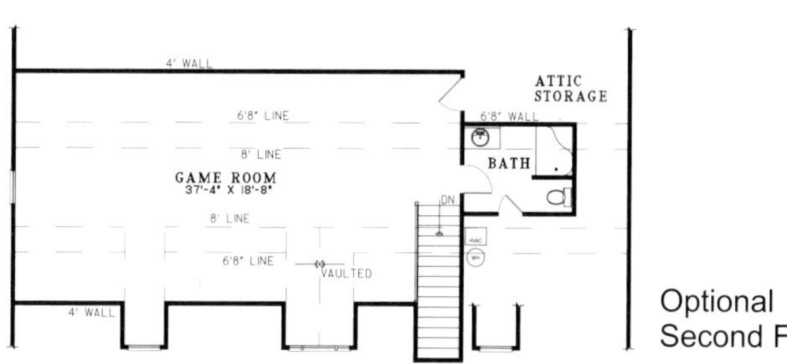

Optional Second Floor

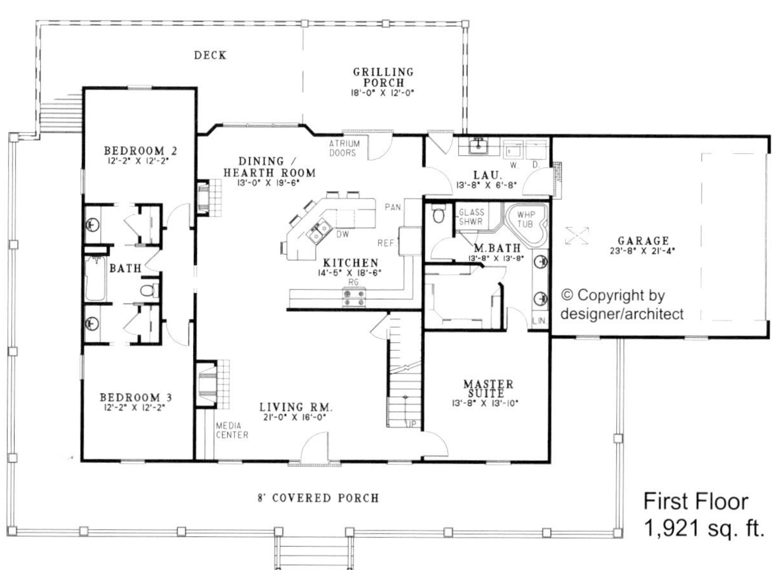

First Floor
1,921 sq. ft.

GRAND PORCH IS INVITING

1,921 total square feet of living area

Width: 84'-0" Depth: 55'-6"

3 bedrooms, 2 baths

2-car side entry garage

Slab or crawl space foundation, please specify when ordering; walk-out basement and basement foundations are available for an additional fee

SPECIAL FEATURES

The secondary bedrooms share a Jack and Jill bath

A massive living room is warmed by a fireplace and includes a built-in media center

The wrap-around kitchen counter with seating opens to the dining/hearth room

The optional second floor has an additional 812 square feet of living space

PRICE CODE C

To order plans, visit the Menards Building Materials Desk or visit www.Menards.com.

KAITLYN

MENARDS®

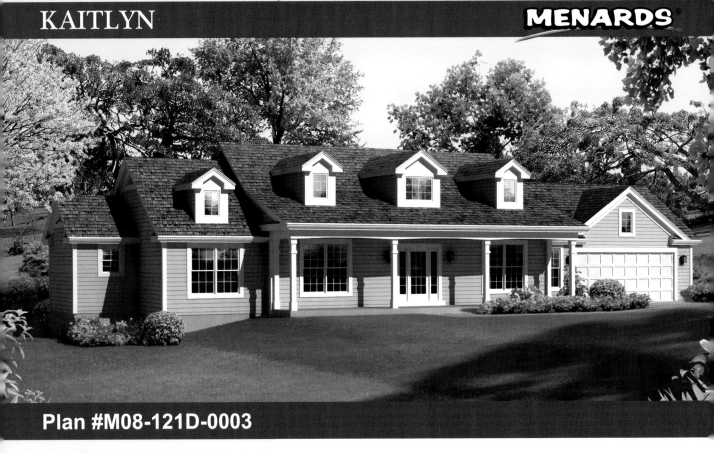

Plan #M08-121D-0003

DORMERS AND PORCH ADD GREAT STRIKING CURB APPEAL

2,215 total square feet of living area

Width: 91'-10" Depth: 52'-6"

3 bedrooms, 2 1/2 baths

2-car garage

Basement foundation

SPECIAL FEATURES

The great room is topped with an inverted vaulted ceiling and shares a see-through fireplace with the vaulted hearth room

The master bedroom features a coffered ceiling along with a bath and walk-in closet

The kitchen has a large wrap-around counter with dining space for five

2" x 6" exterior wall framing available for an additional fee, please specify when ordering

PRICE CODE C

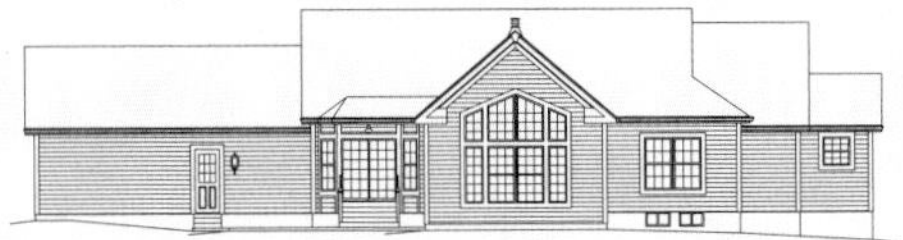

Rear View

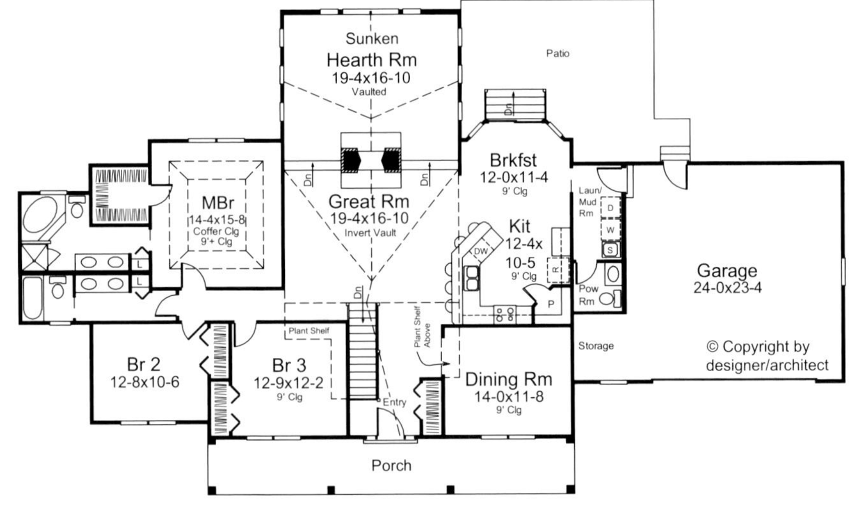

To order plans, visit the Menards Building Materials Desk or visit www.Menards.com.

MENARDS®

MARTIN HOUSE

Plan #M08-013L-0134

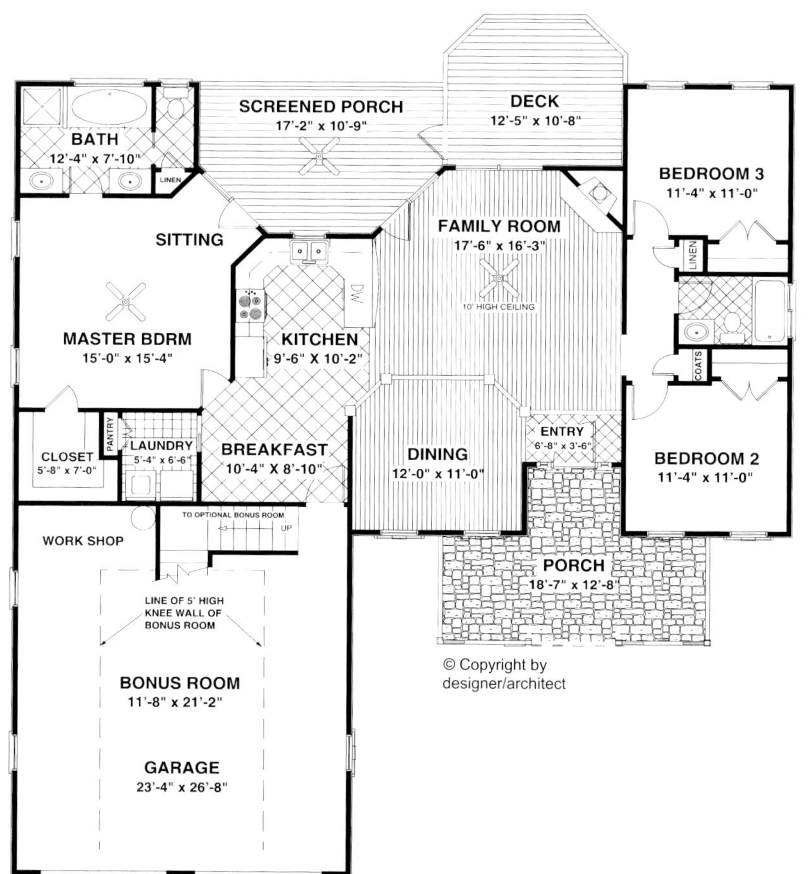

INVITING STONE WALKWAY

1,496 total square feet of living area

Width: 55'-0" Depth: 58'-0"

3 bedrooms, 2 baths

2-car garage

Slab foundation

SPECIAL FEATURES

This country cottage features spacious open rooms and an easy flow from the welcoming front porch stone walkway to the breezy screened porch off of the family room and master bedroom

The family room features a cozy corner fireplace

Isolated from the secondary bedrooms, the master bedroom is an owner's retreat with a sitting area, a large walk-in closet, and a private bath with a separate tub and shower

The bonus room above the garage has an additional 301 square feet of living area

PRICE CODE E

To order plans, visit the Menards Building Materials Desk or visit www.Menards.com.

CASTLECLIFF

MENARDS®

Plan #M08-039L-0025

BEAUTIFUL LANDSCAPING OPPORTUNITIES

1,430 total square feet of living area

Width: 34'-0"   Depth: 60'-0"

3 bedrooms, 2 baths

2-car detached garage

Crawl space or slab foundation, please specify when ordering

SPECIAL FEATURES

All bedrooms enjoy spacious walk-in closets

A large dining room enjoys close proximity to the kitchen

Varied ceiling heights throughout help add character to the interior

PRICE CODE C

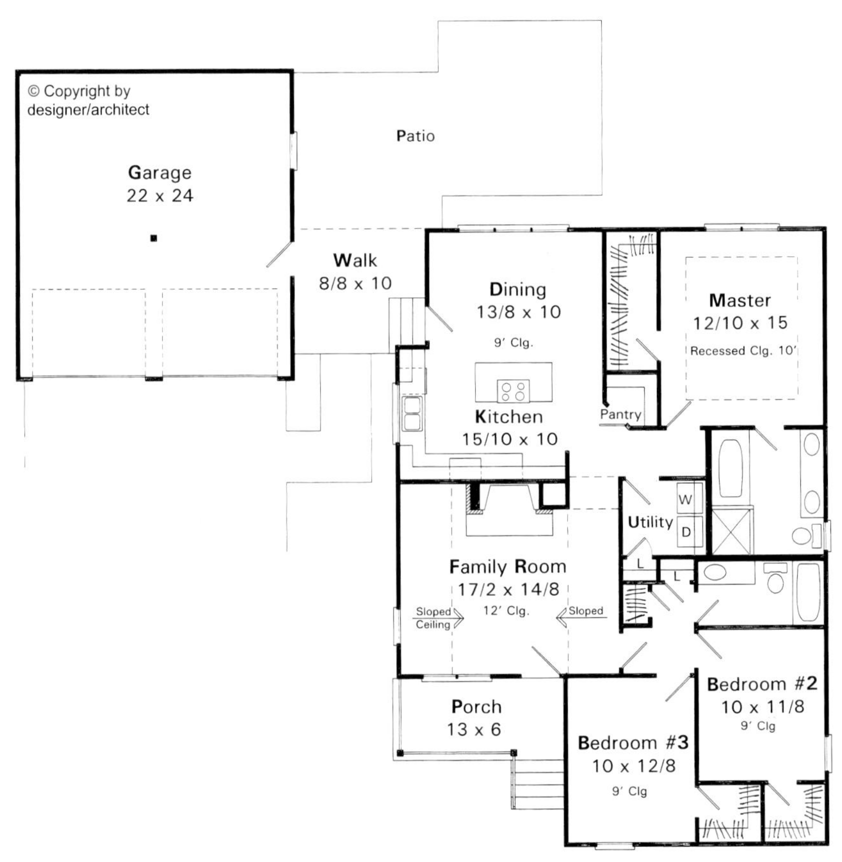

To order plans, visit the Menards Building Materials Desk or visit www.Menards.com.

MENARDS®

SPENCER

Plan #M08-058D-0169

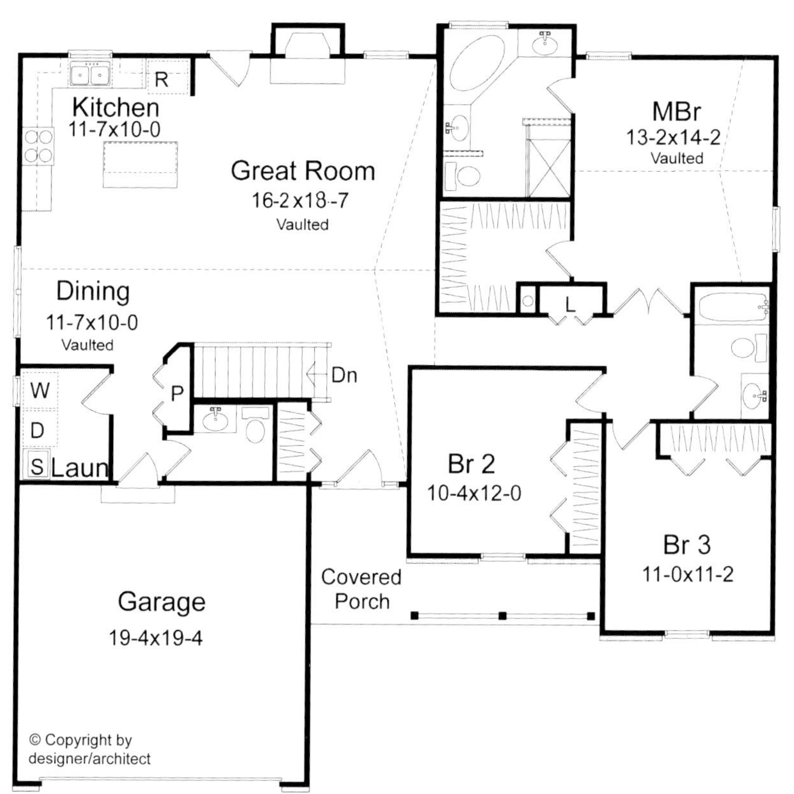

TWIN DORMERS

1,635 total square feet of living area

Width: 51'-0" Depth: 50'-4"

3 bedrooms, 2 1/2 baths

2-car garage

Basement foundation

SPECIAL FEATURES

This country-style ranch is sure to please with an open great room and private bedrooms

The great room enjoys the openness to the kitchen and dining area, a grand fireplace and access to the backyard

A walk-in closet, deluxe bath with whirlpool tub and a vaulted ceiling create a luxurious master bedroom

PRICE CODE AA

To order plans, visit the Menards Building Materials Desk or visit www.Menards.com.

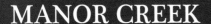

MANOR CREEK

MENARDS®

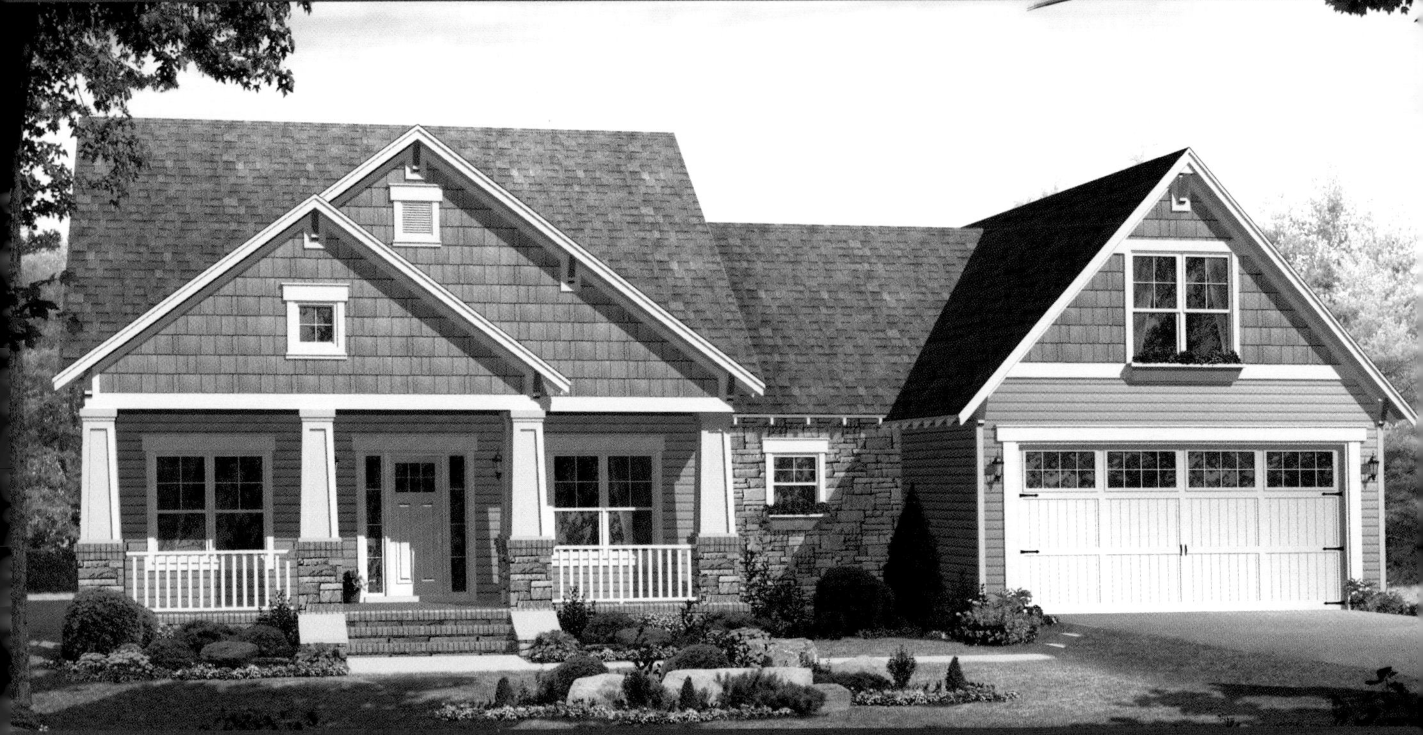

Plan #M08-077L-0140

STYLISH CRAFTSMAN HOME

1,800 total square feet of living area

Width: 65'-0" Depth: 56'-8"

3 bedrooms, 2 baths

2-car garage

Slab or crawl space foundation, please specify when ordering

SPECIAL FEATURES

A large flex space can easily convert to a home office or formal dining room depending on the owner's needs

A large and spacious kitchen has a center island with eating bar and an attached breakfast room with bay window

The corner jet tub in the master bath pampers the homeowners in their private retreat

The unfinished bonus room has an additional 326 square feet of living area

PRICE CODE E

Optional Second Floor

First Floor 1,800 sq. ft.

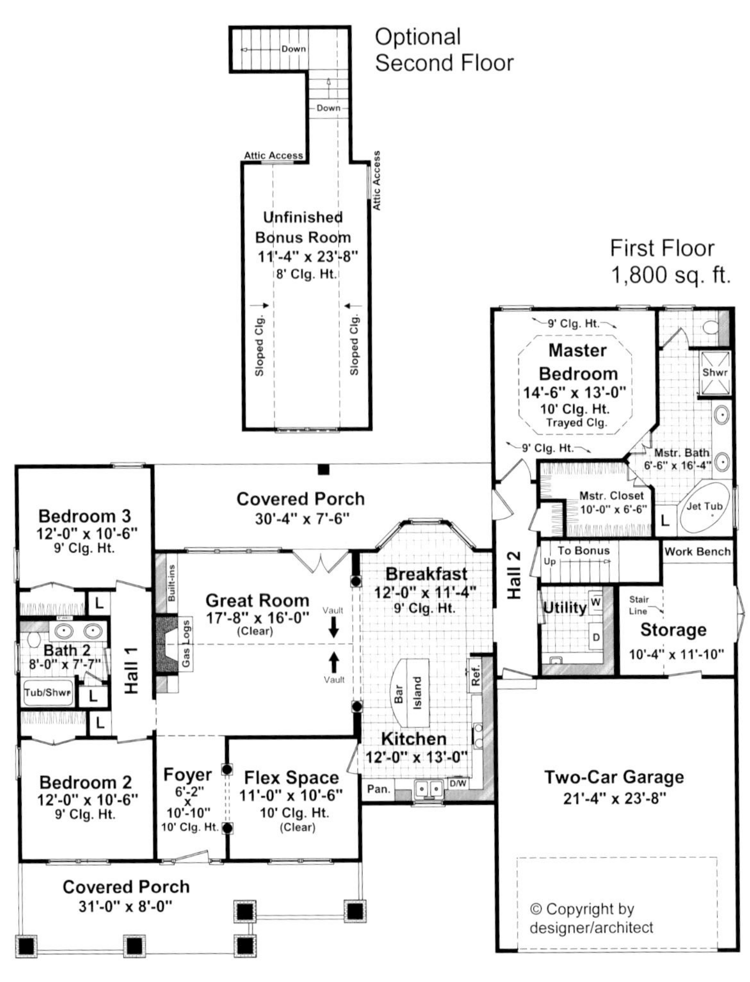

To order plans, visit the Menards Building Materials Desk or visit www.Menards.com.

MENARDS®

LEWISTON

Plan #M08-053D-0051

FAMILY-SIZED KITCHEN IS CENTRALLY LOCATED

2,731 total square feet of living area

Width: 74'-0" Depth: 70'-0"

4 bedrooms, 3 1/2 baths

2-car side entry garage

Basement foundation, drawings also include walk-out basement foundation

SPECIAL FEATURES

The master bedroom enjoys double walk-in closets, a coffered ceiling and bath

Both the dining and living rooms feature coffered ceilings and bay windows

The vaulted family room features a fireplace and access to the rear deck

The secondary bedrooms are separate from the living areas

PRICE CODE C

Rear View

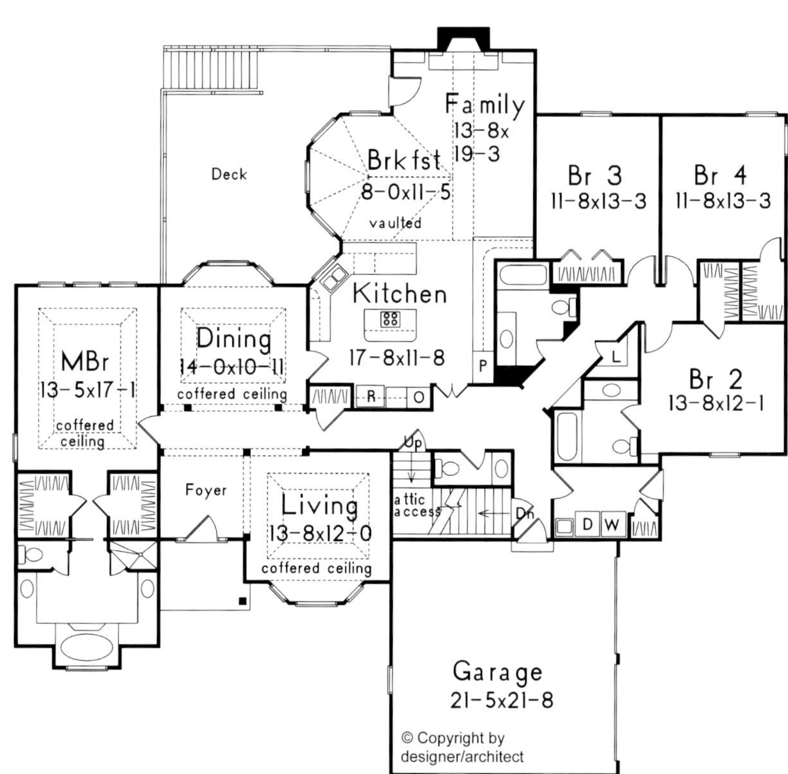

To order plans, visit the Menards Building Materials Desk or visit www.Menards.com.

HUNTINGTON DOWNS

MENARDS®

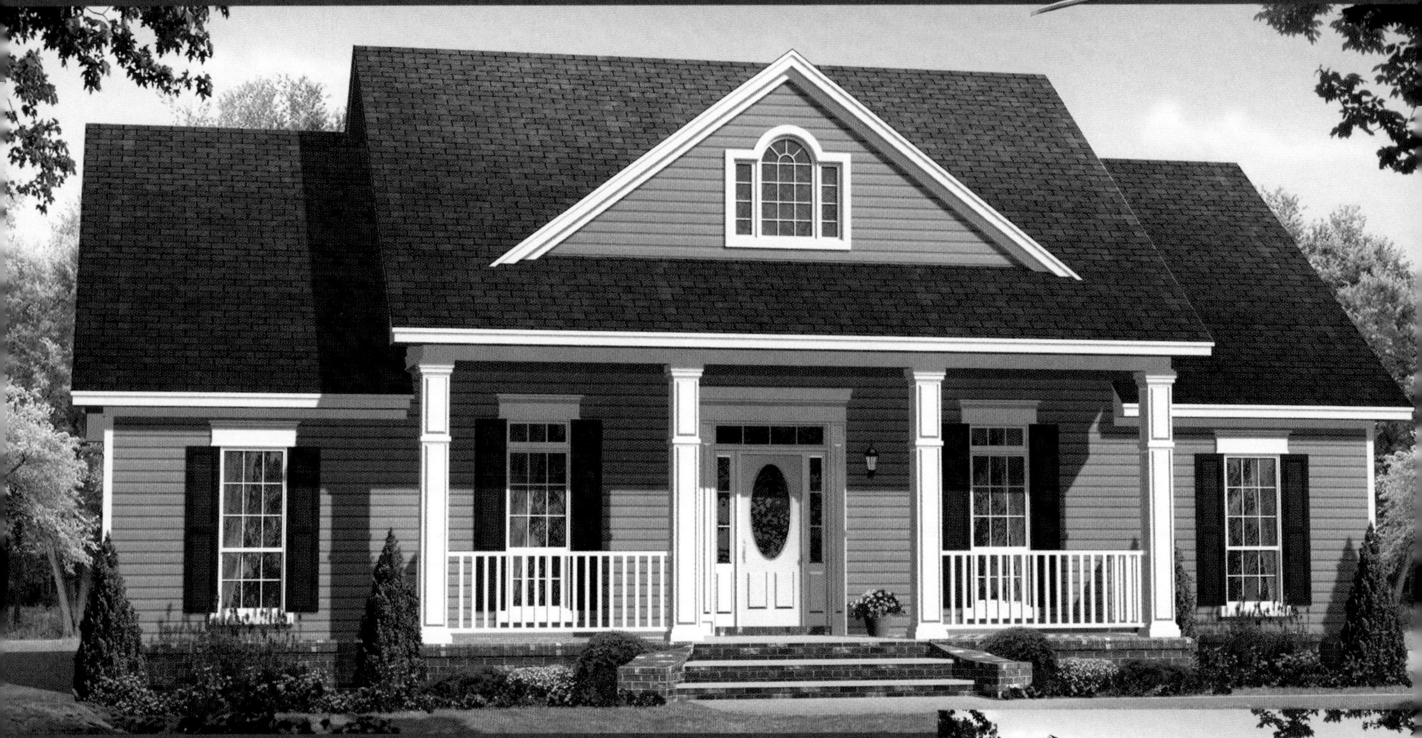

Plan #M08-077L-0122

DELIGHTFUL COUNTRY HOME

1,888 total square feet of living area

Width: 55'-0"   Depth: 70'-0"

3 bedrooms, 2 1/2 baths

2-car side entry garage

Slab or crawl space foundation, please specify when ordering

SPECIAL FEATURES

The generously sized flex space has a half bath nearby and could easily convert to an ideal guest room in a remote location

The eating bar/island combination in the kitchen provides useful dining space and extra workspace for food preparation

The great room is the focal point of this home with a fireplace flanked by built-in bookcases

The optional second floor has an additional 316 square feet of living space

PRICE CODE E

Optional Second Floor

First Floor
1,888 sq. ft.

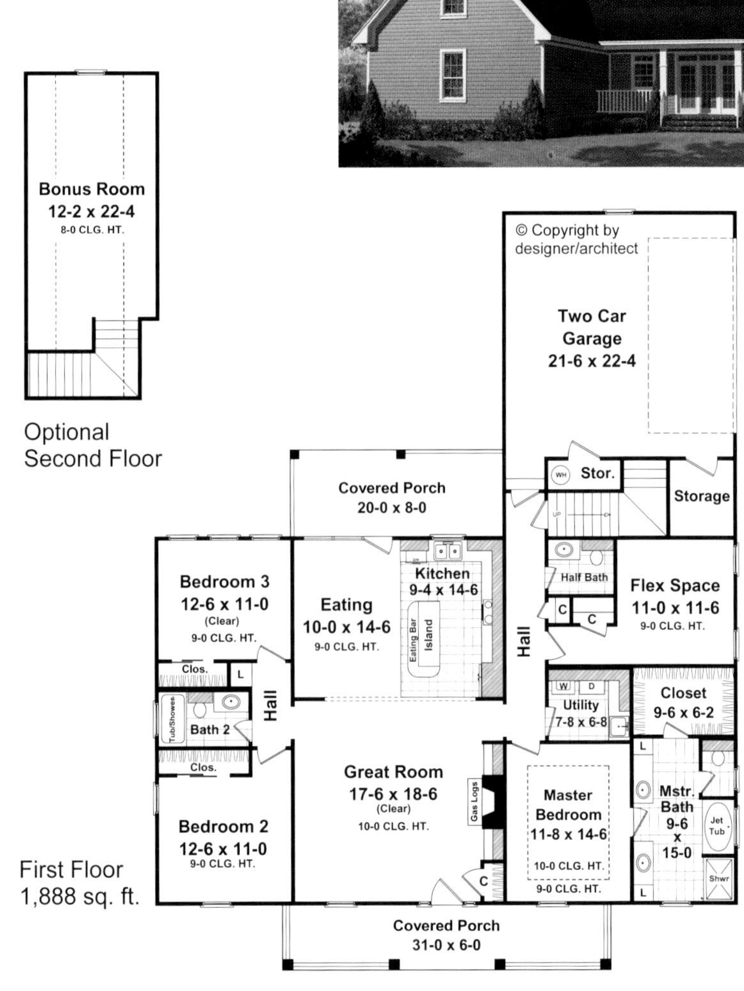

To order plans, visit the Menards Building Materials Desk or visit www.Menards.com.

MULTI-ROOF LEVELS CREATE ATTRACTIVE COLONIAL HOME

1,364 total square feet of living area

Width: 68'-0" Depth: 33'-5"

3 bedrooms, 2 baths

2-car garage

Basement foundation, drawings also include crawl space and slab foundations

SPECIAL FEATURES

A large covered front porch and entry door with sidelights lead into a generous living room

The well-planned U-shaped kitchen features a laundry closet, built-in pantry and open peninsula

The master bedroom has its own bath with a 4' shower

Convenient to the kitchen is an oversized two-car garage with service door to the rear of the home

PRICE CODE A

Mstr Bedrm 12-0x12-0
Family Rm 17-0x12-0
DW
Kit 9-3x 12-0
R
L
Garage 19-8x23-4
Hall
Dn
Pantry
W D
Bedrm 2 10-3x11-8
Bedrm 3 10-6x11-8
Living Rm 23-7x11-8
Porch

To order plans, visit the Menards Building Materials Desk or visit www.Menards.com.

OAKRIDGE

MENARDS

Plan #M08-033D-0012

CENTRAL LIVING AREA KEEPS BEDROOMS PRIVATE

1,546 total square feet of living area

Width: 60'-0" Depth: 43'-0"

3 bedrooms, 2 baths

2-car garage

Basement foundation

SPECIAL FEATURES

The master bedroom is secluded for privacy

The dining room features a large bay window

The kitchen and dinette combine for added space and include access to the outdoors

The large laundry room includes a convenient sink

PRICE CODE C

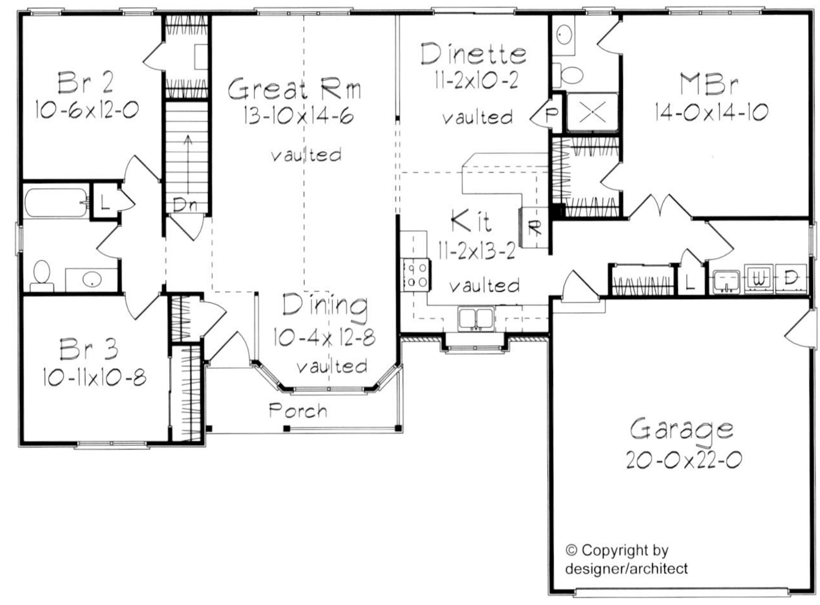

Rear View

To order plans, visit the Menards Building Materials Desk
or visit www.Menards.com.

GEORGIA MANOR

Plan #M08-007D-0231

EXTRAORDINARY DESIGN FOR ENTERTAINING

2,312 total square feet of living area

Width: 77'-0" Depth: 55'-6"

3 bedrooms, 2 1/2 baths

2-car garage

Slab foundation

SPECIAL FEATURES

The great room with fireplace has an ideal sitting room that extends into the covered patio areas, while the adjacent dining room extends into the front porch area

A breakfast room and snack bar adorn the smartly designed kitchen all with views of the rear covered patio through 9' wide sliding glass doors

PRICE CODE E

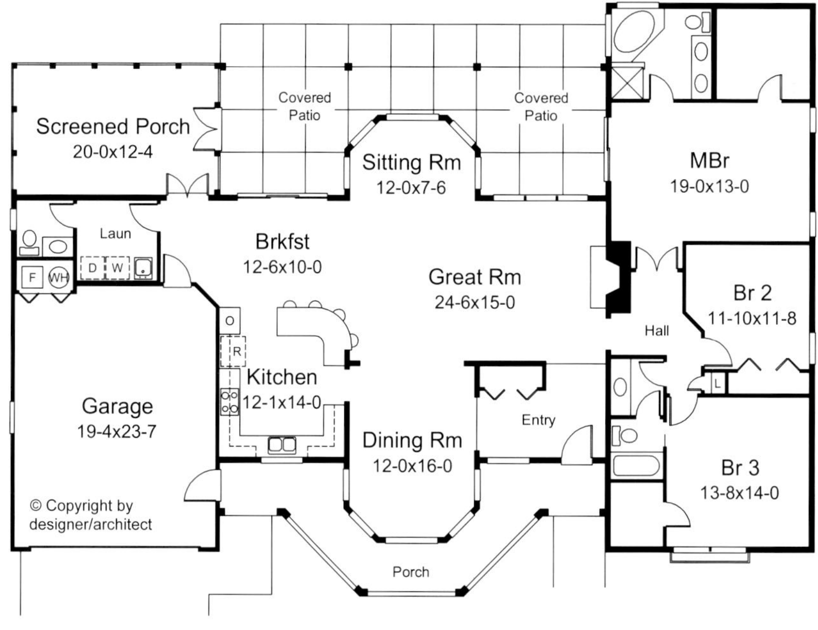

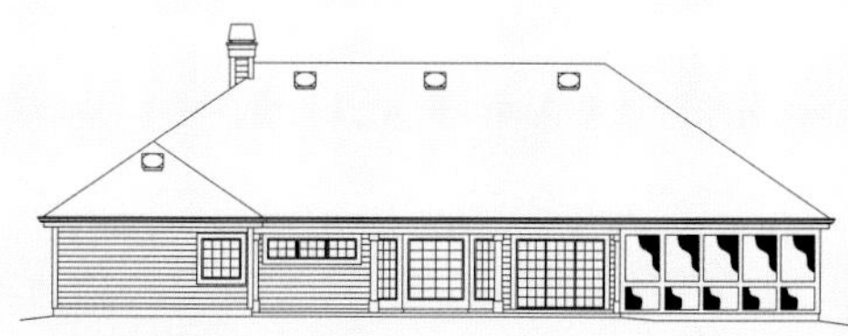

Rear View

To order plans, visit the Menards Building Materials Desk or visit www.Menards.com.

BRAYDEN MANOR

MENARDS®

Plan #M08-007D-0151

PERFECT HOME FOR A LARGE FAMILY ON A BUDGET

1,941 total square feet of living area

Width: 70'-4" Depth: 35'-8"

5 bedrooms, 3 baths

2-car side entry drive under garage

Walk-out basement foundation

SPECIAL FEATURES

Interesting roof lines and a spacious front porch with flanking stonework help to fashion this beautiful country home

The vaulted great room is open to the bayed dining area suitable for friends and a large family

The master bedroom enjoys a big walk-in closet and a gracious bath

PRICE CODE C

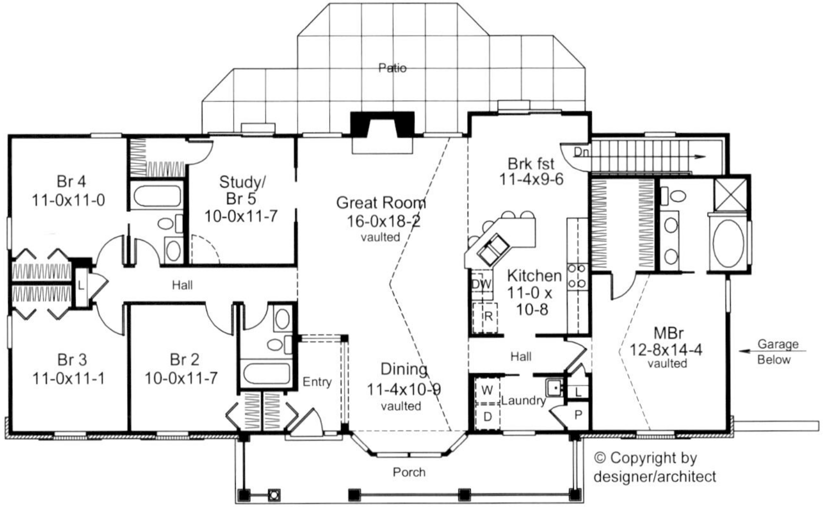

Rear View

To order plans, visit the Menards Building Materials Desk or visit www.Menards.com.

DORMER ADDS CURB APPEAL

1,635 total square feet of living area

Width: 51'-0" Depth: 50'-4"

3 bedrooms, 2 1/2 baths

2-car garage

Basement foundation

Kitchen 11-7x10-0
R
Great Room 16-0x16-6
MBr 13-2x14-2
Dining 11-7x10-0
L
W
D
S
Laun
P
Dn
Br 2 10-4x12-0
Br 3 11-0x11-2
Covered Porch
Garage 19-4x19-4

SPECIAL FEATURES

The open atmosphere of the combined kitchen, dining and great rooms makes this a perfect space to gather with family and friends

When it's time to relax, retreat to the luxurious master bedroom equipped with a deluxe bath

A half bath, laundry room and pantry at the garage entrance add function to this family friendly home

PRICE CODE AA

To order plans, visit the Menards Building Materials Desk or visit www.Menards.com.

STONERIDGE

MENARDS®

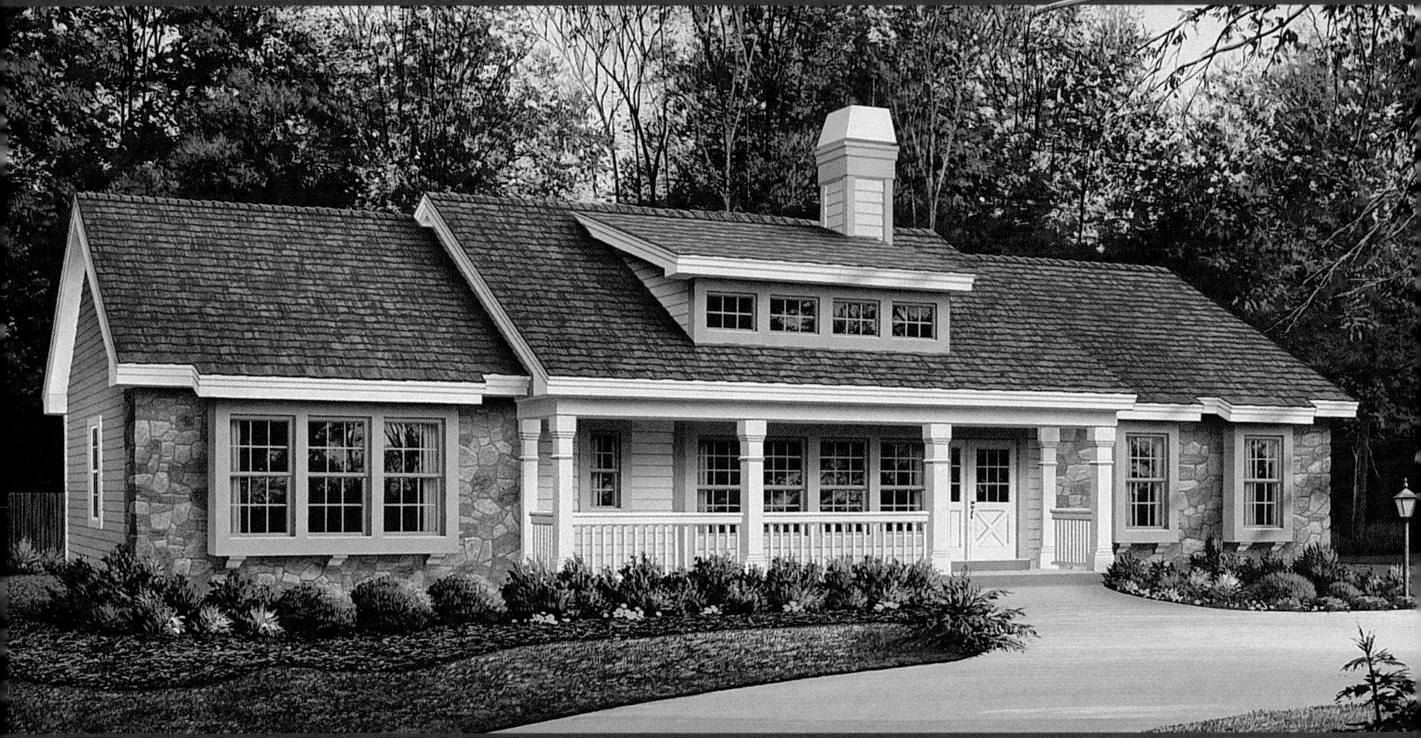

Plan #M08-007D-0101

COUNTRY FLAVOR WITH ATRIUM

2,317 total square feet of living area

Width: 71'-2" Depth: 46'-0"

3 bedrooms, 2 1/2 baths

2-car side entry garage

Walk-out basement foundation

SPECIAL FEATURES

Bracketed box windows create an exterior with country charm

The massive-sized vaulted great room features a majestic atrium, a fireplace, a box window wall, and a dining balcony

The breakfast room has an atrium balcony

1,026 square feet of optional lower level living area with family room, wet bar, bedroom #4 and a bath

PRICE CODE D

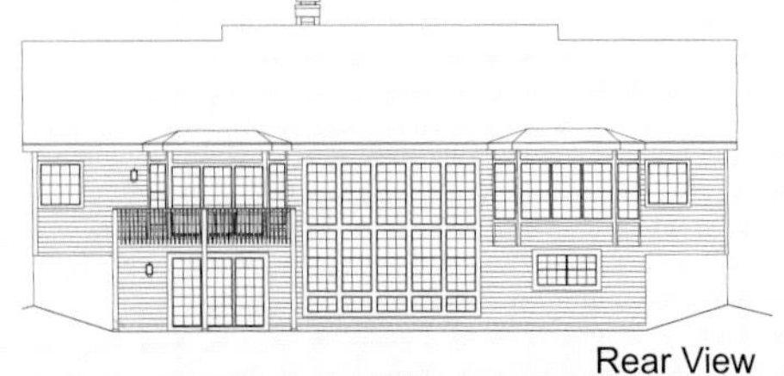

Rear View

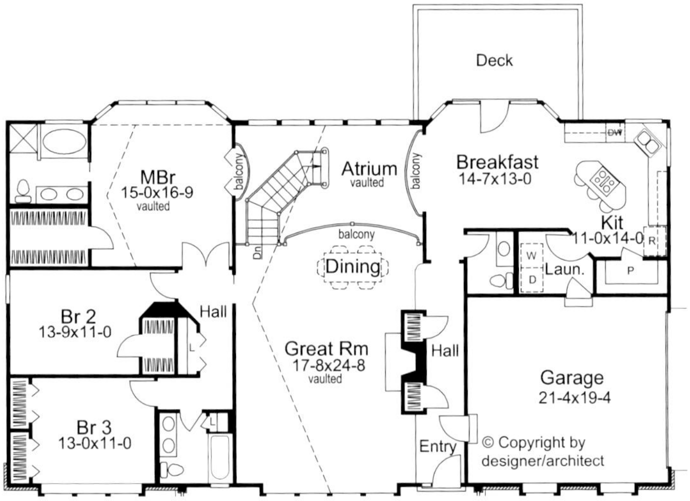

Deck
MBr
15-0x16-9
vaulted
balcony
Atrium
vaulted
balcony
Breakfast
14-7x13-0
DW
Kit
11-0x14-0
R
Dn
balcony
Dining
W
D
Laun.
P
Br 2
13-9x11-0
Hall
L
Great Rm
17-8x24-8
vaulted
Hall
Garage
21-4x19-4
Br 3
13-0x11-0
Entry
© Copyright by
designer/architect

First Floor
2,317 sq. ft.

Patio
Up
Atrium
20-0x12-6
Opt Guest
Bedroom
16-0x17-0
Basement
Bar
Opt Family Rm
20-0x24-4

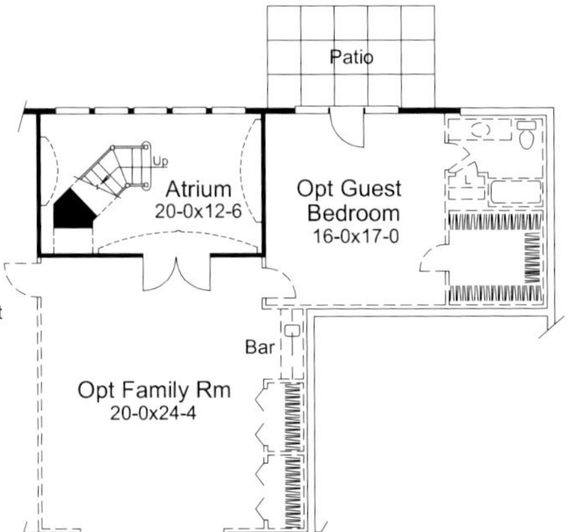

Optional
Lower Level

To order plans, visit the Menards Building Materials Desk
or visit www.Menards.com.

MENARDS®

COCHEPARK MANOR

Plan #M08-007D-0235

UNIQUE DRIVE-THRU BASEMENT GARAGE

2,213 total square feet of living area

Width: 75'-0" Depth: 39'-0"

3 bedrooms, 2 baths

8-car drive under side entry garage

Walk-out basement foundation

SPECIAL FEATURES

The spacious great room has a fireplace, and glass sliding doors to the sundeck

A huge walk-in pantry, a large island, and generous cabinet space are all amenities of the kitchen

The walk-out basement garage has a convenient drive-thru design, abundant storage area or parking for up to 8 cars, and two 9' glass sliding doors for sunlight

PRICE CODE E

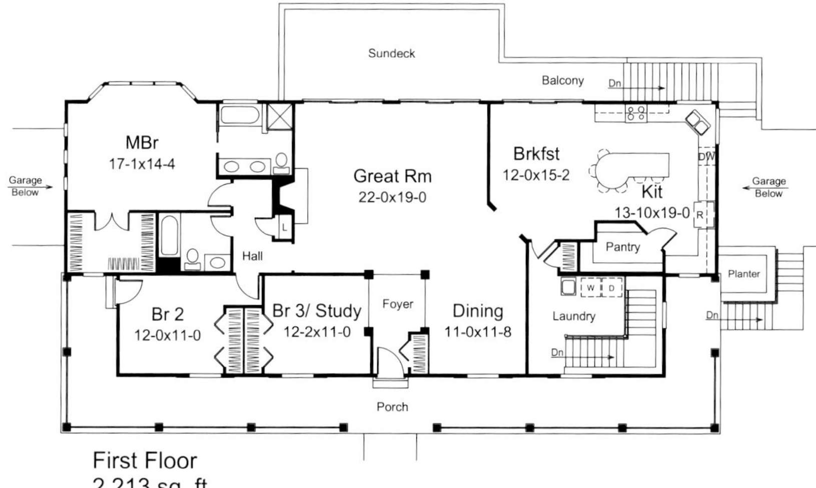

First Floor
2,213 sq. ft.

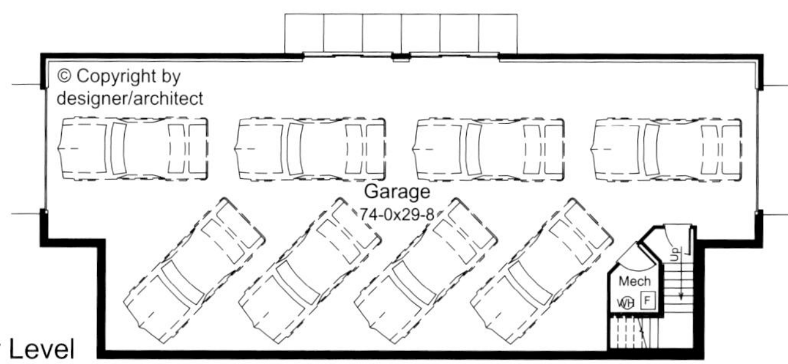

Lower Level

Rear View

To order plans, visit the Menards Building Materials Desk or visit www.Menards.com.

CARROLLSTONE

MENARDS®

Plan #M08-007D-0116

ATRIUM RANCH HOME

3,500 total square feet of living area

Width: 80'-8" Depth: 78'-0"

3 bedrooms, 3 baths

3-car side entry garage

Walk-out basement foundation

SPECIAL FEATURES

A large courtyard with stone walls, lantern columns, and a porch welcomes you

The vaulted great room has a stone fireplace, built-in shelves, and an atrium with a two and a half story window wall

Two walk-in closets, a vaulted ceiling with plant shelf, and a luxury bath adorn the master bedroom suite

The lower level includes a family room, a walk-in bar, a sitting area, bedroom #3 and a bath

PRICE CODE C

Rear View

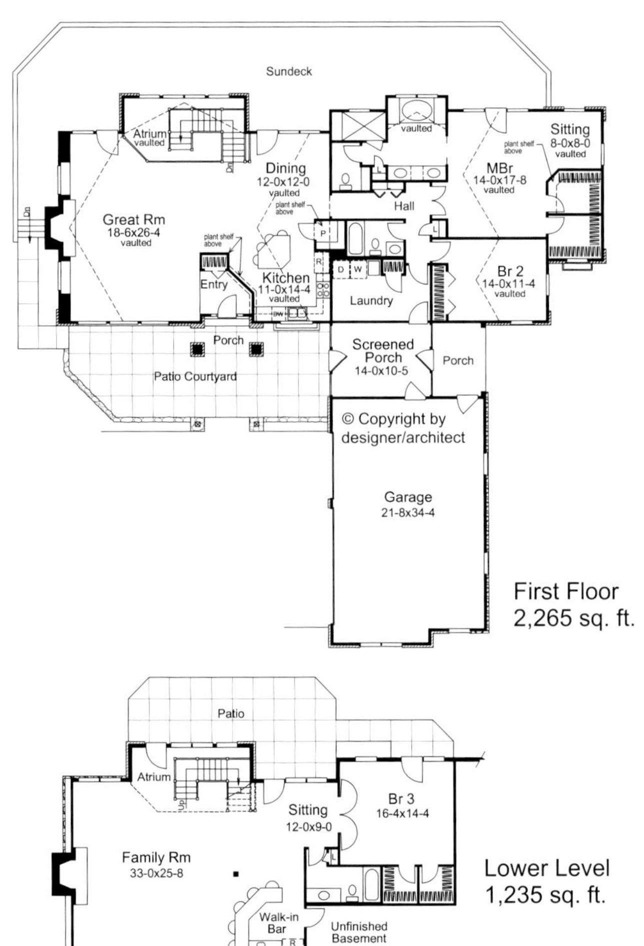

First Floor
2,265 sq. ft.

Lower Level
1,235 sq. ft.

To order plans, visit the Menards Building Materials Desk or visit www.Menards.com.

MENARDS®

CASSANDRA

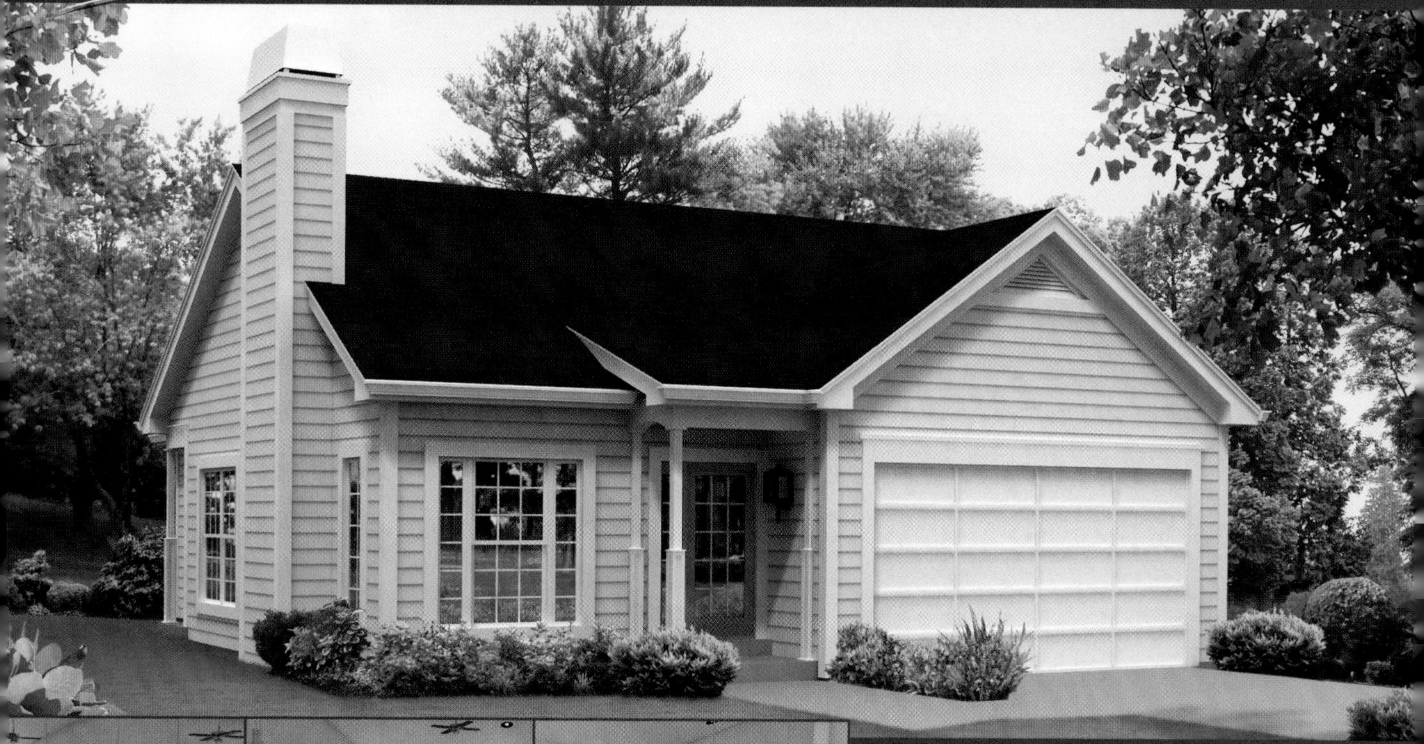

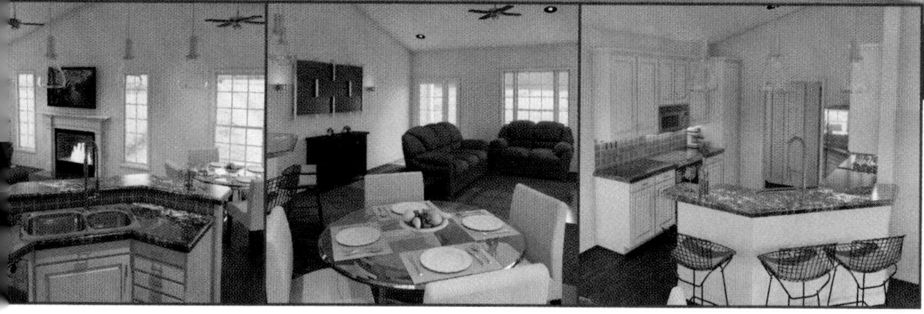

Plan #M08-121D-0010

VAULTED LIVING AREAS FOR ADDED SPACIOUSNESS

1,281 total square feet of living area

Width: 37'-6" Depth: 52'-0"

3 bedrooms, 2 baths

2-car garage

Basement foundation

SPECIAL FEATURES

The functional kitchen has an angled raised counter perfect for casual dining

The vaulted great room and dining area combine, creating an open, airy feel

The vaulted master bedroom enjoys a walk-in closet and its own private bath

PRICE CODE AA

MBr
12-9x14-3
Vaulted
Dn
Br 2
10-4x10-2
Br 3
10-4x10-0
Porch
P
Kitchen
10-6x10-8
Vaulted
L
Dining
10-2x10-8
Vaulted
DW
R
Great Rm
15-2x16-0
Vaulted
Garage
19-4x20-4
E
Porch
© Copyright by designer/architect

Rear View

To order plans, visit the Menards Building Materials Desk or visit www.Menards.com.

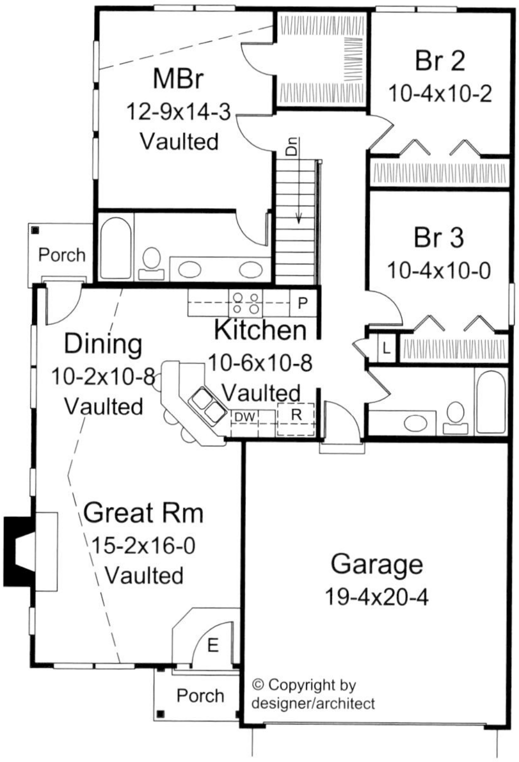

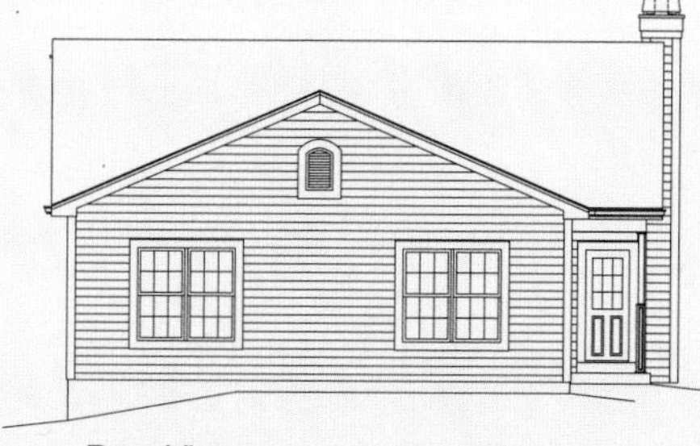

BOLSA KNOLL

MENARDS®

Plan #M08-039L-0014

VAULTED REAR PORCH

1,849 total square feet of living area

Width: 65'-11" Depth: 59'-5"

3 bedrooms, 2 baths

2-car garage

Crawl space or slab foundation, please specify when ordering

SPECIAL FEATURES

An open floor plan creates an airy feeling

The kitchen and breakfast area include a center island, a pantry, and a built-in desk

The master bedroom has a private entrance off of the breakfast area and a view of the vaulted covered porch

PRICE CODE C

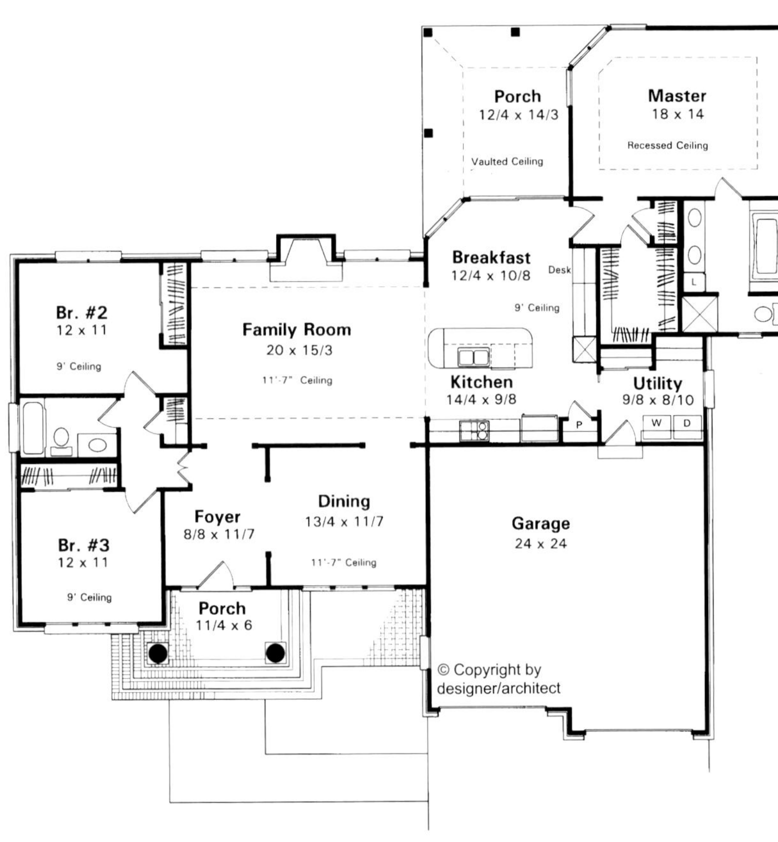

To order plans, visit the Menards Building Materials Desk or visit www.Menards.com.

TERRIFIC DESIGN FOR FAMILY LIVING

1,345 total square feet of living area

Width: 66'-0" Depth: 30'-5"

3 bedrooms, 2 baths

2-car side entry garage

Basement foundation, drawings also include crawl space and slab foundations

SPECIAL FEATURES

Brick front details add a touch of elegance

The master bedroom has a private full bath

The great room combines with the dining area creating a sense of spaciousness

The garage includes a handy storage area that could easily be converted to a workshop space

PRICE CODE A

Br 2
11-6x10-5
Br 3
10-7x9-5
Dining
12-1x9-1
Kit
11-1x8-9
W
D
R
Storage
11-1x9-1
L
Dn
Great Room
20-5x16-3
Garage
21-4x20-3
MBr
11-6x13-10
Porch depth 4-0

To order plans, visit the Menards Building Materials Desk or visit www.Menards.com.

WESTMONT MANOR

MENARDS®

Plan #M08-007D-0170

CLASSIC EXPRESSION

2,154 total square feet of living area

Width: 67'-0" Depth: 55'-8"

4 bedrooms, 2 1/2 baths

2-car garage

Basement foundation

SPECIAL FEATURES

Open to a spacious great room is a breakfast room surrounded by three 6' glass sliding doors leading to covered rear and side patios

The awesome kitchen has an angled breakfast counter, a walk-in pantry, and adjoins a multi-purpose room ideal for a laundry, study, hobby, or exercise room

The vaulted master bedroom has a lavish bath, double walk-in closets, and adjoining study/bedroom #4 with a bay window

PRICE CODE C

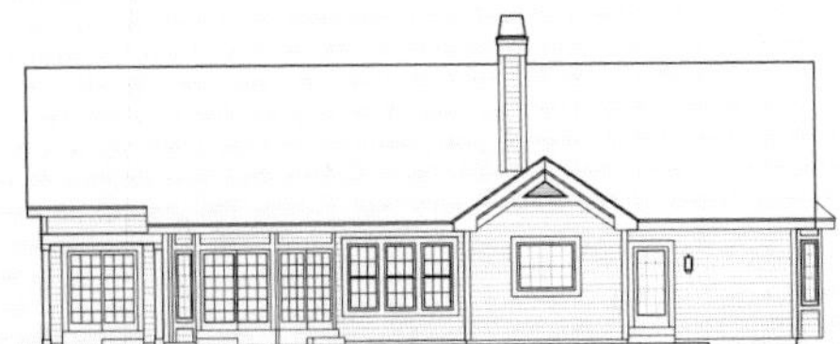

Rear View

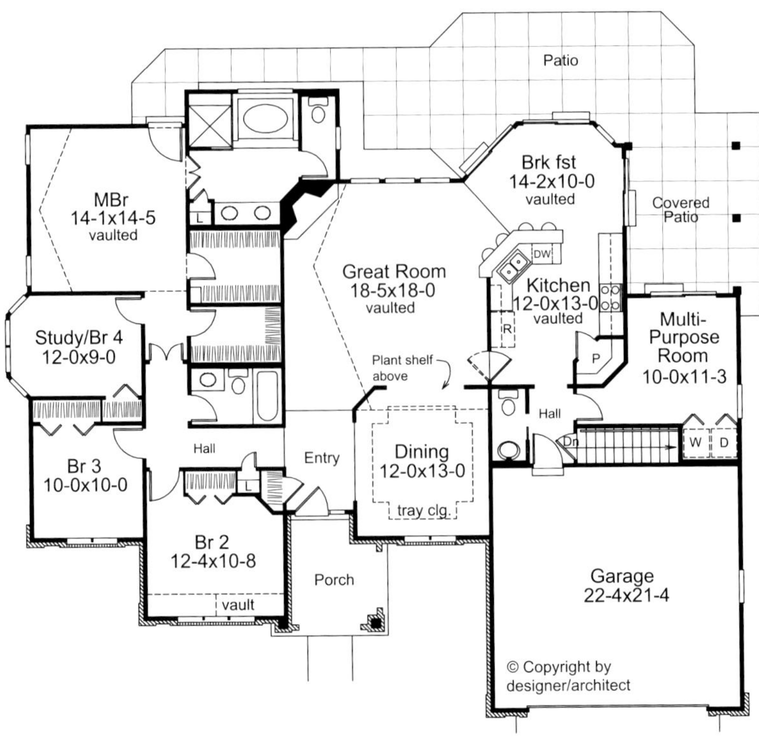

To order plans, visit the Menards Building Materials Desk
or visit www.Menards.com.

MENARDS®

FAIRFIELD LAKE

Plan #M08-055L-0192

FORMAL DINING ROOM

2,096 total square feet of living area

Width: 69'-2" Depth: 74'-10"

3 bedrooms, 2 1/2 baths

3-car side entry garage

Slab, crawl space, basement or walk-out basement foundation, please specify when ordering

SPECIAL FEATURES

The foyer opens to the great room featuring a fireplace and built-in bookshelves

The secondary bedrooms are secluded with a central bath and a laundry room

The grand kitchen has an eating counter, a pantry, an optional island, and connects to the bayed breakfast room

PRICE CODE E

To order plans, visit the Menards Building Materials Desk or visit www.Menards.com.

WELLSHIRE

MENARDS®

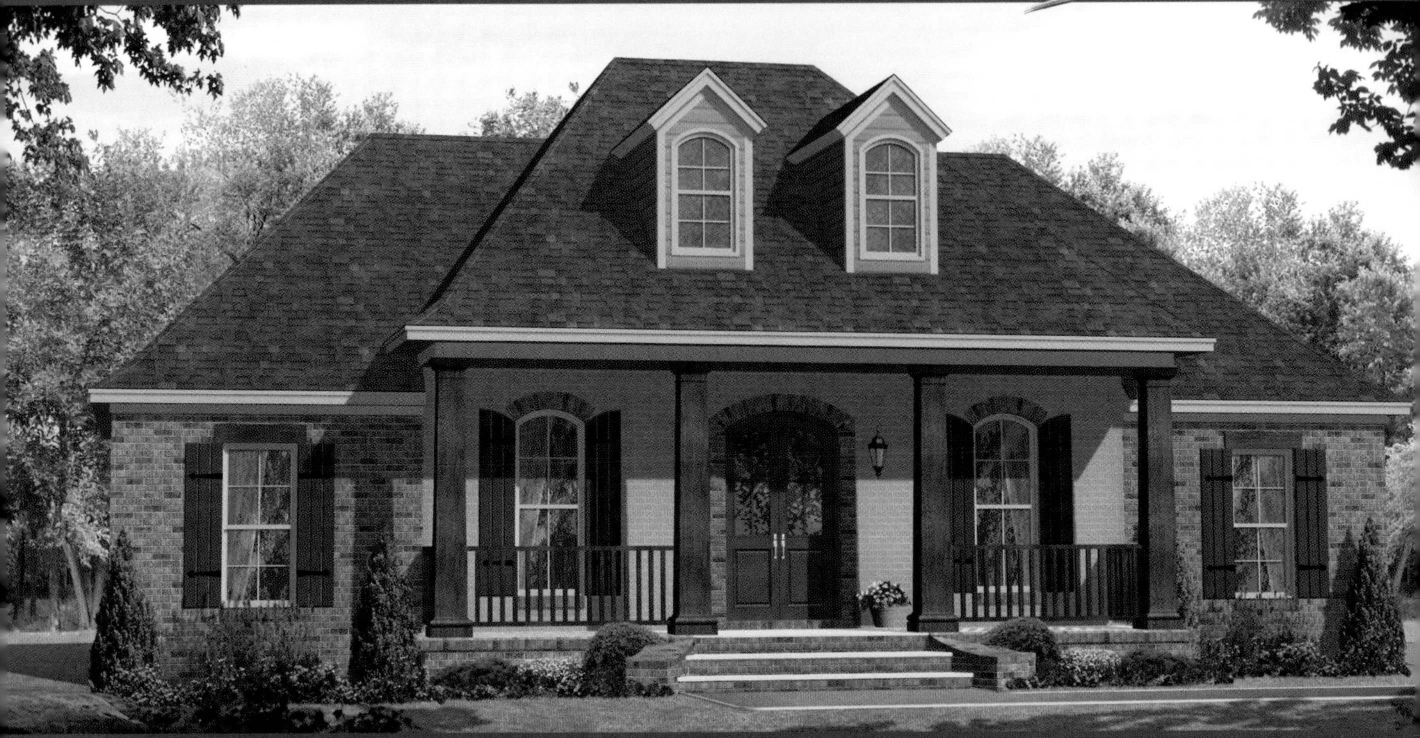

Plan #M08-077L-0156

GRAND ONE-LEVEL

2,200 total square feet of living area

Width: 65'-6" Depth: 79'-6"

4 bedrooms, 2 1/2 baths

2-car side entry garage

Crawl space or slab foundation, please specify when ordering

SPECIAL FEATURES

Step inside this inviting home to find an exquisite great room topped with a tray ceiling and featuring a gas fireplace flanked by built-in shelves

The nearby kitchen is centrally located, offering a walk-in pantry and raised snack bar, and easily serves both the formal dining room and the casual breakfast area

The master bedroom pampers with two walk-in closets and a compartmented bath equipped with a jet tub and twin vanity

The optional second floor has an additional 371 square feet of living area

PRICE CODE F

Optional Second Floor

First Floor
2,200 sq. ft.

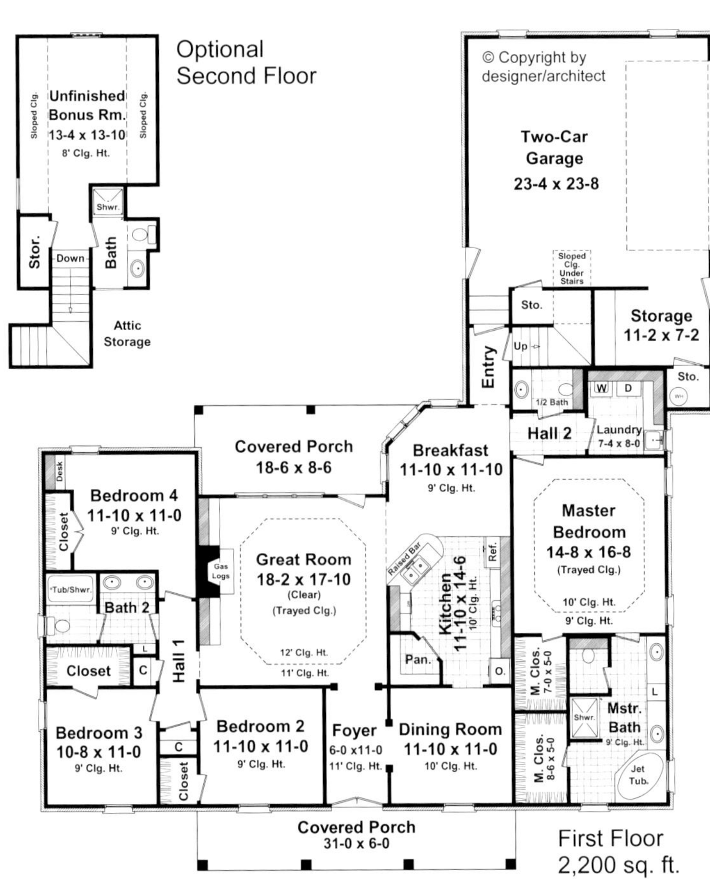

To order plans, visit the Menards Building Materials Desk or visit www.Menards.com.

MENARDS®

LYNNEWOOD PLACE

Plan #M08-007D-0239

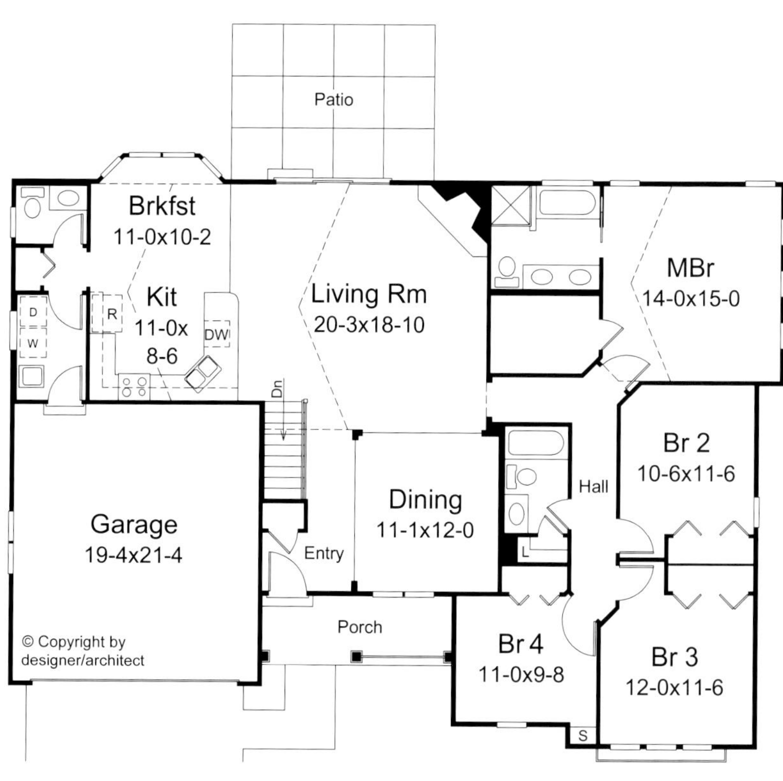

To order plans, visit the Menards Building Materials Desk
or visit www.Menards.com.

SMARTLY DESIGNED FOUR BEDROOM RANCH

1,912 total square feet of living area

Width: 61'-0" Depth: 45'-8"

4 bedrooms, 2 1/2 baths

2-car garage

Basement foundation

SPECIAL FEATURES

The living room, with fireplace and 9' glass sliding doors to a rear patio, is open to the kitchen and bayed breakfast area, all with dramatic vaulted ceilings

Adjacent to the kitchen is a convenient laundry room, coat closet, and half bath

The master bedroom offers a vaulted ceiling, showcase windows, a walk-in closet and a bath with a separate shower

PRICE CODE C

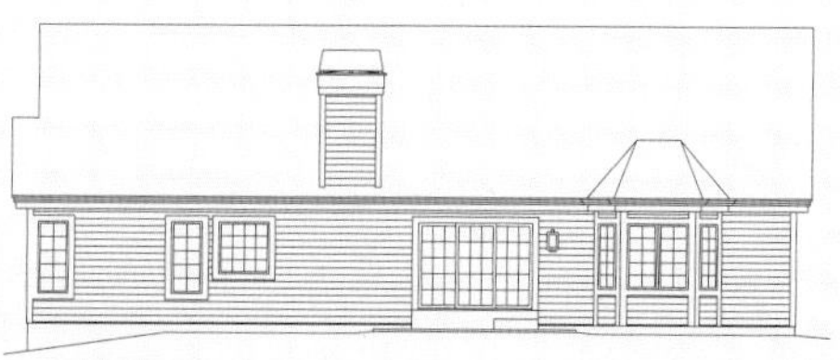

Rear View

HILLSBOROUGH PLACE

MENARDS®

Plan #M08-007D-0178

AFFORDABLE FOUR BEDROOM RANCH

1,203 total square feet of living area

Width: 42'-0" Depth: 48'-8"

4 bedrooms, 2 1/2 baths

2-car garage

Basement foundation, drawings also include slab and crawl space foundations

SPECIAL FEATURES

The vaulted living room has a a fireplace, and a dining area with patio views

The kitchen has an abundance of cabinet storage, a walk-in pantry, and access to the rear yard

The vaulted master bedroom has a private bath with linen storage and a walk-in closet

PRICE CODE A

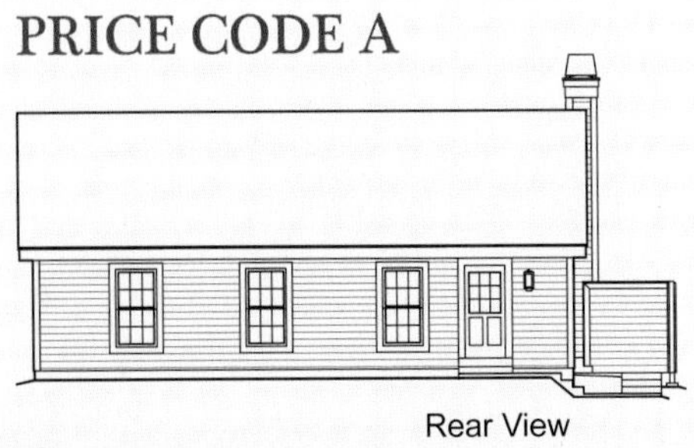

Rear View

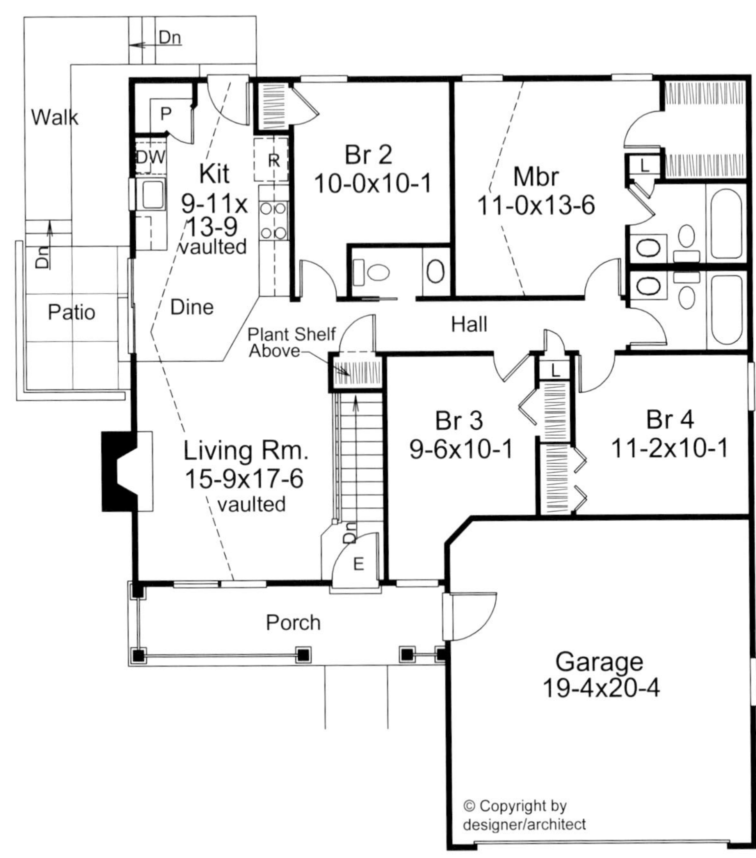

To order plans, visit the Menards Building Materials Desk or visit www.Menards.com.

MENARDS

FOXTON FARM

Plan #M08-008D-0027

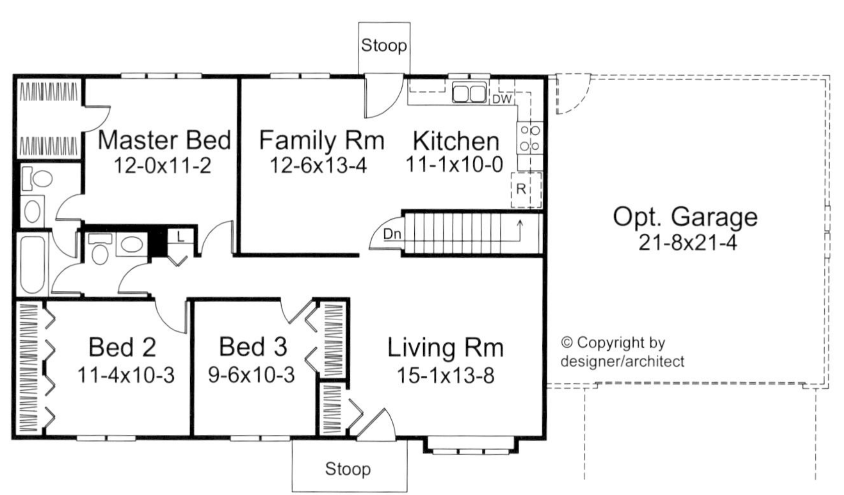

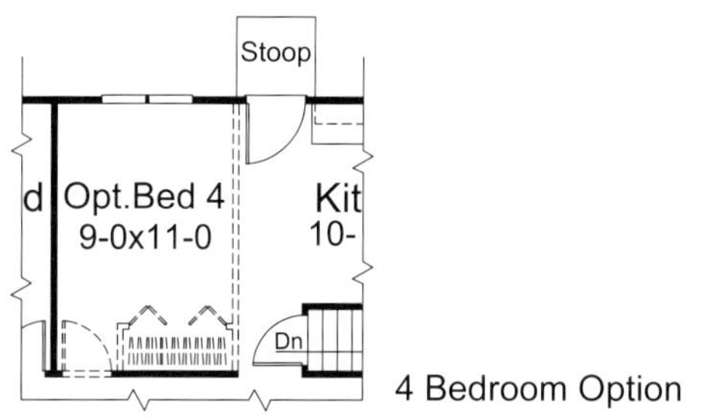

4 Bedroom Option

ENERGY EFFICIENT RANCH

1,176 total square feet of living area

Width: 42'-0" Depth: 29'-0"

3 bedrooms, 1 1/2 baths

Optional 2-car garage

Basement foundation, drawings also include crawl space and slab foundations

SPECIAL FEATURES

The living room features an entry area with a large coat closet and a box-bay window

The kitchen has an eating area and adjoins a very spacious family area

The master bedroom has a huge walk-in closet and shares a compartmented bath with two secondary bedrooms

PRICE CODE AA

To order plans, visit the Menards Building Materials Desk or visit www.Menards.com.

EMILIA

MENARDS®

Plan #M08-121D-0006

EXTERIOR ACCENTS CREATE TIMELESS CURB APPEAL

2,241 total square feet of living area

Width: 68'-4" Depth: 56'-0"

4 bedrooms, 2 1/2 baths

2-car side entry garage

Basement foundation

SPECIAL FEATURES

11' ceilings in the entry, the great room, the kitchen and dining room add spaciousness

Joining the kitchen and great room is a see-through fireplace with built-in shelving

The kitchen has plenty of dining space

2" x 6" exterior wall framing available for an additional fee, please specify when ordering

PRICE CODE C

Rear View

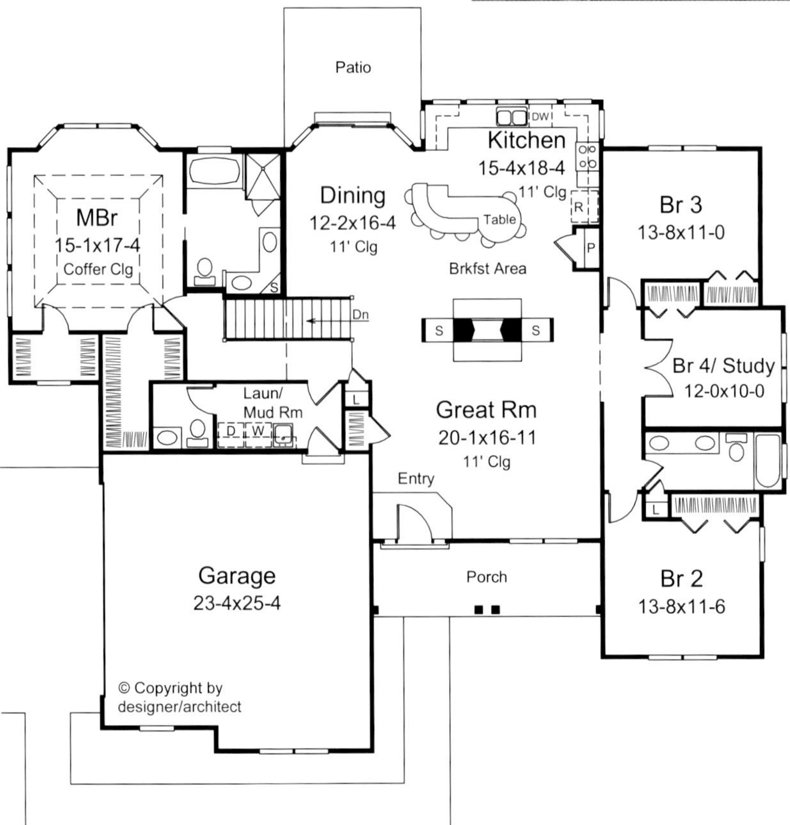

To order plans, visit the Menards Building Materials Desk or visit www.Menards.com.

MENARDS®

SYDNEY

Plan #M08-121D-0025

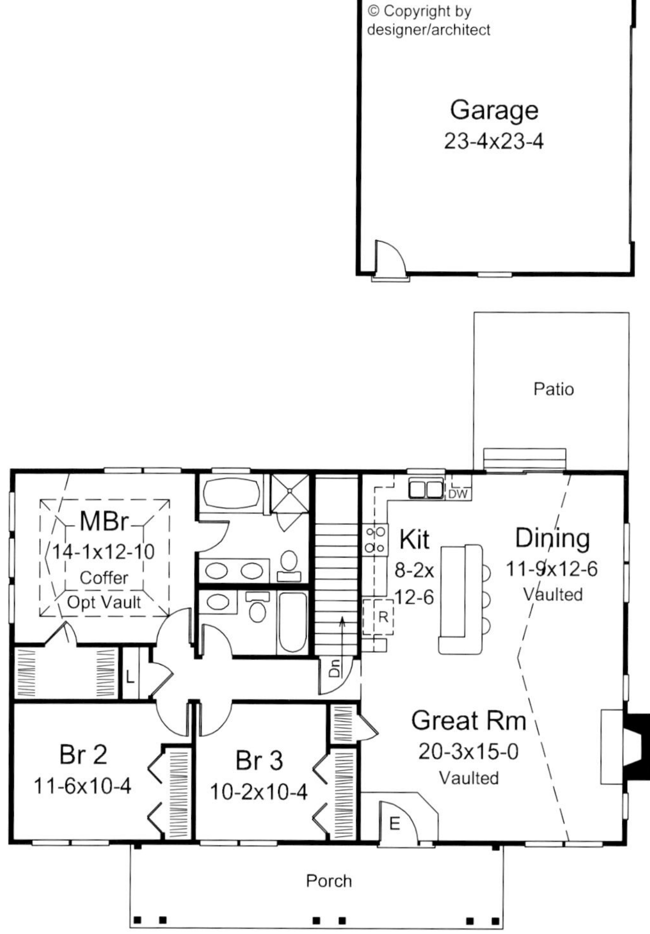

To order plans, visit the Menards Building Materials Desk
or visit www.Menards.com.

BEAUTIFUL COUNTRY RANCH HOME

1,368 total square feet of living area

Width: 50'-0" Depth: 34'-6"

3 bedrooms, 2 baths

2-car detached garage

Basement foundation

SPECIAL FEATURES

The vaulted great room and dining area boast a fireplace and sliding door access to the rear patio

The efficiently designed kitchen enjoys an island with a breakfast bar perfect for casual meals

Multiple windows brighten the master bedroom that has a walk-in closet and a private bath

PRICE CODE AA

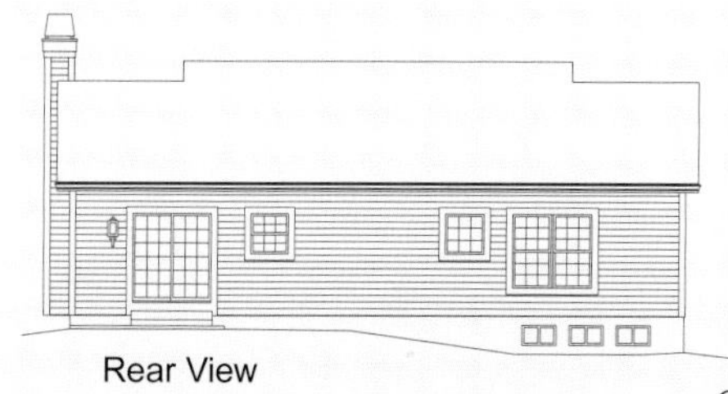

Rear View

SHILOH VALLEY

Plan #M08-007D-0168

LUXURY LIVING IN A COUNTRY HOME

1,814 total square feet of living area

Width: 89'-10" Depth: 40'-2"

3 bedrooms, 2 baths

3-car side entry garage

Basement foundation

SPECIAL FEATURES

This home enjoys a large country porch for a perfect leisurely living area

The vaulted great room, sunny breakfast area and kitchen with snack bar are all open to one another creating a sense of spaciousness

A lavish bath is the highlight of the master bedroom suite and features double vanities with a makeup counter, a 5' x 5' shower with seat, a separate toilet, and a step-up whirlpool-in-a-sunroom

PRICE CODE C

Rear View

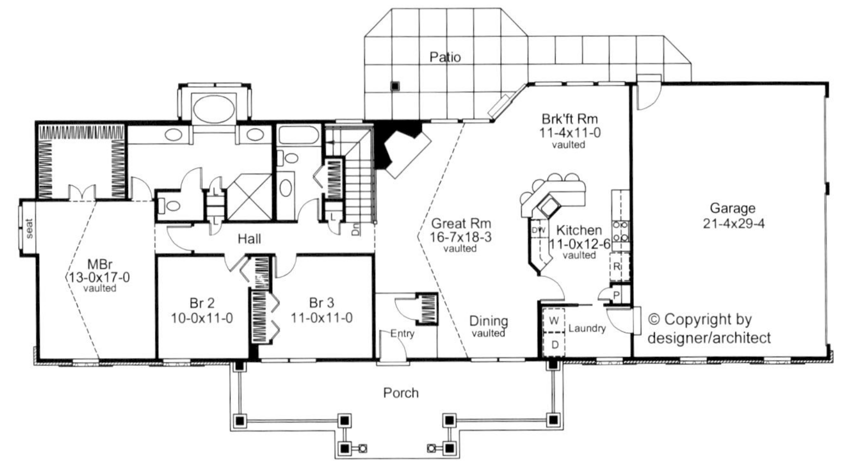

To order plans, visit the Menards Building Materials Desk or visit www.Menards.com.

MENARDS®

REBECCA

Plan #M08-121D-0015

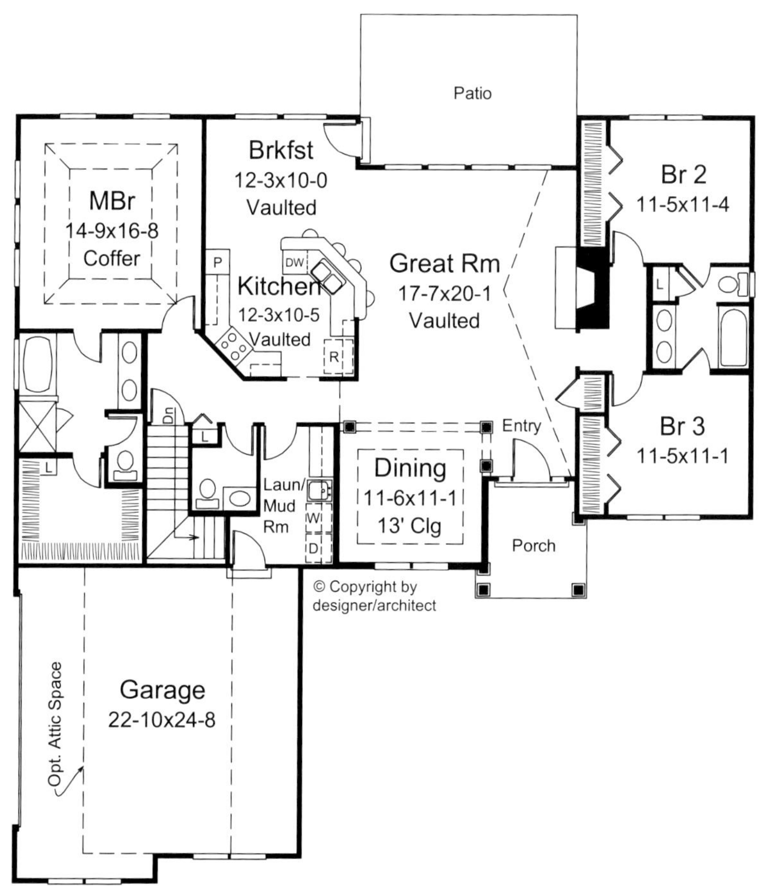

WELCOMING COVERED FRONT PORCH

1,983 total square feet of living area

Width: 60'-0" Depth: 61'-0"

3 bedrooms, 2 1/2 baths

2-car side entry garage

Basement foundation

SPECIAL FEATURES

The vaulted great room offers a fireplace and a wall of windows for an open feel

The master bath has a separate toliet room, a double-bowl vanity, and a large walk-in closet

Bedrooms #2 and #3 share a bath and each have a spacious closet

The optional attic space above the garage has an additional 273 square feet of living area

PRICE CODE B

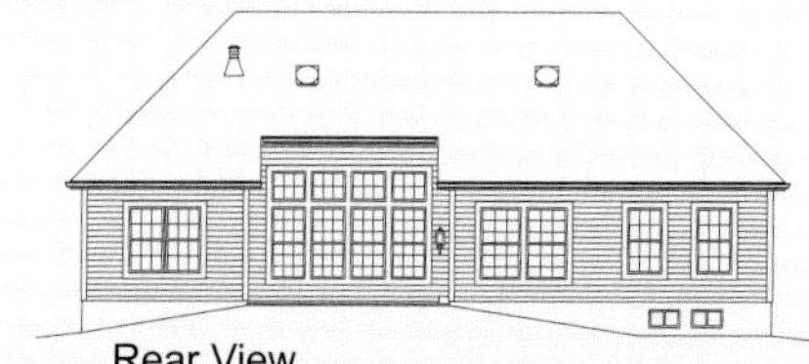

To order plans, visit the Menards Building Materials Desk or visit www.Menards.com.

PRAIRIE LAKE

Plan #M08-007D-0248

IDEAL LAKE HOME

1,763 total square feet of living area

Width: 60'-4"   Depth: 51'-8"

3 bedrooms, 2 1/2 baths

2-car side entry garage

Slab foundation, drawings also include crawl space and basement foundations

SPECIAL FEATURES

The entry with glass double doors and a 10' volume ceiling has a coat closet

A fireplace and 9' glass sliding doors to the patio make the huge great room inviting

The L-shaped kitchen has a snack bar, a desk, a cabinet pantry, and adjacent breakfast and laundry rooms plus a half bath

Double-entry doors, a luxury bath, a large walk-in closet and a glass door to a second private patio are all amenities of the master bedroom

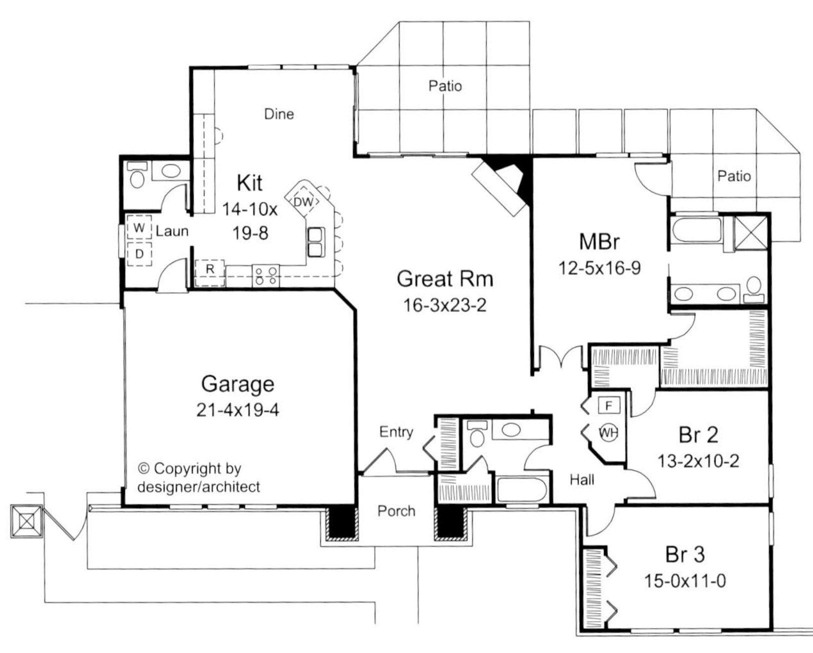

PRICE CODE C

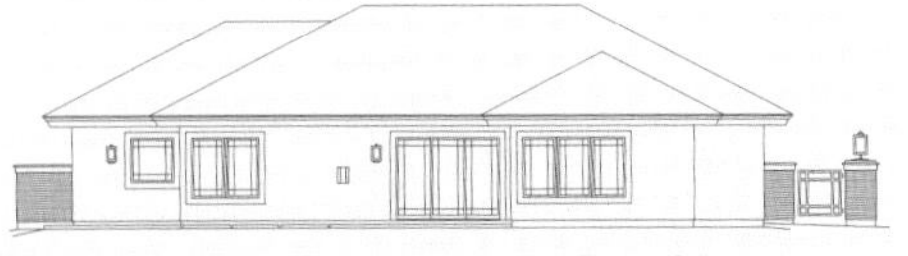

Rear View

To order plans, visit the Menards Building Materials Desk or visit www.Menards.com.

TRIPLE DORMERS CREATE TERRIFIC CURB APPEAL

1,992 total square feet of living area

Width: 66'-2" Depth: 62'-0"

4 bedrooms, 3 baths

2-car side entry garage

Basement, crawl space or slab foundation, please specify when ordering

SPECIAL FEATURES

Interesting angled walls add drama to many of the living areas including the family room, master bedroom and the breakfast area

The rear covered porch includes a spa and an outdoor kitchen with sink, refrigerator and cooktop

Enter the majestic master bath to find a dramatic oversized corner tub

The bonus room above the garage has an additional 299 square feet of living area

PRICE CODE C

BONUS ROOM 10'-7" x 22'-6"
GARAGE 22'-0" x 22'-6"
DECK 24'-8" x 15'-5"
COVERED PORCH 24'-10" x 12'-0"
SINK
REFRIG.
COOKTOP
6' SPA
HIS
MECH.
OPTIONAL STAIRS TO BASEMENT
TV NICHE ABOVE VENTLESS GAS FIREPLACE
SHOWER
SEAT
LIN
TRAY CEILING UP 1' UP 1'
SITTING
CLERESTORY WINDOW ABOVE
BREAKFAST 8'-6" x 11'-0"
HERS
MASTER BEDROOM 19'-0" x 15'-0"
19'-9" HIGH CEILING
DW
KITCHEN 17'-3" x 12'-6"
FAMILY ROOM 16'-0" x 21'-10"
PANT.
OPTIONAL OPENING FOR LIVING
LINE OF 9' HIGH CEILING
BEDROOM 2 11'-0" x 14'-0"
LIVING / BEDROOM 3 11'-0" x 12'-0"
OPEN TO DORMER ABOVE
DINING 13'-8" x 12'-0"
MEDIA / GUEST ROOM 13'-8" x 11'-0"
PORCH 33'-4" x 6'-0"

To order plans, visit the Menards Building Materials Desk or visit www.Menards.com.

CLAYTON MANOR

Plan #M08-007D-0078

RAMBLING RANCH WITH COUNTRY CHARM

2,514 total square feet of living area

Width: 86'-0" Depth: 60'-4"

3 bedrooms, 2 baths

3-car side entry garage with workshop/storage area

Walk-out basement foundation

SPECIAL FEATURES

An expansive porch welcomes you into the foyer, the dining area with bay, and the gallery-sized hall

The U-shaped kitchen is open to a bayed breakfast area, study and family room

The family will enjoy the vaulted sunroom

1,509 square feet of optional living area on the lower level with recreation room, bedroom #4 with bath, and an office

PRICE CODE D

Rear View

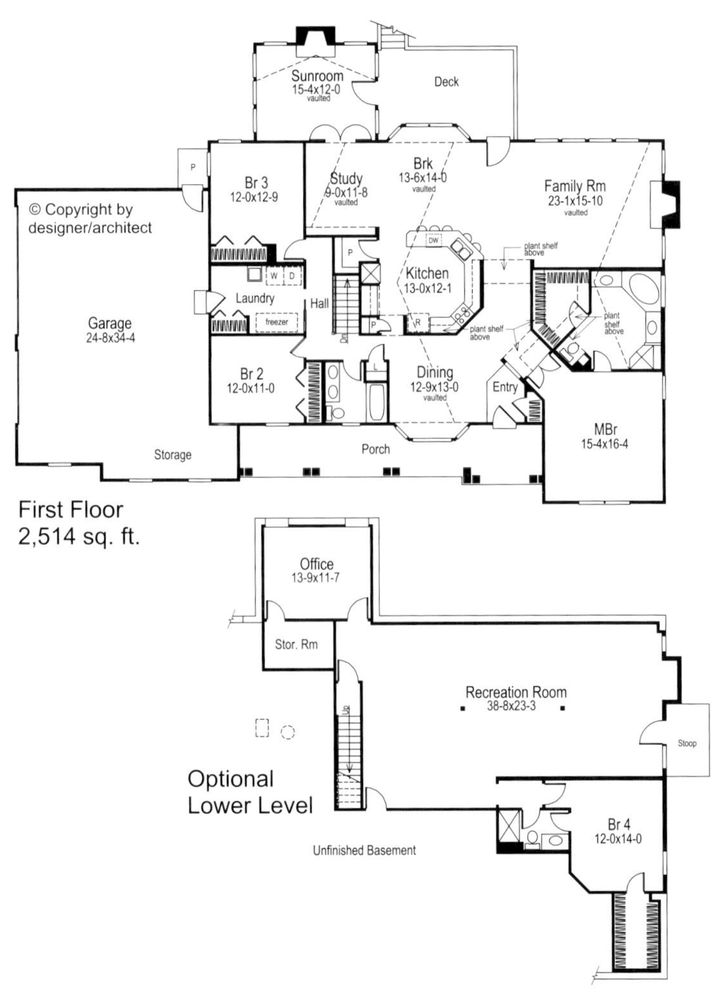

First Floor
2,514 sq. ft.

Optional
Lower Level

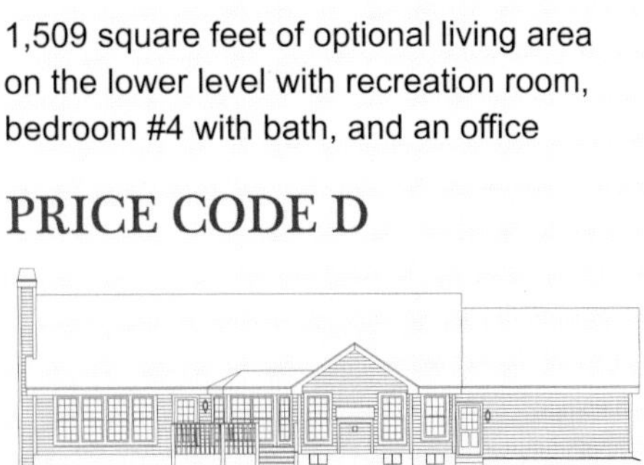

To order plans, visit the Menards Building Materials Desk or visit www.Menards.com.

LILLIAN

Plan #M08-121D-0018

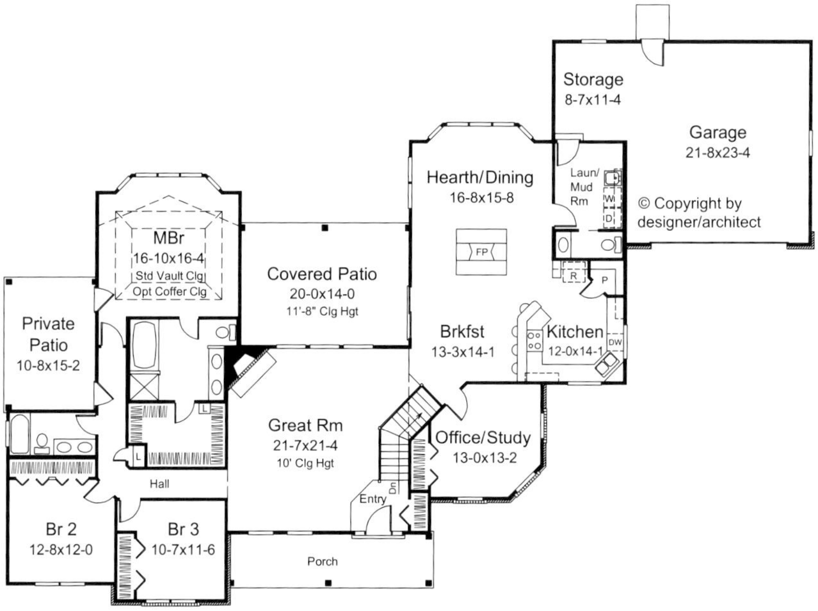

Storage 8-7x11-4
Garage 21-8x23-4
Hearth/Dining 16-8x15-8
Laun/ Mud Rm
© Copyright by designer/architect
MBr 16-10x16-4 Std Vault Clg Opt Coffer Clg
Covered Patio 20-0x14-0 11'-8" Clg Hgt
Private Patio 10-8x15-2
Brkfst 13-3x14-1
Kitchen 12-0x14-1
Great Rm 21-7x21-4 10' Clg Hgt
Office/Study 13-0x13-2
Hall
Entry
Br 2 12-8x12-0
Br 3 10-7x11-6
Porch

EXQUISITE RANCH HOME

2,487 total square feet of living area

Width: 96'-6" Depth: 66'-0"

3 bedrooms, 2 1/2 baths

2-car garage

Basement foundation

SPECIAL FEATURES

A see-through fireplace warms the hearth/dining room, kitchen and breakfast area

The rear covered patio and private covered patio are perfect for enjoying the outdoors and can be enjoyed in any kind of weather

The garage boasts storage space and access to a convenient laundry/mud room

PRICE CODE C

Rear View

To order plans, visit the Menards Building Materials Desk or visit www.Menards.com.

DELMONT

MENARDS®

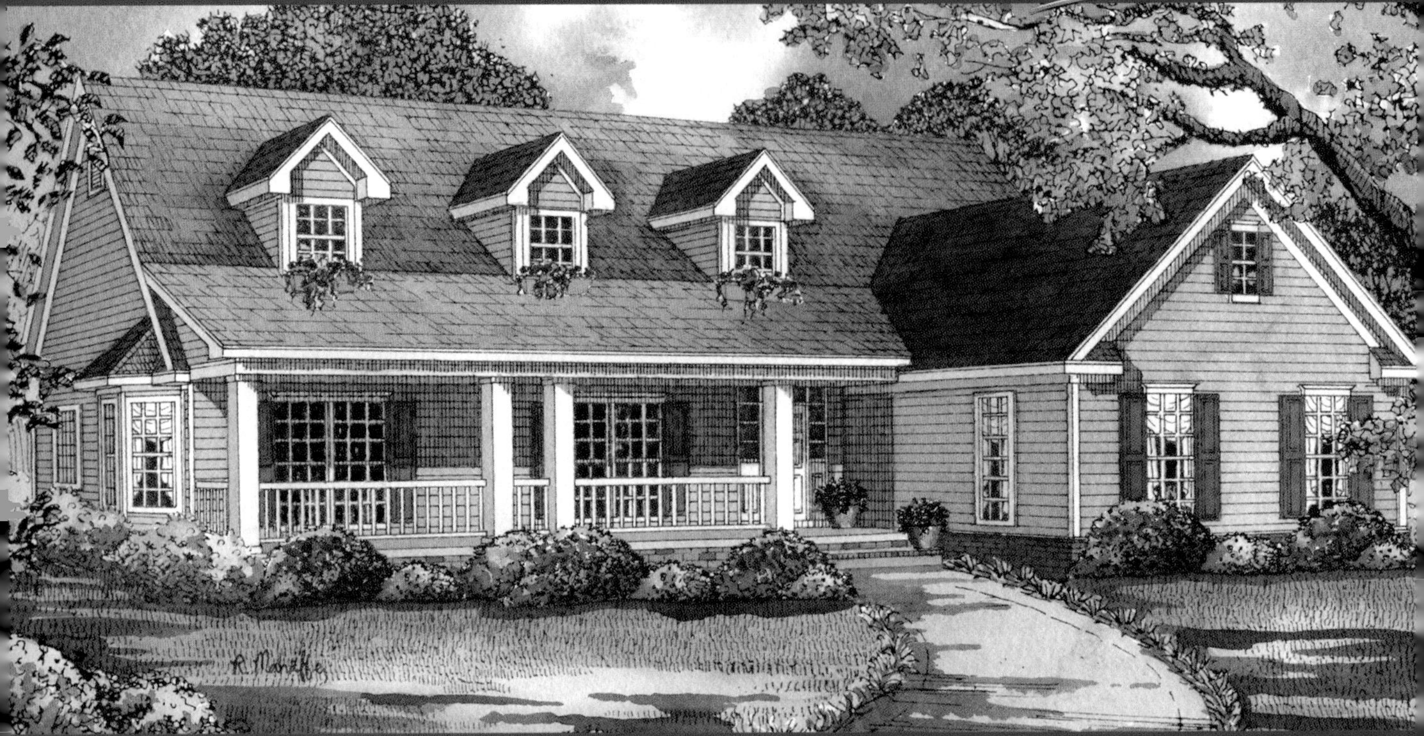

Plan #M08-055L-0193

RELAXING OUTDOOR AREAS

2,131 total square feet of living area

Width: 63'-10" Depth: 72'-2"

3 bedrooms, 2 1/2 baths

2-car side entry garage

Slab or crawl space foundation, please specify when ordering

SPECIAL FEATURES

The kitchen, great room and dining room create an expansive living area

Bedroom #2 features a charming bay window with a built-in seat

The garage includes space for a safe storm shelter

PRICE CODE D

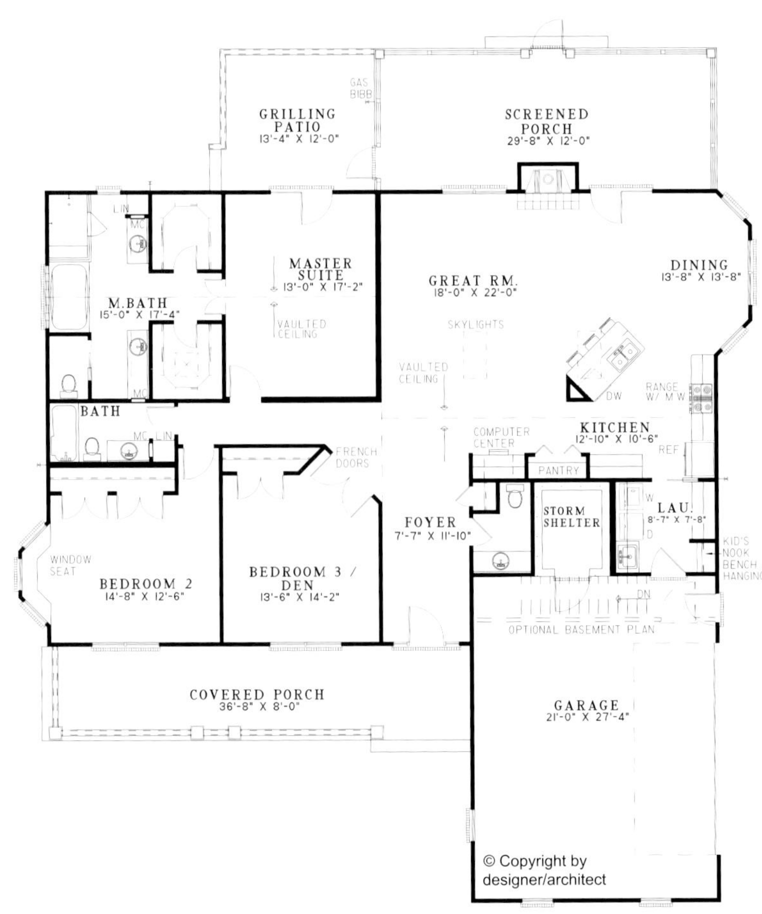

MENARDS®

WHEELERSCREST

Plan #M08-077L-0067

GRACEFUL WINDOWS

2,251 total square feet of living area

Width: 73'-8"   Depth: 58'-4"

3 bedrooms, 2 1/2 baths

3-car side entry garage

Basement, crawl space or slab foundation, please specify when ordering

SPECIAL FEATURES

The highly functional kitchen has ample counterspace, a corner pantry, and a raised breakfast bar

The breakfast room overlooks both of the rear porches

The second floor bonus room features an additional 501 square feet of living space with the option of a bath

PRICE CODE F

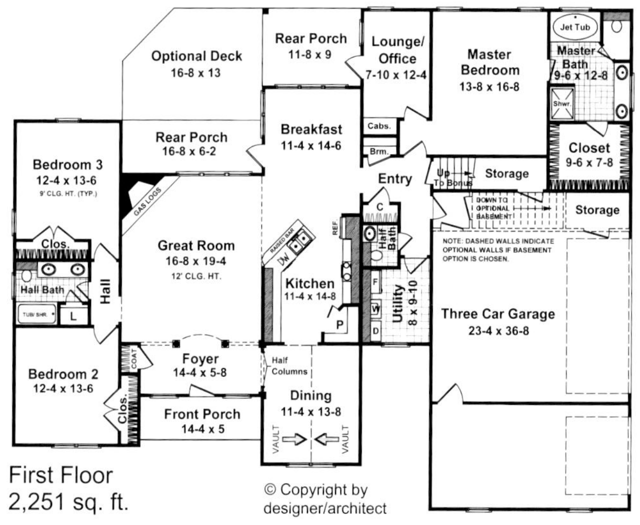

First Floor
2,251 sq. ft.

© Copyright by designer/architect

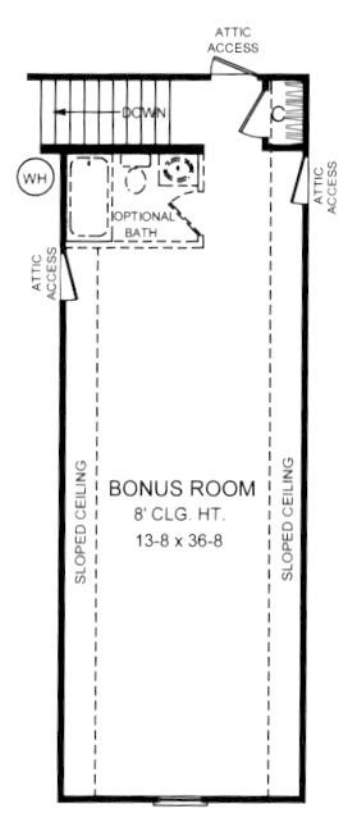

Optional
Second Floor

To order plans, visit the Menards Building Materials Desk or visit www.Menards.com.

DURAND

MENARDS®

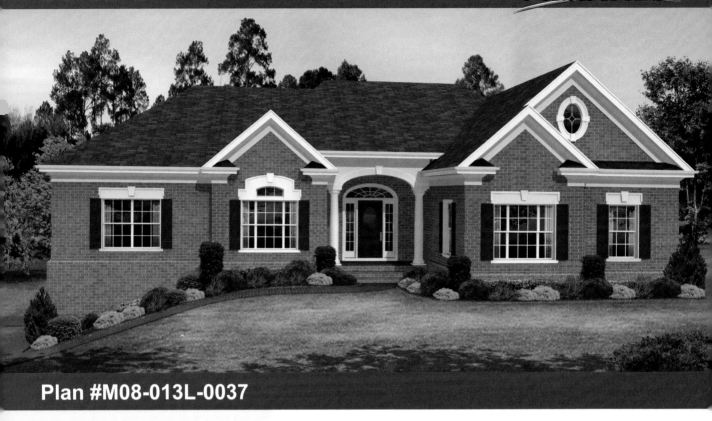

Plan #M08-013L-0037

GRAND ARCHED ENTRY

2,564 total square feet of living area

Width: 72'-0" Depth: 66'-0"

3 bedrooms, 2 1/2 baths

2-car side entry garage

Basement, crawl space or slab foundation, please specify when ordering

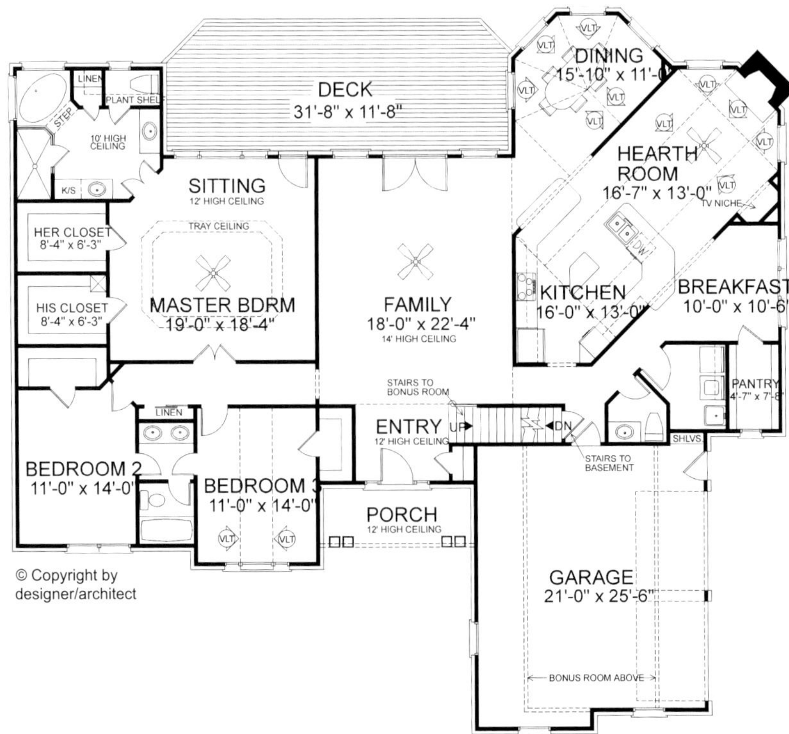

SPECIAL FEATURES

The hearth room is surrounded by the kitchen, dining and breakfast rooms making it the focal point of those living areas

Escape to the master bedroom featuring a luxurious private bath and a sitting area leading to the deck outdoors

The secondary bedrooms share a Jack and Jill bath and both have walk-in closets

The bonus room above the garage has an additional 302 square feet of living area

PRICE CODE E

To order plans, visit the Menards Building Materials Desk or visit www.Menards.com.

REGINA

Plan #M08-065L-0040

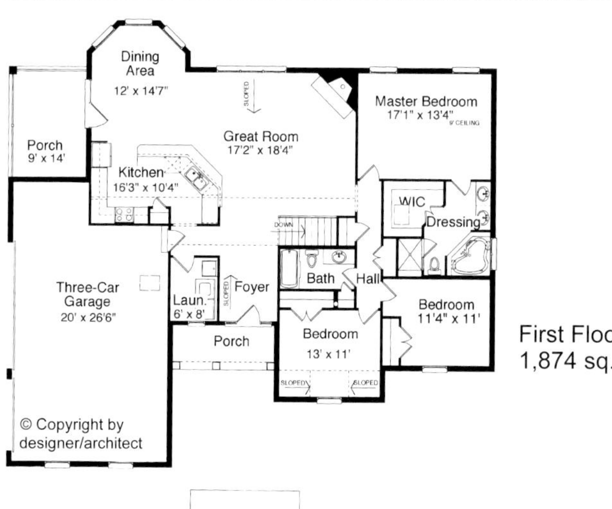

First Floor
1,874 sq. ft.

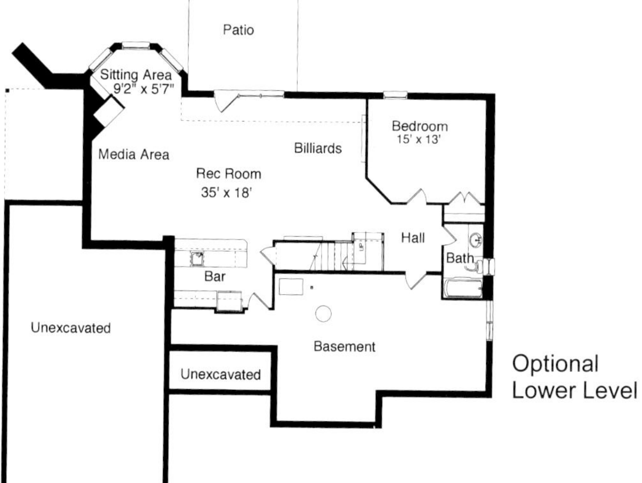

Optional
Lower Level

WARM AND INVITING RANCH

1,874 total square feet of living area

Width: 62'-8" Depth: 56'-7"

3 bedrooms, 2 baths

3-car side entry garage

Walk-out basement foundation

SPECIAL FEATURES

The bayed dining area, kitchen and great room with a fireplace combine for an open living area

The private master bath pampers with a corner whirlpool tub, double vanity and walk-in closet

9' ceilings throughout this home add to the overall spaciousness

An optional lower level has an additional 1,175 square feet of living area

PRICE CODE C

To order plans, visit the Menards Building Materials Desk or visit www.Menards.com.

BROOKMONT

MENARDS®

Plan #M08-007D-0067

SMALL RANCH FOR A PERFECT COUNTRY HAVEN

1,761 total square feet of living area

Width: 57'-0" Depth: 52'-2"

4 bedrooms, 2 baths

2-car side entry garage

Basement foundation

SPECIAL FEATURES

Exterior window dressings, roof dormers and planter boxes add warmth and charm

The vaulted great room, that opens to a pass-through kitchen, boasts a fireplace

The vaulted master bedroom includes a luxury bath and walk-in closet

Home features an abundance of storage

PRICE CODE B

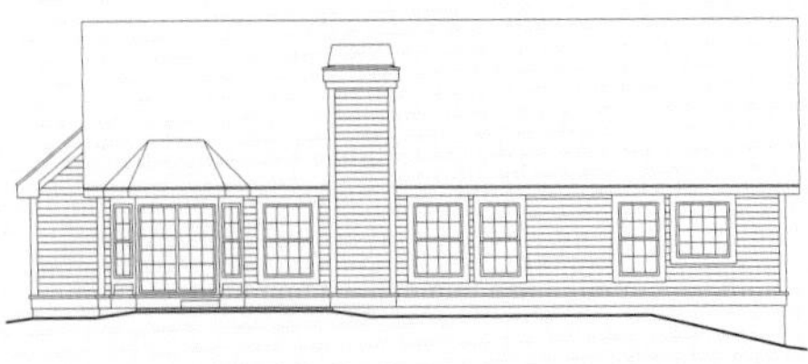

Rear View

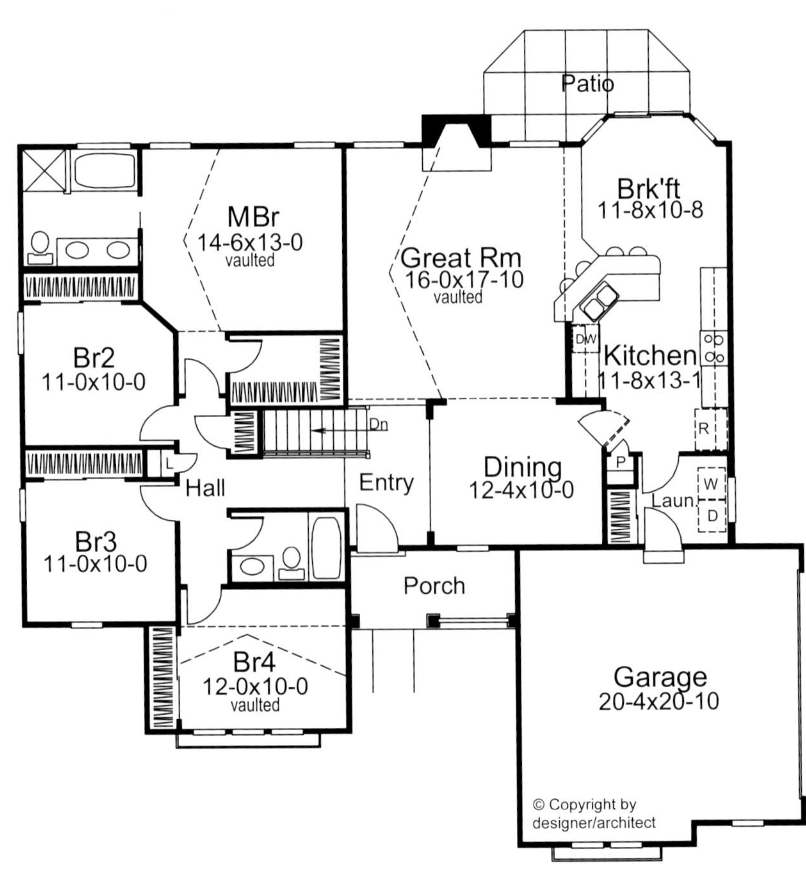

To order plans, visit the Menards Building Materials Desk or visit www.Menards.com.

NOTTINGHAM HILL

Plan #M08-007D-0215

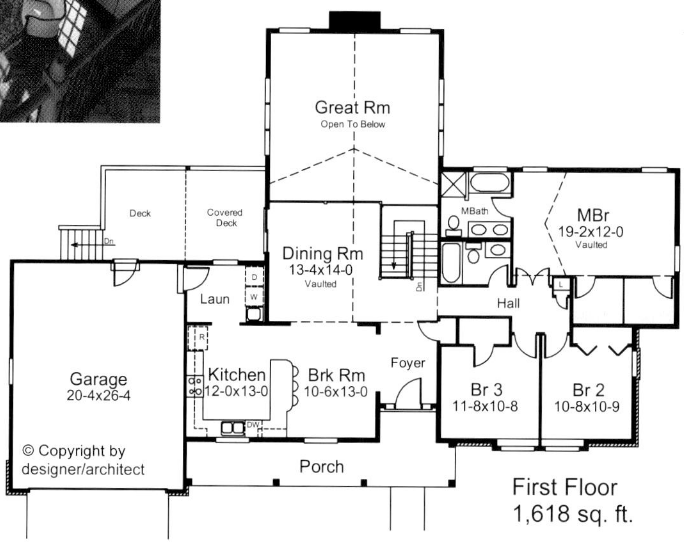

CLASSIC TUDOR HOME

2,541 total square feet of living area

Width: 79'-8" Depth: 56'-4"

3 bedrooms, 3 baths

2-car garage

Walk-out basement foundation

SPECIAL FEATURES

The exterior is complimented by Old English details including stucco, stone, wood trim, and decorative lightning rods

The porch leads into the foyer and the large vaulted living areas featuring a handcrafted staircase

The lower level great room has a two-story vaulted ceiling, a stone fireplace, a game room, its own kitchen and bar, and 9' wide glass doors to the patio

PRICE CODE C

Great Rm Open To Below
Deck
Covered Deck
Dining Rm 13-4x14-0 Vaulted
MBath
MBr 19-2x12-0 Vaulted
Laun
Hall
Garage 20-4x26-4
Kitchen 12-0x13-0
Brk Rm 10-6x13-0
Foyer
Br 3 11-8x10-8
Br 2 10-8x10-9
© Copyright by designer/architect
Porch

First Floor
1,618 sq. ft.

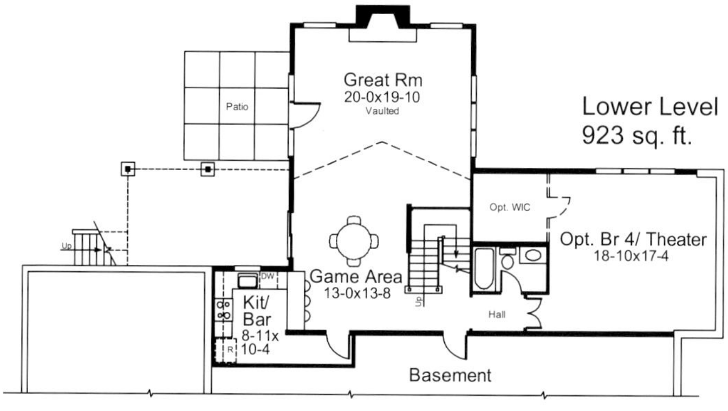

Patio
Great Rm 20-0x19-10 Vaulted
Lower Level
923 sq. ft.
Opt. WIC
Opt. Br 4/ Theater 18-10x17-4
Game Area 13-0x13-8
Kit/ Bar 8-11x 10-4
Hall
Basement

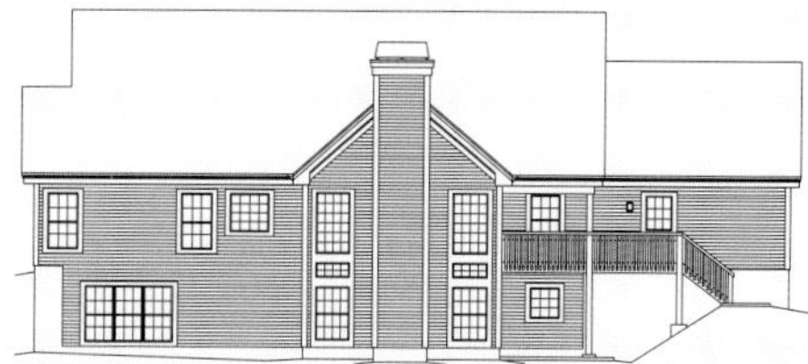
Rear View

To order plans, visit the Menards Building Materials Desk or visit www.Menards.com.

SOUTHFIELD

MENARDS®

Plan #M08-058D-0021

GRACIOUSLY DESIGNED TRADITIONAL RANCH

1,477 total square feet of living area

Width: 66'-8" Depth: 41'-4"

3 bedrooms, 2 baths

2-car side entry garage

Basement foundation

SPECIAL FEATURES

Oversized porch provides protection from the elements

Innovative kitchen employs step-saving design

The kitchen has a snack bar that opens to the breakfast area with bay window

2" x 6" exterior wall framing available for an additional fee, please specify when ordering

PRICE CODE A

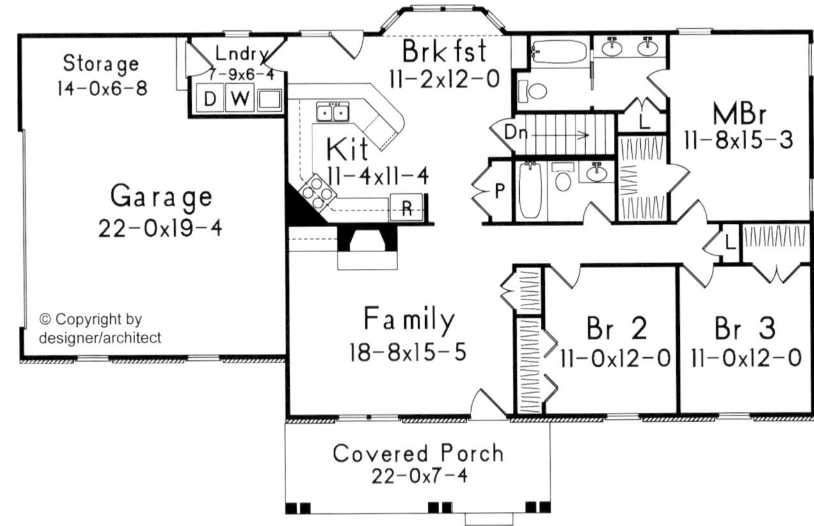

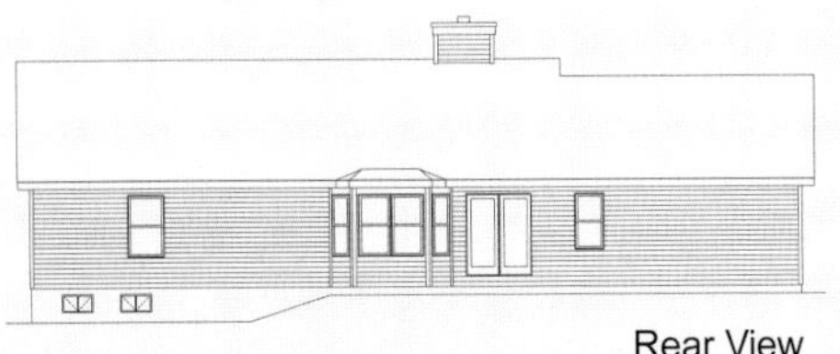

Rear View

To order plans, visit the Menards Building Materials Desk or visit www.Menards.com.

MENARDS®

CHLOE

Plan #M08-121D-0007

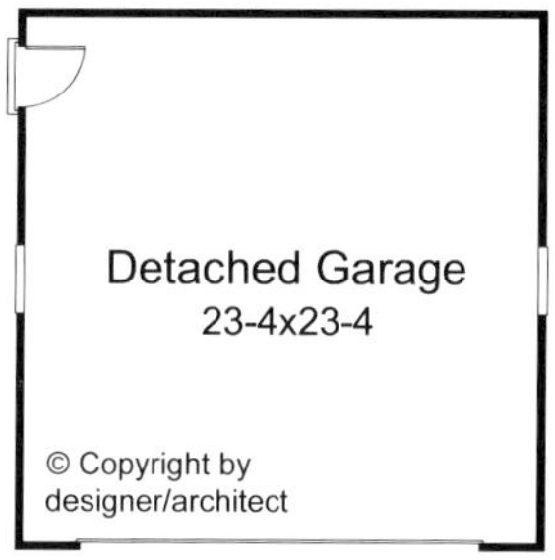

Detached Garage
23-4x23-4

© Copyright by designer/architect

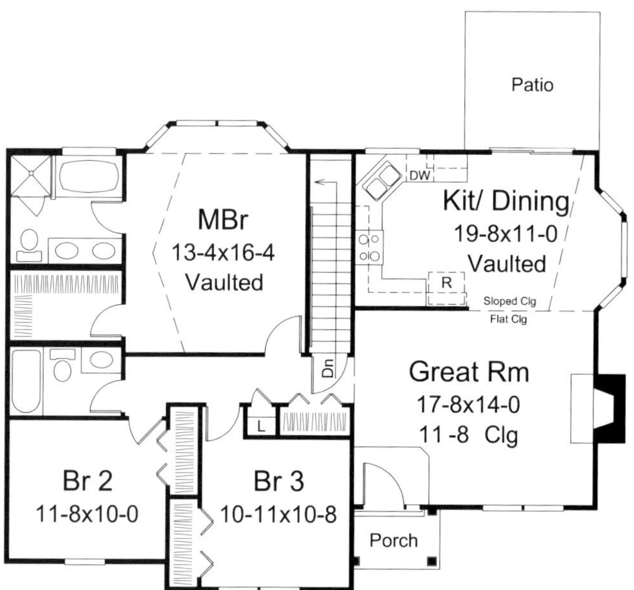

SPACIOUS GREAT ROOM

1,308 total square feet of living area

Width: 46'-0" Depth: 34'-0"

3 bedrooms, 2 baths

2-car detached garage

Basement foundation

SPECIAL FEATURES

A lovely bay window and access to the rear patio are some of the features of the vaulted kitchen/dining area

A tall ceiling and warming fireplace in the great room appeal to every homeowner

The vaulted master bedroom showcases a large walk-in closet, a bay window, and a private bath

PRICE CODE AA

To order plans, visit the Menards Building Materials Desk or visit www.Menards.com.

Plan #M08-068D-0009

INVITING GABLED ENTRY

2,128 total square feet of living area

Width: 56'-0" Depth: 61'-0"

4 bedrooms, 2 baths

2-car garage

Slab foundation, drawings also include crawl space foundation

SPECIAL FEATURES

The kitchen has plenty of entertaining area with a large dining area and counter seating

The luxurious master bedroom has a double-door entry and private bath with a whirlpool tub, double sinks and large walk-in closet

The secondary bedrooms include spacious closets

The coat closet in front entry is a nice added feature

PRICE CODE C

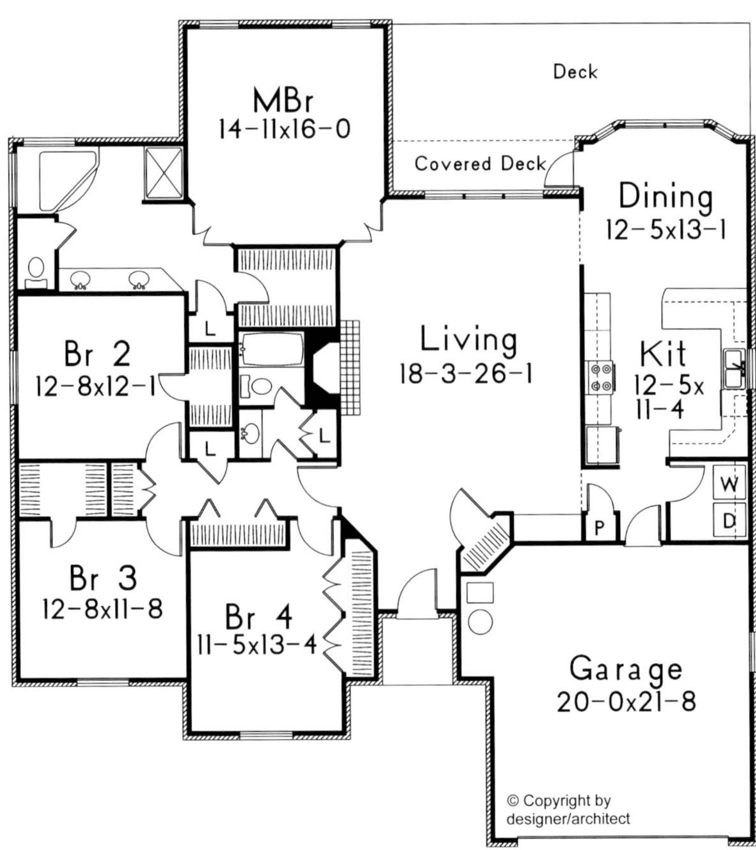

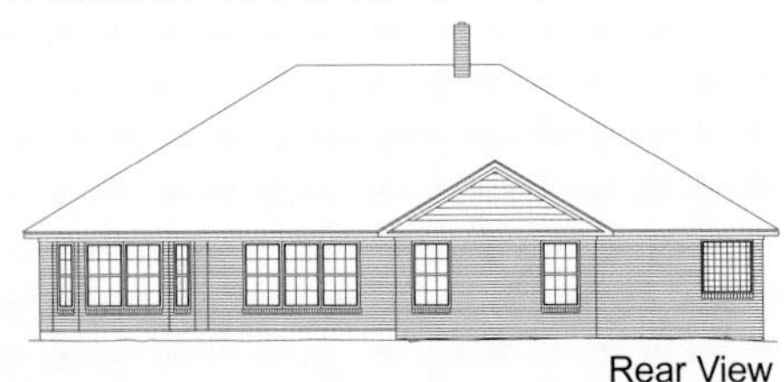

Rear View

To order plans, visit the Menards Building Materials Desk or visit www.Menards.com.

MENARDS®

KENORA PARK

Plan #M08-055L-0214

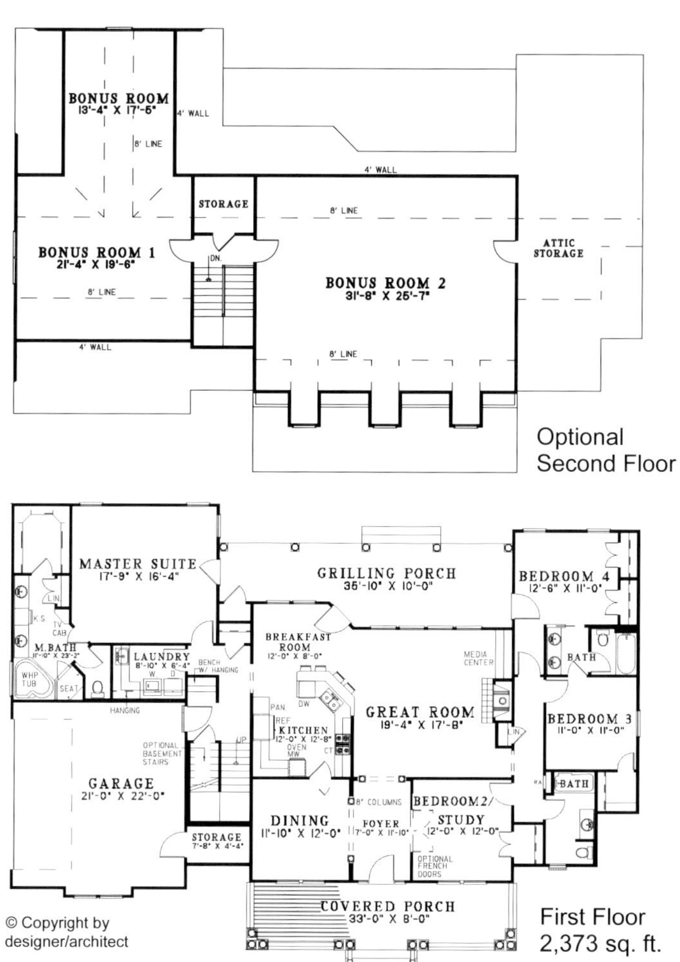

Optional Second Floor

First Floor 2,373 sq. ft.

PORCH AND DORMERS DECORATE EXTERIOR

2,373 total square feet of living area

Width: 76'-10"   Depth: 53'-4"

4 bedrooms, 3 baths

2-car side entry garage

Slab or crawl space foundation, please specify when ordering

SPECIAL FEATURES

The grilling porch extends dining opportunities to the outdoors

The fireplace in the great room also warms the adjoining kitchen and breakfast room

The relaxing master suite enjoys a deluxe bath with a whirlpool tub and a walk-in closet

The optional second floor has an additional 1,672 square feet of living area

PRICE CODE E

To order plans, visit the Menards Building Materials Desk or visit www.Menards.com.

WHITEFIELD

MENARDS®

Plan #M08-008D-0006

UNIQUE SECTIONING FOR ENTERTAINING

1,593 total square feet of living area

Width: 66'-0"   Depth: 36'-0"

3 bedrooms, 2 baths

2-car garage

Basement foundation, drawings also include crawl space and slab foundations

SPECIAL FEATURES

A welcoming porch invites you into a spacious living room

The kitchen and dining room are open to the family room through wood balustrades

The master bedroom offers a private bath and two closets

The laundry room is located directly off the garage with convenient access to the outdoors

PRICE CODE B

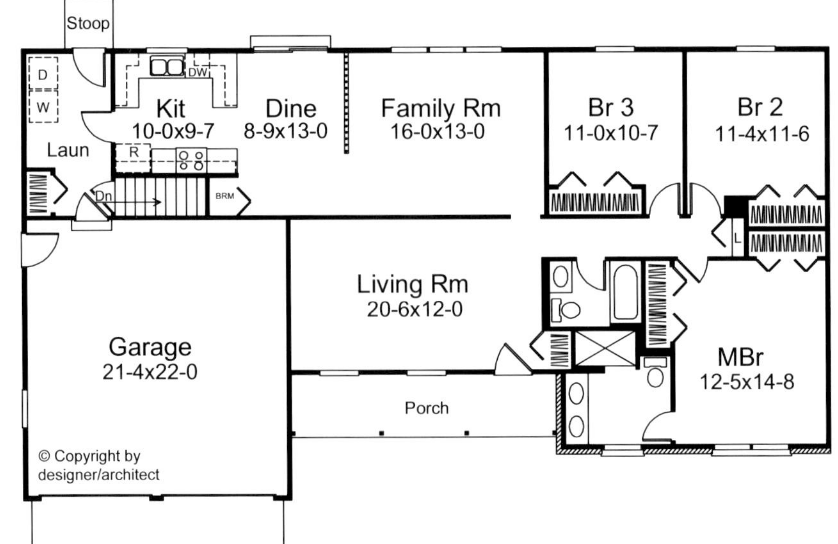

To order plans, visit the Menards Building Materials Desk or visit www.Menards.com.

ASHBRIAR

Plan #M08-007D-0077

CLASSIC ATRIUM RANCH

1,978 total square feet of living area

Width: 76'-8" Depth: 47'-4"

4 bedrooms, 2 1/2 baths

3-car side entry garage

Walk-out basement foundation

SPECIAL FEATURES

Classic Traditional that is always in style

The spacious vaulted great room boasts a dining area, and an atrium with staircase

The lower level has an additional 1,295 square feet of optional living area that consists of a family room, 2 bedrooms, 2 baths and a study

2" x 6" exterior wall framing available for an additional fee, please specify when ordering

PRICE CODE C

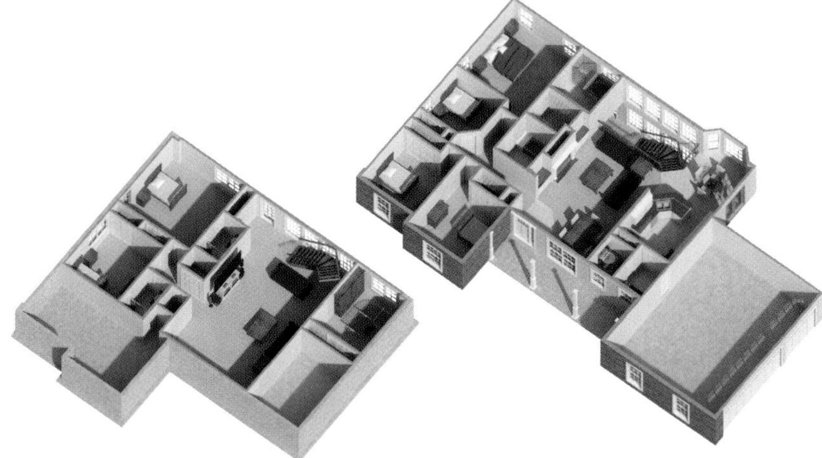

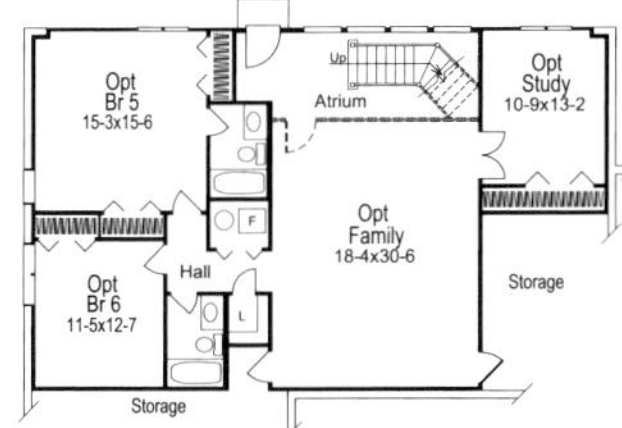

Optional Lower Level

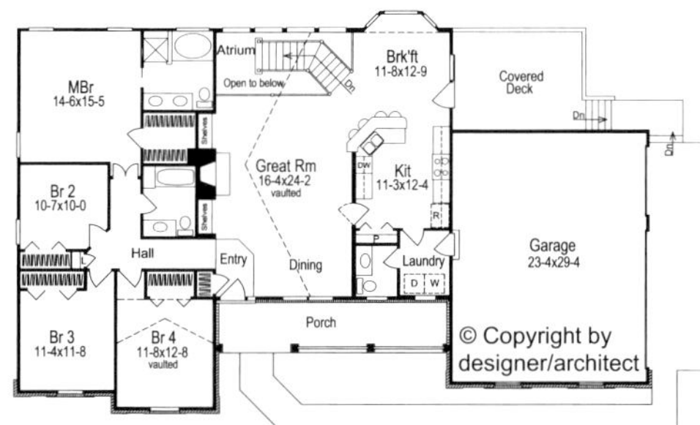

First Floor
1,978 sq. ft.

Rear View

To order plans, visit the Menards Building Materials Desk or visit www.Menards.com.

GRANTVILLE

Plan #M08-058D-0062

PRIVATE BEDROOMS

1,902 total square feet of living area

Width: 71'-0" Depth: 44'-4"

3 bedrooms, 2 1/2 baths

3-car garage

Basement foundation

SPECIAL FEATURES

The wrap-around kitchen counter plus an island provides plenty of counterspace

The foyer opens into the expansive vaulted great room providing an impressive entrance

The laundry area conveniently includes a half bath and a walk-in closet

PRICE CODE C

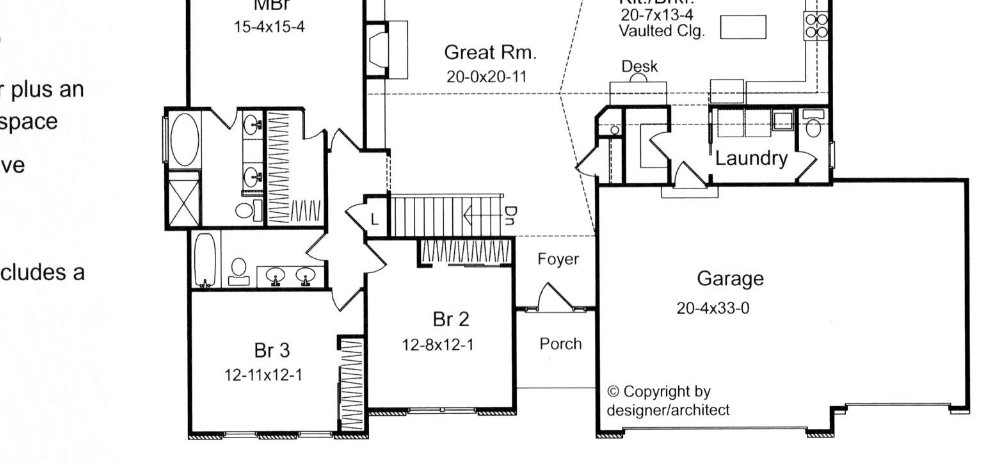

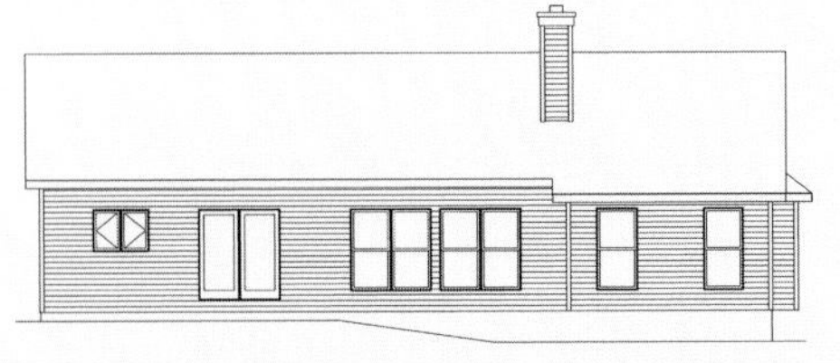

Rear View

To order plans, visit the Menards Building Materials Desk or visit www.Menards.com.

MENARDS®

ANABEL

Plan #M08-121D-0002

DOUBLE DORMERS AND GABLES ADD CURB APPEAL

2,025 total square feet of living area

Width: 70'-4" Depth: 42'-8"

3 bedrooms, 2 1/2 baths

2-car side entry garage

Basement foundation

SPECIAL FEATURES

The great room enjoys a 42" wood burning fireplace, a vaulted ceiling, and 12' wall

The dining room has decorative columns and beams along with a vaulted ceiling

An elegant coffered ceiling tops the private master bedroom

2" x 6" exterior wall framing available for an additional fee, please specify when ordering

PRICE CODE B

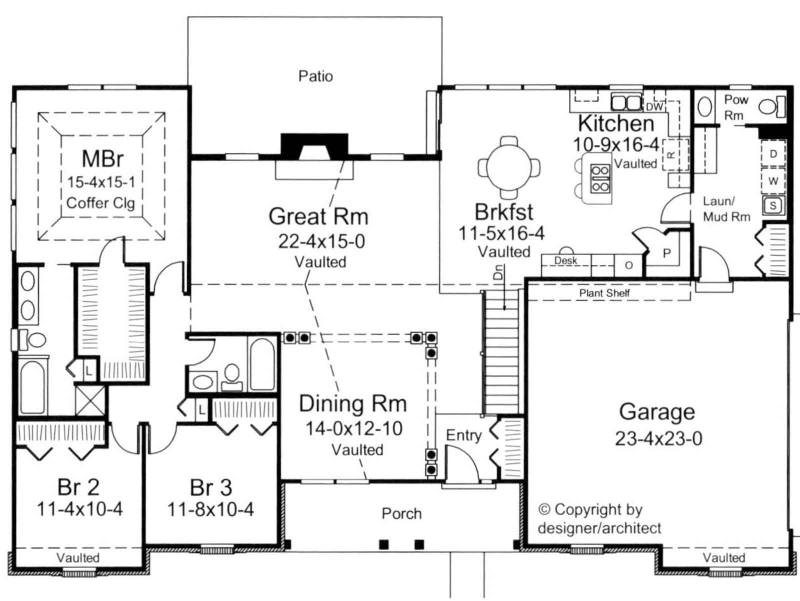

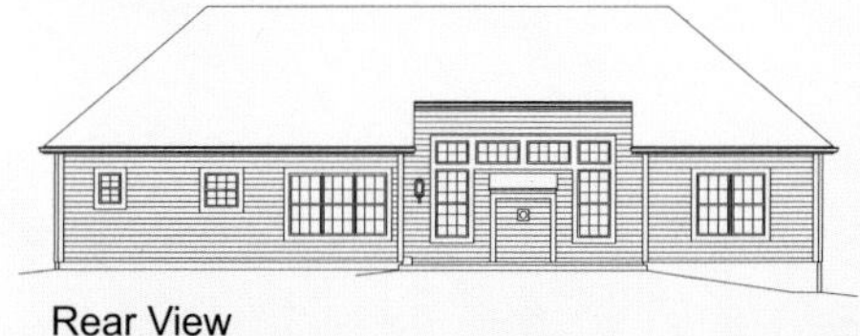

Rear View

To order plans, visit the Menards Building Materials Desk
or visit www.Menards.com.

JEREMY

MENARDS®

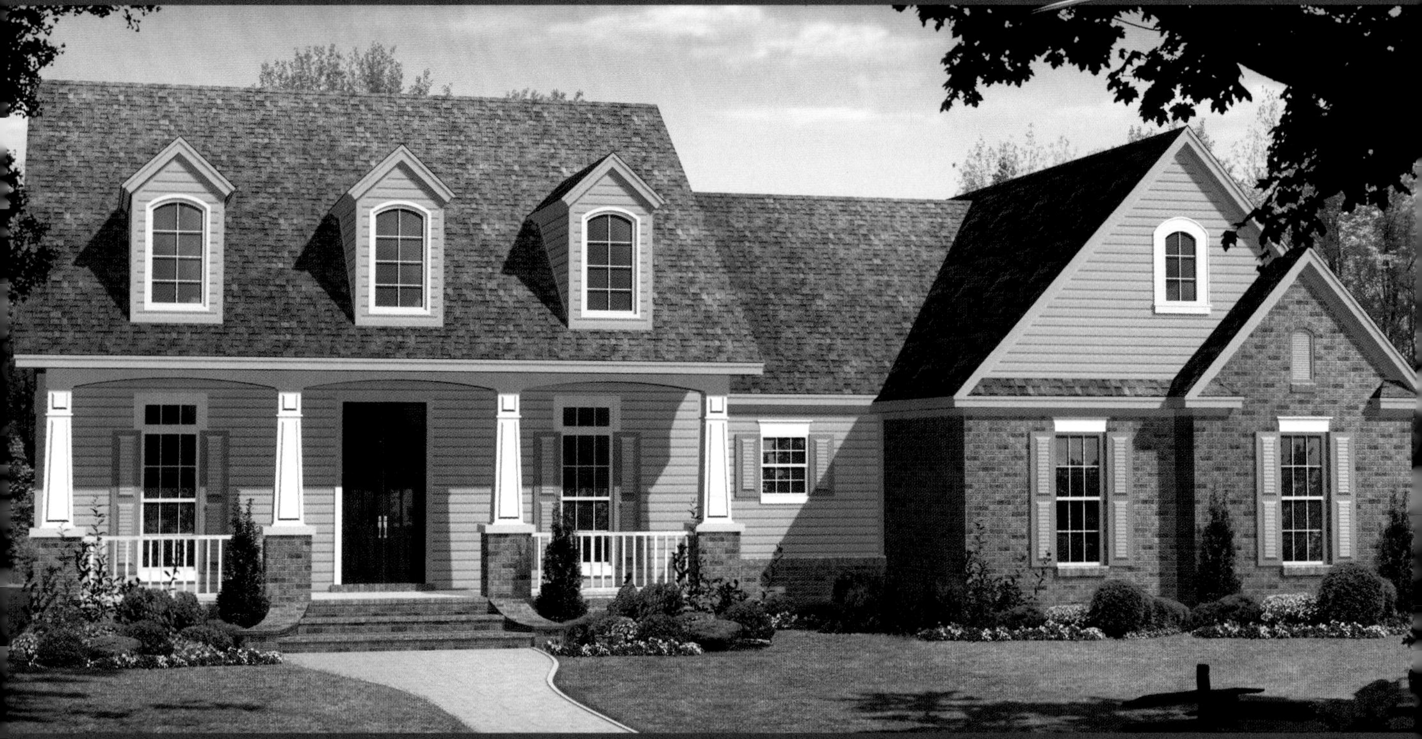

Plan #M08-077L-0101

DORMERS AND PORCHES OFFER COUNTRY CHARM

2,250 total square feet of living area

Width: 66'-8" Depth: 70'-8"

4 bedrooms, 3 baths

2-car side entry garage

Slab or crawl space foundation, please specify when ordering

SPECIAL FEATURES

The kitchen easily serves the casual bayed breakfast room or the formal dining room

The master bedroom enjoys a luxurious bath, two walk-in closets, porch access, and a nearby office/nursery

A large laundry room complete with a sink and counterspace adds simplicity to this household chore

The unfinished bonus room has an additional 310 square feet of living area

PRICE CODE F

Optional Second Floor

First Floor
2,250 sq. ft.

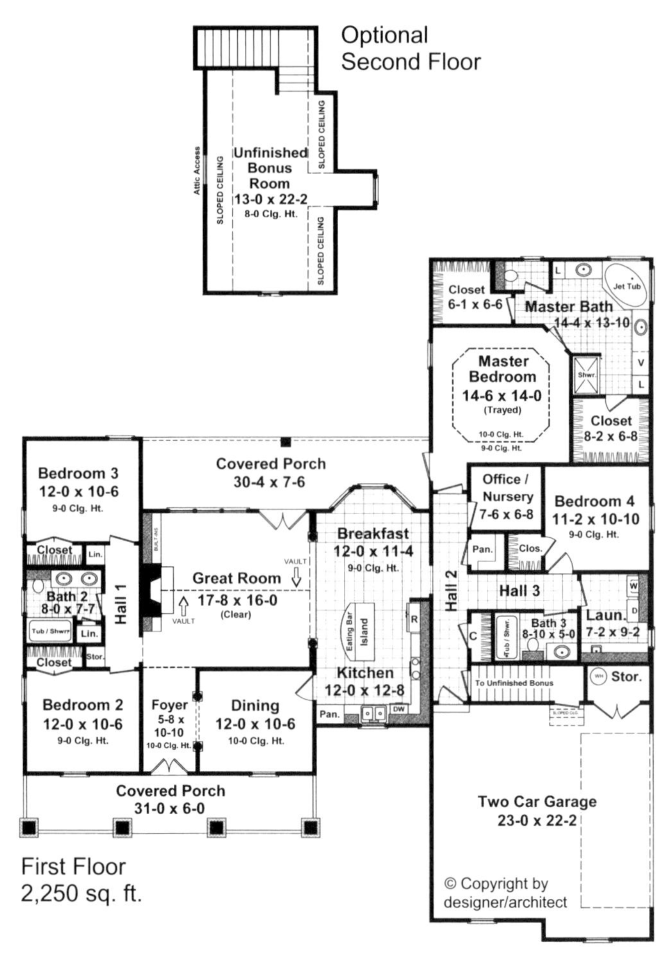

To order plans, visit the Menards Building Materials Desk or visit www.Menards.com.

OPTIONAL GRILLING PORCH
18'-10" X 13'-0"
GARAGE
20'-0" X 26'-10"
SUN ROOM
18'-6" X 7'-8"
FRENCH DOORS
MASTER SUITE
10' BOX CEILING
14'-8" X 14'-8"
M.BATH
8'-6" X 22'-10"
GLASS SHWR
WHP TUB
LIN
KNEE SPACE
MEDIA CENTER
GREAT RM.
10' BOX CEILING
18'-6" X 17'-6"
BUILT-INS
10' ATTIC STORAGE
STORAGE
LAU.
11'-8" X 7'-8"
SEWING
KITCHEN
14'-8" X 14'-0"
ISLAND
PANTRY
BEDROOM 2
10'-10" X 11'-8"
GALLERY
8" COLUMNS
FORMAL LIVING / STUDY
12' CEILING
12'-0" X 12'-4"
FOYER
12' CEILING
6'-8" X 11'-4"
DINING RM.
12' CEILING
12'-0" X 12'-4"
BEDROOM 3
14'-8" X 11'-8"
BUILT-INS
4' PORCH
BRKFST RM. / HEARTH RM.
14'-8" X 10'-0"

LUXURIOUS ARCH WINDOWS

2,525 total square feet of living area

Width: 63'-4" Depth: 59'-10"

3 bedrooms, 2 1/2 baths

2-car side entry garage

Basement foundation; crawl space and slab foundations available for an additional fee, please specify when ordering

SPECIAL FEATURES

A glorious sun room off the great room has French doors leading to the optional covered grilling porch

The enormous laundry room includes a sink and loads of counterspace to make chores much easier

The formal living room/study, as well as the dining room, are accented with decorative columns

PRICE CODE D

To order plans, visit the Menards Building Materials Desk or visit www.Menards.com.

FREEMONT

MENARDS®

Plan #M08-023D-0012

FULLY COLUMNED FRONT ENTRANCE

2,365 total square feet of living area

Width: 67'-6" Depth: 73'-0"

4 bedrooms, 2 baths

2-car carport

Slab foundation

SPECIAL FEATURES

9' ceilings throughout the home add a spacious feel

The expansive centrally located living room is complemented by a corner fireplace

The breakfast bay overlooks the rear covered porch

The master bedroom features a bath with two walk-in closets, a separate tub and a shower as well as a handy linen closet

The peninsula keeps the kitchen private

PRICE CODE D

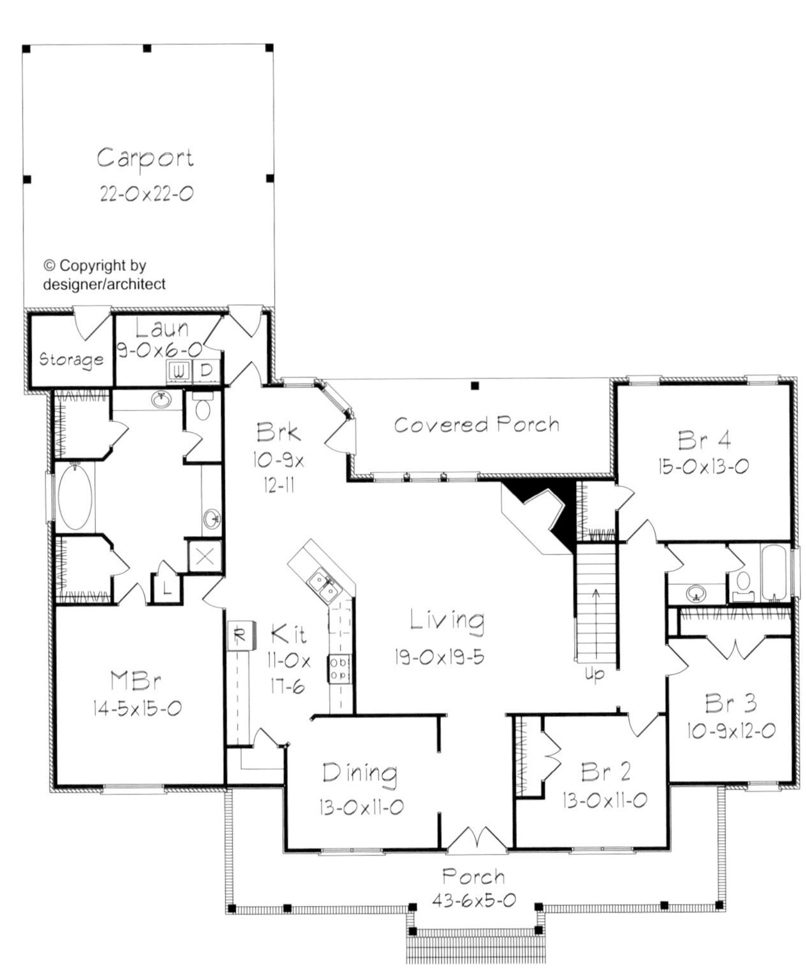

To order plans, visit the Menards Building Materials Desk or visit www.Menards.com.

STEP-SAVING CONVENIENCE

1,498 total square feet of living area

Width: 66'-4" Depth: 44'-10"

3 bedrooms, 2 baths

2-car garage

Basement, crawl space or slab foundation, please specify when ordering

SPECIAL FEATURES

The great room with fireplace and sloped ceiling is visible from the foyer, dining room and kitchen creating a large, open gathering area

The master bedroom enjoys a luxurious bath, a large walk-in closet, and a spacious raised ceiling

A snack bar, walk-in pantry, and nearby laundry room enhance the spacious kitchen

Two generously sized bedrooms share a full bath with a convenient linen closet

PRICE CODE A

Plan #M08-007D-0136

COUNTRY RANCH WITH DRAMATIC ATRIUM VIEWS

1,532 total square feet of living area

Width: 71'-8" Depth: 38'-0"

3 bedrooms, 2 baths

2-car garage

Walk-out basement foundation

SPECIAL FEATURES

The great room has a fireplace and views through a two-story atrium window wall

A covered rear deck is accessed from the breakfast room or garage

The optional lower level has an additional 740 square feet of living area

PRICE CODE B

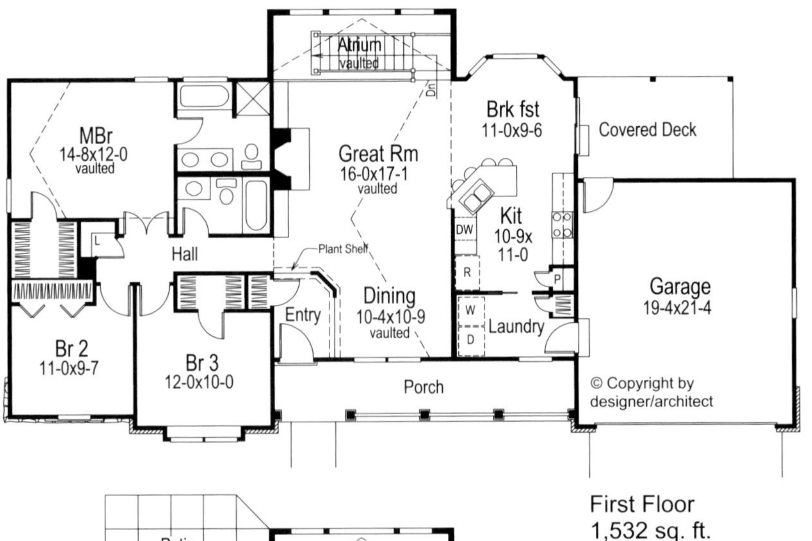

First Floor
1,532 sq. ft.

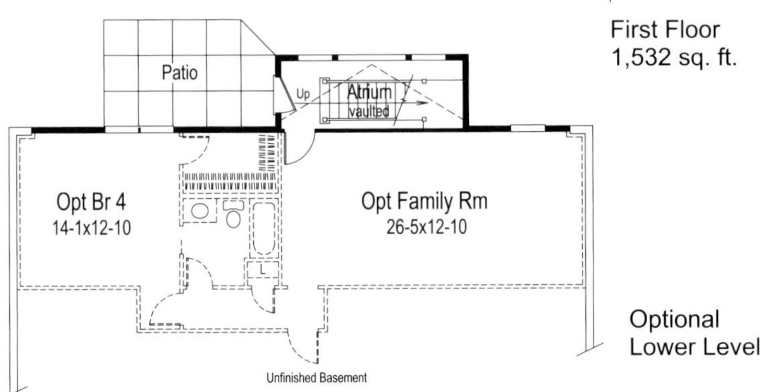

Optional
Lower Level

Rear View

To order plans, visit the Menards Building Materials Desk
or visit www.Menards.com.

EXCELSIOR PARK

Plan #M08-051L-0057

AMENITY-FULL RANCH

2,229 total square feet of living area

Width: 65'-0" Depth: 56'-0"

3 bedrooms, 2 baths

2-car side entry garage

Basement foundation

SPECIAL FEATURES

Energy efficient home with 2" x 6" exterior walls

Home has a welcoming and expansive covered front porch

The dining room enjoys the formality of a tray ceiling

A sunny nook with arched soffit creates an inviting entry into this casual eating space

PRICE CODE D

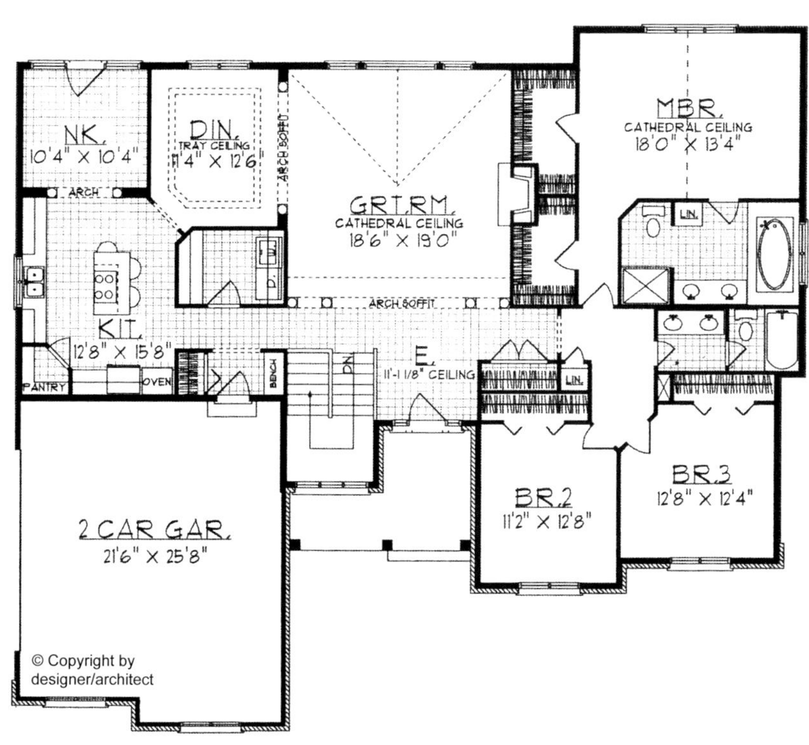

To order plans, visit the Menards Building Materials Desk or visit www.Menards.com.

AUBURN

MENARDS®

Plan #M08-013L-0148

ENCHANTING SCREEN PORCH

1,800 total square feet of living area

Width: 50'-0" Depth: 50'-0"

3 bedrooms, 3 baths

2-car detached garage

Crawl space foundation

SPECIAL FEATURES

Entertaining is simple and easy in the roomy kitchen with an eating nook and serving bar

The dining, office, or guest room is a flexible space that can adapt to fit your family's needs

Tucked away quietly in a corner of this home is a spacious master suite with a sitting area

The bonus room above the garage has an additional 373 square feet of living area

PRICE CODE C

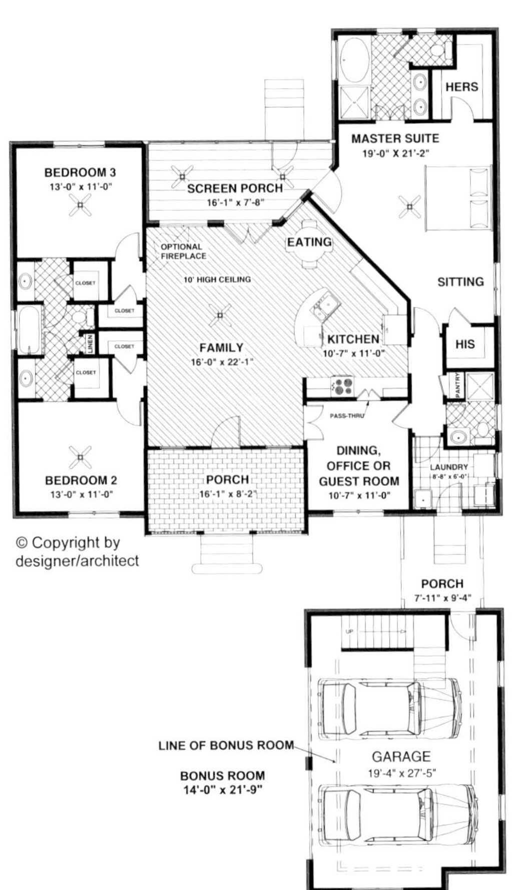

To order plans, visit the Menards Building Materials Desk or visit www.Menards.com.

MENARDS®

ASHMONT PARK

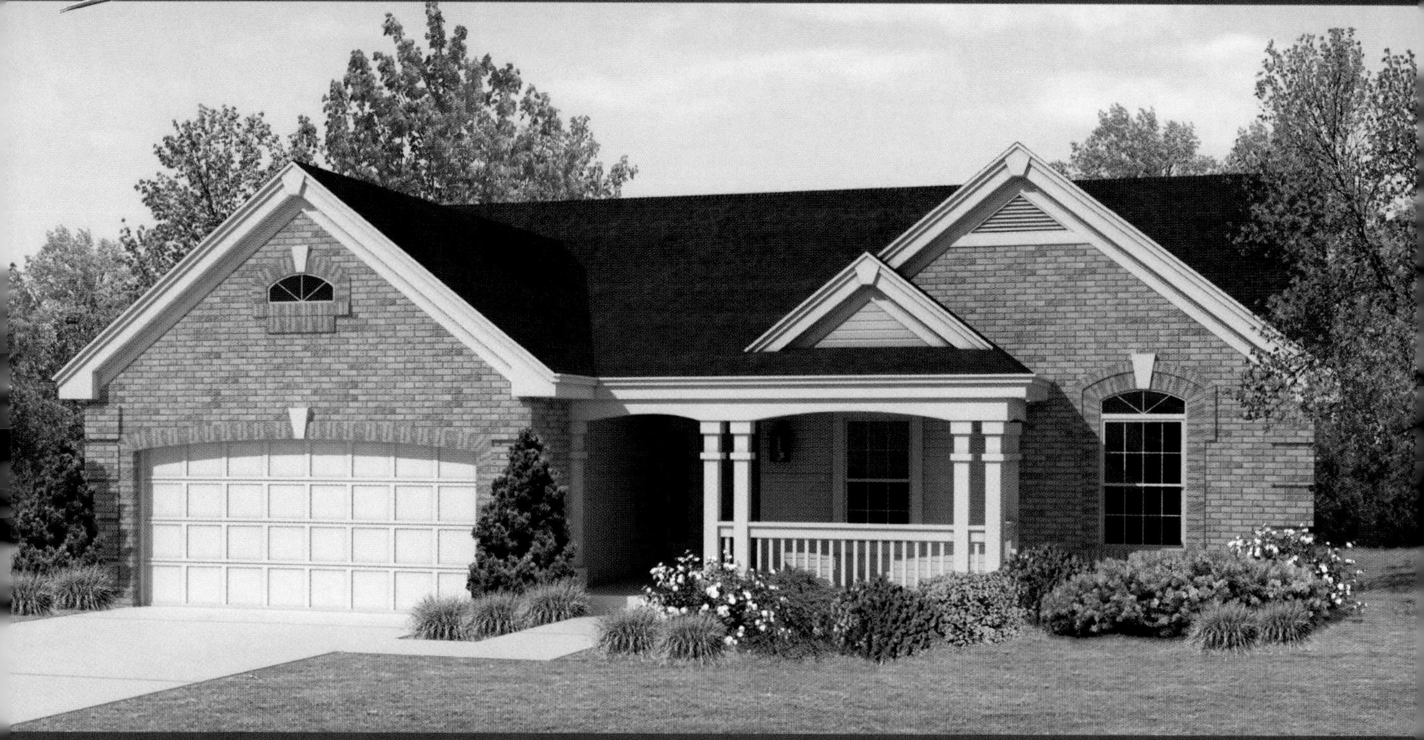

Plan #M08-007D-0163

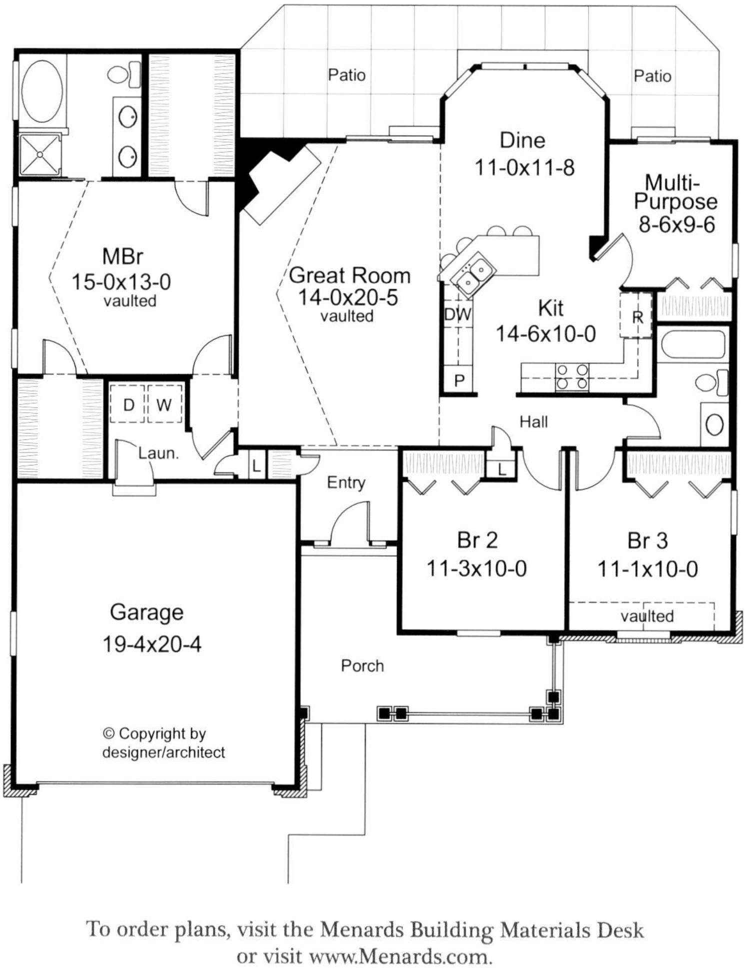

Patio
Patio
Dine
11-0x11-8
Multi-Purpose
8-6x9-6
MBr
15-0x13-0
vaulted
Great Room
14-0x20-5
vaulted
DW
Kit
14-6x10-0
R
P
D
W
Laun.
Hall
L
L
Entry
Br 2
11-3x10-0
Br 3
11-1x10-0
vaulted
Garage
19-4x20-4
Porch
© Copyright by
designer/architect

To order plans, visit the Menards Building Materials Desk
or visit www.Menards.com.

ELEGANCE WITH EFFICIENCY

1,580 total square feet of living area

Width: 50'-8" Depth: 50'-4"

3 bedrooms, 2 baths

2-car garage

Crawl space foundation, drawings also include slab and basement foundations

SPECIAL FEATURES

The large vaulted great room has a corner fireplace, access to the patio and is open to the bayed dining area and kitchen

The spacious kitchen enjoys an adjoining multi-purpose room ideal for a study

The vaulted master bedroom has two walk-in closets and a plush bath

PRICE CODE B

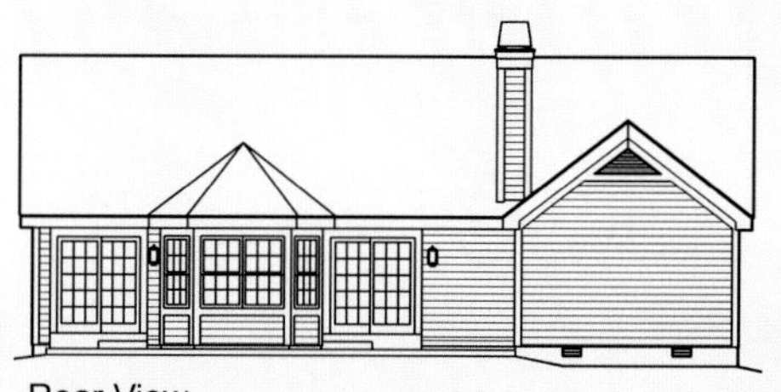

Rear View

CORDER HOLLOW

MENARDS®

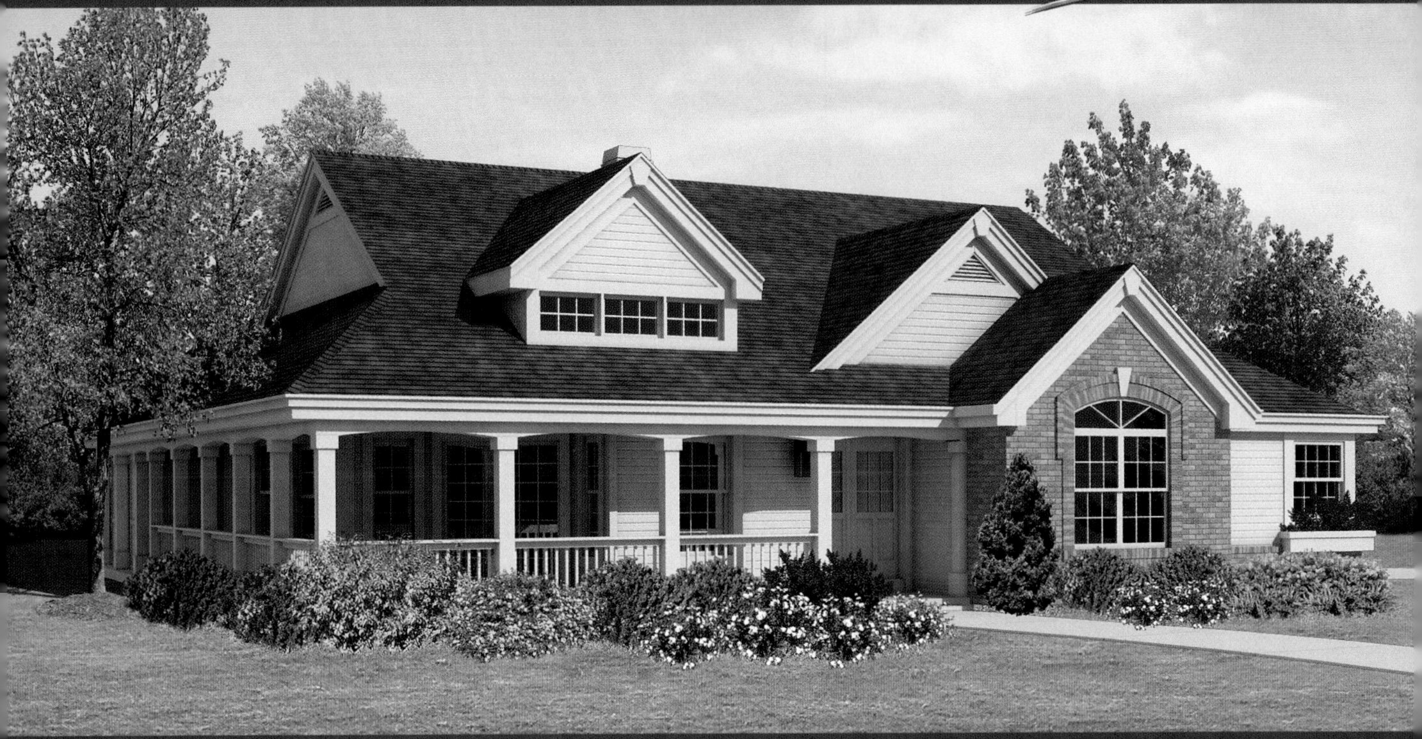

Plan #M08-007D-0172

A PORCH LOVER'S DREAM HOME

1,646 total square feet of living area

Width: 56'-4" Depth: 61'-4"

2 bedrooms, 2 baths

2-car side entry garage

Basement foundation, drawings also include slab and crawl space foundations

SPECIAL FEATURES

The great room has a corner fireplace and views provided by ten windows and doors

A U-shaped kitchen with snack counter is open to the breakfast room and enjoys access to both the side and rear porch

The master bedroom has a luxury bath with corner tub, double vanities with a makeup counter, and a huge walk-in closet

PRICE CODE B

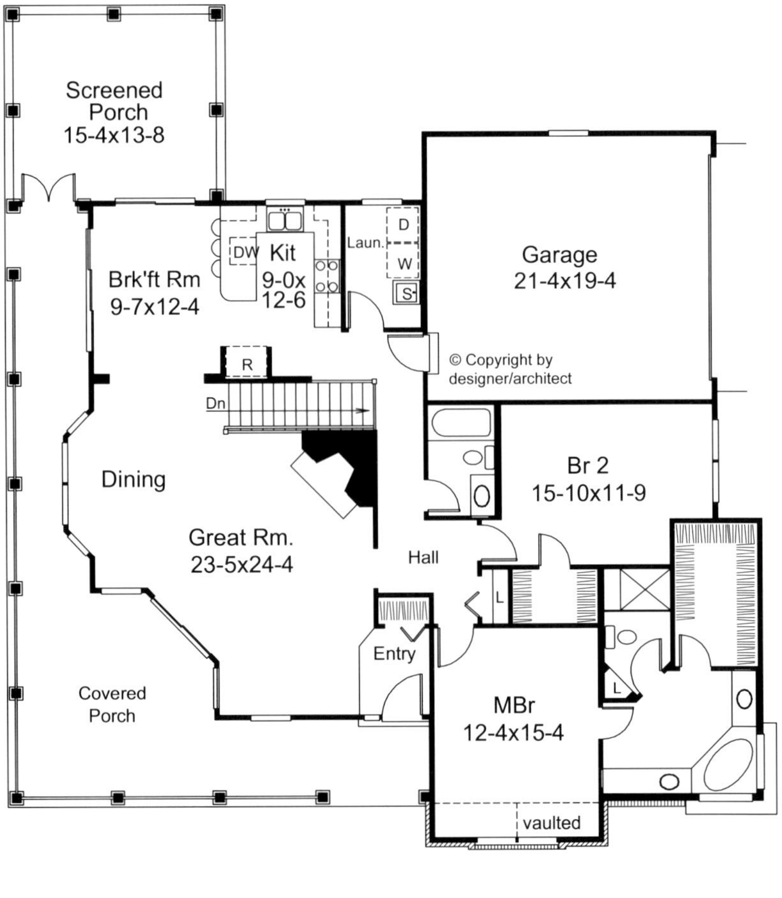

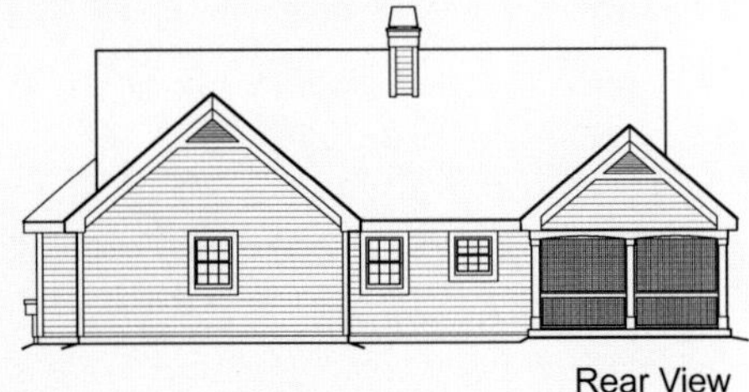

Screened Porch 15-4x13-8
Brk'ft Rm 9-7x12-4
DW
Kit 9-0x 12-6
Laun.
D
W
S
Garage 21-4x19-4
© Copyright by designer/architect
R
Dn
Dining
Great Rm. 23-5x24-4
Br 2 15-10x11-9
Hall
L
Entry
Covered Porch
MBr 12-4x15-4
L
vaulted

Rear View

To order plans, visit the Menards Building Materials Desk or visit www.Menards.com.

SITTING
TRAY CEILING
UP 1'
UP 1'
MASTER SUITE
18'-0" x 19'-8"
CLOSET
5'-0" x 9'-2"
LINEN
DECK
17'-4" x 9'-10"
SCREEN PORCH
17'-4" x 9'-0"
SKYLIGHT
SKYLIGHT
LINEN
BEDROOM 2
13'-0" x 11'-0"
DW
KITCHEN
13'-4" x 11'-8"
SERVING BAR
FAMILY ROOM
18'-0" x 20'-0"
BRKFST
9'8" x 9'0"
PANTRY
COATS
LINEN
STORAGE OR OPTIONAL STAIRS TO BONUS ROOM AND BASEMENT
DN
UP
11' HIGH CEILING

ENTRY
11' HIGH CEILING
BEDROOM 3
13'-0" x 11'-0"
LINE OF BONUS ROOM
14'-2" x 29'-8"
DINING
11'-0" x 13'-4"
12'-8" HIGH CEILING
PORCH
19'-8" x 5'-4"
3 CAR GARAGE
23'-4" x 29'-8"

STYLISH ONE-LEVEL LIVING

1,898 total square feet of living area

Width: 55'-8" Depth: 66'-0"

3 bedrooms, 3 baths

3-car side entry garage

Basement foundation

SPECIAL FEATURES

A large and open family room has a corner fireplace and screen porch access

A stunning corner whirlpool tub provides the ultimate escape in the master suite

A cozy and comforting breakfast area is perfect for intimate meals anytime of day

The bonus room above the garage has an additional 474 square feet of living space

PRICE CODE B

To order plans, visit the Menards Building Materials Desk or visit www.Menards.com.

HILLTOP

MENARDS®

Plan #M08-008D-0110

PALLADIAN WINDOWS DOMINATE FACADE

1,500 total square feet of living area

Width: 52'-8" Depth: 48'-4"

3 bedrooms, 2 baths

2-car garage

Basement foundation

SPECIAL FEATURES

The living room features a cathedral ceiling and opens to the breakfast room

The breakfast room has a spectacular bay window and adjoins a well-appointed kitchen with generous storage

The laundry room is convenient to the kitchen and includes a large closet

The large walk-in closet gives the master bedroom abundant storage

PRICE CODE B

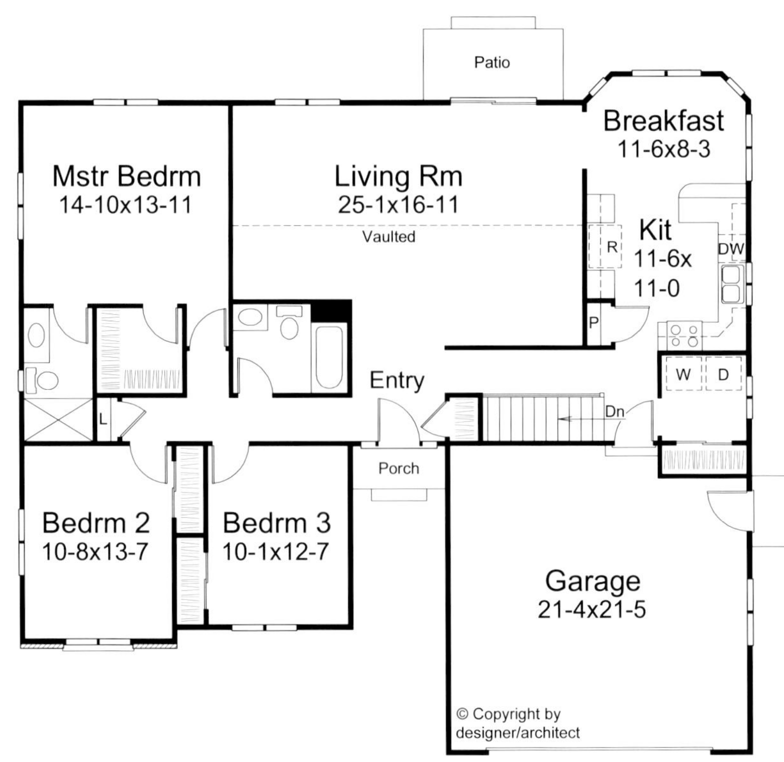

To order plans, visit the Menards Building Materials Desk or visit www.Menards.com.

OAKBURY

Plan #M08-007D-0146

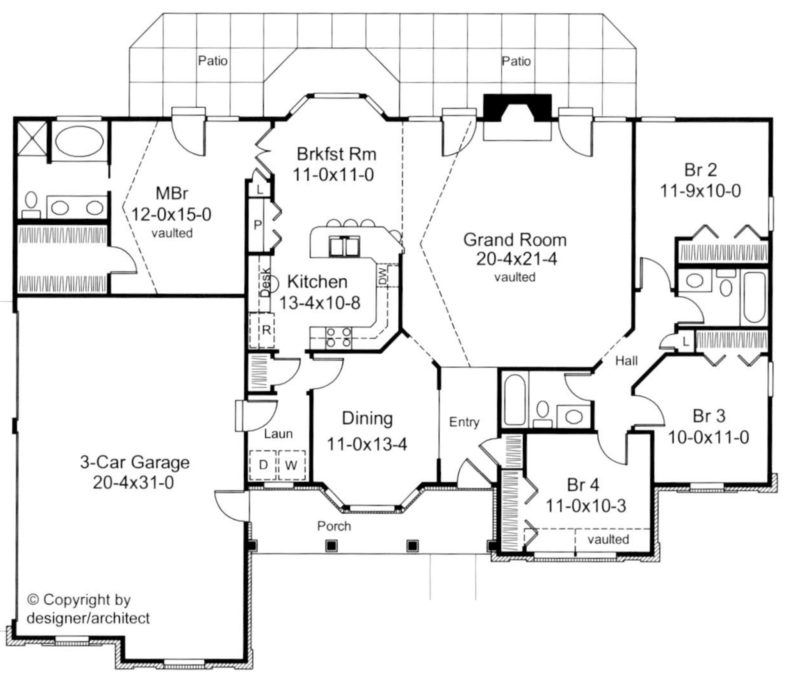

To order plans, visit the Menards Building Materials Desk or visit www.Menards.com.

THE PLAN THAT HAS IT ALL

1,929 total square feet of living area

Width: 68'-0" Depth: 49'-8"

4 bedrooms, 3 baths

3-car side entry garage

Crawl space foundation, drawings also include slab and basement foundations

SPECIAL FEATURES

More than a great room for this size home, the vaulted grand room features a brick and wood mantle fireplace flanked by doors to the rear patio

The state-of-the-art U-shaped kitchen has a built-in pantry, a computer desk, a snack bar, and a breakfast room with bay window

The vaulted master bedroom has a walk-in closet, a luxury bath and patio access

PRICE CODE C

Rear View

ROSE WAY

MENARDS®

Plan #M08-048D-0008

STATELY COVERED FRONT ENTRY

2,089 total square feet of living area

Width: 61'-8" Depth: 54'-0"

4 bedrooms, 3 baths

2-car garage

Slab foundation

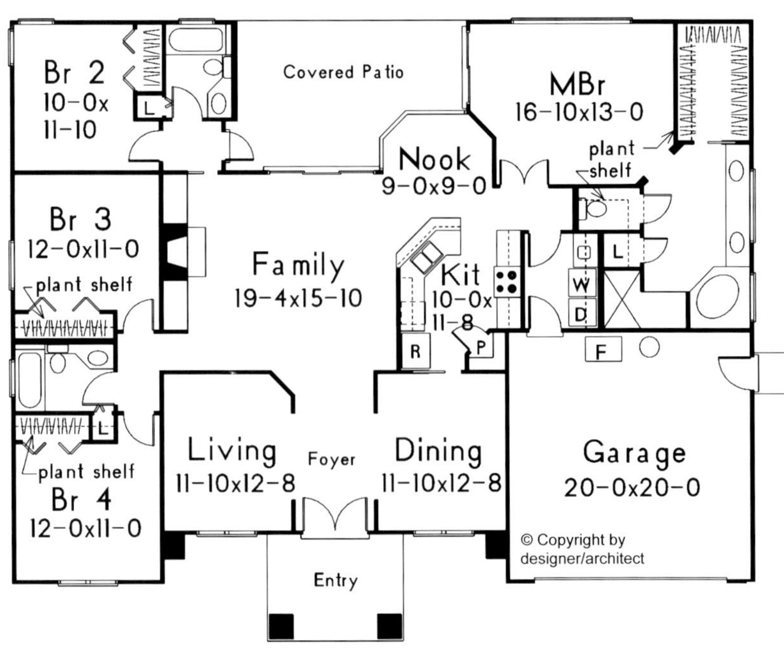

SPECIAL FEATURES

- The family room has a fireplace, built-in bookshelves, and triple sliding glass doors opening to the covered patio
- The kitchen overlooks the family room
- Separated from the three secondary bedrooms, the master bedroom becomes a quiet retreat with patio access
- The master bedroom features an oversized bath with walk-in closet and corner tub

PRICE CODE C

Rear View

To order plans, visit the Menards Building Materials Desk or visit www.Menards.com.

MENARDS®

WHITEHAVEN

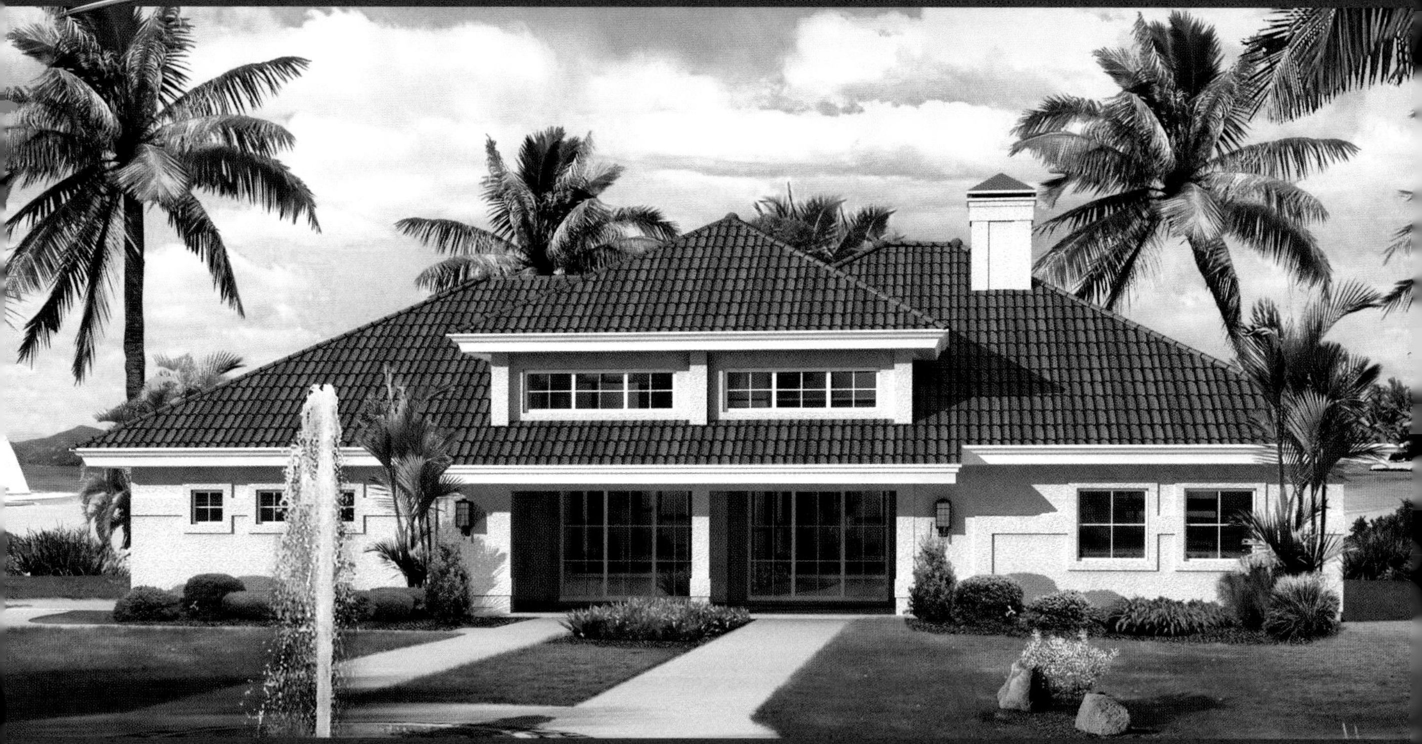

Plan #M08-007D-0229

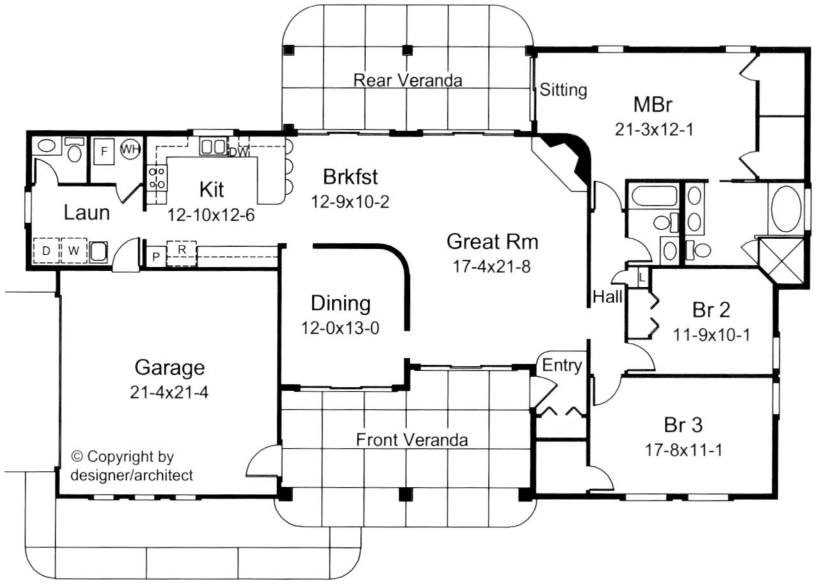

Rear Veranda
Sitting
MBr 21-3x12-1
Brkfst 12-9x10-2
Kit 12-10x12-6
Laun
Great Rm 17-4x21-8
Hall
Br 2 11-9x10-1
Dining 12-0x13-0
Garage 21-4x21-4
Entry
Br 3 17-8x11-1
Front Veranda

EXCITING DESIGN FOR VIEWS

2,014 total square feet of living area

Width: 76'-4" Depth: 43'-0"

3 bedrooms, 2 1/2 baths

2-car side entry garage

Slab foundation

SPECIAL FEATURES

The front veranda, with 15' high ceiling, receives abundant light from the dormer windows above

9' wide sliding glass doors are an awesome feature of the spacious great room

The kitchen excels in cabinet storage and includes a useful snack bar

The master bedroom enjoys two walk-in closets and a luxury bath

PRICE CODE D

Rear View

SPRINGATE

MENARDS®

Plan #M08-058D-0067

LUXURIOUS MASTER BEDROOM

1,587 total square feet of living area

Width: 49'-0"   Depth: 47'-8"

3 bedrooms, 2 baths

2-car garage

Basement foundation

SPECIAL FEATURES

The spacious vaulted family room features a fireplace and a convenient coat closet

The kitchen/breakfast area is brightened by large windows and includes a centrally located pantry

The secondary bedrooms are generously sized and share a full bath

PRICE CODE B

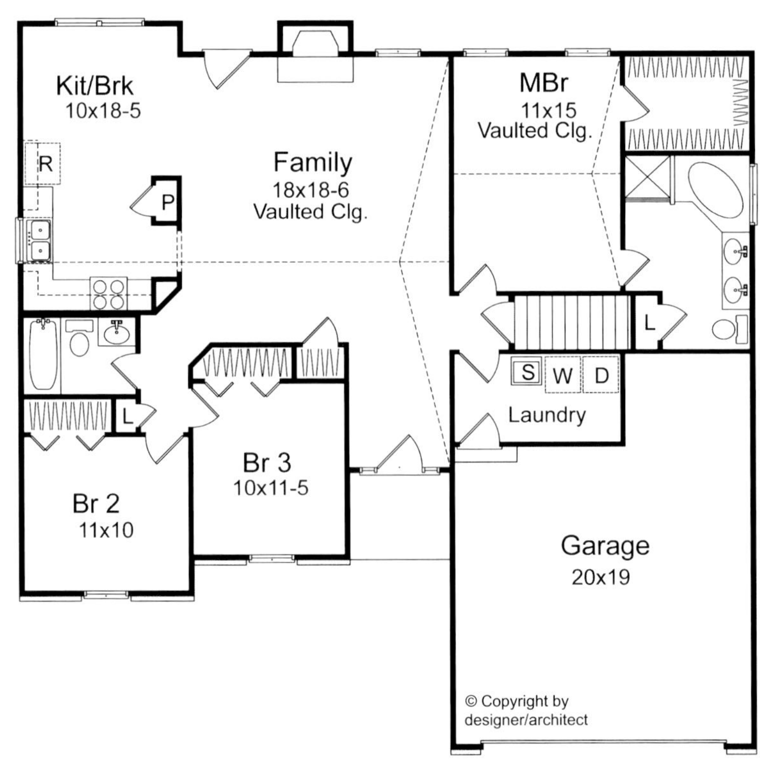

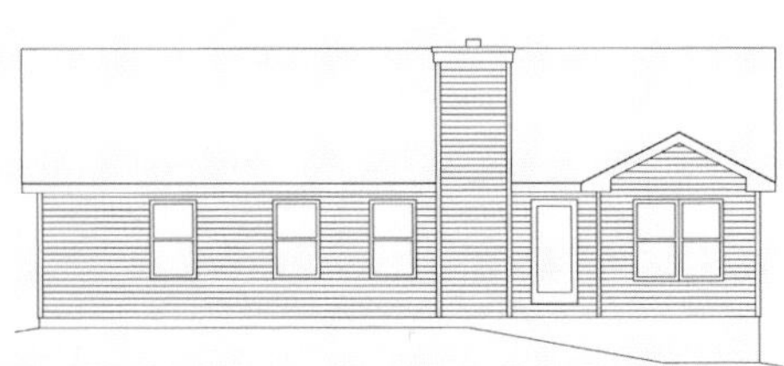

Rear View

To order plans, visit the Menards Building Materials Desk or visit www.Menards.com.

MENARDS

KASINGTON

Plan #M08-007D-0080

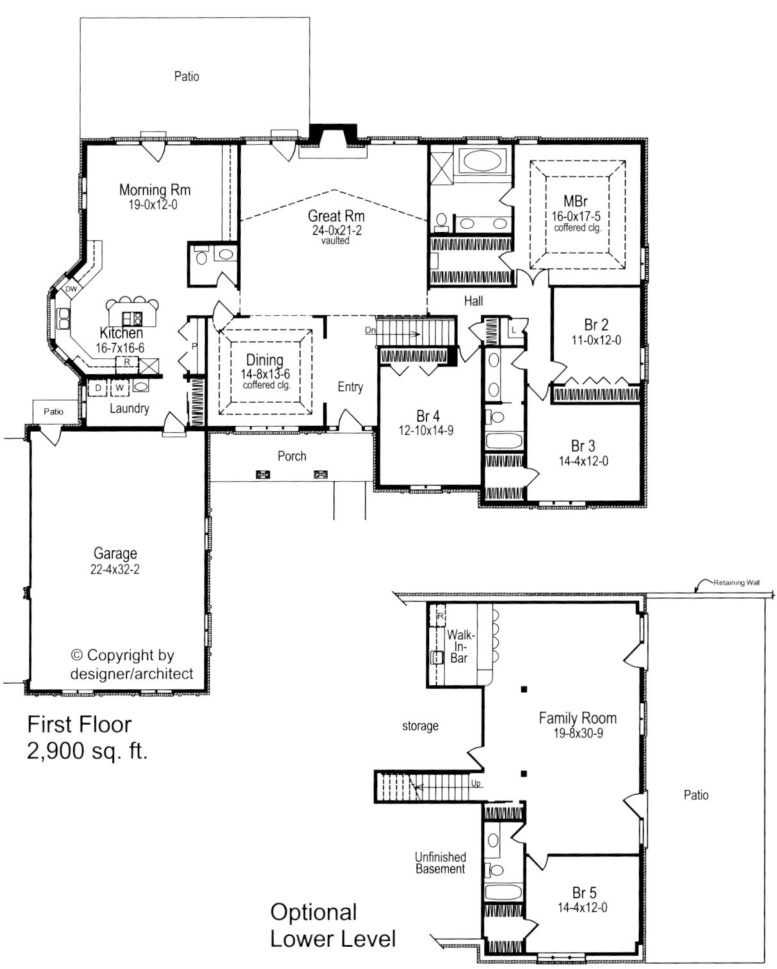

First Floor
2,900 sq. ft.

Optional
Lower Level

To order plans, visit the Menards Building Materials Desk or visit www.Menards.com.

CONTEMPORARY WRAPPED IN BRICK

2,900 total square feet of living area

Width: 79'-0" Depth: 70'-10"

4 bedrooms, 2 1/2 baths

3-car side entry garage

Walk-out basement foundation

SPECIAL FEATURES

Energy efficient home with 2" x 6" exterior walls

The vaulted great room has palladian windows flanking an 8' wide brick fireplace

The kitchen has a picture window above the sink, a huge pantry, a cooktop island, and is open to a large morning room

1,018 square feet of optional living area on the lower level with family room, walk-in bar and a fifth bedroom with a bath

PRICE CODE E

Rear View

RILEY

MENARDS®

Plan #M08-121D-0021

COVERED COUNTRY FRONT PORCH

1,562 total square feet of living area

Width: 65'-0" Depth: 46'-4"

3 bedrooms, 2 baths

2-car garage

Basement foundation

SPECIAL FEATURES

The vaulted breakfast room sits in a sunny bay window with sliding glass doors that access the rear patio

A convenient eating bar in the kitchen is perfect for casual meals

The spacious great room boasts a vaulted ceiling and warming corner fireplace

PRICE CODE A

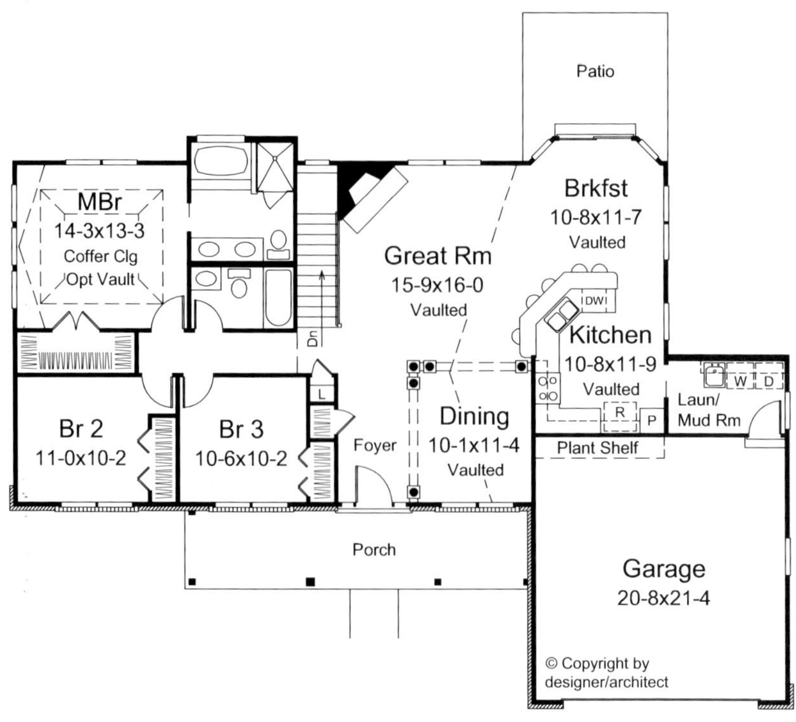

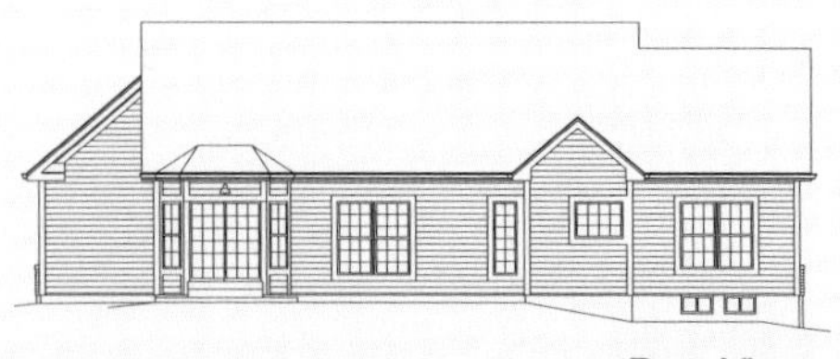

Rear View

To order plans, visit the Menards Building Materials Desk or visit www.Menards.com.

MENARDS

SANTA CLARA

Plan #M08-022D-0005

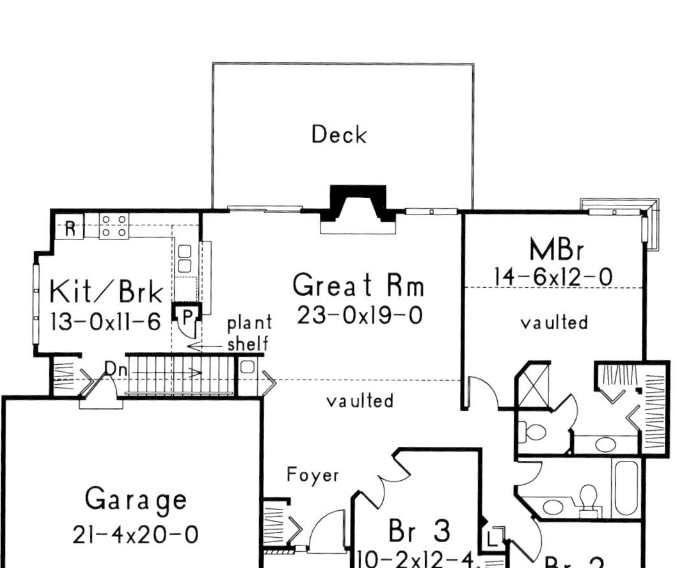

DISTINCTIVE RANCH

1,360 total square feet of living area

Width: 56'-0" Depth: 36'-0"

3 bedrooms, 2 baths

2-car garage

Basement foundation

SPECIAL FEATURES

The foyer opens to the vaulted great room with a fireplace and access to the rear deck

A vaulted ceiling and large windows add openness to the kitchen/breakfast room

Bedroom #3 could easily convert to a den

PRICE CODE A

FORISTELL

Plan #M08-058D-0172

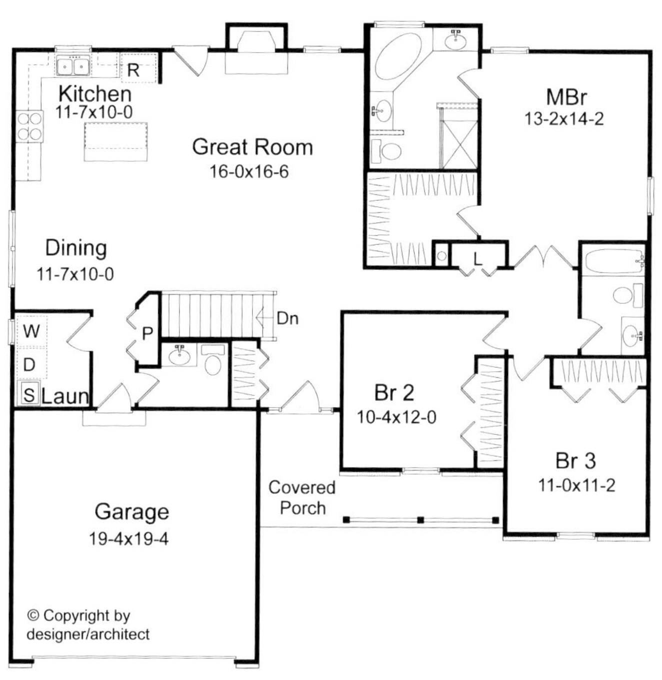

STUNNING FAMILY HOME

1,635 total square feet of living area

Width: 51'-0" Depth: 50'-4"

3 bedrooms, 2 1/2 baths

2-car garage

Basement foundation

SPECIAL FEATURES

The covered front porch creates an inviting facade

A whirlpool tub and twin vanities add elegance to the master bedroom's private bath

The kitchen island provides extra workspace

PRICE CODE AA

To order plans, visit the Menards Building Materials Desk or visit www.Menards.com.

BRIARFIELD

MENARDS

Plan #M08-008D-0010

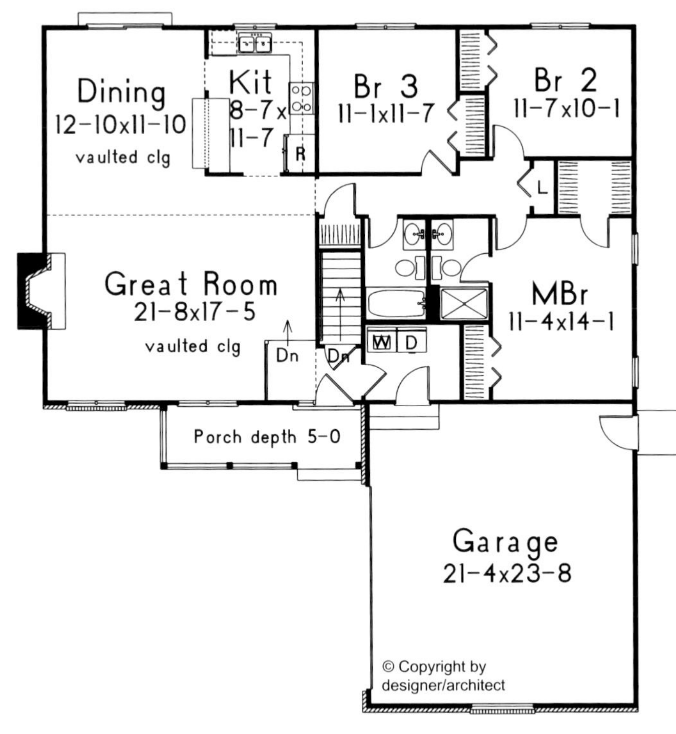

LOVELY RANCH HOME

1,440 total square feet of living area

Width: 50'-0" Depth: 54'-5"

3 bedrooms, 2 baths

2-car side entry garage

Basement foundation, drawings also include crawl space and slab foundations

SPECIAL FEATURES

The huge great room has a sloping ceiling and tall masonry fireplace

The kitchen connects to the spacious dining room

An oversized two-car side entry garage offers plenty of storage for bicycles, lawn equipment, etc.

PRICE CODE A

GRANTWAY

Plan #M08-065L-0095

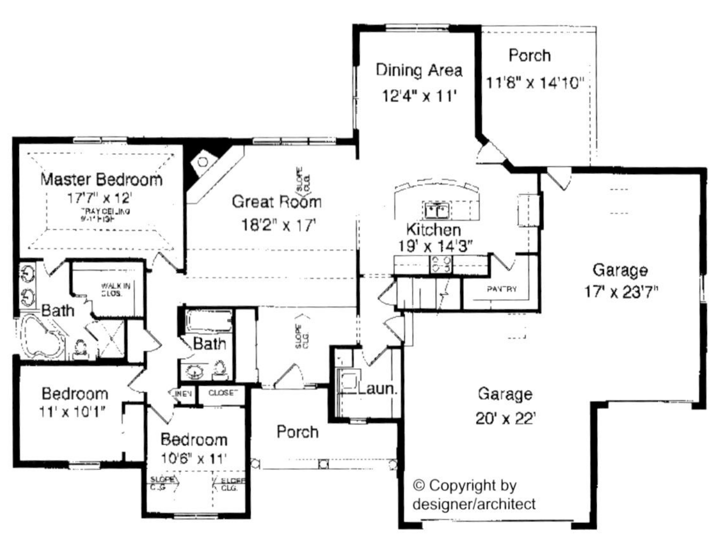

INVITING ARCHED ENTRY

1,824 total square feet of living area

Width: 74'-0" Depth: 52'-0"

3 bedrooms, 2 baths

3-car garage

Basement foundation

SPECIAL FEATURES

The kitchen island is an easy spot for quick meals

The bedrooms are set apart from the rest of the house with a hallway, making them more private

PRICE CODE C

To order plans, visit the Menards Building Materials Desk or visit www.Menards.com.

DELTA QUEEN II

Plan #M08-001D-0068

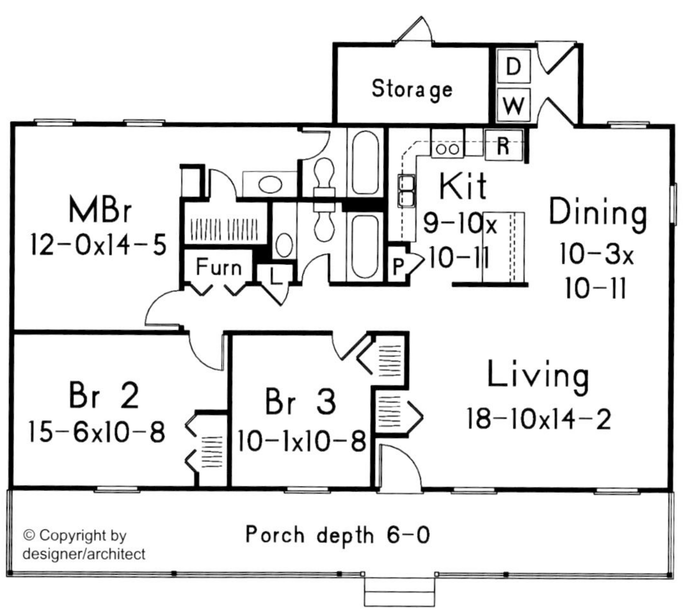

OPEN LIVING AREA

1,285 total square feet of living area

Width: 48'-0" Depth: 37'-8"

3 bedrooms, 2 baths

Crawl space foundation, drawings also include basement and slab foundations

SPECIAL FEATURES

The master bedroom has a dressing area, a private bath, and a built-in bookcase

The kitchen features a pantry, a breakfast bar, and a complete view to the dining room

2" x 6" exterior wall framing available for an additional fee, please specify when ordering

PRICE CODE B

STOVALL

Plan #M08-077L-0019

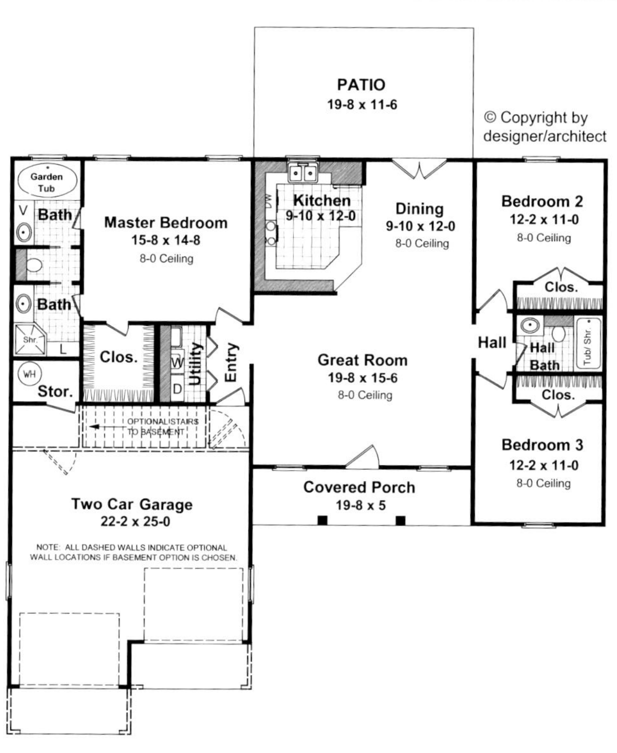

PLEASANT FRONT PORCH

1,400 total square feet of living area

Width: 54'-0" Depth: 47'-0"

3 bedrooms, 2 baths

2-car garage

Slab, basement or crawl space foundation, please specify when ordering

SPECIAL FEATURES

French doors lead from the dining room to the patio

The master bedroom is set apart for privacy

PRICE CODE D

To order plans, visit the Menards Building Materials Desk or visit www.Menards.com.

AMBERDALE

Plan #M08-007D-0240

MENARDS

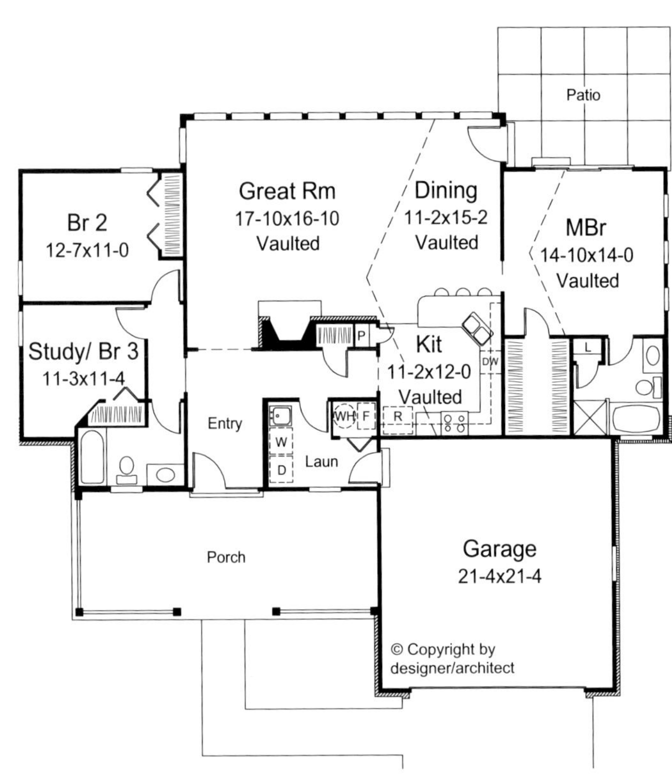

ENCHANTING DORMERS

1,663 total square feet of living area

Width: 60'-8" Depth: 50'-0"

3 bedrooms, 2 baths

2-car garage

Crawl space or slab foundation, please specify when ordering

SPECIAL FEATURES

The vaulted great room offers views through a 30' wide window wall

A snack bar and built-in pantry are features of the efficient U-shaped vaulted kitchen

The vaulted master bedroom has a roomy bath

PRICE CODE C

DELMAR

Plan #M08-053D-0037

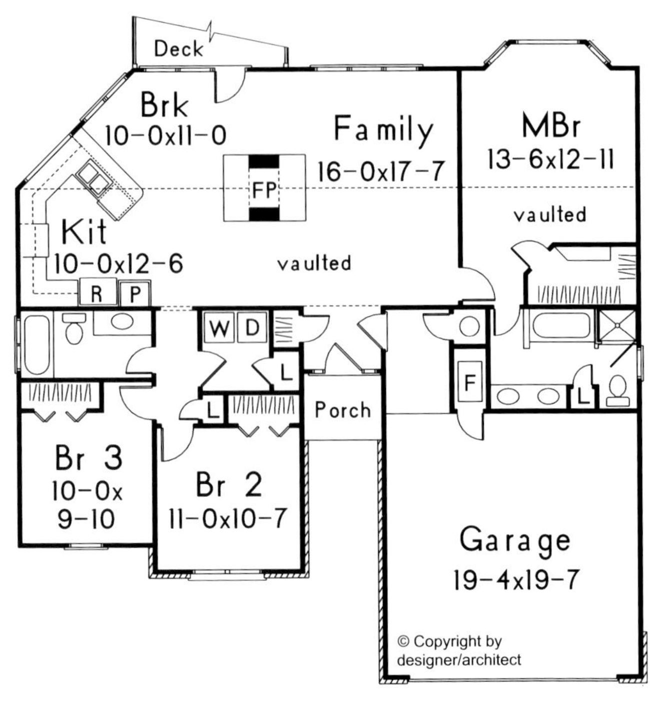

FABULOUS FAMILY LIVING

1,388 total square feet of living area

Width: 48'-0" Depth: 48'-0"

3 bedrooms, 2 baths

2-car garage

Crawl space foundation, drawings also include slab foundation

SPECIAL FEATURES

A see-through fireplace offers a focal point

Many windows throughout this home add sunlight

PRICE CODE A

To order plans, visit the Menards Building Materials Desk or visit www.Menards.com.

EDGEHOLLOW
Plan #M08-008D-0094

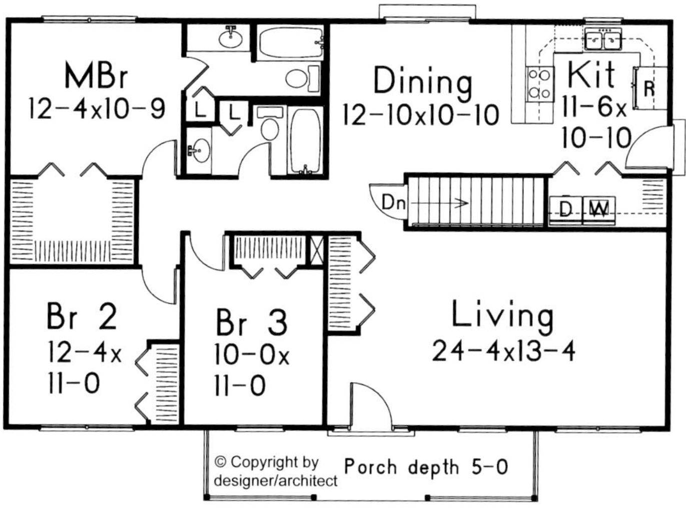

EFFICIENT RANCH

1,364 total square feet of living area

Width: 40'-0" Depth: 34'-0"

3 bedrooms, 2 baths

Basement foundation, drawings also include crawl space foundation

SPECIAL FEATURES

The master bedroom has a spacious walk-in closet and private bath

The living room is highlighted with several windows

The kitchen with snack bar is adjacent to the dining area

This plan includes an optional 2-car garage

PRICE CODE A

IMPERIAL
Plan #M08-008D-0057

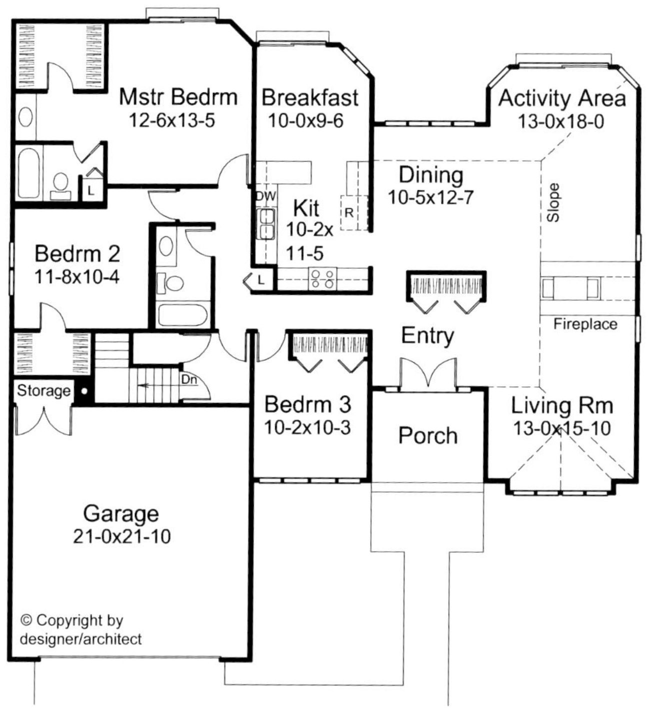

STYLISH RANCH LIVING

1,850 total square feet of living area

Width: 56'-0" Depth: 55'-10"

3 bedrooms, 2 baths

2-car garage

Partial basement/crawl space foundation, drawings also include slab foundation

SPECIAL FEATURES

The well-equipped kitchen enjoys an eating bar

The master bedroom enjoys a compartmented bath

PRICE CODE C

To order plans, visit the Menards Building Materials Desk or visit www.Menards.com.

CHILDRESS HILL

MENARDS

Plan #M08-058D-0050

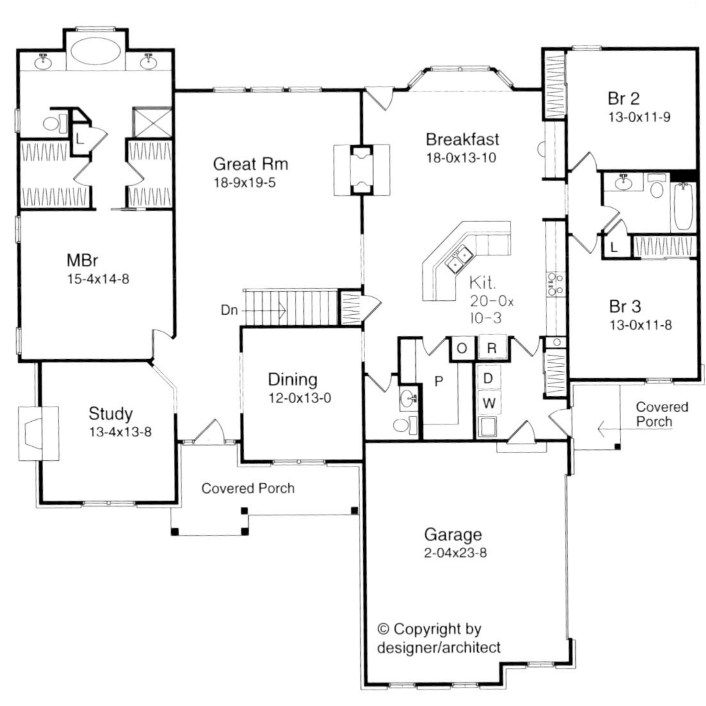

OPEN FLOOR PLAN FOR FAMILY ACTIVITIES

2,598 total square feet of living area

Width: 69'-4" Depth: 65'-4"

3 bedrooms, 2 1/2 baths

2-car side entry garage

Basement foundation

SPECIAL FEATURES

A see-through fireplace warms the great room, kitchen and breakfast area

The master bedroom enjoys two walk-in closets and a private bath with a whirlpool tub

PRICE CODE D

ASHMONT PLACE

Plan #M08-007D-0164

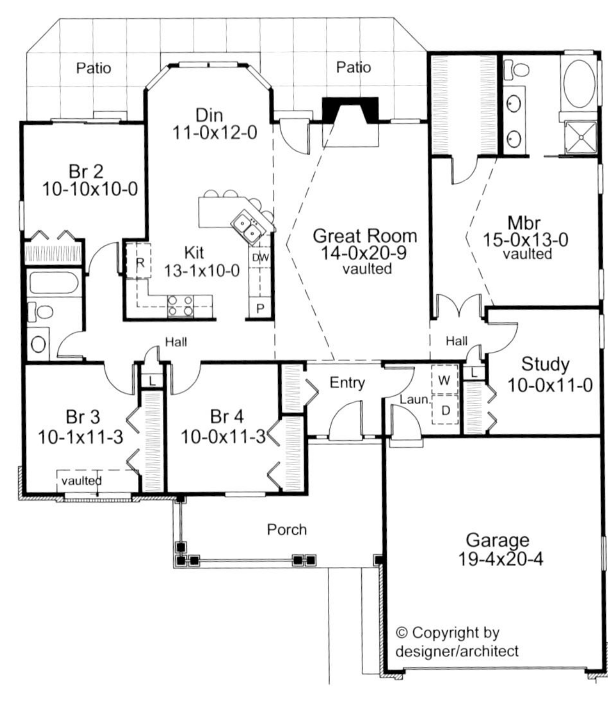

STYLISH RANCH WITH STUDY

1,741 total square feet of living area

Width: 53'-0" Depth: 55'-0"

4 bedrooms, 2 baths

2-car garage

Crawl space foundation, drawings also include slab and basement foundations

SPECIAL FEATURES

The vaulted great room offers a cozy fireplace

The vaulted master bedroom has a walk-in closet

PRICE CODE B

To order plans, visit the Menards Building Materials Desk or visit www.Menards.com.

MENARDS

SUMMERSET
Plan #M08-007D-0055

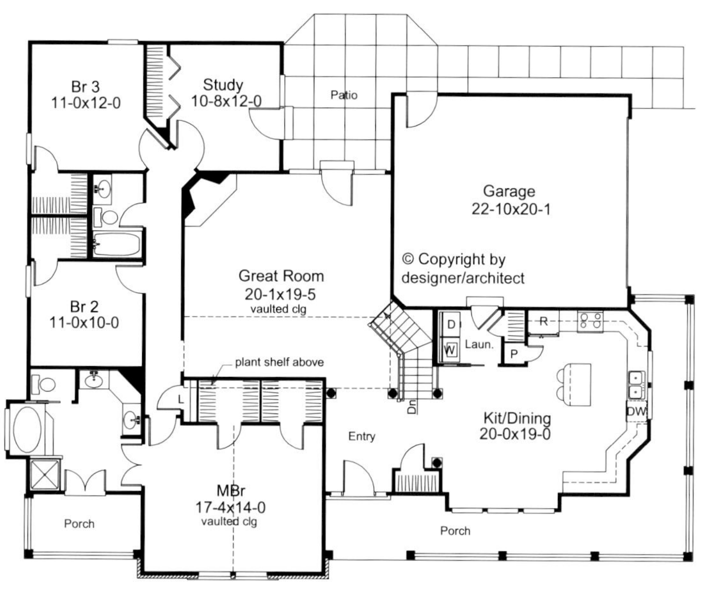

LOVELY COUNTRY HOME

2,029 total square feet of living area

Width: 67'-0" Depth: 51'-4"

3 bedrooms, 2 baths

2-car side entry garage

Basement foundation, drawings also include crawl space and slab foundations

SPECIAL FEATURES

The kitchen/dining area enjoys an island snack bar, a built-in pantry, and multiple tall windows

2" x 6" exterior wall framing available for an additional fee, please specify when ordering

PRICE CODE D

CONWAY GLEN
Plan #M08-077L-0030

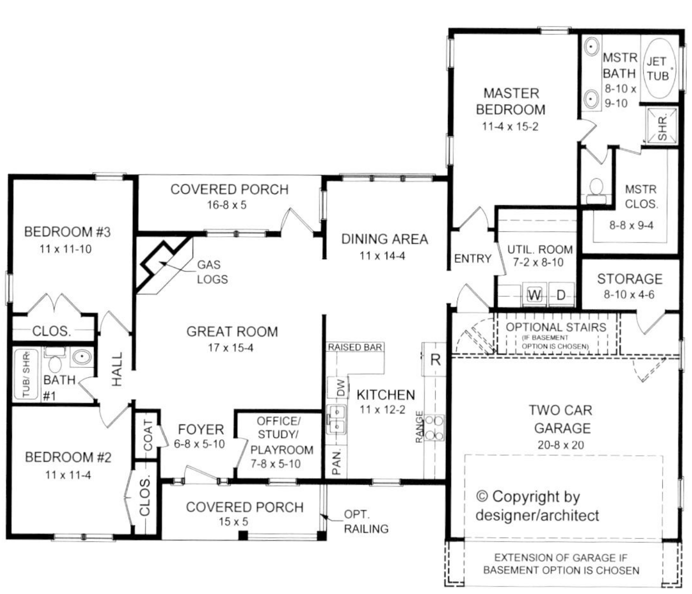

BEAUTIFUL, OPEN DESIGN

1,600 total square feet of living area

Width: 61'-8" Depth: 45'-8"

3 bedrooms, 2 baths

2-car garage

Basement, crawl space or slab foundation, please specify when ordering

SPECIAL FEATURES

Energy efficient home with 2" x 6" exterior walls

The office/study/playroom is a flexible space

PRICE CODE E

To order plans, visit the Menards Building Materials Desk or visit www.Menards.com.

SANDUSKY

MENARDS

Plan #M08-051L-0027

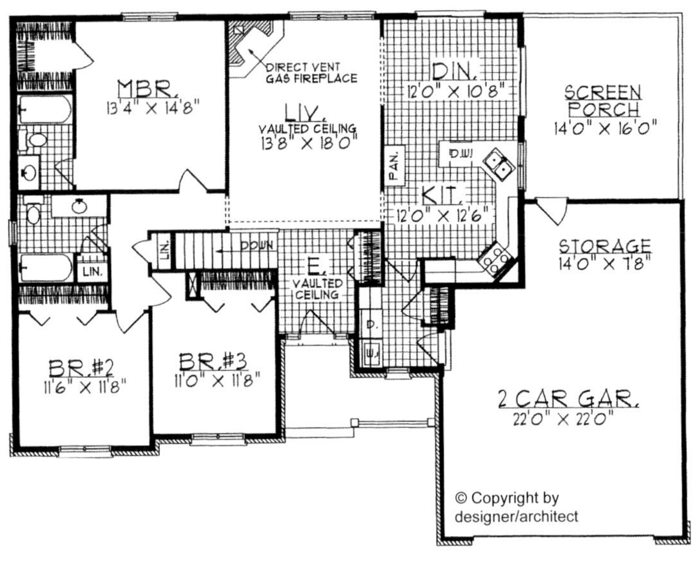

TERRIFIC RANCH

1,520 total square feet of living area

Width: 60'-4" Depth: 46'-0"

3 bedrooms, 2 baths

2-car garage

Basement foundation

SPECIAL FEATURES

Energy efficient home with 2" x 6" exterior walls

The master bedroom has a large walk-in closet

The laundry room is conveniently located between the garage and kitchen

The living room has a cathedral ceiling and fireplace

PRICE CODE E

STRATFORD

Plan #M08-003D-0002

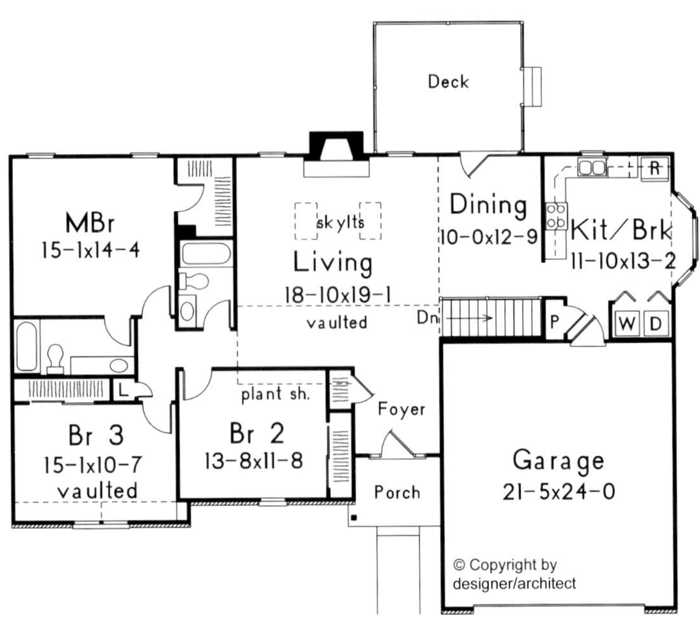

SKYLIGHTS PROVIDE LIGHT

1,676 total square feet of living area

Width: 64'-0" Depth: 44'-0"

3 bedrooms, 2 baths

2-car garage

Basement foundation, drawings also include crawl space and slab foundations

SPECIAL FEATURES

The living area skylights and kitchen/breakfast area with bay window provide plenty of sunlight

The master bedroom has a walk-in closet

PRICE CODE B

To order plans, visit the Menards Building Materials Desk or visit www.Menards.com.

MENARDS
CRAIGLAND HILLS
Plan #M08-007D-0249

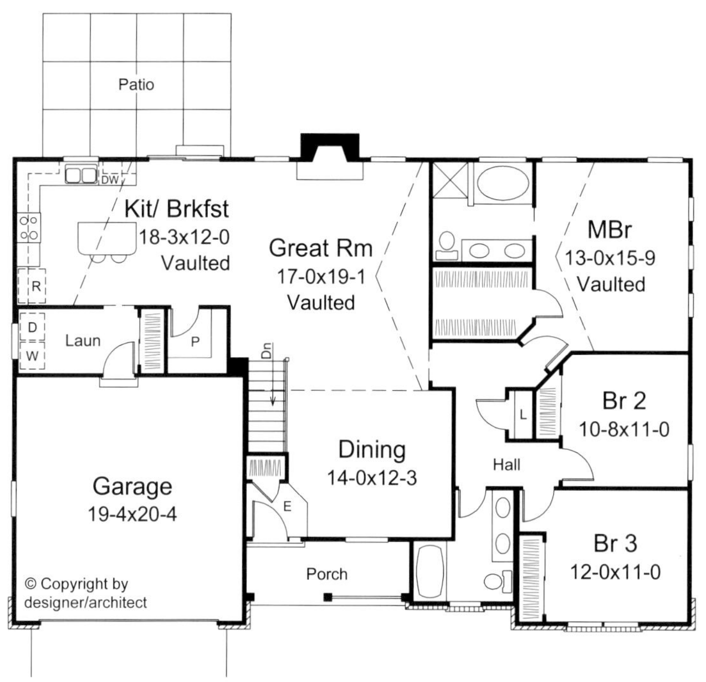

COUNTRY RANCH

1,740 total square feet of living area

Width: 58'-8" Depth: 41'-4"

3 bedrooms, 2 baths

2-car garage

Basement foundation

SPECIAL FEATURES

A protective covered porch and separate entry with guest closet invite you into the vast open living areas

The vaulted great room offers a fireplace

Decorative windows above the bed wall add sunlight to the master bedroom that also enjoys a luxury bath

PRICE CODE C

TWINBROOKE
Plan #M08-037D-0022

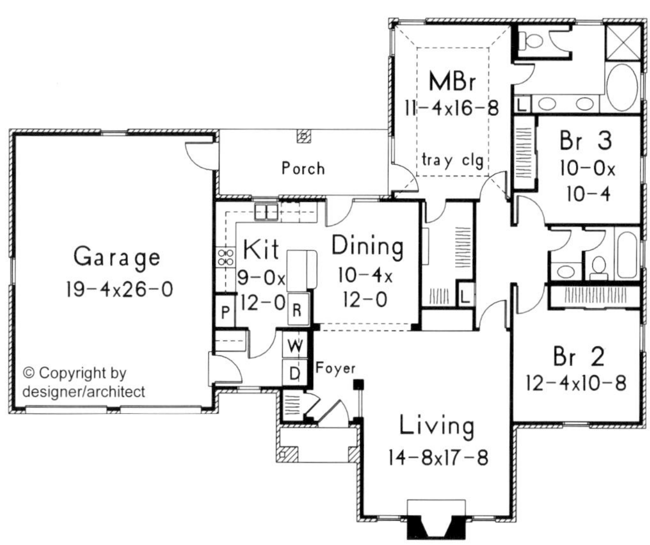

FIREPLACE IS FOCAL POINT

1,539 total square feet of living area

Width: 62'-0" Depth: 49'-8"

3 bedrooms, 2 baths

2-car garage

Slab foundation

SPECIAL FEATURES

The master bedroom has a 10' tray ceiling, access to the porch, ample closet space, and a full bath

The kitchen and dining room share a serving counter

PRICE CODE B

To order plans, visit the Menards Building Materials Desk or visit www.Menards.com.

MADISON MANOR

MENARDS®

Plan #M08-007D-0113

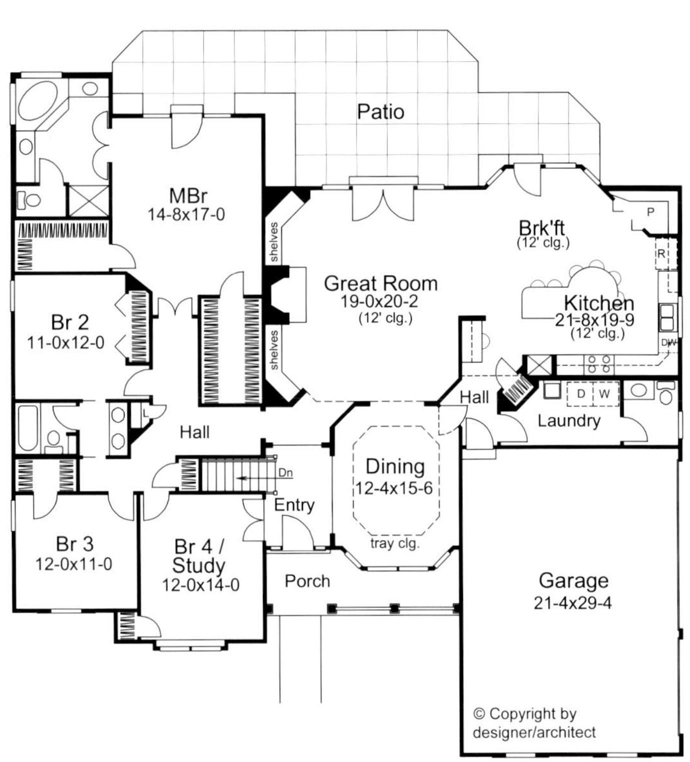

COUNTRY HOME FOCUSES ON PATIO VIEWS

2,547 total square feet of living area

Width: 66'-0" Depth: 66'-0"

4 bedrooms, 2 1/2 baths

3-car side entry garage

Basement foundation

SPECIAL FEATURES

The great room features a 12' ceiling, a fireplace with built-in shelving, and patio doors with transoms

A walk-in pantry, computer desk, large island and breakfast area are features of the kitchen

PRICE CODE D

SYCAMORE

Plan #M08-022D-0011

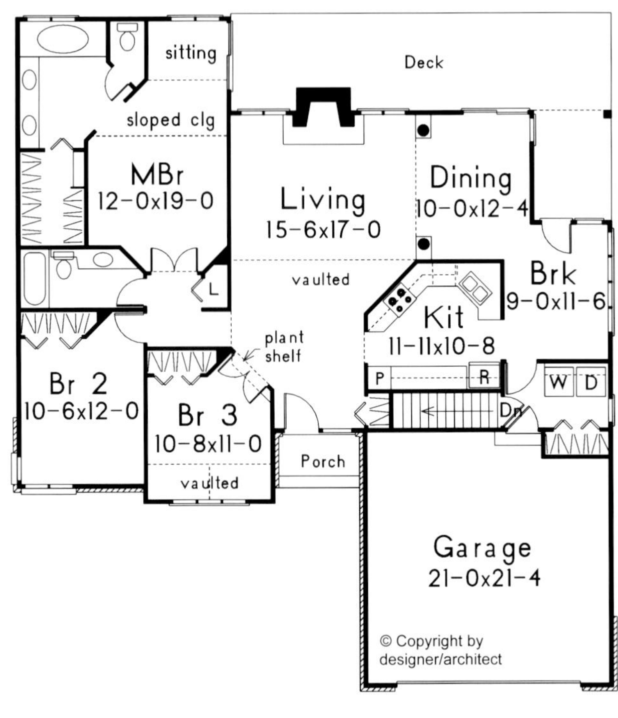

OPEN RANCH DESIGN

1,630 total square feet of living area

Width: 52'-4" Depth: 57'-4"

3 bedrooms, 2 baths

2-car garage

Basement foundation

SPECIAL FEATURES

The wrap-around deck is accessible from the breakfast and dining rooms, and master bedroom

Vaulted ceilings top the living room and master suite

PRICE CODE B

To order plans, visit the Menards Building Materials Desk or visit www.Menards.com.

MENARDS

WOODFORD

Plan #M08-008D-0126

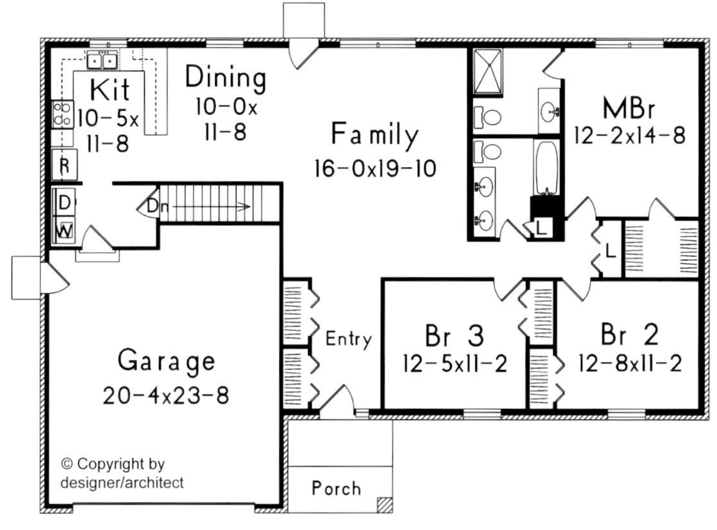

DISTINCTIVE ONE-LEVEL HOME

1,605 total square feet of living area

Width: 58'-10" Depth: 40'-10"

3 bedrooms, 2 baths

2-car garage

Basement foundation, drawings also include crawl space and slab foundations

SPECIAL FEATURES

The detailed entry is highlighted with a stone floor and double guest closets

The well-designed kitchen is open to the family room

Bedroom #3 can be easily utilized as a den

PRICE CODE B

SEYMOUR MILL

Plan #M08-058D-0170

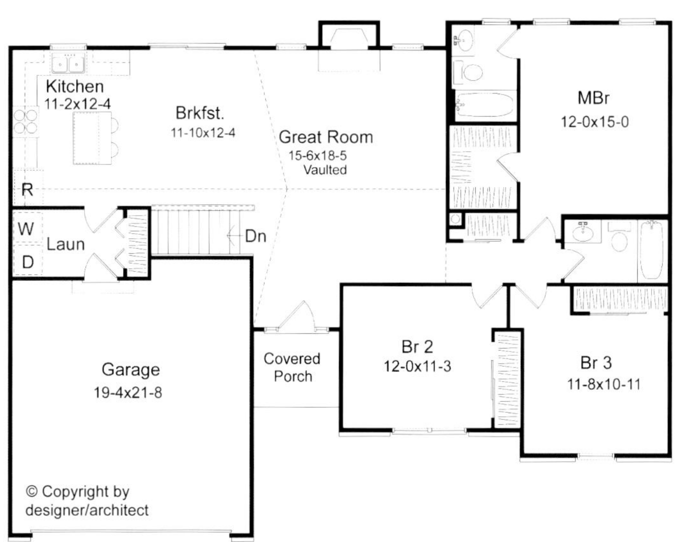

CHEERFUL RANCH

1,418 total square feet of living area

Width: 54'-0" Depth: 41'-4"

3 bedrooms, 2 baths

2-car garage

Basement foundation

SPECIAL FEATURES

The kitchen, breakfast and great rooms combine

All bedrooms are large in size and the master bedroom enjoys a walk-in closet and a private bath

PRICE CODE AA

To order plans, visit the Menards Building Materials Desk or visit www.Menards.com.

DARWIN

Plan #M08-001D-0021

MENARDS

PLEASANT COVERED PORCH

1,416 total square feet of living area

Width: 70'-0" Depth: 40'-0"

3 bedrooms, 2 baths

2-car garage

Crawl space foundation, drawings also include basement foundation

SPECIAL FEATURES

The master bedroom features a private bath

The foyer opens to both a formal living room and an informal great room

The great room has access to the outdoors through glass sliding doors

PRICE CODE A

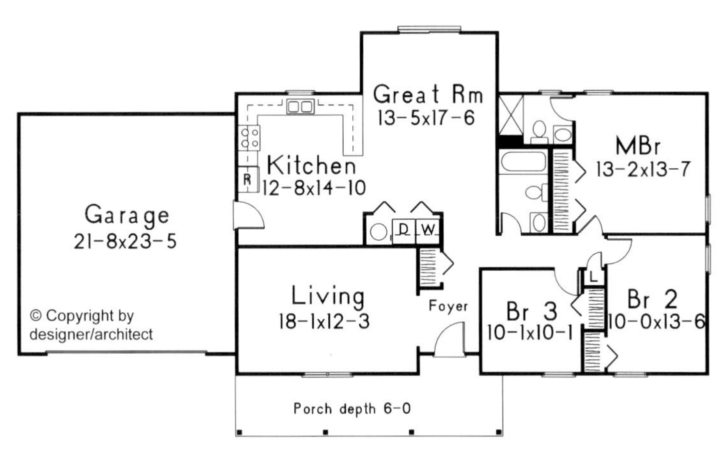

MAPLE GROVE

Plan #M08-051L-0053

COUNTRY FLAIR IN A RANCH

1,461 total square feet of living area

Width: 56'-0" Depth: 42'-0"

3 bedrooms, 2 baths

2-car garage

Basement foundation

SPECIAL FEATURES

The casual dining room is close to the kitchen

Cathedral ceilings in the great room and dining area

A relaxing master bedroom boasts an expansive bath

PRICE CODE A

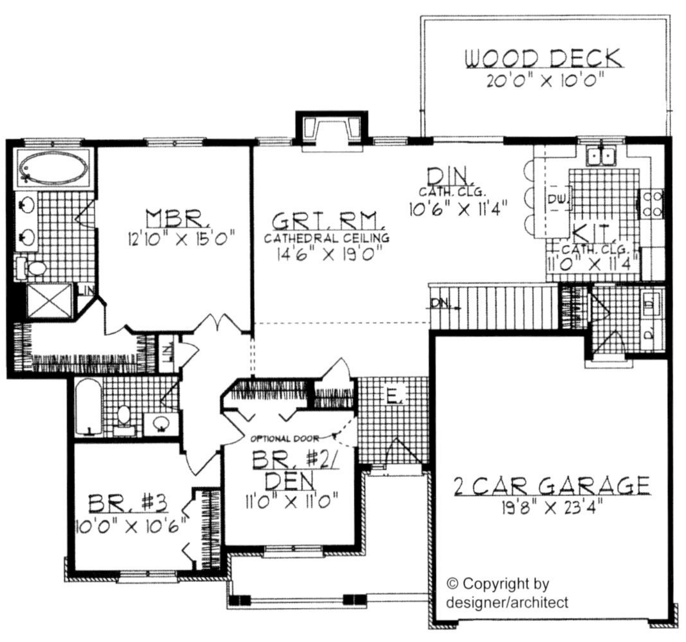

To order plans, visit the Menards Building Materials Desk or visit www.Menards.com.

MENARDS®

Multi-Family HOME PLANS

Multi-family home plans are a popular option for families of all sizes and can range from a two-unit duplex to a plan with over twelve dwellings. A multi-family plan can be a great source of income, energy efficient, and economical to build. They are also a great option for those who need a dwelling that includes in-law quarters. Browse our stylish selection of multi-family home designs in this special collection and find the perfect plan for your needs.

Plan #M08-007D-0022 can be found on page 223.

Plan #M08-007D-0091 can be found on page 218.

Plan #M08-007D-0190 can be found on page 215.

CORAL GABLES

MENARDS®

Plan #M08-007D-0076

ATRIUM DUPLEX WITH ROOM TO GROW

3,484 total square feet of living area

Width: 81'-0"   Depth: 49'-0"

Each unit has 3 bedrooms, 2 baths

Each unit has a 2-car garage

Walk-out basement foundation

SPECIAL FEATURES

An inviting porch and foyer lead to the vaulted living room/dining balcony with atrium window wall

Bedroom #2 doubles as a study with access to the deck through sliding glass doors

An atrium opens to the large family room and third bedroom

Duplex has 1,742 square feet of living space per unit

PRICE CODE H

Rear View

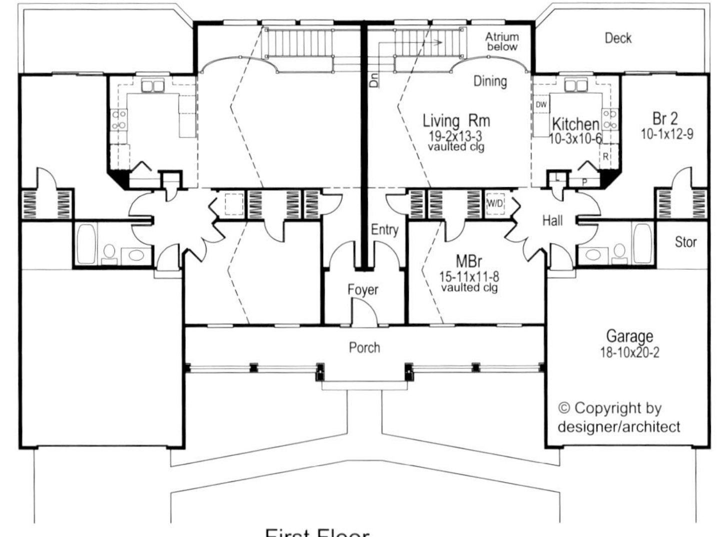

First Floor
1,104 sq. ft. per unit

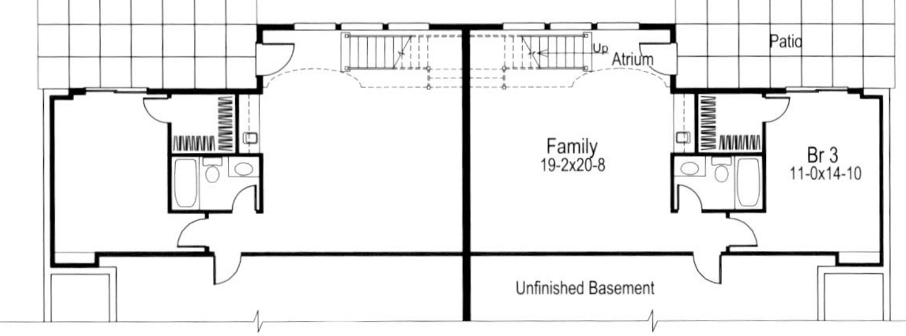

Lower Level
638 sq. ft. per unit

To order plans, visit the Menards Building Materials Desk or visit www.Menards.com.

HICKORY MANOR

Plan #M08-007D-0190

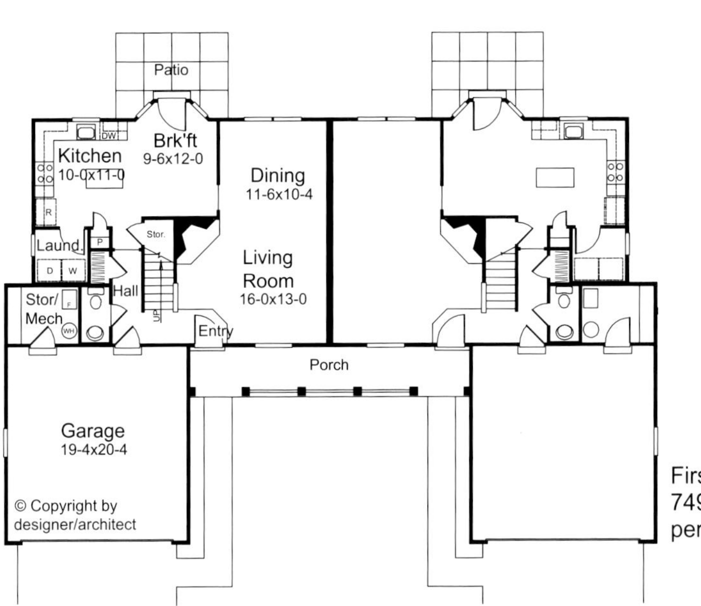

TRADITIONAL TWO-STORY DUPLEX

3,056 total square feet of living area

Width: 70'-0" Depth: 46'-8"

Each unit has 3 bedrooms, 2 1/2 baths

Each unit has a 2-car garage

Crawl space foundation

SPECIAL FEATURES

Multiple gables, a hipped roof, and an elongated porch all help to create this handsome exterior

The large living room has a corner fireplace and is open to the dining area

The laundry room, built-in pantry, and island cabinetry are amenities of the kitchen

Duplex has 1,528 square feet of living space per unit

PRICE CODE D

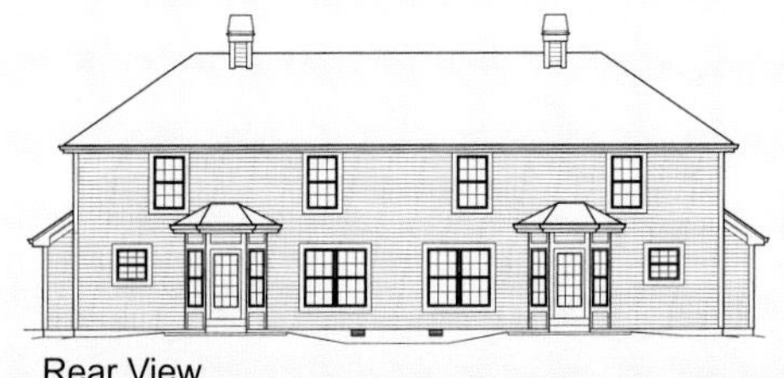

Rear View

To order plans, visit the Menards Building Materials Desk or visit www.Menards.com.

PATTERSON PLACE

MENARDS®

Plan #M08-007D-0094

COMPACT TWO-STORY DUPLEX

2,408 total square feet of living area

Width: 69'-0" Depth: 35'-8"

Each unit has 2 bedrooms, 1 1/2 baths

Each unit has a 1-car garage

Basement foundation

SPECIAL FEATURES

The large great room offers a fireplace and dining area with a view of the patio

Each unit enjoys its own private garage, front porch and rear patio

The second floor bedrooms are large in size and feature spacious walk-in closets

Duplex has 1,204 square feet of living space per unit

PRICE CODE F

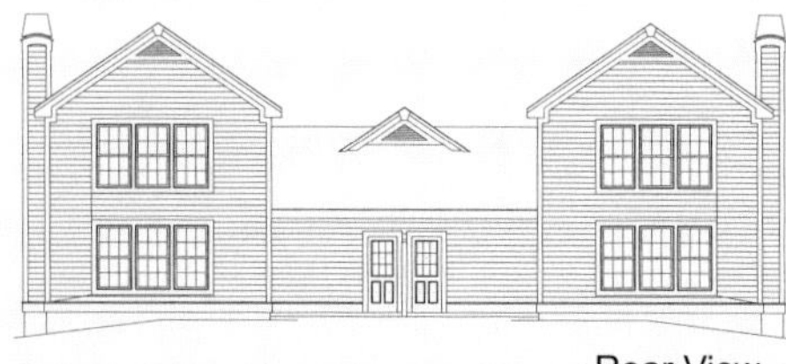

Rear View

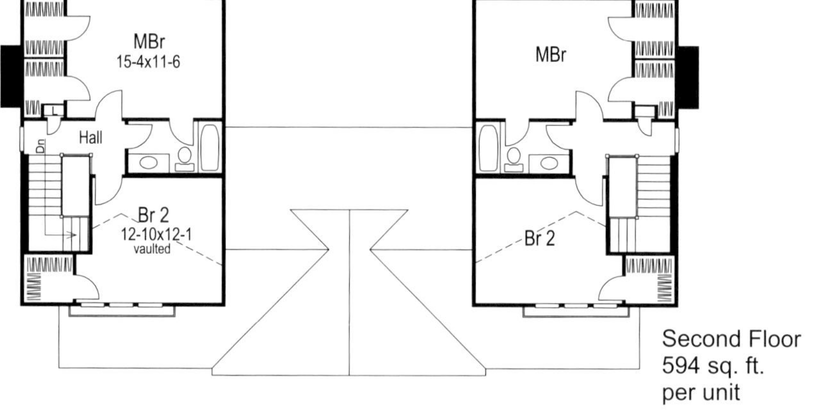

Second Floor
594 sq. ft.
per unit

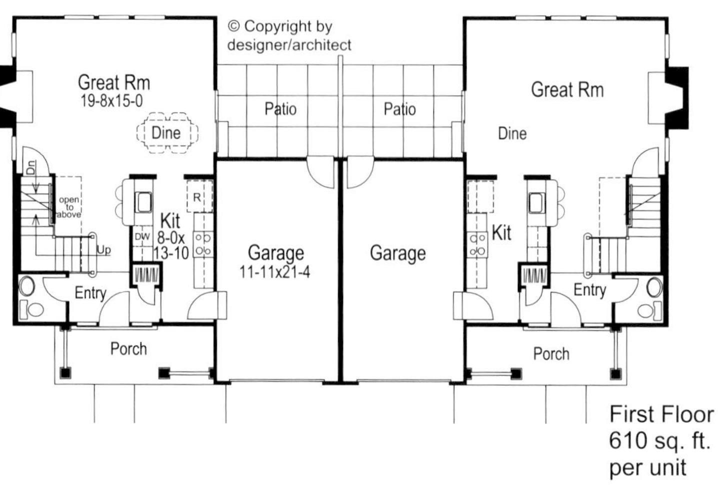

First Floor
610 sq. ft.
per unit

To order plans, visit the Menards Building Materials Desk or visit www.Menards.com.

SHADYDALE

Plan #M08-007D-0020

VAULTED CEILINGS ADD SPACIOUSNESS TO LIVING AREAS

2,318 total square feet of living area

Width: 80'-0" Depth: 42'-8"

Each unit has 3 bedrooms, 2 baths

Each unit has a 1-car garage

Basement foundation

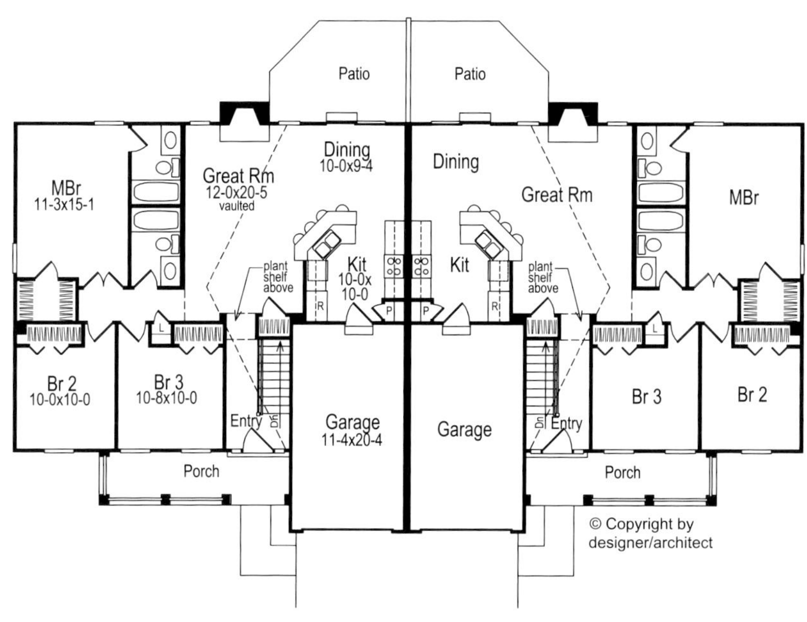

SPECIAL FEATURES

The great room and dining area enjoy a fireplace and patio access

The breakfast bar has a corner sink that overlooks the great room

A plant shelf graces the vaulted entry

The master bedroom provides a walk-in closet and private bath

Duplex has 1,159 square feet of living space per unit

PRICE CODE F

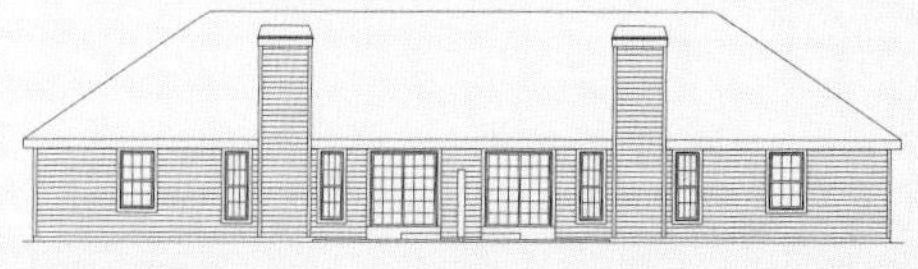

Rear View

To order plans, visit the Menards Building Materials Desk or visit www.Menards.com.

BEDFORD HILL

Plan #M08-007D-0091

DUPLEX WITH A GRAND-SCALE COUNTRY PORCH

3,502 total square feet of living area

Width: 72'-0" Depth: 36'-2"

Each unit has 3 bedrooms, 2 1/2 baths

Each unit has a 2-car drive under garage

Walk-out basement foundation

SPECIAL FEATURES

The two-story entry has a staircase that leads to the living room with a fireplace

The bayed breakfast room has doors to the balcony and a kitchen pass-through

Duplex has 1,751 square feet of living space per unit

PRICE CODE H

Rear View

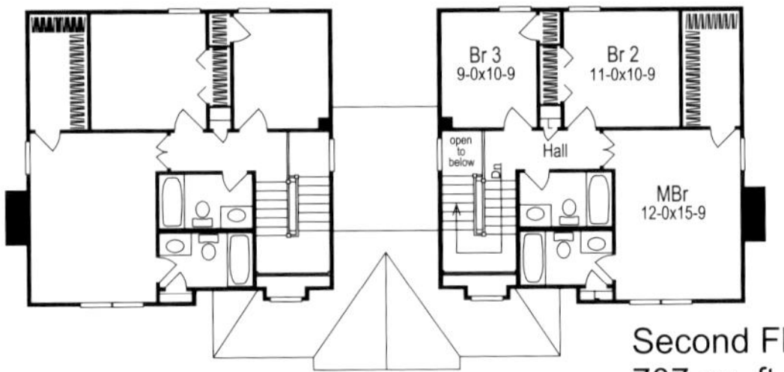

Second Floor
707 sq. ft. per unit

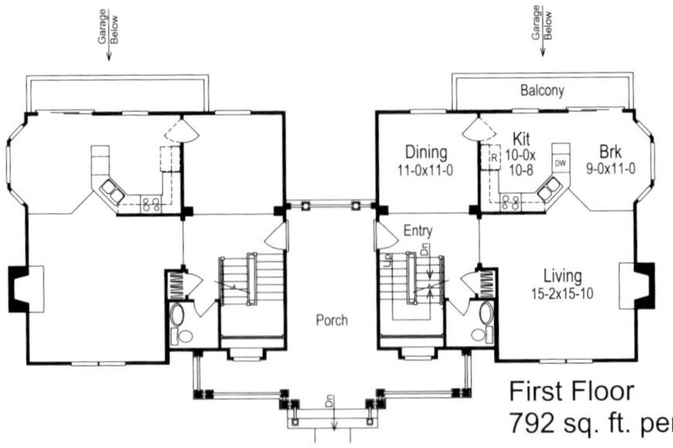

First Floor
792 sq. ft. per unit

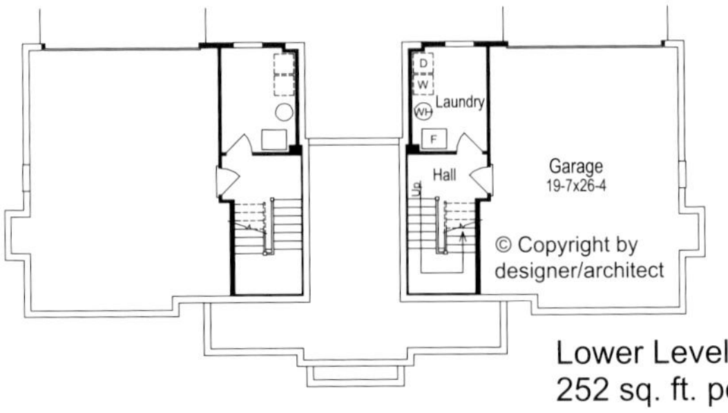

Lower Level
252 sq. ft. per unit

To order plans, visit the Menards Building Materials Desk or visit www.Menards.com.

MENARDS® COUNTRYRIDGE

Plan #M08-007D-0024

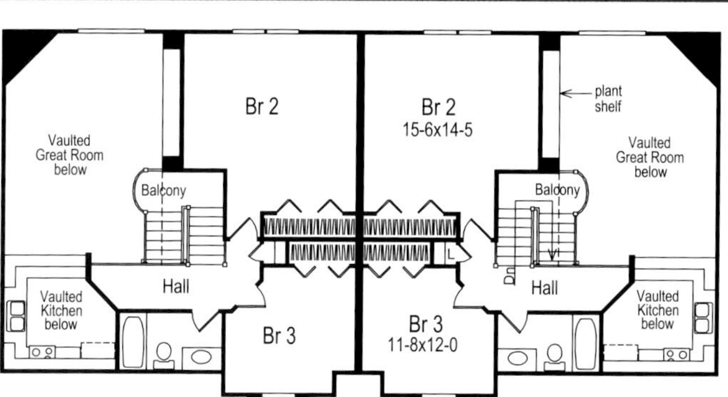

Second Floor
533 sq. ft.
per unit

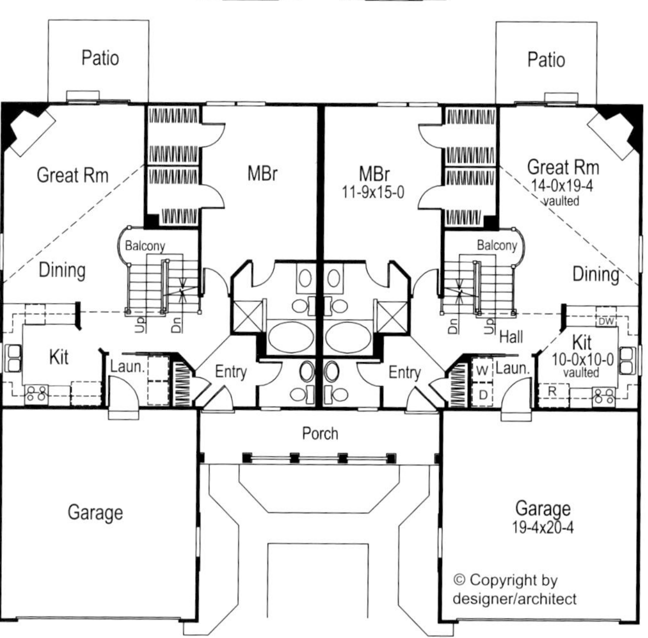

First Floor
960 sq. ft.
per unit

To order plans, visit the Menards Building Materials Desk or visit www.Menards.com.

COUNTRY CHARM IN A DOUBLE FEATURE

2,986 total square feet of living area

Width: 64'-0" Depth: 50'-8"

Each unit has 3 bedrooms, 2 1/2 baths

Each unit has a 2-car garage

Basement foundation

SPECIAL FEATURES

The vaulted great room, kitchen and two balconies add architectural drama

The first floor master bedroom boasts a lavish bath and double walk-in closets

An impressive second floor features two large bedrooms, spacious closets, a hall bath and a balcony overlook

Duplex has 1,493 square feet of living space per unit

PRICE CODE G

Rear View

Multi-Family Plans

LAKESIDE

MENARDS®

Plan #M08-008D-0032

DUTCH HIP ROOF CREATES ATTRACTIVE FACADE

3,674 total square feet of living area

Width: 88'-0" Depth: 42'-0"

Each unit has 3 bedrooms, 2 1/2 baths

Each unit has a 2-car garage

Basement foundation, drawings also include crawl space and slab foundation

SPECIAL FEATURES

The spacious second floor master bedroom has a large walk-in closet

The kitchen has a snack counter that opens to the dining area and great room

Duplex has 1,837 total square feet of living space per unit

PRICE CODE H

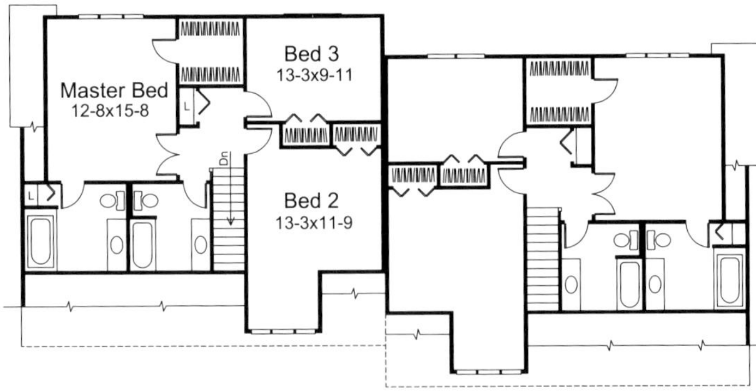

Master Bed
12-8x15-8
Bed 3
13-3x9-11
Bed 2
13-3x11-9

Second Floor
905 sq. ft. per unit

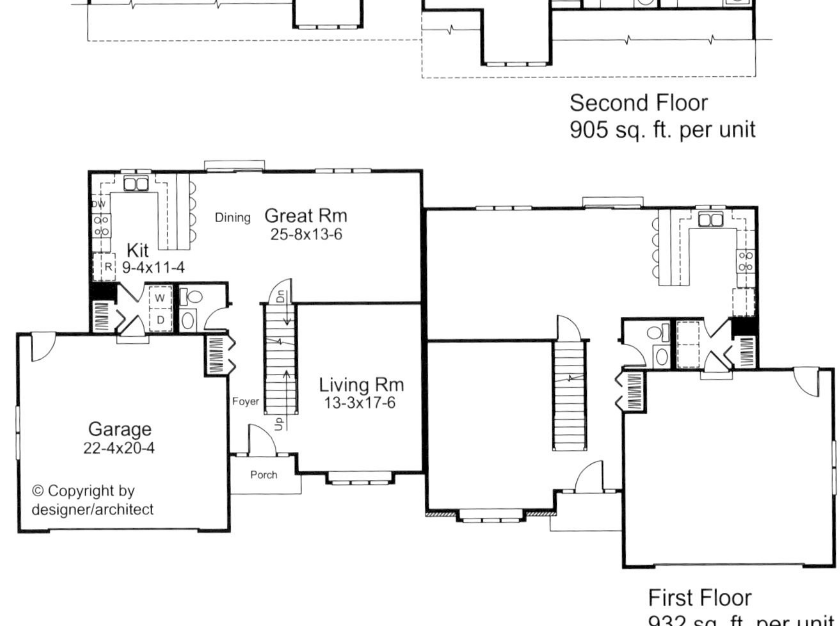

First Floor
932 sq. ft. per unit

To order plans, visit the Menards Building Materials Desk or visit www.Menards.com.

MENARDS

FOREST HILL

Multi-Family Plans

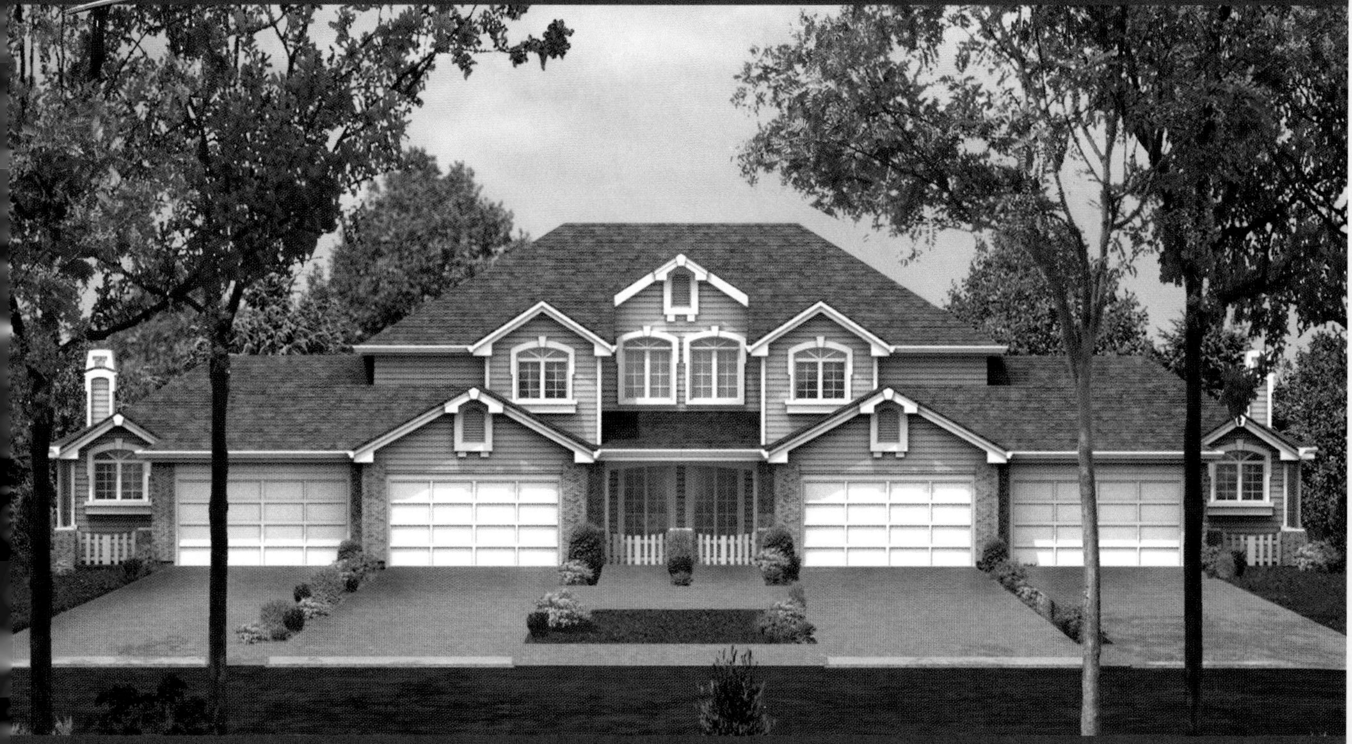

Plan #M08-007D-0023

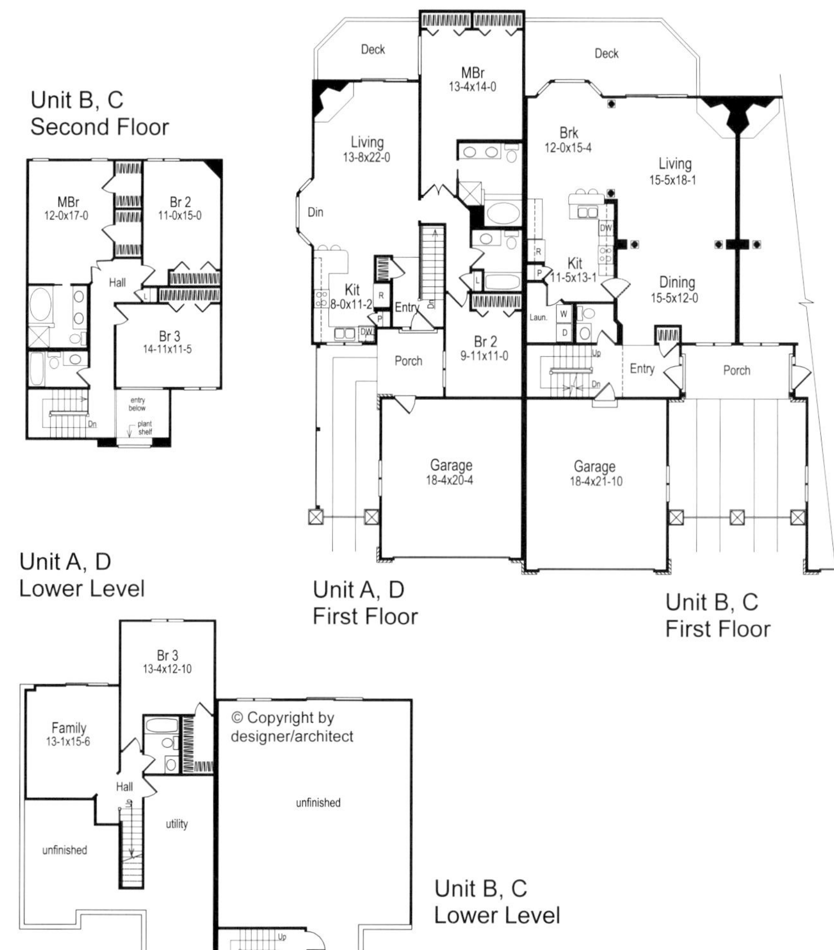

To order plans, visit the Menards Building Materials Desk or visit www.Menards.com.

LOVELY FOURPLEX

7,372 total square feet of living area

Width: 116'-0" Depth: 72'-6"

Walk-out basement foundation

SPECIAL FEATURES

Units A and D have a living/dining combination and master bedroom with lower level family room and third bedroom

Units A and D have 3 bedrooms, 3 baths, 2-car garage with 1,707 square feet of living area and 1,149 on the first floor and 558 on the lower level

Units B and C have a luxury living area and second floor with large master bedroom

Units B and C have 3 bedrooms, 2 1/2 baths, 2-car garage with 1,979 square feet of living area and 1,055 on the first floor and 924 on the second floor

PRICE CODE H

Rear View

HIGHLAND

MENARDS®

Plan #M08-007D-0025

STYLISH LIVING, OPEN DESIGN

1,992 total square feet of living area

Width: 60'-0" Depth: 57'-0"

Each unit has 2 bedrooms, 2 baths

Each unit has a 1-car garage

Basement foundation

SPECIAL FEATURES

A graciously designed ranch duplex with alluring openness

The vaulted spacious kitchen features a huge pantry, plenty of cabinets and a convenient laundry room

The master bedroom includes its own cozy bath and oversized walk-in closet

Duplex has 996 square feet of living space per unit

PRICE CODE E

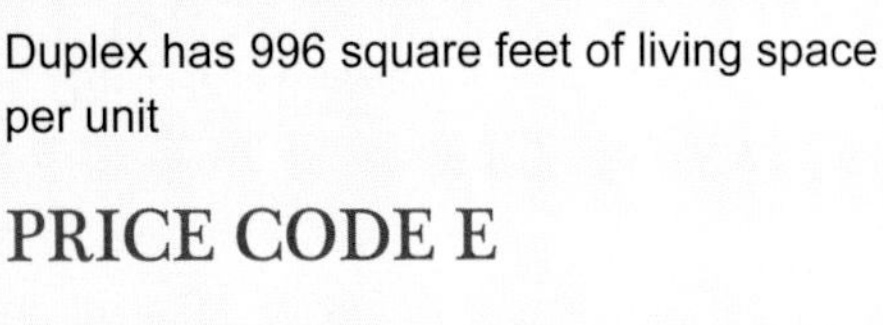

Rear View

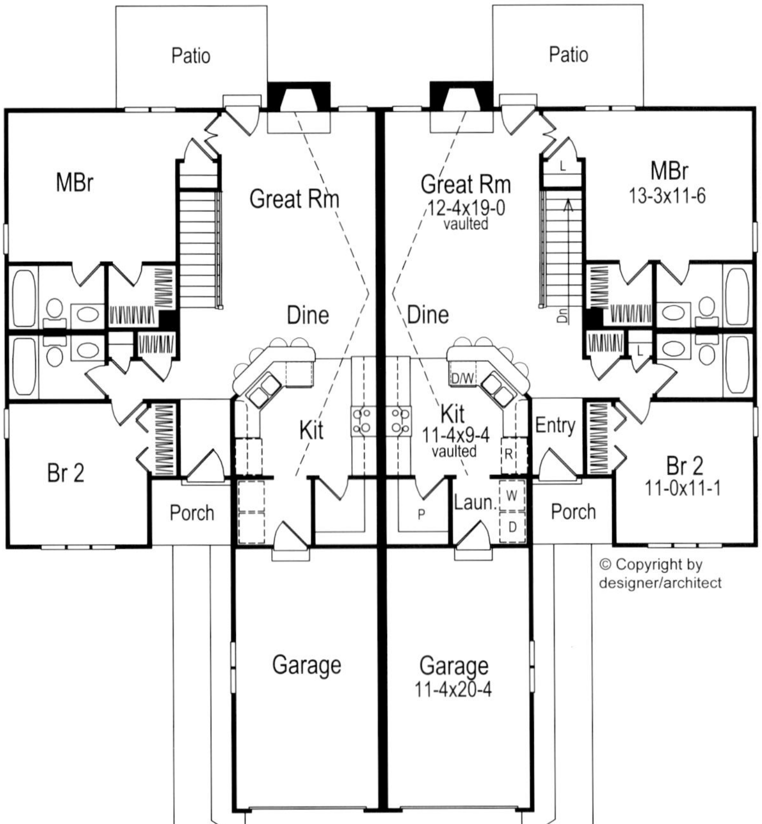

Patio
Patio
MBr
Great Rm
Great Rm
12-4x19-0
vaulted
MBr
13-3x11-6
L
Dn
Dine
Dine
D/W
Kit
Kit
11-4x9-4
vaulted
Entry
L
R
Br 2
Br 2
11-0x11-1
Porch
P
Laun.
W
D
Porch
Garage
Garage
11-4x20-4

To order plans, visit the Menards Building Materials Desk or visit www.Menards.com.

MENARDS®

PASADENA

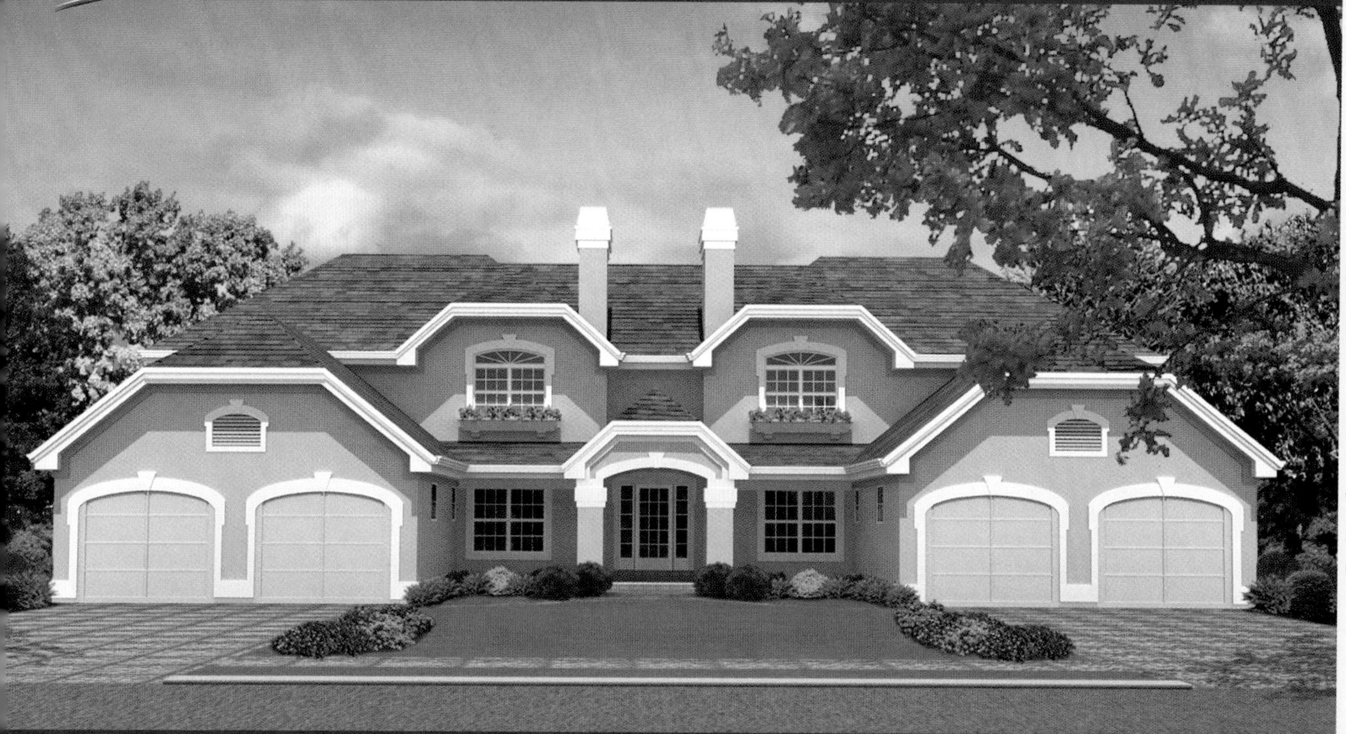

Plan #M08-007D-0022

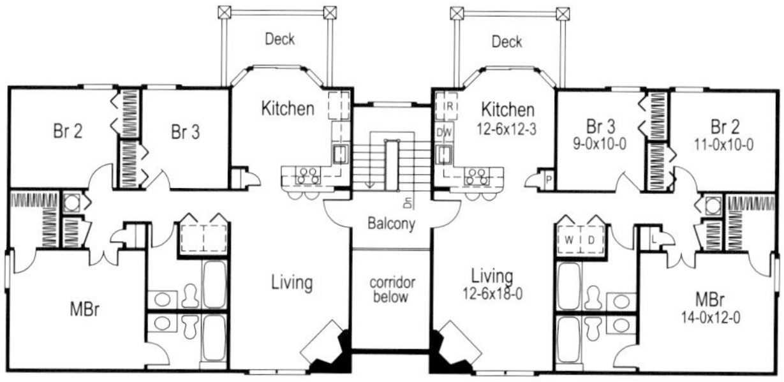

Second Floor
1,060 sq. ft.
per unit

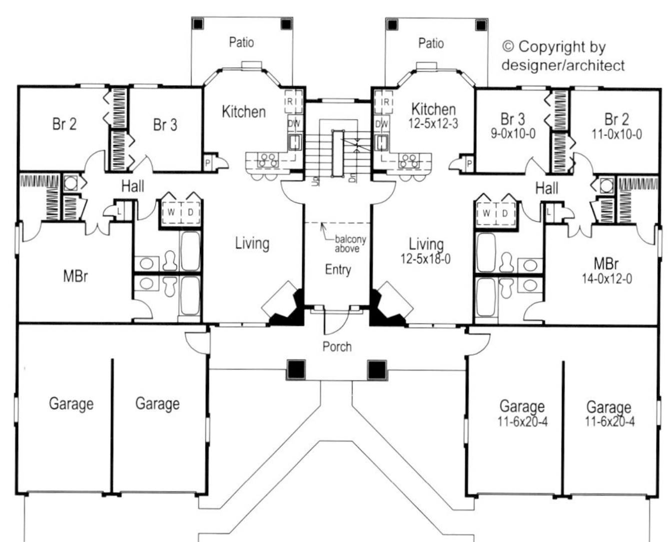

First Floor
1,060 sq. ft.
per unit

To order plans, visit the Menards Building Materials Desk
or visit www.Menards.com.

WELL-DESIGNED FACADE, WELCOMING AND DISTINCTIVE

4,240 total square feet of living area

Width: 80'-0" Depth: 51'-8"

Each unit has 3 bedrooms, 2 baths

Each unit has a 1-car garage

Basement foundation

SPECIAL FEATURES

The kitchen, with a large bay window, accesses a patio on the first floor units and a deck on the second floor units

Bedrooms are separated from living areas

The laundry area is located off the hall for accessibility

Fourplex has 1,060 square feet of living space per unit

PRICE CODE H

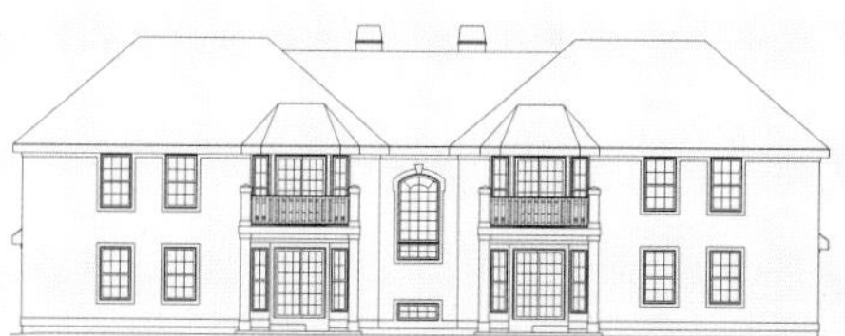

Rear View

HOME PLAN INDEX